BACHELORS, MANHOOD, AND THE NOVEL
1850–1925

Katherine Snyder's study explores the significance of the bachelor narrator, a prevalent but little-recognized figure in pre-modernist and modernist fiction by male authors, including Hawthorne, James, Conrad, Ford, and Fitzgerald. Snyder demonstrates that bachelors functioned in cultural and literary discourse as threshold figures who, by crossing the shifting, permeable boundaries of bourgeois domesticity, highlighted the limits of conventional masculinity. The very marginality of the figure, Snyder argues, effects a critique of gendered norms of manhood, while the symbolic function of marriage as a means of plot resolution is also made more complex by the presence of the single man. Bachelor figures made, moreover, an ideal narrative device for male authors who themselves occupied vexed cultural positions. By attending to the gendered identities and relations at issue in these narratives, Snyder's study discloses the aesthetic and political underpinnings of the traditional canon of English and American male modernism.

Katherine Snyder is Associate Professor of English at the University of California, Berkeley.

BACHELORS, MANHOOD, AND THE NOVEL
1850–1925

KATHERINE V. SNYDER

CAMBRIDGE
UNIVERSITY PRESS

PUBLISHED BY THE PRESS SYNDICATE OF THE UNIVERSITY OF CAMBRIDGE
The Pitt Building, Trumpington Street, Cambridge, United Kingdom

CAMBRIDGE UNIVERSITY PRESS
THE EDINBURGH BUILDING, CAMBRIDGE CB2 2RU, UK   http://www.cup.cam.ac.uk
40 West 20th Street, New York NY 10011–4211, USA   http://www.cup.org
10 Stamford Road, Oakleigh, Melbourne 3166, Australia

© Cambridge University Press 1999

First published 1999

Printed in the United Kingdom at the University Press, Cambridge

Typeset in Baskerville 11/12.5pt [VN]

A catalogue record for this book is available from the British Library

Library of Congress cataloguing in publication data
Snyder, Katherine V.
Bachelors, manhood, and the novel, 1850–1925 / Katherine
V. Snyder.
p.   cm.
Includes bibliographical references.
ISBN 0 521 65046 1 (hardback)
1. American fiction – Men authors – History and criticism.
2. Bachelors in literature.   3. American fiction – 19th century –
History and criticism.   4. English fiction – 20th century – History
and criticism.   5. English fiction – Men authors – History and
criticism.   6. Conrad, Joseph, 1857–1924 – Characters – Bachelors.
7. James, Henry, 1843–1916 – Characters – Bachelors.   8. Masculinity
in literature.   9. First person narrative.   10. Men in literature.
I. Title.
PS374.B34S69   1999
813'.409352041 – dc21   98–45687   CIP

ISBN 0 521 65046 1 hardback

PS
374
.B34
S69
1999

Contents

Acknowledgments

This book, like so many first books, began life as a doctoral dissertation. As a graduate student at Yale University, I benefited from the support of my director, Richard H. Brodhead, and from the input of other members of the faculty, including Wayne Koestenbaum, Linda Peterson, Patricia Meyer Spacks, Robert Stepto, Candace Waid, Bryan Wolf, Mark Wollaeger, and Ruth Bernard Yeazell. My time in New Haven was enhanced by the friendship and feedback of Alison Hickey, Catherine Nickerson, and Susan S. Williams, all of whom remain sources of encouragement and inspiration. While in graduate school and since leaving there, I have received advice and support from colleagues beyond the Yale English department; I would like to mention here Henry Abelove, Peter Agree, Nancy Armstrong, Carol Bernstein, Howard Chudacoff, Peter Gay, Mary Poovey, Catharine Stimpson, and William Stowe. I have also received invaluable responses to the manuscript of the book from Jonathan Freedman, Christopher Looby, Victor Luftig, Joel Pfister, and Hugh Stevens. This is also the place to offer my thanks to my editor, Ray Ryan, for shepherding this project into publication.

The English Department of the University of California at Berkeley has provided a rich and rewarding environment in which to develop this work. I would like to communicate here my appreciation to those who have read portions of the manuscript as it evolved, advised me on strategies for writing, and/or offered camaraderie and much needed diversion. I am particularly grateful to Elizabeth Abel, Janet Adelman, Anne Banfield, John Bishop, Mitchell Breitwieser, Anne Cheng, Jenny Franchot, Catherine Gallagher, Steven Goldsmith, Andrew Griffen, Dorothy Hale, Priya Joshi, Jeffrey Knapp, Sharon Marcus, Samuel Otter, Carolyn Porter, Susan Schweik, and Alex Zwerdling. I have also gained a good deal from the students at Berkeley, especially the graduate students in my fall 1995 James and Conrad seminar and the members of the "Nineteenth Century and Beyond" discussion group. Jeffrey Santa Ana and Freya Johnson provided helpful research assistance, and Jeremy Crean carefully proofread the final draft of the manuscript and indexed the book. I offer here a special thank you to Kerri Smith, undergraduate research assistant extraordinaire, whose contributions were vital to the final stages of manuscript preparation.

I am indebted to the responses of audiences and commentators at the many academic and professional fora in which I have presented portions of this project, including the Modern Language Association Conference (1993 and 1996); the American Studies Association Conference (1994 and 1998); the Interdisciplinary Nineteenth-Century Studies Conference (1995 and 1998); the Annual Meeting of the Organization of American Historians (1996); Narrative, an International Conference (1995); the British Comparative Literature Association Conference (1995); and the Central New York Conference (1992). The 1996–97 Fellows of the Townsend Center in the Humanities offered beneficial feedback at a critical juncture. I am grateful for having had the opportunity to present my work and ideas to students and faculty at Berkeley, at Wesleyan University where I taught in 1992–93, and at Bryn Mawr College where I taught in 1991–92.

The dissertation phase of this project was generously supported by the Mellon Foundation in the Humanities. The University of California at Berkeley has been very generous in material support, and I would like to thank here the English Department chairs who have fostered my work: Frederick Crews, Ralph Rader, and Jeffrey Knapp. This book would never have been completed without release-time from teaching made possible by grants from the Humanities Research Fellowship Program; the Townsend Center in the Humanities; and the Faculty Development Program. A grant from the Hellman Family Faculty Fund and a Regents' Junior Faculty Fellowship also provided welcome material aid. I have benefited greatly as well from research assistance made possible by Research Assistantship in the Humanities Grants; a Junior Faculty Research Grant; a Faculty Mentor Grant; and several grants awarded by the Undergraduate Research Apprenticeship Program.

Last but never least, I want to acknowledge dear friends, especially Erika Milvy and Pearl Soloff, Jerome and M.D. Buttrick, Rick, Rebecca, and Olivia Lowe, Adam Grant, and Laura Payne, who have kept me grounded in life beyond the walls of the academy. For their warmth, encouragement, and good humor, I offer my love and appreciation to my family: Margaret, Robin, Rebecca, Emily, and Jessica Hamilton, and Arthur and Marilyn Snyder. A special thank you to my mother, Elise W. Snyder, for alternately holding my hand and kicking me in the pants, and for doing more than I can say here. No words can express my gratitude to Tim Culvahouse, my husband and my best friend, for being there for me through it all, for making the bad moments better and the good ones truly wonderful.

Abbreviations

BR	*The Blithedale Romance*
C	*Chance*
CT	*The Complete Tales of Henry James*, vols. VI, VII, and IX
GG	*The Great Gatsby*
GS	*The Good Soldier*
LC1	*Henry James: Literary Criticism.* Vol. I: *Essays on Literature, American Writers, and English Writers*
LC2	*Henry James: Literary Criticism.* Vol. II: *French Writers, Other European Writers, and the Prefaces to the New York Edition*
LJ	*Lord Jim*
WH	*Wuthering Heights*

Introduction

Percival Pollard's "The Bachelor in Fiction," a review essay that appeared in *The Bookman* in 1900, begins by asserting the relative rarity of English literature which "concerns itself directly with bachelors."[1] Pollard admits that certain well-known examples of the literature of confirmed bachelorhood do spring to mind, counting among these Israel Zangwill's *The Bachelors' Club*, J. M. Barrie's *When A Man's Single*, and the "famous book" of "Ik Marvel," the 1850 bestseller *Reveries of a Bachelor*, which was apparently so famous that, even in 1900, its title could be left unspecified. But Pollard, in keeping with his persona of the bibliophilic connoisseur, abjures discussion of these obvious instances: "My purpose here is to point not so much to the familiar, famous writings on the state of single blessedness, but to dally rather with certain volumes which the general public either forgets or passes by" (p. 146). The ensuing catalogue brings to light an impressive number of lost or lesser-known bachelor fictions of the 1890s, including Richard Harding Davis's *Van Bibber*, George Hibbard's *The Governor*, F. Hopkinson Smith's *A Day at Laguerre's* and *Colonel Carter of Cartersville*, Robert Grant's *A Bachelor's Christmas*, Edward Sandford Martin's *Windfalls of Observation*, Eugene Field's *The Love Affairs of a Bibliomaniac*, and K. M. C. Meredith's *Green Gates: An Analysis of Foolishness*.

Most of these bachelor books rate only a passing mention, but the last novel in the series, which Pollard lauds as "the most captivating story of bachelordom ... of recent years" (p. 147), receives fuller treatment. Pollard's plot summary of *Green Gates* details the story of a "vain, fastidious, sentimental" bachelor of forty who is roused from his inveterate "thought habit" by a sudden and unrequited love for a girl many years his junior. This ludicrous old bachelor manages to "become fine for one moment of his life, at any rate, when he meddles with the girl's intention to do a foolish thing": "When it is all over, when his meddling has saved the girl from disrepute, if not from death, he goes home to his

1

books – his books, that in the days of his perversity had become perverse themselves and were now in the direst confusion" (p. 148). Although the bachelor preserves the girl's virtue, he can neither save her life nor save himself from his own perversity, which is apparent in the promiscuous mixing upon his library shelves of authors of diverse nationalities, historical periods, and genres. The presence amidst this "unruly jumble" of "that madman Nordau, who, along with the help of Lombroso, has succeeded in classifying himself!" (p. 148) makes the bachelor's very attempt to classify his books seem itself doomed to degeneracy, perhaps even to criminality and madness.[2] He can no more "bring order into his life" (p. 148) than he can successfully bring order to bookshelves that support such depravity.

My study, too, takes as its topic "The Bachelor in Fiction." My reading list and critical aims, however, are worlds apart from Percival Pollard's and, for that matter, from those of the bachelor of *Green Gates*. My selection of texts does not, as Pollard's does, form a subcanon or even a countercanon of literature about bachelors. Rather, I focus upon an array of bachelor texts which are firmly ensconced in our current canon of pre-modernist, proto-modernist, and modernist fiction, a canon that includes such novels as Hawthorne's *The Blithedale Romance* (1852), James's *The Portrait of a Lady* (1880), Conrad's *Lord Jim* (1900), Ford's *The Good Soldier* (1915), and Fitzgerald's *The Great Gatsby* (1925). Nor do I aim, like the *Green Gates* bachelor, to taxonomize or otherwise enforce a normalizing order on the "perverse" fictions that I read here. Rather, I mean to demonstrate how the order of normativity, the proper regulation of boundaries both gendered and cultural, is crucially at issue in these canonical bachelor texts themselves. Much as these fictions of bachelorhood are proper to our current modernist canon, the figure of the bachelor was also at the heart of the bourgeois domestic world that was often the norm for, and a normalizing force in, the novel.[3]

I am concerned here not simply with fiction featuring bachelors, the broader category that Pollard identifies in his study, but with bachelor-*narrated* fiction. Bachelor characters do double duty as first-person narrators in a startling number of texts of the mid nineteenth and early twentieth centuries. Yet bachelor narrators seem to have blended into the background of canonical, British and American fiction, perhaps because of the very familiarity of their voices. The bachelor narrator is a "figure" in the double sense conceptualized by Roland Barthes – both an imaginary subject or character and a narrative device or trope[4] – but this peculiar bridging of the thematic and the formal has virtually escaped critical notice. One aim of this book, then, is to defamiliarize the consummately familiar voice of the bachelor narrator. What does it mean when a bachelor tells the story in a novel? How does narration matter?

This study focuses, moreover, not simply on bachelor-narrated fiction, but mainly on *high-cultural* and *modernist* fictions narrated by bachelor figures. I am concerned here to map the intersections among the historical figure of the bachelor, the use of the bachelor as narrator in pre-modernist and modernist fiction, and a tradition of novelistic authorship which sometimes crossed but more often helped to widen the "great divide" between high and low culture that developed during this era.[5] Not coincidentally, this cultural divide occurred along lines strongly marked by gender differences.[6] The gendered differences – between men and women, and also between men – which were fundamental to the construction of the highbrow/lowbrow split also contributed to the classificatory troubles embodied by the figure of the bachelor.

Bachelors were a necessary resource for the domestic institution of marriage, yet they were often seen by their contemporaries as disruptive to domestic life or sometimes merely extraneous to it. They were thought to be both admirable and contemptible, enviable and execrable, dangerous and defanged. The contradictions evident in and among these pairings evoke the conceptual and practical challenges that bachelorhood presented to nineteenth- and early twentieth-century conceptions of bourgeois marriage, family, and domestic life. A variety of demographic shifts in the United States and Great Britain over the course of the "long nineteenth century," and especially in the latter half of this period, including a rise in average marrying age and a decline in the rate of marriage, contributed to contemporary interest in and worry about bachelors.[7] The fascination with bachelors is evident, for example, in the boom in novels, stories, poems, and essays about bachelorhood published in mass-circulation periodicals during this period.[8] This explosion of popular bachelor discourse attests to the uneven developments that cultural ideologies and institutions of marriage and domesticity were undergoing during this era of rapid urbanization, industrialization, and modernization.[9] Bachelors were a troubling presence within and beyond the already troubled world of the bourgeois family home.

Bachelor trouble was, fundamentally, gender trouble.[10] While they were often seen as violating gendered norms, bachelors were sometimes contradictorily thought to incarnate the desires and identifications of hegemonic bourgeois manhood. The late nineteenth-century figure of the bachelor was thus conceived as "*at the same time* an aspect of a particular, idiosyncratic personality type *and also* an expression of a great Universal": both a separate species of man and a representative modern man.[11] This contradictory status indicates the instability of and competition between different models of manhood. Such uneven developments in gender identities encompassed, but were not limited to, the late nineteenth-century transition from a middle-class ideal of civilized manliness to one of primitive masculinity.

A concomitant of the emergence of new styles of normative and counternormative bourgeois manhood, and of the attendant shifting of the boundaries of what constituted proper bourgeois manhood, was a change in the definition of bachelorhood itself. Eve Kosofsky Sedgwick has theorized a late nineteenth-century transition from bachelorhood understood as a lifestage to bachelorhood understood as a character type. The contest between the character type and the lifestage definitions of bachelorhood – both of which also remained simultaneously in play for the male bourgeois subject – contributed to the paradoxical definition of bachelors as both different from *and* also the same as other, "normal" men. Sedgwick clarifies the homophobic potential of each understanding of bachelorhood, as well as the contribution of the conceptual incoherence of these concurrent definitions to the constitution of the intrinsically homophobic system of homo/heterosexual definition. This system, which is itself based on a conceptual incoherence generated by "minoritizing" and "universalizing" models of sexual identity, was reinforced by the incoherent coexistence of minoritizing and universalizing views of bachelorhood.[12] Sedgwick argues that the mid-Victorian emergence and late Victorian development of the bachelor as a character taxonomy based on "sexual anaesthesia" strategically "desexualized the question ... of male sexual choice," effecting a homophobic erasure of the specificity of male–male sexual desire.[13]

Although the homophobically panicked, sexually anaesthetic bachelor type does appear in some of the texts that I consider, this type is not typical, as my survey of popular writings on bachelorhood in the next chapter shows. Indeed, a rich and polymorphously perverse range of fantasmatic identifications and desires are palpable, though not always explicitly or consciously asserted, in narrative discourse uttered from the gendered subject position of the bachelor. To the extent that such homophobic erasure *is* at work in the bachelor narratives I discuss, I do try to make such panicked occlusions visible by attending to the eroticized activity evident in these figures' narrative utterances. The excesses and occlusions of these first-person narratives often reveal homoerotic desire and its panicked erasure, but they also disclose a wider range of desires and identifications, both transgressive and normative. One could argue, for example, that the unrequited love of the *Green Gates* bachelor for a woman half his age is a coverup, or a displacement, or an expression, of closeted homoerotic desire and homosexual identity. But one might equally well argue that the old bachelor's feelings are based on his identification with and desire for the woman's youth; the difference in age that apparently comes between him and his female object is a salient axis along which his emotional investments travel.[14] Such an age differential is normative in cross-gender relations of the nineteenth century; after all, the marital union of a forty-year old bachelor and an eighteen-year old woman is standard novelistic fare. Yet this bachelor's desires also seem to verge upon the perversely counternormative; in addition to homosexuality, some other unspeakable names for his unrequited love might include pedophilia, incest, and masochism. The key point here is that, both before and after the eruption of his ultimately unconsummated desire, this bachelor does not suffer from an absence of feeling.

The bachelor narrators whom I consider are, similarly, far from anaesthetic in their erotic identifications and desires. In fact, the wide variety and sheer intensity of their erotic and identificatory energies might lead one to describe these figures as voyeuristic, fetishistic, and/or masochistic, psychoanalytic classifications which carry a negative, pathologized valence. The intrasubjective and intersubjective relations by which these figures define themselves and others can be understood as "deviations" from or "perversions" of normative masculine desires and identifications. As such, these relations can be revalorized as gesturing toward alternative, counternormative, or "queer" masculine sexualities and genderings. But the intrasubjective and intersubjective relations by which these figures define themselves and others also signal, perhaps to an even greater extent, the presence of the perverse *within* what has been conventionally demarcated as masculine heteronormativity.[15] What is alternative often turns out to be proper to the mainstream, if necessarily disavowed by its proponents. My primary concern here, then, will be with the paradoxes of the bachelor's relationship to normative domesticity and normative manhood, and with the ways that these paradoxes make this figure so enigmatic as a speaking and/or writing subject of novelistic narrative discourse.

The ambiguities of the bachelor narrator's relation to domestic and gendered norms also make this figure particularly expressive of the ambivalences of male, high-cultural, pre-modernist and modernist literary authorship. Just as the cultural boundaries that defined bourgeois domesticity and hegemonic manhood were permeable and shifting in this period, so too were the boundaries which separated high culture from culture defined as low, mass, or popular and also, as one century segued into the next, the boundaries which separated modernist writing from nonmodernist writing.[16] All the authors considered in this book shine, more or less vividly, as stars in the firmament of current academic literary canons. Yet all struggled, albeit to different degrees and with varying strategies, with what they experienced as competing desires for popular and critical success. These struggles were simultaneous with the historical rise of the popular woman writer and the vast and rapid expansion of literary markets. Correspondingly, many of these male writers experienced their struggles on and against the literary market as "melodramas of beset manhood," in which they performed the part of the long-suffering victim, and sometimes the scrappy survivor, of a debased mob of female readers and writers.[17] One subtlety which this psychic melodrama tends to elide is the fact that economic success and aesthetic success were marked not only by the gendered difference between female and male authorship, but also by the gendered differences between different styles or models of male authorship. Popular writers were not all women; high-cultural writers, and writers who were merely unpopular, were not all men. The male high-cultural authors discussed in the following chapters were not so consistently beset, nor were they beset always by the same people, nor always for the same reasons, as they typically represented themselves.

Another detail which the melodrama of beset high-cultural male authorship tends to obscure is the fact that the trials to which these writers were subject, or to which they subjected themselves, were nuanced by pleasures and privileges. High-cultural literary authorship, like hegemonic bourgeois manhood, exacted sacrifices but it also conferred rewards. While immaterial rewards – prestige, self-esteem, collegiality, the life of the mind – are obvious perquisites of high-cultural artistry, material rewards were not always or entirely ruled out. And when the sacrifice of material comforts and other attainments of normative bourgeois manhood were unavoidable, such asceticism could be re-envisioned by its male subjects as an alternative mode of attaining an exemplary manhood. The self-sacrifice of the artist thus enables that artist to experience the ultimate in self-fulfillment. Ironically, in order to transform the anxieties and hardships of true artistry into sources of emotional satisfaction, male high-cultural writers often psychically enlisted the supposedly low-cultural genre of melodrama, a genre whose queer excesses are seemingly beyond the pale but which exist as a disavowed component within many mainstream cultural narratives.[18]

The contested status of bachelors as figures of luxurious self-indulgence and/or of disciplined self-abnegation made them well-suited to articulate the melodramatic vicissitudes of male, high-cultural authorship. Like the male authors who deployed them, bachelor narrators are themselves given to recasting abjected manhood as manhood triumphant, and to disavowing melancholically the sentimentality that stands both as their own defining trait and as that of the significant others with whom they identify. Bachelor narrators are thus particularly fitted for symbolic use by authors who reinforced, sometimes in the very act of crossing, the borders of the cultural milieus in and against which they defined themselves as writers. Indeed, bachelors often served in cultural and literary discourse more generally as threshold figures who marked the permeable boundaries that separate domesticity, normative manhood, and high-cultural status, from what was defined as extrinsic to these realms.[19]

The liminal function of the bachelor becomes even more pointed when considered through the critical lens of the bachelor as narrator. The first-person bachelor narrators whom I consider are for the most part narrators of the sort Gérard Genette designates "homodiegetic," or present as characters in the stories they tell, as opposed to "heterodiegetic," absent from the stories they tell.[20] As tellers who also appear as characters in their stories, homodiegetic narrators are located both within and beyond the fictional worlds of their stories, serving as intermediaries between diegetic levels within the narrative and also between author and reader. Simultaneously present in separate diegetic spaces, these narrators might also be conceived as divided, or multiplied, within themselves; such a split, or doubling, is most evident between the "I" of the narrative past and the "I" of the narrative present. Saying "I" as a homodiegetic narrator can thus verge on speaking in synchronic and diachronic chorus or call-and-response with oneself, occasioning a spatial and temporal multiplication of subjectivity which would seem to challenge the unitary or monolithic self. Yet homodiegesis is far from an essentially or intrinsically radical form, either aesthetically or politically. The effects of homodiegesis as a narrative technique depend upon the specific uses made of its potential for confirming or confounding the boundaries within, and also between, individuals.

Authors are not the only ones upon whom the containing and/or subverting effects of homodiegetic narrative depend. Readers also make vital contributions to the aesthetic and political meanings of homodiegetic narrative. As a reader who is a narratological critic, Genette assumes the impermeability and hierarchical grounding of individual subjectivity, an assumption evident in his further narratological distinction between two varieties of homodiegesis:

> one where the narrator is the hero of his narrative (*Gil Blas*) and one where he plays only a secondary role, which almost always turns out to be a role as observer and witness: Lockwood [in *Wuthering Heights*], the anonymous narrator of Louis Lambert, Ishmael in *Moby Dick*, Marlow in *Lord Jim*, Carraway in *The Great Gatsby*, Zeitblom in *Doctor Faustus* – not to mention the most illustrious and most representative one of all, the transparent (but inquisitive) Dr. Watson of Conan Doyle. It is as if the narrator cannot be an ordinary walk-on in his narrative: he can be only the star, or else a mere bystander. For the first variety (which to some extent represents the strong degree of the homodiegetic) we will reserve the unavoidable term *autodiegetic*.[21]

One glance at my Table of Contents will reveal that my bachelor narratives are mostly of Genette's second variety: non-autodiegetic homodiegetic narrative in which the bachelor narrator tells someone else's, often another man's, story. But the distinction Genette asserts between the autodiegetic narrator who is "the hero of his narrative" and the homodiegetic narrator who "plays only a secondary role ... as observer and witness" is not so clear. Indeed, the ideological stakes, and particularly the gendered stakes, of this so-called "secondary role" are already suggested by Genette's labelling of the first variety as the "strong degree." We might surmise that not only the narratives told by non-hero narrators are of the "weak degree," but also the non-hero narrators themselves who are weak, unheroic, not fully manly. Genette's evaluative descriptor betrays the ideological bias that is intrinsic to but disguised by the formalism of traditional narratology.

The bachelor narrators I consider in this book are for the most part well described as observers and witnesses, yet I do not accept Genette's assumption that he who is not the hero of his own narrative is automatically and uncomplicatedly a "mere bystander," diminished by the full measure of inconsequentiality that phrase implies. (I am puzzled, I admit, by Genette's distinction between an "ordinary walk-on" and a "mere bystander," although in his hierarchy the former does seem preferable to the latter.) In the chapters which follow, I call attention to the heavily freighted relations between the bachelor narrators and the significant others whose stories they tell. Enacted in the space and time of narration, these relations repeat but also revise the gendered relations that construct the main plots of these fictions. The bachelor and his narrative thus effect discursive supplements which destabilize the texts' dominant fictions of manhood and domesticity.[22] The activity of the bachelor narrators in both the novels' story and their discourse constitute alternatives to hegemonic masterplots and hegemonic manhood.

While these narratives can be construed as offering a rhetorical challenge to the predominance of protagonists, whether individual or paired, and their plots, the very rhetoric of the "challenge" predisposes the critic to read the bachelor narrative as a story of contest in which the bachelor ultimately reveals himself as a better man than the nominal hero. Such a reading practice would merely invert the ideology of Genette's narratological model, recasting the "mere bystander" as the hero of his own narrative. Were a critic to proclaim Dr. Watson the true mastermind of Baker Street, for example, this inversion would merely transform weak homodiegesis into strong autodiegesis, and the implicitly weak homodiegetic narrator into an implicitly strong autodiegetic narrator, without questioning the ideological valences of those categories. While competition between the homodiegetic narrator and his narrative's significant others, or even between narrative and plot, is far from irrelevant to the bachelor narratives I consider, I believe it is crucial to attend to the other modes of relation, real and especially imaginary, that animate these narratives.

Therefore, in attending to the figure of Oedipal plotting which emerges from the domestic and familial carpet of many of the novels considered here, I look beyond the classical account which identifies the son as a murderous competitor with the father for possession of the mother. In so doing, I take my cue from Eve Sedgwick's influential account, following Gayle Rubin, of the traffic in women effected by erotic triangles consisting of two men and one woman, a configuration that holds a place of privilege in Freud's psychoanalytical theory, Lévi-Strauss's anthropological theory, and René Girard's literary theory in *Deceit, Desire and the Novel*.[23] Because it heeds the differentials of power and gender at issue in mediated desire, Sedgwick's theorization of a homosocial continuum of male desire disrupted by homophobic panic allows us to see disavowed homoerotic energies at work in heterosexual rivalries between men. As other critics have pointed out, however, Sedgwick's emphasis on homosocial desire between men obscures the potential for female trafficking (where women occupy one or more of the points of erotic triangulation) and for male trafficking which does not involve women (where men occupy all three points of erotic triangulation). To redress the latter elision, I attend in some of my readings to a story which we might call the "other Oedipus": the Oedipus of loving brothers rather than, or as well as, patricidal sons. Desirous and identificatory collaboration, rather than sibling rivalry, crucially defines such fraternal relations. This "other Oedipal" plot and the classic homosocial Oedipal plot together make up a multilayered story of masculine subject formation based on mutuality as well as hostility; reciprocity as well as manipulation; equality as well as hierarchy.[24]

My readings of the triangulated dynamics of desire and identification are complemented by attention to other multilayered mythic paradigms, including the myriad myths of Orpheus which figure in James's "The Aspern Papers" and the manifold figure of the Medusa's Head in Conrad's *Under Western Eyes*. The utility of these mythic paradigms resides in their explicit emphasis on the visual, on seeing and not-seeing as ways of knowing, having, or being. They make newly and differently visible the basis of mediated desire in systems of exchange, especially those that involve the trading of gazes, looks, and glances. For example, the performance of bachelor narrators as onlookers at the triangulated love plots which are the stock-in-trade of novelistic fiction reveals mediated desire as not merely triangulated, but as fundamentally *quadrangulated*. In *Wuthering Heights*, for example, Lockwood assumes, among other subject positions, that of a "third man" who observes the male-male-female triangles consisting of Heathcliff, Edgar, and Catherine in the first generation, and Hareton, Linton, and Cathy in the second generation. In this text and others, the bachelor onlooker is a figure of surplus value, one who is apparently in excess of the requirements of a homosocial market in Oedipalized desire. The specular relations of the bachelor creates a speculative market, one whose value depends upon the interest invested in it by a figure who is not a primary producer, consumer, or even an object of consumption, within this economy. The bachelor narrator as witness is invested in what he sees and tells, yet his identity within the narrative *mise en scène* is not solely constituted in terms of his competition on the marriage market of the novel's plot. Bachelor narration thus might be said to represent an alternative economy of manhood, even while it also participates vicariously and, one might argue, decisively in the exchanges that constitute the narrative transactions of novelistic discourse.

In departing from a conventional psychoanalytic vocabulary here, I mean to signal my awareness of the limits of psychoanalysis as a methodology, as well as the value of non-Oedipal, or even anti-Oedipal, theories of desire.[25] One could legitimately object to the use of psychoanalytical paradigms for reading bachelor narratives on the grounds that the product of any given set of social conditions has limited ability to critique other products of those same conditions; in this context, those "products" include psychoanalysis, the bourgeois family, and also the bachelor as a cultural figure constructed in relation, however vexed that relation may be, to the historical and discursive framework of the family. One could even argue that the bourgeois family itself *is* the social condition that produced psychoanalysis, and hence psychoanalytical paradigms can hardly be expected to do other than reproduce the conditions of their making when used to consider novelistic representations of bachelorhood.

There is, however, another way of looking at this relation. I would contend that the historical adjacency, or even direct mutual causality, of the family and psychoanalysis makes the latter particularly amenable for understanding the former. Psychoanalytically informed critical approaches seem to me especially well calibrated for taking the measure of the family as a machine for the production of gendered subjectivities, including those of bachelors. It is, of course, necessary to correct for the inevitable biases in traditional psychoanalytic precepts and practices. For example, recent correctives to the reductive assumption that desire and identification must necessarily have differently gendered objects have had a revitalizing effect, one which is crucial to the viability of this methodology for reading bachelor narratives.[26] Recent reconceptualizations of identification as having the potential to trouble, rather than simply reinforce, the boundaries of individual subjectivity, have also contributed to the utility of psychoanalytical methodologies. Judith Butler argues that "identifications belong to the imaginary; they are phantasmatic efforts of alignment, loyalty, ambiguous and cross-corporeal cohabitation; they unsettle the 'I'; they are the sedimentation of the 'we' in the constitution of any 'I,' the structuring presence of alterity in the very formulation of the 'I'."[27] Such a rethinking of identification as the dynamic basis of identity-formation allows us to read the incorporations and introjections of bachelor narrators as alternative or supplementary models of masculine subjectivity. When intrasubjective relations are understood to depend upon, even to be coextensive with, intersubjective ones, bachelor narratives can be understood as having the potential not only to buttress conservative identities and interactions, but also to generate alternative models of masculine subjectivity and gendered relations. Just as considering the identifications and desires of bachelors psychoanalytically can open up new understandings of the formation of gendered intersubjectivity, considering bachelors in relation to the dominant fiction of the domestic family can open up new understandings of families themselves, revising the traditional psychoanalytic abstraction of the family as a closed, nuclear unit.

As the preceding comments on economic markets and intersubjective relations have doubtless already made apparent, this book is more than a strictly narratological study. In this regard, I follow the practice of recent critics who bring to bear on the narratives they consider such contextual issues as the emotional and material effects of historically constructed gender norms and subjectivity.[28] But this study is also more than strictly narratological because I refuse to maintain – frankly, quite often, I simply cannot see – the division between story and discourse, or between *histoire* and *récit*, which is fundamental to narratological approaches. Although narratologists acknowledge that such divisions are only approximations, theoretical constructs meant to describe the complexities of real texts, this approximation seems particularly untenable in homodiegetic narratives, narratives in which the story/discourse dualism is embodied within a single character. It is not only a matter of the practical difficulty of distinguishing with certainty between the narrative past and the narrative present, but one of the theoretical impossibility of separating the story from its telling. This study is predicated on my critical conviction that story and discourse, the "what" and the "way," of bachelor narration are so deeply and mutually constitutive that they cannot be surgically separated without doing irreparable damage. The critical portmanteau of "bachelor narrative" does not so much yoke together a cultural type and a narrative form as it reveals the abiding, indivisible connection between ideology and form.

By affirming the ideology of form, my aim is not to equate male author with male narrator. Rather, I mean to investigate the narrative and authorial effects that their differences as well as their similarities may have had. Such representations may occur within the boundaries of gender but not apart from the bounds of difference. For this reason, I have included only one full-scale reading of a novel by a female author, even though many well-known women novelists of the period – including all three Brontë sisters, George Eliot, Harriet Beecher Stowe, Edith Wharton, and Willa Cather – deployed single or married male narrators, used male pseudonyms, or otherwise assumed masculine identifications in their pursuit of authorship.[29] Much compelling work has been done and remains to be done on such cross-gendered representations, as well as on representations that transpire across the boundaries of class and race. Without minimizing the importance of such projects, I believe that it is of vital importance to attend to issues of same-gender representations within our current canon of modernist male authorship. What it means for a male author to speak in the voice of a male narrator does not go without saying.

While attending to certain differences among bachelor-narrated texts written on different continents and sometimes separated by more than half a century, this study is predicated on their similarities. The premise here is that we can productively read texts so disparate as these – sketches and short stories together with novels; narratives that feature heterodiegesis with focalizing bachelor reflectors along with homodiegetic bachelor narratives; a female-authored novel among male-authored ones; books by American and British authors and by an expatriate Pole writing in English; even a novel that features a married but virginal male narrator – as bachelor narratives. If the diversity of material gathered here under the rubric of bachelor narrative seems willfully broad, this study makes certain exclusions that may seem equally willful. Poetry enters only obliquely, even though the personae – both dramatic monologists and less fully dramatized speaking voices – assumed by many poets in the period sing in harmony with the chorus of novelistic bachelor narrators. I have focused upon prose fiction because of the centrality of marriage plotting to the novelistic tradition treated here, even while recognizing that comparable conventions crucially inflect poems both narrative and lyric. This study is meant to open up a field larger than what it encompasses. I hope that the inevitable exclusion of texts that might be considered under the rubric of bachelor narrative will stimulate other critics to examine these texts along lines comparable to the ones sketched here.

The structure of this book is roughly chronological, following the arc of modernism from the mid nineteenth to the early twentieth century. The book does not, however, argue for a unified historical trajectory of bachelor narrative; rather, it takes the case study as its method. While close readings of individual texts are the general *modus operandi*, heterogeneity in the structure and focus of the chapters allows for attention to broader historical contexts, to authorial careers, and to the intricate workings of literary narrative. Thus chapters 2 and 5 each cluster together several novels which share an historical moment and a thematic focus, while chapters 3 and 4 each focus on individual authors. Whereas chapter 3 takes a comparatively wide-angle view of the author's career, chapter 4 takes a close-up look at a single moment and a single text. Chapter 1 might be said to zoom in from a consideration of external perspectives on bachelors as represented in popular texts, especially nineteenth-century mass-circulation periodicals, to the inside perspective on the bachelor imaginary presented by the immensely popular mid-century *Reveries of a Bachelor*. Chapter 1 thus provides both an historical framework for and an historical point of entry into the remaining chapters; it also makes a methodological movement inward which sets the sights of the following chapters on the intrapsychic and intersubjective relations of bachelors as effected by their narratives.

Chapter 1, "Trouble in paradise: bachelors and bourgeois domesticity," begins with an overview of the demographic, economic, and cultural changes in England and America that contributed to the popular and literary fascination with bachelors and bachelor representations over the long nineteenth century. This overview prepares the way for a discussion of the paradoxical expectations of domestic ideology for middle-class men, and the ways that bachelors were viewed by their contemporaries as diverging from normative bourgeois masculinity. The vexed relation of bachelors to bourgeois domesticity and manhood is particularly visible in the history and representation of urban housing, as I show in the next section of the chapter. This section traces the contemporary association of bachelors with multiple-occupancy urban housing in England and America; the perceived incompatibility of such residential forms with family life; and the contribution of such institutions as the men's club and the bachelor apartment building to contemporary critiques of married domesticity. The last section of the chapter considers the narrative negotiations of domestic ideology and practice in the 1850 bestseller, *Reveries of a Bachelor* by Donald Grant Mitchell (a.k.a. "Ik Marvel"). In its negotiations of intimacy and distance, fantasy and reality, normativity and perversity, Mitchell's text is an important precedent for the bachelor narrations that I consider in the later chapters of the book. The liminality of reverie – hovering between waking and sleeping, the bachelor in his reveries is paradoxically represented as both active and passive, working and playing, producing and consuming – exemplifies the function of the bachelor as a threshold figure, one who both demarcates and subtly alters the placement and permeability of the boundaries of domesticity and domestic selfhood. The bachelor's reveries mark this figure as both within and beyond the worlds of bourgeois family life and manhood.

Chapter 2, "Susceptibility and the single man: the constitution of the bachelor invalid," extends chapter 1's ultimate focus on the bachelor's gendered subjectivity as represented by and in first-person narration. Here I consider three nineteenth-century novels that imagine bachelors as invalids and narrative intermediaries: *Wuthering Heights* (1847), *The Blithedale Romance* (1852), and *The Portrait of a Lady* (1880). In all three novels, the visual perspectives of these bachelor invalids and the different voices in which they speak are inflected by the fragility of their health and the spectacle of death, a spectacle which each bachelor either vicariously witnesses or himself performs. The ex-centric masculinity of these bachelor invalid narrators reenacts, both repeats and revises, the permeability of identity and the proper regulation of boundaries between individuals at issue in these novels' plotting of the gendered relations of marriage and alternatives to marriage. I consider the differences between the homodiegetic first-person bachelor narration of *Wuthering Heights* and *Blithedale* (whose narrative situations also differ significantly from each other) and *Portrait*'s heterodiegetic third-person narration which employs a supplementary yet crucial bachelor "center of consciousness," which I call an "off-center of consciousness" in recognition of Ralph Touchett's eccentric masculinity. The perspectives of all these bachelor narrators and reflectors reveal their constant negotiations between sympathy and detachment, between proximity and distance, and also between specular vicariousness and spectacular self-display, negotiations that inform our understanding of these novels' gendered authorship.

Chapter 3, "An artist and a bachelor: Henry James, mastery and the life of art," proceeds from chapter 2's reading of the bachelor reflector in *The Portrait of a Lady*, to argue that the figure of the bachelor vitally informs the persona of the high-cultural male artist that James himself assumed in his life and writing. This chapter examines a wide range of James's writings, with a particular emphasis on his mid-career "tales of literary life," "The Lesson of the Master" (1888), "The Aspern Papers" (1888) and "The Figure in the Carpet" (1896), and on his literary criticism, especially his 1907 essay on Shakespeare and his 1914 essay, "The New Novel." I begin by analyzing James's critical objections to first-person narration in longer works of fiction, demonstrating James's association of this narrative technique with a self-contradictory range of sexual and gender identities, cultural ranks, and genres: femininity and masculinity, lowbrow and highbrow, autobiography and romance. James's multiple and inconsistent readings of this narrative technique in his own and others' writings provide insight into his attempts to reclaim literary fiction as an arena of properly regulated masculine endeavor. The aesthetic "life of art" appears in James's fiction and criticism as a source of both gendered normativity and counternormativity, a tension evident both in the conflict and collusion of the man with the artist. The man and the artist are figures which stand in James's work sometimes for internal self-division, sometimes for interpersonal male-male relations, and sometimes for both simultaneously. I focus throughout on the gendered interplays of specular vicariousness and spectacular self-display, self-discipline and self-indulgence, and hierarchy and equality, all of which sustain the intrapsychic and intersubjective formation of masculine desire and identification in James's writings.

Chapter 4, "A way of looking on: bachelor narration in Joseph Conrad's *Under Western Eyes*," argues that national and racial differences are not the only differences at issue in the "translation" which is offered by this novel's bachelor narrator. This narrator speaks across explicitly gendered divides, border lines which separate masculine from feminine and also mark the difference between as well as the proximity among a range of masculine subject positions. The double binds of male specularity and male feminism in both the novel's plot and its narration reflect a related gendered double bind which Conrad experienced in writing this novel. I demonstrate how "The Secret Sharer," which Conrad dashed off in December of 1909 while struggling to finish *Under Western Eyes*, crystallizes the competing and internally conflicted models of manhood at issue both in this novel and in the Marlow-narrated novels that preceded and followed its publication. These conflicts play themselves out in the bachelor narrator's use of the figure of the Medusa's Head, an uncanny figure whose long-standing association with artistic representation, with unruly women, and with revolution, were not lost on Conrad. The aesthetic, the erotic, and the nationalistic implications of this figure for the narrator's representation of the novel's heroine, reveal Conrad's own authorial anxiety that something would be lost in translation.

Chapter 5, "The necessary melancholy of bachelors: melancholy, manhood, and modernist narrative," widens the view of Conrad's corpus of work by taking up two novels narrated by Conrad's most famous bachelor narrator and by grouping these two Marlow-narrated texts with two highly canonical, early twentieth-century bachelor-narrated novels which are equally marked by a melancholic sense of lack. "The Necessary Melancholy of Bachelors," the title of a 1908 essay that appeared in *Putnam's Magazine*, reveals a vital historical context for the more familiar melancholy which pervades much of modernism, particularly male modernism, and even more specifically the two-protagonist form that gives shape to an influential strand of modernist narrative. The melancholy of these modernist narratives which bear the name of "another man" – *Lord Jim* (1900), *The Good Soldier* (1915), and *The Great Gatsby* (1925) – can be traced to the narrators' disavowal of the sentimentality of their abjected male objects and of themselves, a melancholic investment reinforced by their reliance upon familial and especially fraternal metaphors to describe their attachments and resentments. The compensatory efforts which disrupt their narratives reveal an irresolvable tension between desires for affiliation and autonomy, and for merger and separateness, a tension that also reveals a contest between homoerotic desire and its homophobic disavowal. Similar tensions animate *Chance* (1913), in which Conrad revived Marlow for his swan song more than a decade after his penultimate appearance as the narrator of *Lord Jim*, and which, ironically enough, garnered Conrad his first popular success. The figure of the "good uncle" in *Chance* provides a point of entry to the quasi-familial and quasi-domestic status of bachelor narrators in this period and thus returns us to the liminal status of the bachelor in relation to domestic life and hegemonic manhood.

In their ways of telling, bachelor narrators delineate the thresholds of bourgeois domesticity and manhood, thereby enabling themselves and their authorial creators to mark the boundaries of normativity while simultaneously going out of bounds. I like to think of the bachelor as a figure who stands in the doorway, looking in from the outside and also looking out from within. This double perspective provides readers a privileged vantage upon the world of the novel, a fictional world that both reflected and crucially shaped the real world beyond. The "I" of the bachelor, a masculine subject position that is at once both within and beyond the pale, reveals the novels to be considered in the chapters which follow as both representative modernist texts and truly singular fictions.

CHAPTER I

Trouble in paradise: bachelors and bourgeois domesticity

"The Bachelor in Fiction" was hardly news when Percival Pollard published his review essay of that title in 1900. An 1859 Wilkie Collins sketch entitled "The Bachelor Bedroom," published anonymously in the English periodical *All the Year Round*, indicates that as early as mid-century the bachelor in fiction had long been a conventional topic: "The bachelor has been profusely served up on all sorts of literary tables; but, the presentation of him has been hitherto remarkable for a singularly monotonous flavour of matrimonial sauce. We have heard of his loneliness, and its remedy, or his solitary position in illness, and its remedy; of the miserable neglect of his linen, and its remedy."[1] Deploring the monotonous insistence on marriage as the sole remedy for the ills of bachelor life, Collins asserts that there is "a new aspect of the bachelor left to be presented . . . a new subject for worn-out readers of the nineteenth century whose fountain of literary novelty has become exhausted at the source":

But what have we heard of him in connexion with his remarkable bedroom, at those periods of his existence when he, like the rest of the world, is a visitor at his friend's country house? Who has presented him, in his relation to married society, under those peculiar circumstances of his life, when he is away from his solitary chambers, and is thrown straight into the sacred centre of that home circle from which his ordinary habits are so universally supposed to exclude him? (p. 355)

The topic proposed as an antidote to the hackneyed representation of bachelorhood is not so innovative as he would have it. This "new subject for worn-out readers" falls short of newness, for one thing, because Collins shares with his literary predecessors the assumption that married life is a crucial frame of reference for bachelorhood, if not simply its remedy. This sketch, like the profusion of written representations of bachelorhood before it, concerns itself primarily with the bachelor's vexed "relation to married society," and to conventional familial and domestic life more generally.

It was precisely the bachelor's ambiguous distance from or, rather, his ambiguous proximity to "that home circle from which his ordinary habits are so universally supposed to exclude him" (p. 355) that made this figure a "fountain of literary novelty" to nineteenth-century readers. Whether staying in other people's homes, residing in homes of their own, or occupying indoor or outdoor spaces that were anything but domestic, bachelors were represented primarily in terms of hegemonic marital, familial, and domestic ideologies, practices, and spheres. Bachelors were seen as both proper and improper to conventional married, bourgeois domesticity, much as the remarkable bedrooms and other spaces with which they were so insistently associated were often located either dangerously close to or threateningly far from, sometimes even simultaneously within and beyond, the "civilised residences" (p. 355) of married people and families.

The conceptual incoherence produced by the figure of the bachelor is particularly vivid against the background of domestic life. Bachelors were often thought to be the antithesis of domesticity yet they were also sometimes seen as its epitome. This paradox results in large part from the self-contradictory status of the private sphere itself within bourgeois domestic ideology. That is to say, the private was both the center of meaning for bourgeois domestic life and also marginal to it, trivial in comparison to the "real world" of the public sphere. By the mid nineteenth century, the private, domestic household was defined as ideally beyond the marketplace and market relations, yet the household was itself the very type, or imaginary origin, of economy, a term that derives from the Greek "oekonomia" which refers to household management.

For bourgeois men, the conflicted relation of the private household to the public marketplace was particularly perplexed and perplexing. *Patresfamilias* were, in theory at least, the kings of their castles and yet they were often dispossessed within "the empire of the mother."[2] Men, moreover, were defined and were expected to define themselves in relation to subcultural contexts – work and home, public and private – whose explicit values were often opposed. That these spheres were not always so separate as their nineteenth-century constituents and twentieth-century commentators assumed – neither so different in ethos nor so spatially distinct as the ideology of separate spheres would suggest – only compounded the confusion. Under hegemonic domestic ideologies, home may have been idealized as a haven from a heartless world or even a veritable heaven on earth, but there was trouble in paradise. The presence of bachelors *within* bourgeois homes and the existence of paradises of bachelors – versions of domesticity and quasi-domesticity enacted by bachelors in chambers, men's clubs, and bachelor apartment buildings – only meant more trouble.

THE TROUBLE WITH BACHELORS: AN HISTORICAL OVERVIEW

The figure of the bachelor was not invented in the nineteenth century. Indeed, the bachelor appears as a stock character in seventeenth- and eighteenth-century writing, a figure that partakes of other contemporary types of eccentric manhood such as the rake, the beau, the fop, and, somewhat later, the sentimental man of feeling. But the genealogy of the bachelor goes back even further. The *Oxford English Dictionary* gives "bas chevalier" as the conjectural etymology of the term: "a young knight, not old enough or having too few vassals to display his own banner, and who therefore followed the banner of another... Hence knight bachelor, a knight of the lowest but most ancient order." This meaning, which holds from the fourteenth century through to the sixteenth, overlaps with another denotation of the term, used from the fourteenth century through to the nineteenth. This slightly later denotation refers to "a junior or inferior member, or 'yeoman,' of a trade guild or City Company" or to "one who has taken the first or lowest degree at a university, who is not yet a master of the Arts."[3] The *OED* also records that bachelor was used in the seventeenth century to refer to an inexperienced person or novice. Only in the mid eighteenth century did the current primary meaning arise: an unmarried man of marriageable age. The pre-eighteenth-century uses of the term – knight, guildsman, student – all have a primarily vocational register with connotations of youthfulness. These early uses register the centrality of an apprenticeship system in which the bachelor serves a master in hopes of later assuming a position of authority himself. While unmarried status may be necessary for these pursuits, bachelorhood here primarily refers to the man's vocational status.

The eighteenth-century shift of the primary denotation of bachelorhood to unmarried status moved the definitional context of bachelorhood into a world and a set of relations – the private sphere, the family, marriage – from which bachelors themselves were nominally excluded. This striking shift to a meaning more or less parallel to our contemporary usage occurred at roughly the same time that middle-class masculinity itself was coming to be equated with the emerging concept of occupation.[4] Bachelorhood was not an occupation, yet such phrases as the "freedom, luxury, and self-indulgence of a bachelor's career" suggest something like a substitute or alternative vocation, even while gesturing towards the bachelor's violation of the norms of bourgeois masculinity, especially with respect to an ideal of male productivity.[5] The larger cultural and historical context of the emerging concept of occupation is, of course, the formation of the middle class itself and its attendant ideology of separate spheres.[6] Bourgeois domesticity as an ideology was not based on marriage *per se*, but on the gendered division of labor and the construction of a private realm as the locus of true selfhood, a realm separate from that of the marketplace.[7] Although home and marriage were not literally synonymous, their ideologies were so intricately interwoven that they were virtually interchangeable, at least rhetorically. Alterations in nineteenth-century marriage patterns were understandably considered to have an inevitable impact, either immediate or delayed, on domestic ideologies and practices.

During the second half of the nineteenth century in England and America, there was a decline, probably real and certainly perceived, in the "popularity" of marriage. In America, the marriage rate declined until the turn of the century.[8] Moreover, between 1890 and 1920, the proportion of American men over age fifty-five who had never married was actually increasing, even while the overall marriage rate was beginning to climb again. There was no overall decline in the marriage rate in England, but the unequal numbers and uneven distribution of men and women there and elsewhere contributed to concerns about the future of domestic life. The 1851 census showed 405,000 more women than men in England, an imbalance famously addressed in W. R. Greg's now notorious 1862 essay, "Why Are Women Redundant?" By 1871, there were 593,000 more women than men in England, and by 1901, there were over a million more.[9] By contrast with the increasingly skewed sexual proportions in England, the sex ratio in the United States remained essentially even, at 51 men per 49 women, throughout the second half of the nineteenth century.[10]

While bachelors were in short supply in England, there was a "surplus" of them in Canada, Australia, and the United States. The effects of these imbalances were exacerbated by uneven local and regional distributions of single men everywhere. "Bachelor subcultures," which often included married men, a problem of nomenclature that I will discuss later, were found in cities and frontier areas, on land and at sea. Proposed solutions to the so-called redundancy problem included female emigration and bachelor taxes, solutions meant to boost the marriage rate, not to provide alternatives to traditional marital domesticity.[11] A 1907 editorial in *The North American Review*, "Why Bachelors Should Not Be Taxed," comments:

From time to time, special taxes have been imposed upon single men in Great Britain and Ireland, but only, it was always carefully stated, for the purpose of increasing revenues. In France, on the other hand, fear of depopulation is said to be at the root of the present movement, unsuccessful thus far, to exact toll for celibacy. It will be seen, then, that the actuating causes have varied widely; but, generally speaking, the discrimination has rested upon the Spartan principle that it is the duty to the state of every citizen to rear up legitimate children, although there is room for suspicion that, in some instances, the hen-pecked married men who made the laws felt that bachelors should pay well for happiness that seemed to them exceptional.

This anti-tax writer appears to question the "Spartan principle" itself, but he concludes that there is no real "danger of matrimony itself falling into disfavor as an avocation," and hence no need for a bachelor tax.[12] By contrast, a 1908 bachelor-tax advocate argues in *The Westminster Review* that the bachelor does indeed shirk his civic duty since "[o]wing to his not being a householder the single man escapes another burden – the Inhabited House duty, levied upon all houses rate at £20 and upwards." Noting the practical difficulty of redressing the bachelor's unfair economic advantage through income taxes and other indirect taxation, this writer argues that a special tax "levied at age 25 or 30" on bachelors "possessed of a certain income" would make these unmarried men "bear their fair share of . . . the national and local burdens."[13]

Anxieties about what this 1908 writer solemnly referred to as "the strength and security of the State" were also provoked by a late-century rise in marriage age.[14] Like so-called old maids, "old bachelors" were not necessarily elderly, just older than the normative marriage age. In the late nineteenth century, a man merely in his early thirties might be labeled an old bachelor. The average British and American marriage age is estimated to have been lowest at mid century. Sometime between the 1850s and the turn of the century, people began to marry later than previous generations had or than later generations would.[15] This graying trend peaked slightly earlier, sometime between 1890 and the 1900s, in the United States than in England, where the turning point came around 1910.[16] The anxieties elicited by the rise in marriage age were compounded by the dramatic decline in fertility rates which began early in the century.[17] The later marrying age alone did not account for the nineteenth-century decline in fertility; Banks, among others, has persuasively demonstrated that the use of contraception and other methods of family planning made significant contributions to this decline. Both smaller families and families started later in life augmented anxieties about the future of domesticity.

These demographic shifts and their attendant anxieties were particularly great for the middle and upper classes. Since there is some evidence that many working-class demographic trends ran in the opposite direction, the situation in the higher socio-economic reaches may have been more pronounced than the statistical record shows.[18] In both countries, middle-class men married later on average than working-class men, remaining at home longer or living in lodgings often until their late twenties or even early thirties.[19] Moreover, new educational opportunities in the second half of the nineteenth-century had a particularly pronounced impact on the lives of middle- and upper-class women; the marriage rate of female college graduates was strikingly lower than that of the general population of women, a trend that contributed to fears about the future of bourgeois marriage.[20] Also fanning the flames of fear, changes in the legal and economic condition of married and single women of all classes heightened awareness of the multiple and sometimes conflicting definitions of marriage as a religious sacrament, a legal contract, and a private union. While not everyone took the situation so seriously, a distinct sense of urgency is evident in the words of one 1880s commentator: "our present marriage customs set at defiance all the rules which ought to be followed in order to secure that the race shall not deteriorate."[21] The double threat of extinction and degeneracy, that is, the risk of ruining both population quantity and "quality," are suggested by this image of racial deterioration, a variation on the class- and nation-centered specter of "race suicide."[22]

The high cost of living, especially of married living, was commonly believed to be the chief cause of the feared deterioration of the bourgeois family. The middle-class standard of living rose rapidly in the second half of the nineteenth century, as did expectations that newly married couples would live in the same comfort or luxury they had enjoyed in their parental homes.[23] Bachelors often delayed marriage in order to develop their careers and to accumulate the capital necessary not merely to support their wives, but to keep them in comfort. Indeed, the emergence in the 1840s of the idea of the "proper time to marry" signals an acceptance of and even a desire for prudent delay. As this trend intensified, it gave rise to new worries.[24] Young women often were criticized for their materialistic expectations and the marriage-postponing or marriage-eliminating effects thereof. They were chastised, for example, in pieces as diverse as a 1910 survey of 500 bachelors published in *Good Housekeeping* and plaintively entitled "Bachelors – Why?"; an 1877 *Temple Bar* essay "On the Excessive Influence of Women, by an Old Fogey"; and an 1859 *Harper's* piece, "Single Life Among Us," which argued that

so far as our women are concerned, the standard of average expectation rises far beyond the standard of wealth, and society is full of young ladies whose tastes are wholly out of keeping with their domestic condition and prospects. Their evident desire for a delicate way of life at once alarms the unpretending class of suitors, and discourages the very habits of thrift and self-reliance that might make them helpers of worthy young husbands through years of modest frugality to years of peaceful independence... We must set down a false feminine fastidiousness as a very prominent cause of celibacy.[25]

Just as often, the unreasonable desire of bachelors for luxury before or instead of marriage bore the brunt of popular criticism. Thus an 1893 article claims that "To marry ... means a terrible falling-off in the standard of comfort, and the one luxury which these pleasant fellows religiously deny themselves is that of a wife."[26]

The influence of the high cost of living on both the marriage rate and marriage age was magnified by the rise of the professions. Certain occupations were linked to prolonged bachelorhood, particularly those professions which required years of training and then a protracted period for establishing a practice. Thus, in the popular fiction of the era, bachelor medical and law students appear with predictable frequency, as do bachelor doctors and lawyers.[27] Doctors seemed to their contemporaries to be in special need of the respectability of marriage since their work, like that of clergymen, brought them into the female-coded space of the home and sexually charged space of the bedroom. Yet some writers argued that there were valid reasons for doctors and other professionals to avoid married life. An 1861 letter published in the *British Medical Journal* put the situation in these terms:

It has often occurred to us, that most medical men would be the better if they remain single... [I]n the present state of society, in which expensive luxury forms a constant element, it is next to impossible for a general practitioner to support a proper appearance in the world from nothing more than the proceeds of his professional exertions... [I]t is owing to the cares of matrimony that many, who would otherwise have been philosophers, devoted to their profession, end by becoming nothing better than routineers or professional tradesmen. In moments of real illness and danger the public do not ask whether the doctor rides or walks, is married or unmarried. All they require is that he should be at hand when he is wanted, and should be capable of performing all that is required of him.[28]

Both the health of the doctor and the well-being of his patients are endangered by his marrying. While the author of this last piece is willing to excuse some medical men from the obligation to wed, his self-consciously extreme position, braced against the current of popular opinion, suggests that the ideological web that bound marriage to bourgeois manhood, and especially to professional manhood, was tightly woven indeed.

Middle-class manhood was not an uncontested ideal, a static backdrop against which the figure of the bachelor stood out as an aberration. There was no single ideal of normative manhood, but multiple models that were continually changing over time, and also overlapping and competing with other models at any given time. For example, historians of British culture describe a shift from an early nineteenth-century intellectually and emotionally earnest "Christian manliness" to "a more spartan, athletic, and conformist 'muscular manliness' at the close of the century"; they link this shift to such national conditions as imperialist and industrial expansion.[29] American historians describe a comparable shift from mid-century "civilized manliness" to turn-of-the-century "primitive masculinity," a new style of bourgeois manhood modelled on ideals of independence, physical roughness, and sexual expressiveness previously associated with non-white and working-class men.[30]

However useful such descriptions of broad shifts in dominant styles of manhood are, they tend to obscure the presence of competing ideologies and practices within and between styles of manhood throughout the period. For example, Timothy Gilfoyle and others demonstrate that a "sporting male subculture" with its attendant ideology existed in New York and elsewhere in America as early as the 1820s. This male subculture

displaced older rules and traditions governing sexual behavior for young, married, and "respectable" men. By the age of the Civil War, the writer George Ellington could conclude that many "fashionable bloods and old fogies, known rakes and presumedly pious people, wealthy bachelors and respectable married men, fast sons and moral husbands" consorted with prostitutes. If this became widely known, Ellington feared, it would "convulse society."

Gilfoyle describes how sporting male culture, "resting on an ethic of sensual pleasure," cut across class boundaries and thereby "promoted a certain gender solidarity among nineteenth-century urban males."[31] Like Gilfoyle, Elliott Gorn in *The Manly Art* and George Chauncey in *Gay New York* emphasize that American bachelors who were sporting men were, or at least were perceived to be, anti-domestic. Chauncey, for example, argues that "many of the men of the bachelor subculture ... forged an alternative definition of manliness that was predicated on a rejection of family obligations ... [e]mbodying a rejection of domesticity and of bourgeois acquisitivism alike."[32]

This bachelor subculture, which "broadly equated sexual promiscuity and erotic indulgence with individual autonomy and personal freedom," offered men an alternative or complement to domestic culture.[33] "*Bachelor* subculture" is a misleading label, however, since both married and unmarried men actively participated in them.[34] While bachelor subcultures does seem apt in relation to American cities with their "surplus" of migrant and immigrant single men, "homosocial male subcultures" or even "sporting male subcultures" make even more suitable terms, given the homosocial climate of British and American cities and of nineteenth-century British and American culture more generally. The prevalence of men's clubs, associations, and secret societies in the last third of the nineteenth century is just one register of the continuing salience of homosociality during this period. Homosociality was both a social norm for all-male activities and the basis for culture-structuring bonds more generally, a larger continuum of gendered power relations in which, as Eve Sedgwick has so persuasively theorized, both male–female and male–male bonds ultimately serve the exchange and consolidation of power among men.[35] But the key point here is that middle-class men, unlike middle-class women, could with relative impunity shuttle between the world of the street and the world of the home.[36] W. R. Greg censoriously acknowledges that

[A]mong the middle and higher ranks [men are not] compelled to lead a life of stainless abstinence ... Unhappily, as matters are managed now, thousands of men find it perfectly feasible to combine all the freedom, luxury, and self-indulgence of a bachelor's career with the pleasures of female society and the enjoyments they seek for there.[37]

In Oscar Wilde's 1891 *The Picture of Dorian Gray*, Lord Henry essentially concurs with Greg's observation, though in a tone more amusedly blasé than aggrieved: "Nowadays all the married men live like bachelors and all the bachelors live like married men.''[38] English men, both married and single, like their American counterparts, could participate actively in homosocial or sporting male subcultures whose values departed from those of hegemonic domestic ideology, and still be considered respectable.

Although they were the beneficiaries of a sexual double standard, middle-class men were nevertheless subject to conflicting expectations under domestic and other, overlapping and separate, subcultural regimes. While home and work, private and public life, were supposed to be natural and mutually sustaining complements, their values frequently clashed. Stephanie Coontz observes that while secular vocation increasingly came to replace the old notion of a man's spiritual calling, the *means* of achieving success in the marketplace often ran counter to prevailing notions of virtue.[39] The marketplace asset of autonomy conflicted with the home virtue of uxoriousness. Similarly, the public values of independence, competitiveness, and aggressiveness ran counter to the private requirements of mutuality, reciprocity, and even deference to the moral authority of wives and mothers.[40] While fathers were the nominal heads of the household, and their homes supposedly their castles, the domestic empire was in many ways subject to a different sovereign.[41] Moreover, as the ideology of marriage late in the century shifted from a more communal ethos to a more individualist one, from social duty to romantic self-fulfillment, these conflicts surely intensified for many individual men and for middle-class culture more generally. There was increased pressure on men to spend their leisure time with their wives, as a more affectional, companionate style of marriage came to replace the more hierarchical, patriarchal model. Yet the fear that "too much" contact with women would feminize men, a fear exacerbated by the demands of the new style of primitive masculinity, put new pressures on men to find their identities and pleasures outside of marriage. Torn between competing ideals of marriage, between the competing demands of home and work, and between competing models of normative masculinity, it is no wonder that middle-class men sometimes felt that their lives were in crisis.

While the paradigm of a crisis in masculinity has been used by some historians to describe the impact of competing and shifting models of manhood, it has been questioned by others.[42] Gail Bederman skillfully adjudicates between the contributions of both "crisis-thesis" and "anti-crisis-thesis" historians, agreeing with the former that "[m]iddle-class men were unusually obsessed with manhood at the turn of the century," while concurring with the latter that "despite virile, chest-thumping rhetoric, most middle-class men did not flee to the Western frontier, but remained devoted to hearth and home." Bederman persuasively argues against describing this obsession with manhood as a crisis because "to imply that masculinity was in crisis suggests that manhood is a transhistorical category or fixed essence ... rather than an ideological construct which is constantly being remade." Many late nineteenth-century men may well have been anxious about their own or others' manhood, but the notion of an actual, discrete masculinity crisis obscures the ways that manhood is always multiple, conflicted, and changing. As a corrective to the insufficient theorization of gender as "a collection of traits, attributes or sex roles," Bederman describes gender as an "historical, ideological process" which may serve a range of overlapping and not always consistent cultural functions.[43] While the process of gender may well have been particularly active at the *fin de siècle*, it is clear that the nineteenth and twentieth centuries were roiled throughout with conflicting expectations of and by men. These conflicting expectations were generated within domestic ideologies, and also by tensions between these ideologies and rival ideologies of manhood.

If married men had difficulties in coordinating these conflicting demands, how did the bachelor fare in the morass of proscriptions and prescriptions enjoined upon him by normative bourgeois definitions of manhood? Not surprisingly, nineteenth-century writers usually portrayed bachelors, both confirmed and temporary ones, as diverging from the admittedly conflicting norms of bourgeois manhood. The polymorphic variety of negative bachelor stereotypes reveals no single trajectory of aberrance, but any number of ways in which bachelors, especially those "old bachelors" who seemed to have run permanently off the rails of the marriage track, were seen as veering away from an acceptable performance of manhood. The binaries by which bachelors were stereotyped are most notable for their contrariness: superannuated and boyish; worldly and callow; gregarious and reclusive; overrefined and coarse; sophisticatedly decadent and atavistically primitive; clingy and remote; self-indulgent and miserly; unfeeling and oversensitive; fastidious and slovenly; errant and unbudging; inconsistent and rigid.

Popular representations also posed, and attempted to answer, a host of questions about the nature and meaning of bachelorhood: Was the bachelor born or did he acquire his bachelor traits? Was bachelorhood chosen as an act of conviction or imposed by an accident of fate? Was the bachelor's behavior volitional or nonvolitional, an issue of will or defect, badness or weakness? Was he like or unlike other men? Was he normal or abnormal? Indeed, was there such a thing as a "normal bachelor"? Was bachelorhood a justifiable or an illegitimate condition? Were bachelors useful and if so how? Was there an intrinsic connection between bachelorhood and high achievement in political, intellectual, aesthetic, or spiritual arenas? Did society benefit from the existence of bachelors? What were their uses or contributions? And did these uses or contributions justify their bachelorhood? Could anything justify bachelorhood? Clearly, these questions are all over the map, and the answers given to them are equally multiform and often incoherent. But the list of questions *does* give a sense of how and also why popular writers were troubled by bachelors.

Some contemporary trouble-shooters created their own typologies of bachelorhood as a way of managing the trouble with bachelors. There is little or no consistency in the ways these popular typologies were organized. For example, an 1853 *Southern Literary Messenger* article, "On Old Bachelors," presents us with four types of bachelors: Involuntary, Sentimental, Misogynistic, and Stingy; an 1898 article, "Famous Bachelors," which appeared in the British journal *The Woman at Home*, surveys five kinds: the misogynist, the sentimental, the irresolute, the timid, and the hopeful; and a 1913 *Good Housekeeping* article, entitled simply "Bachelors," makes a tripartite division of bachelordom into "men who are born bachelors," "men who achieve bachelorhood," and others who "have bachelorhood thrust upon them."[44] These three "nonfiction" pieces make their taxonomizing particularly explicit, although similar and disparate taxonomies implicitly obtain in other examples and other genres. While certain motifs appear throughout the period, there is no clear pattern, no clear sense of continuity or development across time. This lack of clarity results in part from the same taxonomic labels, such as "misogynist" or "sentimental," being used to describe different traits; to indicate cause or effect; to defend bachelorhood or to mark it as indefensible. The very incoherence of these troubled taxonomies registers the difficulties that bourgeois writers and readers experienced in attempting to account for a group that they described as a class, a race, a tribe, and even a species.

Within and beyond these troubled taxonomies, economic explanations were frequently offered as a way of accounting for bachelorhood:

Therefore, if marriage be a man's object, let him not forget that a sufficient income – not pleasant badinage, nor fluent speaking, nor a good seat – is the first essential condition.

"Cupid has definitely located his arch enemy: he is the High Cost of Living," observes a Boston investigator of the allied subjects of economics and romance.[45]

As often, economic considerations were seen as rationalizations for the bad characters of bachelors:

In coming to this important decision [i.e., marriage], the bachelor is often influenced by selfish or pecuniary decisions.

Is the hesitation of so many bachelors before the problem of matrimony owing wholly, or mainly, to the high cost of living?[46]

To this rhetorical question, the answer was invariably "No."

[Bachelors are] unsocial beings who would selfishly live for their pleasure alone.

To read of themselves would be infinite pleasure/ As they loved their dear selves they knew beyond measure/ And themselves, their own selves, were their heart's greatest treasure.

[S]ome of the most artistic, luxurious and beautiful rooms in New York are the bachelor quarters where members of my selfish class lead their not always useless and selfish lives.

A bachelor must be, to a certain extent, selfish; he cannot help it; he thinks of himself in some shape or another from morning till night; and selfishness begets self-indulgence and hard-heartedness.[47]

This sampling of pronouncements, which span the long nineteenth century and which I have selected primarily for their brevity, demonstrates the tight conceptual fit between bachelors and home economics. Far from being insulated from market relations, the marital home was the marketplace's *sine qua non*. Hence, "selfishness" was seen as the principal defect of bachelors. Self-centeredness, the wish for luxury, the desire to evade responsibility, stinginess, the love of comfort, the longing for glory – all these and more are considered under the rubric of bachelor selfishness. One might say that in the Victorian era, "selfish bachelor" was a redundancy.

Even *apologias* for bachelorhood conceded the inevitable selfishness of bachelors. Consider this defense of bachelorhood offered in an 1880s *Temple Bar* piece, "Why We Men Do Not Marry, By One of Us":

Each year I have some money to save or to spend. Shall I spend it on a wife and children; on millinery bills and boot bills; on doctor's bills and schoolmasters' bills[?] I prefer to dispose of it otherwise. I prefer to keep a horse; I prefer a comfortable annual trip on the continent, or to America; I prefer pictures and china, shilling cigars and first-rate hock. Very selfish, no doubt. Yet not so altogether. I am a professional man, my work makes heavy demands on my nervous system. A glass of generous wine or the subtle enjoyment of a good Havana may save me from an opiate or a doctor's visit. So it is with my annual holiday. I am exhausted by a year's labour; my holiday is absolutely necessary... In the stress and strain of this tense civilisation, luxury has been drawn close to necessity. I might, it is true, dispense with these solaces, but I should break down the sooner.[48]

While many contemporary writers condemned the craving for luxury as a sign of bachelors' defection from the values of thrift and self-restraint, the psychological necessity of luxury is offered here as a moral justification for bachelorhood. "Very selfish no doubt. Yet not so altogether": given "the stress and strain of this tense civilization," this writer counts luxury as a necessity so basic that marriage itself comes to seem an imprudent, even dangerous, extravagance.

Profligacy and stinginess are flipsides of the same coin which bachelors were seen as reserving for their own selfish use. Bachelors were as often accused of miserliness as of extravagance: "John Bachelor Stingybones, Esq ... is excessively close and saving – and take my word for it, that is the reason why he has never married."[49] Thus, the bachelor was popularly imagined as a figure of improper expenditure, as one who either spends too much – "A bachelor who has been accustomed to spend all his income or wages upon himself will not have much to spare for a family" – or spends too little, hoarding his money in a miserly, antisocial fashion, as an 1839 poem describes "The Old Bachelor" who leaves behind nothing after his death "But wealth, and ill health, and his pelf and his self."[50]

Improper expenditure is not merely a matter of too much or too little, but of the particular uses to which spending is put. While the improper objects of bachelor spending include anything that is not within the purview of the familial or the marital, the most commonly conceived improper object of spending is the bachelor himself. Indeed, the selfishness ascribed to bachelors has primary connotations of both self-centeredness and dissipation. We see this double register in an 1869 *Temple Bar* poem, "The Bachelor: A Modern Idyll," in which a married man insists to a doubting bachelor that the "selfish joys" of bachelor self-indulgence pale beside the pleasure of seeing "contentment beam in six-and-twenty eyes," even though "we have to live without some things we'd like."[51] The double register of bachelor egocentricism and degeneracy also appears in the 1859 *Harper's* piece cited above, which claims that "Too many old bachelors abandon love and take to their bank-book and bill of fare – not to name baser indulgences – for their solace." Here indulgence at the dinner table goes hand-in-hand with miserliness, since eating and saving are both forms of acquisitiveness.[52] Significantly, the underspending of the bank-book and the overspending of the bill of fare are linked to unnamed "baser indulgences," a rhetorical indirection that nonetheless clearly alludes to nonprocreative and extramarital sexual activity.

These representations of bachelor economics can be understood as figures for bachelor sexuality. Specifically sexual bachelor "energies" or "resources" and those that were not specifically sexual were used as metaphors for each other.[53] Just as bachelors were imagined as spending their money on the wrong objects or for the wrong reasons, they were also imagined as channelling, or dissipating, their sexual energy in a variety of nonmarital "dead ends." Particularly in the first half of the century, bachelors were thought to be especially susceptible to masturbation.[54] The nonproductive, pleasure-driven, and self-oriented qualities of masturbation were thought to constitute a serious danger, a material and moral drain on a finite, bodily "spermatic economy" as well as a drain on the domestic economies of the nation, race, and class. Worse still, masturbation was regarded as a major cause of spermatorrhea or "bachelor's disease." This imaginary malady – the involuntary loss of seminal fluid in nocturnal emissions or through the urine – was, with the possible exception of masturbation, "the single most discussed problem in instructional books for boys and young men."[55] First diagnosed in 1836, spermatorrhea came in the later nineteenth century to be associated with neurasthenia and other forms of nervous exhaustion that seemed to plague the urban business classes. Thought to deplete the male body of its limited supply of vital forces, spermatorrhea was represented by many legitimate physicians as well as quacks as a scourge that would result in consumption, epilepsy, insanity, feeble-mindedness, or death, unless nipped in the bud. With the rise of social purity and social hygiene movements during the second half of the nineteenth century, male continence was increasingly prescribed as a treatment for spermatorrhea, especially for single men. But throughout this period and particularly with the turn into the twentieth century, there was a countervailing emphasis, especially in medical and psychiatric discourse, on the normal need for men to express their "pent-up" sexual energies.[56] Sexual intercourse within the bounds of marriage was considered the last stage in the treatment of spermatorrhea as well as the ultimate goal of the treatment.

The notion that male sexual release was conducive to good health did not, of course, mean that any form of sexual activity was permissible. Indeed, the idea of healthy or therapeutic release made bachelors newly suspect since they had no sanctioned sexual outlet. While there had been a tacit recognition of the inevitability of male commerce with prostitutes, this form of sexual activity was increasingly associated with sexual deviance. In fact, one form of deviance linked to consorting with prostitutes, both female and male, was *the* paradigmatic turn-of-the-century perversion, which Christopher Craft has evocatively called "the perversion with a future": homosexuality.[57] This linkage resulted in part from the nineteenth-century prosecution under prostitution statutes of men who engaged in same-sex activities.[58] By the turn of the century, all forms of nonprocreative sexual activity including masturbation, bestiality, and pederasty, even the *absence* of sexual activity within or beyond the bonds of marriage, were coming increasingly to be seen as possible signs of homosexuality.

Not all bachelors were considered homosexuals, although "bachelor" came to be used often as an slurring insinuation against gay men or as an insider's codeword by them. But the epistemological indeterminacy of bachelorhood both preceded and postdated what Sedgwick describes as a "sudden, radical condensation of sexual categories" by which the gender of object choice emerged at the turn of the century as "*the* dimension denoted by the now ubiquitous categories of 'sexual orientation.'"[59] Whether as a specific type of sexual deviant or as a more generalized locus of trouble, the bachelor disrupted the proper regulation that defined home economics throughout the nineteenth century and into the twentieth. The disorderly potential of the bachelor may well indicate the susceptibility of this home economy to elements that many would have wanted to consider extrinsic to it. The insistent representation of bachelors in relation to conventional domesticity served partly to regulate, and thus to control, their disruptiveness, yet the very prevalence of such representations suggests a lack of control, or failure to contain, the trouble with bachelors. Representations of bachelors at home, living in or visiting other people's houses, or residing in homes of their own, did multiple and sometimes contradictory cultural tasks. While often deployed in order to contain the volatile manhood of bachelors, the discourse of bachelor domesticity itself provided opportunities for bachelors to go out of bounds.

BACHING IT: HOUSING AND THE QUESTION OF
BACHELOR DOMESTICITY

Of all possible connotations that a verb derived from the noun "bachelor" might have, it is no accident that the primary one has to do with housing and home-making. The locution "baching it," like its close but now obsolete cousin "bachelorizing," arose in the context of early nineteenth-century emigration to frontier areas of British colonies and American territories; it referred specifically to the residences and living styles of single men who were making new homes in these new worlds.[60] The prevalence of stories, poems, and essays with titles such as "Bachelor's Bedroom," "Bachelor's Wing," "Bachelor's Den," "Bachelor's Hall," throughout the period attests to the fascination that "baching it" held for its observers and participants.[61] These popular texts, as well as many others that dwell on the living arrangements of bachelors, combine an eroticized fixation on the private lives of single men with anxiety about the future of domesticity in a rapidly modernizing, urbanizing and industrializing age. The question of whether true domesticity could be found in the modern era and especially in the modern city overlapped with the question of whether bachelors could or should make "real homes."

Both the image of the bachelor and the meaning of domesticity changed significantly during this era, in ways that are almost certainly correlated. While bachelorhood came to appear more compatible with domesticity during the course of the nineteenth century, domesticity itself came to look more like the bachelor version of it. Although still rooted in a notion of the home as the center of woman's life and feminine virtue, domesticity was changing to encompass a more self-expressive, pleasure-centered, consumer-oriented, even luxurious ideal by the beginning of the twentieth century, a shift associated with the larger cultural transition from a producer-based economy to a consumer-based one.[62] Although a home continued to depend, according to hegemonic domestic ideologies, on the presence of a woman, the appearance and behavior of this woman was changing. At mid century, the ideal domestic woman was the wife-as-mother; by the turn of the century, the wife-as-mother had been partially supplanted by the wife-as-companion. If a new companionate style of married "masculine domesticity" accompanied the expansion of the suburbs in the last third of the nineteenth century, then the rise of urban bachelor apartment buildings and the proliferation of men's clubs during this period also

created new opportunities for domesticity and quasi-domesticity practiced by single men alone, in pairs, or in groups.[63]

While bachelor domesticity may have increased in practice and
accrued new ideological meanings toward the turn of the century,
counter-discourses and alternative styles of bachelor domesticity existed
throughout the century. Even in the early nineteenth century, as, for
example, in an 1828 *Blackwood's Magazine* feature entitled "The Bachelor's Beat," bachelors were sometimes imagined as exemplars of domestic life. In one installment of this four-part series, bearing the highly
conventional title "The Bachelor's Christmas," the old bachelor saves
his nephew, and the nephew's marriage, from the dangerous influence
of a party of "sportsmen" and "dashers":

> "Uncle," said Philip, in a tone of manly firmness, "you will assist me to get
> civilly rid of yonder host of idlers, and the false friend who hoped, by their
> means, to disgust me with my country, and estrange me from my bride. You
> shall make me an Englishman after your own heart."
> "Uncle," whispered Lady Jane, with the most insinuating softness' "you will
> invite us to your cottage, won't you, till a few more comforts are added to our
> home, to make it all that an English home should be?"

Earlier in the story, this bachelor uncle laments the "cheerless meal and
silent vigil of my own bachelor home." Yet his description of his
bachelor home, especially in combination with the happy outcome of
the nephew's marriage plot, defies any simple sense of domestic lack:

> And yet it is a beloved home, – hallowed by fond recollections, and rich in
> present enjoyments; endeared by the shelter it afforded to the green loveliness
> of a mother's old age, which had nothing of age save its sanctity; hallowed, as
> the scene of a transition which had nothing of death but the name; adorned by
> her own exquisite taste, and my solicitude for her comfort, with a thousand little
> refinements which few bachelor homes can boast.[64]

The assertion that these "thousand little refinements" are anomalous in
a bachelor home is a stock gesture of nineteenth-century bachelor
discourse, as is the implication that a "bachelor home" itself is a kind of
oxymoron. When there are so many exceptions to the rule of the
non-domesticity or even anti-domesticity of bachelors, the rule itself
becomes questionable. Throughout the century, bachelors in their residences were imagined as embracing but also rejecting, adapting to but
also transforming, conventional domestic ideologies and practices,
which were themselves undergoing uneven developments.

For the vast majority of nineteenth-century middle-class British and
American citizens, marriage and family meant home, and home meant

a single-family house. Although some bachelors resided in and/or owned such houses, they were not customarily associated with them. In English cities, "chambers" were the type of housing most often associated with bachelors, probably "because the best-known sets of chambers in London were those provided for the exclusively male entrants into the legal profession at Temple and Lincoln's Inns."[65] Chambers designated a range of accommodations that varied widely in cost, comfort, services, and space. The modest end of the spectrum may be represented by Dick Swiveller's "bachelor establishment" in *The Old Curiosity Shop*:

By a . . . pleasant fiction his single chamber was always mentioned in the plural number. In its disengaged times, the tobacconist had announced it in his window as "apartments" for a single gentleman, and Mr Swiveller, following up the hint, never failed to speak of it as his rooms, his lodgings, or his chambers, conveying to his hearers a notion of indefinite space, and leaving their imaginations to wander through long suites of lofty halls, at pleasure.[66]

Whereas Dick Swiveller orders his meals from a nearby eating house, the mysterious "single gentleman" lodger in this Dickens novel cooks his meals on a remarkable, self-contained "cooking apparatus."[67] By contrast, well-established chambers offered dining in commons or in private dining rooms. This other end of the chambers spectrum is well represented by the "very perfection of quiet absorption of good living, good drinking, good feeling and good talk" enjoyed at one of the Inns of Court by the narrator of Melville's 1855 "The Paradise of Bachelors."[68] A mid-century London *Landlord's and Tenant's Guide* emphasizes the "independence" afforded by chambers to "young bachelors not yet wishing to be troubled with housekeeping, and old bachelors who have renounced all thoughts of it"; an 1876 letter to the editor of *The Builder*, England's foremost architectural journal, stresses their comfort and convenience: "There are few men who have lived in good suites of chambers who do not contrast unfavourably with them the houses they are compelled to occupy when they get married and settled."[69]

While *The Builder* correspondent looks to certain aspects of chamber life as a model for married domesticity, there was no thought that such accommodations should actually be inhabited by bourgeois English families. Flats were accepted as housing for the working classes and the unmarried, but for the middle classes they "continued to be associated with 'bachelor chambers,' such as those in *The Albany*."[70] Similar prejudices against multi-unit and multi-family dwelling existed in the United

States, although Americans ultimately proved more accepting of such housing. This acceptance was not, however, without reservation. Delores Hayden observes that while workers in the United States lived in crowded tenements with several families to a floor, before 1860 "it would have been unthinkable for a family of even modest social aspirations to live in anything but a private dwelling, however humble such a house might be."[71]

Since home-ownership was a bourgeois ideal, if largely an unfulfilled one, one minor objection to families lodging in chambers and, later, in flats in purpose-built apartment houses was that these residences were rented.[72] But the principal objection to chambers and flats was that they crossed lines, often imaginary but nevertheless highly charged, which separated middle-class from working-class residential styles, residential spaces from commercial ones, and different families from each other. Privacy *within* the family was not generally at issue in the first half of the century, although it became increasingly so later on.[73] But when individuals of different families or households shared exterior spaces including sidewalks and building entrances, and interior spaces such as lobbies and hallways, and sometimes even sitting-rooms and dining-rooms, the supposedly inviolable privacy *of* the family, a central tenet of bourgeois domesticity, seemed to be jeopardized. Just as working-class tenements required different families to share facilities for bathing and laundry, living arrangements that were shocking to middle-class sensibilities, chambers and flats also occasioned the unacceptable crossing of established social and spatial divides.[74] Elizabeth Cromley suggests that the gradual acceptance of boarding as a residential option for middle-class and married Americans made boundary-crossings of certain kinds even more likely:

[By mid century], a broad cross-section of occupations and varied "family status" (married and single) could occupy a single house. Indeed, this "mix" was sometimes seen as volatile, not solely because of cross-class conflicts but also because of differences in marital status; for example, Junius Browne's 1869 guidebook *Great Metropolis* represents single men as threatening to married couples in boardinghouse settings through their double position as an example to the husbands of "freedom" and as potential seducers of the wives.[75]

The promiscuous mingling of individuals of different walks of life, sexes, and marital statuses, was particularly threatening because it took place across the boundaries of the family, supposedly the dwelling place of one's truest, most private, inner self.

Bachelors were thus represented as a danger against which other multi-unit dwellers, single and married, male and female, had to gird themselves. The dangers of sharing a residence with bachelors are illustrated in the 1859 Wilkie Collins sketch, "The Bachelor Bedroom," mentioned at the beginning of this chapter. This bachelor bedroom provides only temporary quarters for the bachelors who serially occupy it, and hence it differs from the full-time and closer proximity of the boarding house. Yet the permanent assignment of a bedroom to bachelors in this upper-class English countryhouse suggests that, as in the boarding house, bachelors are a regular feature of this world, not excluded from it.[76] Like the bachelors who abide there, the bachelor bedroom is at once integral to this "civilised residence" and yet fundamentally at odds with it: "It started in life, under Sir John's careful auspices, the perfection of neatness and tidiness. But the bachelors have corrupted it long since . . . He is a rigid man and resolute in the matter of order, and has his way all over the rest of the house – but the Bachelor Bedroom is too much for him" (pp. 355–6). Just as the respectable house contains a "slovenly and unpresentable" (p. 355) bachelor bedroom, so too does each outwardly respectable bachelor reveal his true, inner nature within its confines. The hypochondriacal "Mr. Jollins," for example, betrays "a horrible triumph and interest in the maladies of others, of which nobody would suspect in the general society of the house" (p. 357). And when the door of the bachelor bedroom closes behind the ultra-refined "Mr. Smart," "the jolliest, broadest and richest Irish brogue" replaces this bachelor's "highly-bred English with the imperturbably gentle drawl," and "wild and lavish generosity suddenly bec[omes] the leading characteristic of this once reticent man" (pp. 357–8).

Similarly, the bachelor "Mr. Bigg," who seems "altogether an irreproachable character," undergoes a transformation inside the bedroom:

But what is Mr. Bigg, when he has courteously wished the ladies good night, when he has secretly summoned the footman with the surreptitious tray, and when he has deluded the unprincipled married men of the party into having an hour's cozy chat with them before they go upstairs? Another being – a being unknown to the ladies, and unsuspected by the respectable guests. Inside the Bedroom, the outward aspect of Mr. Bigg changes as if by magic; and a kind of gorgeous slovenliness pervades him from top to toe. Buttons which have rigidly restrained him within distinct physical boundaries slip exhausted out of their button-holes; and the figure of Mr. Bigg suddenly expands and asserts itself for the first time as a protuberant fact. His neckcloth flies on to the nearest chair, his rigid shirt-collar yawns open, his wiry under-whiskers ooze multitudinously into view, his coat, waistcoat, and braces drop off his shoulders. If the two young ladies who sleep in the room above, and who most unreasonably complain of the ceaseless nocturnal croaking and growling of voices in the Bachelor Bedroom, could look down through the ceiling now, they would not know Mr. Bigg again, and would suspect that a dissipated artisan had intruded himself into Sir John's house. (p. 356)

I quote this marvelously rich passage in its entirety to show the range of threats, real and imaginary, posed by this bachelor in his bedroom. He seduces the married men into nocturnal excesses; he annoys, and possibly endangers, the young ladies by his audible proximity, the improper absence or permeability of boundaries between male and female spaces evoked here by the fantasy of a see-through ceiling; his resemblance to a "dissipated artisan" suggests an improper transgression of class boundaries; the "nocturnal croaking and growling" even suggests a transgression of the boundary between animal and human. These transgressions are abetted by the boundary-crossing that characterizes Mr. Bigg's body: his "wiry underwhiskers ooze" out and his figure, released by his buttons from "distinct physical boundaries," "expands and asserts itself . . . as a protuberant fact." His body breaches the bounds of a sexualized propriety, much as this bachelor intruder breaches the security of proper domesticity, adding to the profusion of ways in which a bachelor may be in, yet not fully of, the home.

Bachelors in other people's homes are not only a threat to others; they sometimes present a threat to themselves. The threatening social and physical expansiveness demonstrated by Mr. Bigg within the confines of the Bachelor Bedroom has a counterpart, though an inverse one, in the threatening constriction of a bachelor who cannot make himself fully at home in his London lodgings. The titular bachelor of this 1850s *Harper's* story, yet another "A Bachelor's Christmas," moves out of the Inner Temple in search of quieter surroundings more conducive to studying for the bar.[77] He is initially well pleased with the "solitude of lodgings" where he relieves himself from the rigors of Blackstone with Montaigne, Congreve, Pope, Shakespeare, and Milton. With only the companionship of his books, "my dearest, my only associates," and his landlady, whom he tolerates despite her prying and petty thievery, he describes himself as becoming "egotistic and lazy": "There was a selfish pleasure in the conviction that my case was so much better than that of thousands of the toilers and strugglers of the earth" (p. 399). His satisfaction, however, is transformed into misery when he must endure such minor inconveniences as late meals and noise as his landlady prepares a Christmas holiday celebration for her friends and relations. Far from his own home in Scotland, he is overcome by loneliness, "sick at heart – stupidly and profoundly dejected" (p. 400), maddened by "envy at the exuberant mirth," and "furious at the sympathy which my loneliness created." This increasingly "nervous and irritable" (p. 401) bachelor seems to be on the verge of a breakdown.

The moral of the story is not, as one might expect, that the bachelor should have accepted the offers of hospitality from downstairs. In fact, the narrator never explains his unwillingness to join the party, although class prejudice coupled with studiously respectable reserve is the most likely explanation. Rather, he recalls "vow[ing] solemnly that I would not pass another Christmas day in solitude, and in lodgings – and I didn't" (p. 401). In the coda to the story, he tells how he and his bride manage to move from their temporary lodgings in furnished apartments to their new home in a suburban villa in time for Christmas. The likelihood that this home of their own is rented does not seem to mitigate their domestic bliss. What seems crucial to the attainment of domesticity is, rather, the privacy enabled by the single family residence, as well as the presence within that dwelling of a woman of his own, the former bachelor's wife.

The dangerous isolation of this solitary bachelor in his lodgings might be also considered the flipside of the dangerous companionship enjoyed by a group of bachelor tenants in a *Harper's* piece of the same decade, an 1853 cartoon entitled "Scenes in Bachelor Life." Here, reckless dissipation rather than maddening loneliness constitutes the primary threat to bachelor well-being. The first panel shows three figures standing near a fireplace in a room devoid of furnishings, with a caption reading "Messrs. Briggs, Brown and Bangs admire their apartments and anticipate 'Great Times'." By turn, they engage in fencing, boxing, and wrestling until the landlady knocks at the door, requesting the "Gentlemen to make less noise." They think they'll "take a little" after their exertions, and proceed to "imbibe" punch made in an apparatus resembling a chafing dish.[78] In their drunken state, they accidentally set the place on fire and they are shown running out the door: "Exit Messrs. Briggs, Bangs, and Brown. The 'Good Time' is postponed."[79]

The alcohol-fueled, sports-oriented carousing of these bachelors in their rented digs – culminating in a conflagration metonymically linked to the bachelors' enflamed appetite for pleasure – is a far cry from the studious and ultimately depressive isolation of the bachelor lodger in "A

Bachelor's Christmas." In that story, it is the bachelor who is disturbed by the landlady's audible merrymaking, whereas here it is the landlady who complains about the bachelors' noise. In the first story, the bachelor seeks true domesticity with a wife, whereas here the bachelors seek only to escape the dangerous effects of their riotous behavior, with no promise, implicit or explicit, of domestic reform. Yet both pieces are cautionary tales. Baching it proves dangerous to the well-being of these bachelors, the differences in the outcome of their stories notwithstanding. The need for the domestic reform of bachelors is evident to the reader of both pieces, if not necessarily to the bachelor characters portrayed in them.

Other writers envisioned bachelors not as the source of domestic disorder, but as domestic reformers. Oliver Bell Bunce's 1881 *Bachelor Bluff: His Opinions, Sentiments, and Disputations* opens with a challenge to the conventional wisdom "that domestic bliss is something which bachelors neither understand nor appreciate."[80] Bunce's Bachelor Bluff goes on to argue that:

refined and perfect domestic comfort is understood by men only . . . Women are not personally selfish enough to be fastidious in these things . . . They are neat because they constitutionally hate dust, not because neatness is important to their own selfish comfort. Women are rarely epicureans. They have no keen enjoyment of eating and drinking, in dreams and laziness; they do not understand intellectual repose. (pp. 19–20)

Bunce's bachelor does not despair of women, but rather hopes to enlist them to his cause:

What I hope to do is to convince "lovely woman" that, if we are to continue to marry her, she must endeavor to work up to our ideals of domestic felicity. She must try and find an outlet for her energies, so that at home she can fall into our luxuriousness, our love of repose, our enjoyment of supreme ease. (p. 25)

In the 1880s, the most plausible outlet for middle-class women's virtuous energies was not the paid work force, but the volunteer charitable work which was increasingly being performed by "public mothers."[81] Bachelor Bluff's suggestion that women leave the home to reform the world is ultimately less radical, however, than his argument that men must reform the home. It takes a man's "active ideas at work" (p. 26), strangely enough, to "create a paradise of indolence, to fill the mind with an ecstasy of repose, to render home a heaven of the senses – women are usually too virtuous to do this. Daintiness in man takes an artistic form; in woman it assumes a formidable order, a fearful cleanliness, a precision of arrangements that freeze us" (p. 27). If women are needed as public mothers, then men must be private fathers. Only the artistic daintiness of men can create a paradise on earth, a home which is a "heaven of the senses" (p. 27).

Men in general and bachelors in particular assume a guiding role in Bunce's vignettes, reversing the traditionally gendered order of the mid-century domestic empire of the mother. Bunce's "heaven of the senses" appropriates some of the features of the spiritual heaven of the home, but he inverts their meanings. Traditional virtues including cleanliness, industriousness, selflessness and virtuousness itself, are re-imagined here as *obstacles* to achieved domesticity. For Bunce, aesthetic refinement and material comfort, leisure and repose, are not antithetical to virtue, but sources of value in themselves, the very heart and soul of domesticity. While refinement and comfort had a place in more traditional domestic ideologies and practices, here they assume a different ontological status. They become the ends as well as the means of domesticity. This modification can be understood in terms of a synchronic difference between bachelor domesticity and more conventional marital domesticity. It can also be understood in terms of a diachronic shift from domesticity-as-virtue to domesticity-as-pleasure, a shift which might be said to culminate with the House Beautiful aestheticism of Charles Eastlake, Clarence Cook, Oscar Wilde and others.[82]

In propounding his aesthetic domestic reform, Bunce's bachelor was part of a much larger cultural chorus registering dissatisfaction with various aspects of traditional domesticity. Not surprisingly, one of the foremost objects of criticism for nineteenth-century domestic reformers was the tradition of single-family housing.[83] When envisioning a viable alternative to the single-family home, the writer of an 1888 *Temple Bar* article, "Why We Men Do Not Marry, By One of Us," turned to the residential system of British colleges:

I can imagine a number of families living together in a building constructed and managed on the principle of a college ... There should be a common dining-hall, a common recreation-room, a common garden, a common billiard-room. On each staircase, around the quadrangle, should live a family ... There would be vastly more comfort and vastly less cost. In all the great dead [sic] expenses, co-operative principles would effect the usual reduction.

Build me then no more flats; though these are good in their way. But build me a college quadrangle; and perhaps I will marry and live therein.[84]

Although this writer recommends the college quadrangle as a model for married living, the enhancements of unmarried life represented by these residential halls were not far to seek. Other alternatives to traditional married domesticity were evident in the settlement house movement in the latter part of the century and in utopian experiments in communal living throughout the century.

Urban men's clubs, while far from self-consciously reformist, also helped to remodel domestic possibilities for men both married and single. Like the utopian community and the settlement house, the men's club reimagined the traditional division of space into public and private spheres by moving a range of social and solitary activities out of the home and into the club. The concepts of private and public hardly disappeared later in the century – indeed, one might argue that the distinction between them was heightened – but the boundaries demarcating them were not stable. When the lines shifted, what properly belonged to each sphere was redefined. In this respect, the club was a particularly charged institution, since it was understood as both private and public, as both home and world. An example of this kind of ambiguity can be found in John Seymour Wood's 1891 "The Story of an Old Beau," published in *Scribner's Magazine*. The bachelor protagonist of the story treasures his club as "my only home," but the authorial narrator challenges the domestic potential of this realm: "This is the way in clubs, where men have no business to be pitiful, and no desire to be merciful. The club is after all but a miniature of the world."[85] These conflicting assessments of the club as both home and world are left unresolved, with the protagonist ultimately rejecting the unsympathetic familial home of his sister and niece, forfeiting the luxurious but equally unforgiving home of his club, and rebuilding his fortune in California. In this story, being a "real man" means never being at home.

The last third of the nineteenth century was the heyday of the men's club in the principal cities of both America and England. It has been estimated that "[a]t the turn of the century there were more than 200 clubs in London, half of which had been founded within the previous 30 years," and that "by 1873 there were nearly one hundred clubs in New York, giving it the largest number of any city in the world except London."[86] While there were some clubs specifically for bachelors, most clubs had a mix of married and unmarried members.[87] Married clubmen, moreover, were in the majority at most clubs in America and probably in England as well.[88] There was, however, a widely perceived linkage between bachelors and these all-male social institutions. Thus a

1911 history of London clubs observes with satisfaction that "[t]he growth of the club system undoubtedly effected a great revolution in the domestic life of men generally, and especially in that of the younger ones . . . It was, however, in the life of the bachelor that the introduction of this state of affairs caused the greatest change."[89]

Clubs offered to bachelors, as they did to married men, an all-male arena for activities, interactions, and emotions that had been formerly, and still were ideally, associated with the conjugal and familial home: rest and recreation, solitude and sociability, privacy and companionship. In her recent study of American clubs, Anne Henry suggests that comfort was the crucial offering of British and American men's clubs, including such amenities as leather armchairs, blazing hearths, great windows, libraries full of books, morning papers, good food, and good wine. Both British and American clubs provided men with the opportunity for playing at cards and billiards, smoking and drinking, reading and conversation; for good dining in an attractive setting, and for lounging and viewing (a window with a prime view of the street was particularly valued). While the physical amenities offered by British and American clubs were comparable, Henry notes that "[p]art of an English club's comfort derived from its members' privacy, while for Americans, comfort was equally found in society."[90] The contrast between American sociability and British solitariness is highlighted in an 1891 *Scribner's* article comparing London clubs to those in America: "Much has been said in the course of this paper about sociability; that is, indeed, the characteristic difference between English and American clubs."[91] The unsociable character of the English club is deliciously spoofed, for example, in Sherlock Holmes's description of "the queerest club in London":

There are many men in London, you know, who, some from shyness, some from misanthropy, have no wish for the company of their fellows. Yet they are not averse to comfortable chairs and the latest periodicals. It is for the convenience of these that the Diogenes Club was started, and it now contains the most unsociable and unclubbable men in town. No member is permitted to take the least notice of any other one. Save in the Stranger's Room, no talking is, under any circumstances, allowed, and three offences, if brought to the notice of the committee, render the talker liable to expulsion.[92]

Overall, popular representations of the period stereotyped British clubmen as unsociable or antisocial, while American clubmen tended to be stereotyped as overly gregarious or hypersocial.

Such stereotyping, whether venomous or affectionate, fulfills an ideological function extending beyond the enforcement of national differences. American gregariousness and British taciturnity are both represented as excessive because the need for companionship and privacy were understood to be ideally fulfilled within the conjugal home. French feminist and socialist Flora Tristan, who visited several London clubs in 1840 while disguised as a man, claimed that these clubs "make men more self-centered and egotistical . . . [I]f they [the clubs] did not exist, men would frequent society more and stay with their families."[93] Men could better find the privacy they crave within the home, she suggests, while also learning there to be more sociable. An American bachelor quoted in the 1910 *Good Housekeeping* survey, "Bachelors – Why?", also compared the camaraderie of clubs unfavorably with the truer companionship of home: "the club is all right so far as food and comfort of body go, but that is as far as it is of any use. A home is a place that gives these comforts, and love and sympathy as well. The club can never do this. The man of deep feelings, therefore, had better avoid the club. It is fit only for vapid triflers."[94] Clubs, like the bachelors with whom they are metonymically linked, are perceived as both antisocial and hypersocial. The excessive sociability and excessive withdrawal fostered by clubs is not just a problem of degree, but crucially one of kind. Clubmen, like bachelors, expend their limited fund of male energies on the "wrong people," that is, on other men or women whom they have no intention of marrying, and toward the "wrong ends," that is, the extramarital and nonprocreative.

While some writers argued that the rise of the club system was causing the rejection of matrimony, others defended clubs against such charges, affirming that clubs constituted a "preparation and not a substitute for domestic life."[95] Yet the availability of residential accommodations in clubs clearly made them potential alternatives, as well as supplements, to married domesticity. Although lodging, both temporary and permanent, was available only on a limited scale in American clubs, these clubs were nonetheless widely understood as providing homes for bachelors, as Henry Nelson suggested in 1890 when he described New York's Union Club as "not only the first club in the city . . . [but] the first club intended to be a home for bachelors and to furnish the creature comforts found by clubless men in taverns."[96] By the 1890s, two other housing institutions that were changing the face of urban domesticity joined the club as refuges for middle- and upper-class American bachelors: the apartment hotel and the bachelor-flat building.

The term "apartment hotel" originated as a neologism that enabled developers to take advantage of a loophole in an 1890s law restricting the height of apartment buildings, but not of hotels. Although the law was changed in 1901 to allow taller apartment buildings, the "apartment hotel" designation was retained to distinguish this type of residence from family apartment buildings, which did not provide all the services of hotels, and also from hotels, which did not offer as much privacy for dining and entertainment of guests. In addition to cleaning and other services, apartment hotels featured communal kitchens which furnished either private meals or a bill of fare in the house restaurant, thereby eliminating the individual kitchen or supplementing it with alternative dining options. According to Cromley, the most successful apartment hotels were those designed specifically for bachelors. By the turn of the century, these accommodations were supplemented by suites set aside for unmarried men in many smaller buildings like The Chelsea and also in such massive apartment houses as the Ansonia and the Dakota; by bachelor apartments on the upper floors of midtown buildings with street-level stores or deluxe restaurants such as Delmonico's and Sherry's; and by apartment buildings designed specifically for bachelors, including the Percival, the Century, the Carlyle Chambers, and the Benedict.[97]

The pleasures and dangers of the New York bachelor apartment building are evident in Edith Wharton's *The House of Mirth* when Lily Bart impulsively accompanies Lawrence Selden home for tea. This impromptu visit precipitates Lily's inexorable tumble down the socio-economic ladder and ultimately results in her death:

He ushered her into a slip of a hall hung with old prints. She noticed the letters and notes heaped on the table among his gloves and sticks; then she found herself in a small library, dark but cheerful, with its walls of books, a pleasantly faded Turkey rug, a littered desk, and, as he had foretold, a tea-tray on a low table near the window. A breeze had sprung up, swaying inward the muslin curtains, and bringing a fresh scent of mignonette and petunias from the flower-box on the balcony.

Lily sank with a sigh into one the shabby leather chairs.

"How delicious to have a place like this all to one's self! What a miserable thing it is to be a woman." She leaned back in a luxury of discontent.[98]

Lily enviously indulges herself in "a luxury of discontent," but a single woman without a fortune cannot afford even this small luxury, at least not in the upper reaches of New York society. Selden can afford greater luxuries than Lily, not despite his bachelor status, but because of it. After all, Selden lives in The Benedick, Wharton's barely disguised name for the luxury bachelor apartment building on Washington Square designed by the architectural firm of McKim, Mead, and White and the residence of the architect and notorious bachelor, Stanford White. In historical fact as well as in Wharton's fiction, being a bachelor meant that one could enjoy the freedoms of privacy *and* have a comfortable home of one's own.[99]

The self-styled "bachelor home-maker" of Frank Chaffee's 1892 collection of sketches, *Bachelor Buttons*, enjoys comparable pleasures in his own New York bachelor apartment:

> a cheerful log burning on my old fire-irons, make up an establishment not so unhomelike as might be, and when, of an evening, the "blond young man" drops in and we draw our chairs before the fire and enjoy that tête-à-tête of intimates, which needs no effort of entertaining, puffing great fragrant clouds of smoke, gazing into the fire and indulging in the always delightful reveries of a bachelor, the whole thing is, as our friends across the briny would say, "not half bad." . . .
> Fancy a man reverizing with a wife beside him, arguing the desirability of a new kind of weather strip or urging the merits of a patent clothes wringer.[100]

Luxuriating in the comfort of "an establishment not so unhomelike," he alludes to an American bachelor past famously envisioned in Donald Grant Mitchell's *Reveries of a Bachelor*. Chaffee's bachelor rhetorically places the quasi-domestic fireside communion enjoyed with his "blond young man," a type identifiable as homosexual to those who could read the code, within longer-standing traditions of bachelor quasi-domesticity, both "across the briny" and in the United States. While Chaffee's bachelor finds it ludicrous to imagine "a man reverizing with a wife beside him," it is worth noting that Mitchell's bachelor would have found it equally inconceivable to "reverize" with another man beside him since mid-century reverie was primarily conceived as a solitary vice, not a dyadic one. But whether practiced singly, in same-sex or cross-sex pairs, or in groups, bachelor domesticity enabled bachelors to cross certain boundaries while staying safely at home. This paradoxical combination of being at once an errant wanderer and a devoted homebody is particularly pronounced for the narrator of Mitchell's *Reveries*. This bachelor is most at home when lost in his dreams.

TELLING DREAMS: DONALD GRANT MITCHELL'S *REVERIES OF A BACHELOR*

While the popular success of *Reveries of a Bachelor, or a Book of the Heart* came nowhere near the sensational sales of such mid-century bestsellers as Stowe's *Uncle Tom's Cabin* (1851–2) which sold 300,000 copies in the year of its publication, or even Dickens's *Bleak House* (1852–3) which sold 35,000 copies in each of its monthly installments, *Reveries* did cause a mild sensation. In its first year, the book sold 14,000 copies and continued to sell throughout the century, ultimately appearing in over 50 editions apart from those issued by its authorized publisher, as well as in a variety of foreign language editions.[101] One of its many admirers was the young Emily Dickinson, who counted *Reveries* among her favorite books. "Ik Marvel," a pseudonym assumed by the author who was himself a bachelor at the time of publication, received a flood of fan mail from readers in America and abroad: letters praising the book, asking for advice on love affairs, proposing marriage. Poems and even a French polka were dedicated to Ik Marvel.[102]

Reveries, moreover, spawned a host of imitations by authors attempting to capitalize on the popularity of the bachelor as a narrative persona and as a subject of literary representation more generally. Among those mid-century writers who took a leaf from Mitchell's *Book of the Heart* were Oliver Bell Bunce, author of the 1881 *Bachelor Bluff*, who also published *A Bachelor's Story* in 1859, and Nathaniel Hawthorne, whose Coverdale of the 1852 *The Blithedale Romance* displays a distinct family resemblance to Mitchell's bachelor persona.[103] We can also see the influence of *Reveries of a Bachelor* on the many short pieces published during the 1850s in *Harper's New Monthly Magazine*, where the first reverie of Mitchell's book had been reprinted after first appearing in the *Southern Literary Messenger* in 1849. Mitchell was an editor at *Harper's* where he founded the long-running "Editor's Easy Chair" feature; he occupied this comfortable seat from 1851 until replaced in 1855 by George W. Curtis, the second most popular male sentimental author of the 1850s. The many *Reveries*-influenced pieces that appeared in *Harper's* during this era include ones cited earlier in this chapter: the 1859 essay "Single Life Among Us"; Melville's 1855 diptych, "The Paradise of Bachelors" and "The Tartarus of Maids"; the 1853 cartoon "Scenes in Bachelor Life"; and the 1851 story "A Bachelor's Christmas."

The bachelors depicted in all of these pieces have certain traits in common with Mitchell's bachelor. The depressing isolation of the studious bachelor in his London lodgings in the 1851 "A Bachelor's Christmas" can be seen, for example, as a dysphoric version of the dreamy solitariness of Mitchell's bachelor. The house-proud satisfaction that this bachelor, once married, takes in his refurbished suburban villa, also resembles the pride and joy that Mitchell's bachelor derives from his own "quiet farm-house in the country," which he visits each winter to review his tenant's farm accounts.[104] Although he takes great pleasure in the comforts of this country home, replete with its "cosy-looking fireplace – a heavy oak floor – a couple of arm-chairs, and a brown table with carved lion's feet ... [and] a broad bachelor bedstead" (p. 15), the bachelor of *Reveries* exhibits a negligence toward his house which recalls the behavior of the roughhousing cartoon bachelors in lodgings in the 1853 "Scenes from Bachelor Life." This bachelor does not burn his house down, as the incendiary cartoon bachelors do, but he does manage to do considerable damage:

It happens to be the only house in the world, of which I am *bona-fide* owner; and I take a vast deal of comfort in treating it just as I choose. I manage to break some article of furniture, almost every time I pay it a visit; and if I cannot open the window readily of a morning, to breathe the fresh air, I knock out a pane or two of glass with my boot. I lean against the walls in a very old armchair there is on the premises, and scarce ever fail to worry such a hole in the plastering, as would set me down for a round charge for damages in town, or make a prim housewife fret herself into a raging fever. I laugh out loud with myself, in my big arm-chair, when I think that I am neither afraid of one, nor the other. (p. 16)

In subordinating prudent delay to immediate gratification and privileging aggressive self-assertion over circumspect decorum, Mitchell's bachelor tarnishes his image as a "*bona-fide* owner": not as an owner *per se*, but an owner in good faith, one who maintains both in word and deed a proper bourgeois respect for private property. For Mitchell's bachelor, having a home of his own means having the right to trash it.

In the passage cited above, the bachelor tellingly lumps together the owner of a rented-out town residence with the "prim housewife" as representatives of proper behavior and attitudes toward property. He arms himself against their power of influence with the knowledge of his own right of ownership. But the lumping together of landowner and housewife reveals the difficulty of determining to whom the house properly belongs. Under most state laws at mid-century, a house was considered the legal property of the man of the house, but "belonging" is not simply a matter of legal ownership. The housewife is not the legal owner, yet she is the one who "frets herself into a raging fever" when the plastering has a hole "worried" into it. The house thus "belongs" to the housewife under hegemonic domestic ideology; her practical responsibility for such domestic spaces signifies her moral authority over them and those who inhabit them.[105] The house may belong to Mitchell's bachelor, yet he does not seem fully to belong to the world of domesticity.

The meaning of home ownership for Mitchell's bachelor is further complicated by his announcement, at the beginning of his fourth and final reverie, that he will never be able to return home again:

> It is a spring day under the oaks – the loved oaks of a once cherished home, – now alas, mine no longer!
>
> I had sold the old farm-house, and the groves, and the cool springs, where I had bathed my head in the heats of summer; and with the first warm days of May, they were to pass from me forever. Seventy years they had been in the possession of my mother's family; for seventy years, they had borne the same name of proprietorship; for seventy years, the Lares of our country home, often neglected, almost forgotten, – yet brightened from time to time, by gleams of heart-worship, had held their place in the sweet valley of Elmgrove.
>
> And in this changeful, bustling American life of ours, seventy years is no child's holiday. (pp. 149–50)

While no precise explanation for the sale is ever given, one gathers from the contrast between "changeful, bustling American life" and the traditional and retired quality of this old Elmgrove home that an earlier familial and affective economy, an economy linked in this text to the mother's family, is no longer viable. The old homeplace cannot compete in, or against, a modern world that puts a premium on mobility, acquisition, and competition. Complete with gloomy gestures toward architectural rack and ruin – "the cornice is straggling . . . the porch has fallen . . . the stone chimney is yawning with wide gaps . . . all is going to decay" (pp. 152–3) – this nostalgic backward glance is a standard of sentimental discourse.[106]

The sentimental nostalgia engendered by the decay and fall of the ancestral house of this bachelor does not necessarily conflict with his destructive behavior within this dwelling. His melancholy can be read, for instance, as a cover-up for his emphatic rejection of the responsibilities of home ownership. One might well interpret the bachelor's sale of his family home, like his window-smashing and plaster-gouging, as a repudiation of the duties of the bourgeois householder. Likewise, the morbid speculations of the book's first reverie can easily be seen as thinly veiled expressions of hostility toward the imaginary wife and children whose deaths the bachelor mournfully – or is it zestfully? – conjures up. He begins his reverie by reflecting on the annoyances and discomforts of married life, maintaining that any real wife or children must pale beside the imaginary ones "which a brilliant working imagination has invested time and again with brightness, and delight" (p. 20). At one point, the bachelor allows himself to wonder whether the connection he asserts between single life and the "gorgeous realm making" of his dream-like reveries is, in fact, inevitable: "My fancy would surely quicken, thought I, if such [a wife] were in attendance. Surely, imagination would be stronger, and purer, if it could have the playful fancies of dawning womanhood to delight it" (p. 32). But this train of thought inexorably leads him to reflect that a wife could comfort you if your friend, sister, or mother were to die. The death toll rises: if you were to die, she would attend you; worse still, the children and even she herself might die first. The bachelor's conclusion: "Blessed, thought I again, is the man who escapes such trials as will measure the limit of patience and the limit of courage!" (pp. 43–4). In other words, better to partake of pleasurably melancholy sentiments in one's imagination than to experience actual, painful loss.

Yet to argue that Mitchell's bachelor is flatly anti-domestic, anti-marriage, and anti-wife requires one to overlook, or to flatten, a good deal of evidence. For one thing, the bachelor himself distinguishes clearly between the house as a material object and the home as a source of spiritual and affective meaning:

A home! – it is the bright, blessed, adorable, phantom which sits highest on the sunny horizon that girdeth Life!... It is not the house, though that may have its charms; nor the field carefully tilled, and streaked with your own foot-paths; – nor the trees, though their shadow be to you like that of a great rock in a weary land; – nor yet is it the fireside, with its sweet blaze-play; – nor the pictures which tell of loved ones, nor the cherished books, – but more far than all these – it is the Presence. The Lares of your worship are there; the altar of your confidence there; the end of your worldly faith is there; and adorning it all, and sending your blood in passionate flow, is the ecstasy of the conviction, that *there* at least you are beloved; that there you are understood; that there your errors will meet ever with gentlest forgiveness; that there your troubles will be smiled away; that there you may unburden your soul, fearless of harsh, unsympathizing ears; and that there you may be entirely and joyfully – yourself! (pp. 90–1)

The catalogue of the material accoutrements of domestic pleasure at the beginning of this passage inarguably bestows a certain preeminence upon these physical comforts. One might compare this loving itemiz-ation of household objects, for example, to the book's second paragraph which effectively maps the interior space and furnishings of the bach-elor's house, leading up to, then into, his bedroom with its "saucy colored lithographic print of some fancy 'Bessie'" (p. 15). But both passages ultimately subordinate such tangible assets, both human and inanimate, to what they signify spiritually and emotionally. The emphasis on the immaterial in this ecstatic paeon locates the essence of selfhood in the spiritual heaven on earth which is home. Home is imagined here as an originary spiritual center that radiates its life force into and through the self, but also rings round the self as "the sunny horizon that girdeth Life!" (p. 90), enclosing it and yet connecting it to the infinite. In this vision, being "entirely and joyfully yourself" (p. 91) is not a dutiful means to a virtuous end, but the joyful end itself. The performance of domestic selfhood is its own reward.

The bachelor champions the home and the wife as prime movers of domestic selfhood, but his emphasis on their immateriality cuts both ways. Despite his yearning gesture toward the millennial heaven of making oneself at home, he seems to prefer, in fact to need, the home with the wife within it to remain "a bright, blessed, adorable, phantom" (p. 90). Thus the correct, indeed the necessary, answer to his rhetorical questions – "When shall [home] be reached? When shall it cease to be a glittering day-dream, and become fully and fairly yours?" (p. 90) – must be "Never." The marital and familial home retains its preeminence as the source of life's meaning, but for the bachelor of *Reveries* it is the source of life's meaning by virtue of its imaginary rather than actual status. The bachelor's real estate in Mitchell's *Reveries* is not the house that he literally inhabits, but the dreamy state of mind, the reveries that preoccupy him. The bachelor's real life is a "Dream Life," also the title of the sequel Mitchell wrote in the immediate wake of *Reveries*'s success.

Dream life is not precisely an alternative to domestic life for the bachelor narrator of *Reveries*, but rather a crucial form of vicarious access to it. In his original Preface, Mitchell wryly notes his inclination "to think bachelors are the only safe and secure observers of all the phases of married life" (p. vi), suggesting that bachelorhood is a position for looking and that married life is the primary object of the bachelor's gaze. In this text, however, the bachelor's onlooking takes place entirely within his mind's eye, within the apparently self-enclosed world of his reveries. Mitchell's bachelor "makes an opera glass of [his] imagination," as *Blithedale*'s Zenobia describes the characteristic habit of mind of that novel's bachelor narrator, but *Reveries*'s bachelor does so without the benefit of visual aids.[107] In many of the fictions I will discuss in the following chapters, bachelors play onlooking and sometimes facilitating roles in the marital and familial plots they narrate, sustaining a distanced intimacy with or an intimate distance from the denizens of conventional domestic life. In contrast to these bachelor narrators,

Mitchell's bachelor seems to be located more definitively beyond the gravitational pull of that "Presence" (p. 91) which is home.

Yet the bachelor of *Reveries*, too, stands on the domestic threshold. The liminality of reverie, a condition that hovers somewhere between sleeping and waking, aptly evokes the bachelor's liminal relation to domestic life, and also to the public, marketplace world that is the private realm's supposed antithesis and complement. Indeed, the presence of this bachelor at the domestic threshold indicates the very ambiguity that confounds the status of the private within bourgeois domestic ideology, especially for bourgeois men whose inner selves were contradictorily defined as both intrinsic and extraneous to this sphere. The bachelor's vexed positioning with respect to bourgeois domesticity, and ultimately with respect to normative bourgeois manhood, is suggested by another passage that links the bachelor's reverie-making habit of mind to his tendency towards spectatorship:

Shall he who has been hitherto a mere observer of other men's cares, and business – moving off where they made him sick of heart, approaching whenever and wherever they made him gleeful – shall he now undertake administration of just such cares and business, without qualms? . . . Shall this brain of mine, careless-working, never tired with idleness, feeding on long vagaries, and high, gigantic castles, dreaming out beatitudes hour by hour – turn itself at length to such dull task-work, as thinking out a livelihood for wife and children? (p. 20)

Bachelorhood is initially defined in opposition to the responsible, wage-earning labor of the bourgeois married man, yet the bachelor observer is not entirely idle. The language that describes his strangely disembodied brain – "careless-working, never tired with idleness . . . hour by hour" – suggests activity, even industriousness. In the bachelor's "brilliant working imagination" we can recognize the ethos of productive masculine labor, as well as an implicit class distinction between intellectual and aesthetic labor and menial labor. The disavowal of brain work as real labor, characteristic of antebellum discourse validating the cultural status of professional authors, both potentially compromised the masculine status of these writers and redefined the bounds of normative masculinity. The activity of this bachelor's brain is apparently divorced, furthermore, from any material effect on anyone other than himself; his reveries are a leisure activity whose only product is his own amusement. Indeed, his brain is portrayed as a consumer as much as a producer, vampiristically "feeding on long vagaries and high gigantic castles"

(p. 20), accumulating images in "the *omnium gatherum* of your own brain," stocking "the private larder of your head" (p. 21). The status of the reverizing bachelor imagination is uncertain: is the bachelor in his reveries at work or at play? productive or consumptive? active or passive? Bachelor and reverie alike confound these ordering binarisms of masculine, bourgeois, and domestic life, at once demarcating and crossing the lines that mark the boundaries of these realms.

The text's rhetorical equation of reverie with its written representation compounds these indeterminacies, ultimately effecting a comparable challenge to the boundaries that define individual subjectivity. In his original Preface to the book, Mitchell never uses the term "sketch" to describe his writing. Rather, he alludes to the pieces that make up his book as if they were themselves the reveries: "This book is neither more, nor less than it pretends to be; it is a collection of those floating Reveries which have, from time to time, drifted across my brain" (p. v). This rhetorical move accords with a basic premise of the sketch as a form: that it is not a literary conceit at all, but a mental impression merely jotted down or spewed forth without labor or calculation.[108] In his Preface, Mitchell also asserts the honesty of his literary mode of production: "If they [the Reveries] had been worked over with more unity of design, I dare say I might have made a respectable novel; as it is, I have chosen the honester way of setting them down as they came seething from my thought, with all their crudities and contrasts, uncovered" (p. v). Mitchell implies here that his writing does not take any literary or generic form at all, but that it is an unmediated transmission, a telegraphing of thought and emotion, an infusion of the fluid medium of his reveries themselves. The readers of *Reveries*, according to this logic, experience the bachelor's reveries first-hand; the act of reading joins them with the author in a realm that is at once mental and textual.

The double life of reveries as both mental state and written text shades into their equally mixed status as both psychic and somatic. In a book that disdains the material realm as "crude, – a mere reduction of ideality to sense, – a transformation of the spiritual to the earthly, – a levelling of soul to matter" (p. 56), the products of the bachelor imagination are strikingly, if still metaphorically, physical. The reveries that come "seething from my thought," like the "fancies thronging on my brain," seem strangely fluid: both liquid and mobile. And the brain across which the bachelor's reveries drift and where his fancies throng seems as much a physical location as a body part. The bachelor's brain in these passages, like his heart elsewhere in this *Book of the Heart*, is portrayed as a bodily organ that produces, accumulates, and ultimately releases pent-up reveries.[109]

Indeed, popular advice manuals and tracts written by mid-century "male purity" advocates explicitly linked reverie to masturbation.[110] In a recent *American Literature* article, Vincent Bertolini convincingly compares the narrative rhythms of the *Reveries* to the erotic rhythms of masturbation, citing a passage from the second reverie in which the bachelor, having returned from his Wood Fire in the country to his City Grate, imagines the teasing of a "coquette":

> And so, with my eye clinging to the flickering blaze, I see in my reverie a bright one dancing before me with sparkling, coquettish smile, teasing me with the prettiest graces in the world; – and I grow maddened between hope and fear, and still watch with my whole soul in my eyes; and see her features by and by relax to pity, as a gleam of sensibility comes stealing over her spirit; – and then to a kindly, feeling regard: presently she approaches, – a coy and doubtful approach – and throws back the ringlets that lie over her cheek, and lays her hand – a little bit of white hand – timidly upon my strong fingers, – and turns her head daintily to one side, – and looks up in my eyes, as they rest on the playing blaze; and my fingers close fast and passionately over that little hand, like a swift night-cloud shrouding the pale tips of Dian; – and my eyes draw nearer and nearer to the blue, laughing, pitying, teasing eyes, and my arm clasps round that shadowy form, – and my lips feel a warm breath – growing warmer and warmer –
>
> Just here the maid comes in, and throws upon the fire a panful of Anthracite, and my sparkling sea-coal Reverie is ended. (pp. 78–9)

In the "repeated short phrases and the accelerating pace that builds towards a climax," it is hard *not* to see masturbatory eroticism as a defining feature of reverie.[111] It is also hard to miss the tension between an eroticized single life, epitomized by the fantasized finger-play of bachelor and coquette, and a de-eroticized domestic life, embodied in the chambermaid's brusque and deflationary *interruptus*. But if the maid is no coquette, it is worth noting that the coquette is herself distinguished from the "city flirt," a "coarse-grained soul" whose "frittering passions fuse all that is sound and combustible into black, sooty shapeless residuum." The coquette's sparkle, by contrast, "will flicker around a true soul like a blaze around an *omelette au rhum*, leaving the kernel sounder and warmer. Coquetry, with all its pranks and teasings, makes the spice to your dinner – the mulled wine to your supper" (p. 78). The bachelor here fantasizes about a woman who could bring some spice to married domesticity. Similarly, the maid's arrival on the scene, though sadly ill-timed, is not meant to extinguish the bachelor's fire; she is trying, albeit unsuccessfully, to stoke it with a different fuel. After a slow start, the maid's Anthracite coal glows with "true and earnest constancy" (p. 82), "with a pure and steady flame" (p. 83): "The heart that with its glow can light up, and warm a garret with loose casements and shattered roof, is capable of the best love, – domestic love" (p. 86). Domestic homefires and the fires of sexual passion are not necessarily mutually exclusive, although both seem to be best enjoyed vicariously and alone: viewed in the shadows cast by the flames upon the fire screen, and in the images cast by the projected light of the bachelor's reverie.

The insistent metonymic association of reveries with fire in this text also contributes to the bachelor's vexed relation to marital domesticity, a relation that is imaginatively invested yet necessarily distanced, at once engaged with and divorced from married home life. The hearth is not only what we might call Mitchell's *synedoche qua non* for the familial home, it is also the site where Mitchell's bachelor narrator most often indulges in his reveries. Each of the reveries is organized around, and subtitled for, a different fire motif. The first reverie, "Over a Wood Fire," is divided into three sections: "Smoke, Signifying Doubt," "Blaze, Signifying Cheer," and "Ashes, Signifying Desolation." The second reverie, "By a City Grate," consists of "Sea Coal" and "Anthracite." The Third Reverie, "A Cigar Three Times Lighted," puns on good matches and match-making with "Coal," "A Wisp of Paper," and a "Match." The last reverie, "Morning, Noon, and Evening," extends the already overextended fire metaphor to the diurnal cycle of that ultimate heat source, the sun. Like the heart in this "Book of the Heart," fire is a privileged emblem for both conventional domesticity and for the bachelor's imagination, a metonymic signifier which draws these spheres together while giving point to their differences.

The bachelor's proclivity for reverie is metaphorically as well as structurally associated with his habit of cigar-smoking, a blatant emblem of male sexual self-indulgence which nevertheless binds the bachelor to more conventionally domestic home fires.[112] At the opening of the third reverie, the bachelor portrays himself at home with his spinster "Aunt Tabithy," a familial audience-in-the-text who censures his smoking as "dirty" and "a filthy abomination."[113] Her epithets evoke the association of smoking with illicit and supposedly anti-domestic sexual practices. The bachelor and his aunt strike a bargain, sealing their deal with a clasping of hands which parodies the marriage contract: "our right hands joined; – my left was holding my cigar, while in hers was tightly grasped – her broomstick. And this Reverie, to make the matter short, is what came of the contract" (p. 102). If he cannot bring her to tears by telling his reveries, he will give up the cigars which she abhors; if he can, and of course he does, she must allow him to smoke his cigars on the front porch, a liminal space that marks a permeable boundary of domesticity. His reverie, "all twisted out of the smoke" (p. 101) of his cigar, enables the bachelor to stake a claim in domestic territory, or at least on its threshold.

When the bachelor defends his right to smoke in, or at least near, the house, he reveals the potential contradiction in the ideological opposition of domestic ideals and the self-indulgence of feeling, whether erotic or sentimental. Tellingly, the bachelor's defense of his cigar-smoking habit – "It is clean and sweet ... and a most pleasant soother of disturbed feelings; and a capital companion; and a comforter" (p. 100) – resembles his defense of his reverizing habit:

I know not justly, if it be a weakness or a sin to create these phantoms that we love, and to group them into a paradise – soul-created. But if it is a sin, it is a sweet and enchanting sin; and if it is a weakness, it is a strong and stirring weakness. If this heart is sick of the falsities that meet it at every hand, and is eager to spend that power which nature has ribbed it with, on some object worthy of its fulness and depth, – shall it not feel a rich relief, – nay more, an exercise in keeping with its end, if it flow out, – strong as a tempest, wild as a rushing river, upon those ideal creations, which imagination invents, and which are tempered by our best sense of beauty, purity and grace? (p. 81)

While the bachelor may obtain relief by allowing his reveries to "flow out – strong as a tempest, wild as a rushing river," these apparently unregulated emissions nonetheless take a proper course, much as cigar-smoking "makes a man meditative; and gives a current to his habits of contemplation" (p. 100). These "phantoms" may not be real, but they are nonetheless proper objects, "tempered by our best sense of beauty, purity and grace," and hence linked to the conventionally domestic, if necessarily imaginary, ideals of home and wife.

These products of the bachelor's imagination are also linked to a different sphere of "beauty, purity and grace." The passage continues:

– Useless, do you say? Aye, it is as useless as the pleasure of looking hour upon hour, over bright landscapes; it is as useless as the rapt enjoyment of listening with heart full and eyes brimming, to such music as the *Miserere* at Rome; it is as useless as the ecstasy of kindling your soul into fervor and love, and madness, over pages that reek with genius.

There are indeed base-moulded souls who know nothing of this; they laugh;

they sneer; they even affect to pity. Just so the Huns under the avenging Attila, who had been used to foul cookery and steak stewed under their saddles, laughed brutally at the spiced banquets of an Apicius. (pp. 81–2)

This defense connects the emotional and physical pleasures of reverie to the aesthetic pleasures of sublime landscape, music, and literary genius. This justification is not far from the philosophy that Pater would famously expound in his 1868 "Conclusion" to *The Renaissance*. When he celebrates "kindling your soul into fervor and love and madness," Mitchell demonstrates a critical sensibility reminiscent of Pater who recommends that one "burn always with this hard, gem-like flame, to maintain this ecstasy."[114] Both images sustain the opposition of sanity and insanity but reverse their assigned values to effect an essentially Romantic revision of Victorian masculinity. Like Pater's defense of art for art's sake, Mitchell's art-for-sentiment's-sake defense of reverie finds true "success in life" in the realm of the aesthetic, thereby suggesting an alternative to the economic rewards and respectability of conventional bourgeois masculinity. By making anarchy into an avatar of culture and not its antithesis, Mitchell sets his aesthetic bachelor above and against crass "Huns" who, like Arnold's Philistines, are characterized by a materialistic yet impoverished insensibility to true culture. Like the Arnoldian man who celebrates "the best which has been thought and said in the world," and the Paterian man who gets "as many pulsations as possible into the given time," the bachelor of *Reveries* is finally a bachelor of art.[115]

Mitchell's aesthetic defense of reverie is, at heart, a defense of the sentimental relations that imaginative creativity enables. In what is perhaps this text's most radical move, the solitary vice of reverie is touted as affording not only a virtuous communion with oneself, but a vitalizing community of feeling with others. In order to accomplish this startling reversal of expectations, Mitchell's narrator must go beyond his equation of mental reverie with its written representation and his elision of the distinction between physical and mental generativity. He must ultimately valorize writing over speech, claiming for writing a truth which is at once more artistic and more natural than that of spoken words. Mitchell's narrator makes this crucial move in the opening passage of his second reverie:

Blessed be letters! – they are the monitors, they are also the comforters, and they are the only true heart-talkers! Your speech and their speeches, are conventional; they are moulded by circumstance; they are suggested by the observation, remark, and influence of parties to whom the speaking is addressed, or by whom it may be over-heard.

Your truest thought is modified half through its utterance by a look, a sign, a smile, or a sneer. It is not individual: it is not integral: it is social and mixed, – half of you, and half of others. It bends, it sways, it multiplies, it retires, and it advances, as the talk of others presses, relaxes, or quickens.

But it is not so of Letters... Utter it then freely; – write it down – stamp it – burn it in the ink! – There it is, a true soul-print! (pp. 53–4)

The bachelor's desire to forestall "lip-slang" (p. 54) signals a possible aversion to the physical presence of other people, but his anxiety about the potential influence of "a look, a sign, a smile, or a sneer" indicates neither indifference to nor independence of others. Rather, his preference for the written word can be traced to his excessive susceptibility to the influence of others. The act of writing, construed along these lines, is a way of coping with or managing this over-sensitivity, a way for the bachelor to avoid getting too mixed up by, or with, others: "there you are, with only the soulless pen, and the snow-white, virgin paper. Your soul is measuring itself by itself, and saying its own sayings . . . nothing is present, but you, and your thought" (p. 54). The image of resolute authorial self-reliance evoked by this passage is mitigated by the fact that the "glory, the freedom, the passion of a letter" (p. 54) affords communion between the writer and his readers. Indeed, this encomium to the written word is Mitchell's acknowledgment of correspondence from the readers of the 1849 "A Bachelor's Reverie," now the book's "First Reverie."

In the introductory section of the second reverie, Mitchell describes a range of readers who have sent him what we now call fan mail: a mother who has lost a child; another mother who is afraid of losing hers; a wife whose family is still intact; a young girl who has not yet found love; and a father who "has laid down the book, overcome by its story of his own griefs" (p. 57). Mitchell's bachelor keeps these "Souvenirs du Coeur" (p. 58) from his readers in a packet of saved letters from his own mother and sister, thereby making an extended family of his reading audience. This quasi-familial reading public might also be described as a decidedly "private public"; although he gladly outlines the domestic situations described in the letters of these writing readers, Mitchell contends that "[I]t would be cold, and dastardly work to copy them; I am too selfish for that" (p. 55), making a conspicuous display of keeping the letters to himself. This public performance of privateness is reinforced by the contrast Mitchell draws between the feeling responses of his quasi-familial audience and the "cold praise of newspaper paragraphs, or the critically contrived approval of colder friends" (p. 58). His disdain for intellectualizing and aestheticizing professional readers fleshes out his preference for those readers who have already internalized the lessons of sentimental education or who are ready for conversion.

Strangely absent from the roster of correspondents who complete the sentimental circuit are those whom, as Samuel Otter notes, Mitchell "most explicitly and earnestly addresses in *Reveries*, the young men who are or whom he hopes to render men of feeling."[116] Yet these young male addressees *are* present in the text, in the second-person "you" whom Mitchell's first-person narrator inserts into or encloses within his reveries. As Otter compellingly contends, "second only in the 1850s to Whitman ... Mitchell is a master of the intricate rhetoric of 'I' and 'you,' the intimate choreography between writer and implied reader ... What I feel you shall feel, asserts Mitchell, for every feeling belonging to me as good belongs to you."[117] David Leverenz describes the textual activity of a rhetoric of "I and you" in the work of the five most canonical male writers of the American Renaissance, linking this rhetoric to these writers' development of "premodernist styles to explore and exalt their sense of being deviant from male norms."[118] While some contemporary reviewers did criticize "the almost feminine delicacy of Mr. Mitchell's nature,"[119] Mitchell displayed little or no anxiety about joining the "damned mob of scribbling women" so resented by Hawthorne and Melville. Unlike his currently canonized male contemporaries, whose agon of professional authorship may be their distinguishing shared trait, Mitchell embraced wholeheartedly the nascent mass audience which his writing helped to shape. The rhetoric of "I and you" in *Reveries* effects a sentimental commerce between author and his readers which finally troubles the boundaries of individuality and the bounds of normative manhood.

Reveries's rhetoric of "I and you" engenders imaginary unions between a bachelor "I" and a "you" who is most often represented as male; these male-male unions are also represented as essentially incompatible with the union of man and wife. Once married, "you" and "your" affections inevitably undergo a change of heart that precludes the wider world of masculine feeling available to bachelors. Although the affections of the married man gain "a finer tone and touch" from "domestic attachments" (p. 44), the husband is doomed by the enervated overrefinement of his feelings, especially given the inevitable demise of his wife and family. The married man is cut off from the more extensive, more varied, and essentially male "community of feeling" that had been enjoyed by the bachelor:

You do not now look men in the face as if a heart-bond was linking you – as if a community of feeling lay between. There is a heart-bond that absorbs all others; there is a community that monopolizes your feeling. When the heart lay wide open, before it had grown upon, and closed around particular objects, it could take strength and cheer, from a hundred connections that now seem colder than ice. (p. 44)

Whitman probably would not have approved of Mitchell's expression, but surely he would have shared his sentiment. A heart which has not been monopolized or "closed around particular objects" is able to contain multitudes and to merge with them, to bond fully in what Whitman also called "adhesive love" and "fervid comradeship."[120] The bachelor's affections, precisely because they are so "wide-spread and superficial," are able to survive and even flourish outside the "forcing glass of the home-roof," "shoot[ing] out tendrils into barren world-soil and suck[ing] up thence strengthening nutriment" (p. 44), this last eroticized image suggesting both the flexibility and the reciprocity of these male-male relations.

While the community of feeling that Mitchell associates with single men's lives in the wider world is explicitly non-domestic, it strikingly resembles the quasi-familial "heart-bond" that binds Mitchell to that diverse community of readers who write to him. Like the bachelor "you" in the text who is able to give and receive feelingly, these other readers-in-the-text are able to see the truth of reveries and to respond in kind:

It is enough to say that they, the kind writers, have seen a heart in the Reverie – have felt that it was real, true. They know it; a secret influence has told it. What matters it pray, if literally, there was no wife, and no dead child, and no coffin in the house? Is not feeling, feeling; and heart, heart? Are not these fancies thronging on my brain, bringing tears to my eyes, bringing joy to my soul, as living, as anything human can be living? (pp. 56–7)

This is not a denial of the fictionality of the reveries but an assertion that what the bachelor and his readers have imagined and felt, though fictional, is real. The preeminence of emotional and imaginative generativity in this passage, and in Mitchell's text as a whole, establishes an alternative ontology, an ontology in which dreams are more real than what elsewhere counts as reality.

A world in which fantasies are "as living as anything human can be living" might well be viewed as a damagingly self-enclosed world, a dream world fatally cut off from other people in its smug insistence upon itself, and particularly its own aesthetic forms and sentimental feelings, as its only justifications. However valid such a critique of Mitchell's aestheticism and sentimentalism may be, we should not allow it to occlude the cultural and conceptual work that this text does accomplish. The text's elision of the difference between reveries and the *effects* of reveries upon their imaginary (both imagining and imagined) subjects is precisely what enables *Reveries* to conceive of the bachelor's dream world as a visionary ideal of emotional communion. The epistemological indeterminacy produced by the text's alternative ontology of "dream life" contributes to an alternative economy of meaning: not a finite system of limited resources, but an infinitely renewing process of incessant speculation which is a proper end in itself. In this alternative economy, the bachelor's reveries are themselves both a form of labor and a commodity, at once the means of exchange and the objects of endless circulation, just as the bachelor, like his readers, is both consumer and producer of private lives. The bachelor imaginary in Mitchell's *Reveries* is both a home industry and a psychic interior that is decidedly domestic, a space which reveals the imaginary boundaries between private and public, between home and work, and even between mind and body. In the bachelor's liminal relation to domestic life, the contradictions upon which domestic ideology itself depends become evident.

Implicit in the alternative ontology and the alternative economy of this text is an alternative model of manhood. Just as the bachelor's dream world stands as a utopian image of emotional communion, the dreaming bachelor is himself an exemplar of feeling. The bachelor in his reveries is defined by the intensity of his inner life, an inner life which imaginatively crosses the divides between fantasy and reality, and between self and other. The bachelor imaginary does not dispense with the proper regulations associated with normative bourgeois manhood, but it does reconceive the nature of proper regulation; the bachelor imaginary shifts the boundaries of identity by reimagining the extent of their allowable permeability. The susceptibility to the spheres of others, as well as the tendency toward vicarious consumption and imaginative production, that characterize the subjectivity of Mitchell's bachelor narrator links this figure to the mid-century invalid bachelor narrators of Emily Brontë and Nathaniel Hawthorne that I will discuss in the next chapter. The alternative style of masculinity enacted by Mitchell's bachelor in the realms of aesthetic production and consumption, more-over, stands as a model for the cultural and gendered hierarchies asserted by the male, high-cultural novelists I will discuss in the re-mainder of this book. In the chapters which follow, I aim to elucidate the ways in which those fictional narratives represented as issuing forth from the not-so-separate sphere of bachelorhood are themselves telling stories.

CHAPTER 2

Susceptibility and the single man: the constitution of the bachelor invalid

The author of an 1871 essay, published in the popular British periodical *Once a Week* and entitled "Bachelor Invalids and Male Nurses," summarizes his three-fold purpose in writing:

This point I shall endeavour to prove – in the first place, to mitigate the real anxiety which women naturally feel when they know that their bachelor friends or relations are ill, and left to the tender mercies of hirelings and the rougher sex; in the next place, to divert the freely bestowed compassion of susceptible and impulsive natures from useless channels; and lastly, in the hope that some reminiscences of bachelor sick-rooms may be found entertaining, and not altogether uninstructive.[1]

The set of aims he describes – to mitigate anxiety, to divert compassion from useless channels, and to entertain – might well describe the charge of the nineteenth-century sick-nurse. The male writer of this essay claims that he does not believe that men make better nurses than women: "Far be it from me to underrate the merits of female nurses, or to depreciate the fortitude, patience, and devotion with which thousands upon thousands of them are continually sacrificing time, rest, and health in tending sufferers. My aim is to show that men can, at a humble distance, follow their example" (p. 318). Particularly in cases of "dangerous or protracted illness out of which it is, in my opinion, impossible to extract any kind of amusement" or in cases of "unhinging of the nervous system," he emphasizes the prudence of deferring to "feminine aid" (p. 318). Yet, this writer inevitably downplays the effectiveness, and thereby undercuts the authority, of female nurses. He does so, not surprisingly, in terms that reveal the gendered implications of both illness and the care of invalids in this period.[2]

According to this writer, female nursing of bachelor patients is dangerous to both parties. Even though "every woman is at heart a nurse"

(p. 320), a play on Pope's animadversion which suggests the erotic nimbus of the sickbed, female nurses are doubly at risk. While the "marked isolation of bed-rooms in family dwelling houses" endangers women attending bachelor convalescents, a still greater danger resides in insufficient rather than excessive distance: "they love a sick-room; and the more marked its distinctive characteristics are, the more do they feel in their element." The "unconscious gratification" (p. 320) of the female nurse in her power over the bachelor invalid may prevent him from getting better, may even make him worse, and may also do her harm in the process.

Male nurses are not as susceptible as female ones to the "conservative proclivities of the domestic state [which] encourage the exaggeration of invalidism" (p. 320). Just as men are less likely to partake of what we might call the nurse's "powers of the strong," they are also less likely to indulge in the invalid's "powers of the weak" since "before their own sex they try to bear up; and the effort is highly beneficial if nothing is seriously amiss" (p. 320). In one anecdote in which the author himself helps to nurse a convalescent bachelor, male nurses and male patients all seem to benefit from "the masculine system of therapeutics" (p. 318): "We certainly did not find the nursing irksome or fatiguing, nor did we acquit ourselves any the worse for being thoroughly comfortable and cheerful over it. Neither had our charge any reason to accuse himself of "vampirism," as Mr. Lowell calls it, as none of us exhibit any of the physical symptoms of incipient angelhood" (p. 319). If the bachelor patient is innocent of "vampirism," then so are his male nurses; far from sapping the life from their patient, their good humor serves a salutary function. The absence of "physical symptoms" in the male nurses suggests the security of the boundaries between the identities of nurse and patient, as well as between body and spirit, between one individual and another, between illness and health, and between life and death.

The boundaries so confidently asserted by the author of this 1871 essay are less secure in three nineteenth-century novels that also imagine bachelors as invalids: *Wuthering Heights* (1847), *The Blithedale Romance* (1852), and *The Portrait of a Lady* (1880). These novels do not feature their bachelor invalids among the starring players in their dramas, but rather use these figures in more of a framing capacity, as sidelined onlookers who witness the multiple, overlapping erotic triangles and marriage plots that animate these fictions. The bachelor invalids in all three novels sustain important differences in the severity of their illnesses as well as in the functions of their illnesses. Whereas *Portrait*'s Ralph

Touchett dies of what ails him, Lockwood in *Wuthering Heights* and Coverdale in *Blithedale* are only temporarily indisposed. And while Ralph serves as a privileged "focalizer" in James's third-person narrated (or heterodiegetic) novel, Lockwood and Coverdale are first-person (or homodiegetic) narrators.

What these bachelors have in common is a permeability of identity associated with their illnesses, which confounds the divisions which normally separate one individual from another, and also separate body from spirit and life from death. Such boundary-crossing is not the exclusive domain of bachelor invalids; such crossings are also evident in the gendered relations of marriage and marital alternatives featured in the novels' plots. But the movement of the bachelor invalids across the borders of domestic selfhood and domestic life discloses the stakes of the proper regulation of boundaries within and between individuals. To the extent that these bachelor figures diverge in their crossings from the patterns of gendered identity and relation that they witness, they enact a style of masculine identity that is, potentially at least, more reciprocal and unhierarchical than that of the main male protagonists.

It is nonetheless vital for us to recognize the homophobic potential of fictional portrayals of bachelor as invalids. Such portrayals set influential precedents for "our culture's inclination to regard gay men as marked men" in the age of AIDS, as deathbed victims who emanate an aura of doom from deep within themselves.[3] Late twentieth-century Western culture's ways of looking at counternormative styles of manhood have had devastating effects. One way to resist the death sentence, I would maintain, is to recuperate the nineteenth-century figure of the bachelor invalid.

We can begin this critical act of recuperation by recognizing the tensions within these texts between form and content, tensions that render unstable conventional moralizing and thereby infuse new life into plotted dead ends. These novels link the invalid status of their bachelors to these figures' narratorial function, forging connections among illnesses, convalescence, and the acts of seeing, hearing, and/or telling. The perspectives of these bachelor invalids reveal their constant negotiations between sympathy and detachment, between proximity and distance, and also between specular vicariousness and spectacular self-display. Ultimately, these negotiations of identity and relation bear as heavily on the gendered authorship of these novels as they do on the gendered relations of sickroom and deathbed in their plots. The bachelor invalid narrators or reflectors of these novels do not simply stand in for the novels' authors; they also stand between the world of the text and the world beyond it, at once within and without the plots that they repeat and revise. The mediative function of the bachelor invalid narrator or reflector is thus metonymically associated with the liminal status of the bachelor in relation to domestic life and of the convalescent invalid in relation to health. The bachelor invalid and the unreliable narrative with which he is associated finally constitute discursive supplements which destabilize the texts' dominant fictions of bourgeois manhood.

UNRELIABILITY, INELIGIBILITY, INVALIDISM: *WUTHERING HEIGHTS* AND *THE BLITHEDALE ROMANCE*

One would be hard put to mistake the author of *The Blithedale Romance* for the author of *Wuthering Heights*. Longevity (of life, not authorial reputation), nationality, gender, and marital status are only the most conspicuous among the many differences that distinguish Nathaniel Hawthorne from Emily Brontë. But their bachelor narrators bear an uncanny resemblance to each other. Among other traits, Lockwood and Coverdale share a distinctive combination of self-reflexivity and unselfconsciousness; imaginative engagement and emotional distance; acuteness and obtuseness of perception. One could attribute this paradoxical combination of traits to a split in these figures' narrative function, a disjunction between their powers of observation and their powers of interpretation. And, indeed such a split has been used to understand these narrators as quintessentially unreliable.[4]

What has been less fully understood is the gendered dimension of these narrators' unreliability. That is to say, there is a constitutive link between narrative unreliability and the gendered eccentricity or "excentricity" of the narrators. The discrepancies between what these narrators claim for themselves and what we as readers infer about them raise questions about the normativity of their performance of bourgeois manhood. For example, both bachelor narrators portray themselves as thwarted suitors when neither is anything of the sort.[5] While it is easy to see how self-portrayal as a contender in the arena of courtship could work as a bid for manly consequence, such an interpretation overlooks the ways that both figures make the inaccuracy of their self-portrayal as contenders so conspicuously evident to readers. It is not simply their failure to succeed in the arena of marital courtship that undercuts these narrators' self-presentations. Rather, it is their insistent self-display as nonstarters, their patently evident reluctance or inability to enter the lists, that complicates their self-portrayal. While their self-presentations as thwarted suitors makes these bachelor narrators into abjected spectacles-in-the-text, this same self-presentation gains each the privileged position of spectator-in-the-text, a kind of runner-up prize for the suitor who does not prove himself finally to be the better man. In so obviously miscasting themselves as thwarted suitors, and thereby assuming the positions of spectacle and spectator, these bachelor figures visibly diverge from ideal or even acceptable manhood.[6]

Consider Coverdale's last words at the end of *Blithedale*, his "confession" to the reader after he describes his confrontation with Priscilla and her now husband, Hollingsworth: "I – I myself – was in love – with – *Priscilla!*" (*BR*, p. 247). Coverdale's melodramatically stage-whispered confession does not, as he claims it will, "throw a gleam of light over [his] behavior throughout the foregoing incidents," nor does it satisfactorily account for the ensuing "inactive years of meridian manhood," by which he means both his permanent "bachelorship" and his idle "lack of purpose" (*BR*, p. 247). Rather, his "foolish little secret" confirms the reader's suspicions that his narration has been marked throughout by intentional withholdings as well as by unintentional disclosures. Paradoxically, it corroborates our sense of the narration's unreliability in the very moment of the narrator's avowed full disclosure. It is a self-asserting last bid for consequence, for the confidence of his readers in his integrity as narrator and in his integral role in the novel's marriage plotting. It is also a self-effacing display of inconsequentiality: "It is ... an absurd thing ever to have happened, and quite the absurdest for an old bachelor, like me, to talk about" (*BR*, p. 247). Much like the insufficient moral to the story that Coverdale draws in the penultimate chapter, this greatest secret of the bachelor narrator's heart makes a conspicuously flimsy and irrelevant conclusion to the tragic love triangle that dooms Zenobia, Hollingsworth, and Priscilla.

Yet Coverdale's suggestion of a possible mismatch in the novel's romantic couplings is not utterly implausible since, in contrast to the superabundance of marriages in *Wuthering Heights*, *The Blithedale Romance* comes up one romance short. *Blithedale* does not culminate with that most blissful of endings for a Victorian novel, the double wedding, despite the romantic possibilities suggested by its two matched sets of "light" and "dark" protagonists, male and female. These symmetrical pairings have generated, for example, the long-standing critical tradition of reading Coverdale's declared love for Priscilla as a displacement from his frighteningly powerful erotic attraction to Zenobia.[7] A more recent critical interpretation pairs Coverdale with Hollingsworth, noting the homoerotic charge of Coverdale's attraction to the man whom he desires for a "death-bed companion," and whose sexual ambiguity Coverdale perceives, or perhaps wishes to perceive: "There was something of the woman moulded into the great, stalwart frame of Hollingsworth" (*BR*, p. 42).[8] A third interpretive take on the novel's romantic mismatchings sees Zenobia as the "right" woman for Hollingsworth; when this "bad mother" is eliminated by her own hand, the "daughter's seduction" is consummated, fulfilling the marriage plot but uniting the wrong pair of characters.[9]

All these critical understandings of Coverdale's dramatic avowal of love for Priscilla acknowledge the centrality of a love triangle in the novel, whether that triangle consists of two men and one woman, or one man and two women; whether the competition is between two men, two women, or a man and a woman; whether the erotic object of this eroticized rivalry is male or female. They fail, however, to acknowledge the ways in which the erotics of this novel are crucially *quadrangulated*, not merely triangulated. Coverdale adds a fourth to a crowd already made up of three. In his quadrangulating role, this bachelor narrator plays a part that is the quintessence of superfluity, yet speaks to his desire for indispensability, or at least consequentiality. As the spectator of an already existing erotic triangle, the bachelor narrator exceeds the requirements of mediated desire yet also epitomizes the dynamics of such desire. The very act of imaginatively participating in this already triangulated relationship reveals Coverdale's limited purchase on and relevance to it. He thereby creates the paradoxical effect of simultaneously bolstering and undermining his gendered status as a sexual contender.

A similarly paradoxical effect is produced by the vicarious quadrangulations of *Wuthering Heights*'s Lockwood, who makes a superfluous fourth to the second-generation love triangle consisting of Cathy II, Hareton, and Linton, and an even more superfluous fifth to the abutting love triangles in the first generation composed of Catherine, Edgar, Heathcliff, and Isabella. I will, however, refrain from labeling this "quintangulation," having already coined the egregious "quadrangulation." When Lockwood vicariously squares the first-generation triangles consisting of Heathcliff, Edgar, and Catherine, and of Heathcliff, Catherine, and Isabella, he imaginatively inserts himself into a polymorphous variety of subject and object positions. The most insistent of these, however, is his erotic identification with Heathcliff, his desire both to be and to have Heathcliff. Moreover, Lockwood most vividly enacts his erotic identification with Heathcliff via his self-portrayal as a thwarted suitor for the hand of Cathy II, when he imagines himself as Hareton's rival after Linton's death leaves an opening in the erotic triangulation of the second generation. By envisioning himself as Heathcliff's successor or heir – an identification which also reinforces his resemblance to Linton, who manages to get the girl despite, or even because, of his status as an oversensitive invalid[10] – Lockwood imaginatively occupies an Oedipalized position that both subordinates him yet also implies his eventual rise to patriarchal power. He wishfully casts himself as a second edition of Heathcliff, for example, in his reflection at the end of the novel's first volume upon the dangerously seductive "fascination that lurks in Catherine Heathcliff's eyes": "I should be in a curious taking if I surrendered my heart to that young person, and the daughter turned out to be a second edition of the mother" (*WH*, p. 191). Catherine is thus not the only character in this novel whom one can imagine passionately announcing, or at least thinking, "Nelly, I *am* Heathcliff"!

Lockwood again tries to pass himself off as a second-generation Heathcliff when he returns to Wuthering Heights in the fall of 1802 and is surprised to find Cathy and Hareton united. This "epilogue" resembles Coverdale's unexpected encounter with Priscilla and Hollingsworth several years after the action of the story. Within Brontë's novel, it also recalls Heathcliff's own belated return to Wuthering Heights after Catherine has married Edgar:

[T]hey had stationed themselves not far from one of the windows. I could both see them and hear them talk before I entered, and looked and listened in consequence, being moved thereto by a mingled sense of curiosity and envy that grew as I lingered . . . [Having witnessed them kissing and preparing for a walk on the moors,] I supposed I should be condemned in Hareton Earnshaw's heart, if not by his mouth, to the lowest pit in the infernal regions if I showed my unfortunate person in his neighbourhood then, and feeling very mean and malignant, I skulked round to seek refuge in the kitchen. (*WH*, pp. 338–9)

The language and imagery of the passage – Lockwood's reference to "infernal regions"; the animal metaphor ("Skulker" is the name of the dog that bites Catherine's ankle early in the novel [*WH*, p. 90]); seeking refuge in or being banished to the servants' quarters – all these recall Heathcliff and his thwarted striving for the first Catherine. Lockwood's representation of this domestic scene from outside looking in through a window also evokes the scene in which the young Heathcliff peers in through the window at Thrushcross Grange, giving the narrative an outsider's perspective upon the enticing warmth and luxury into which Catherine has been accepted and from which he has been forcibly excluded.

In the penultimate scene of the novel, Lockwood once again peeps at the young lovers and then sneaks away once more, though this time he is on the inside looking out: "As they stepped onto the door-stones, and halted to take a last look at the moon, or, more correctly, at each other, by her light, I felt irresistibly impelled to escape them again; and, pressing a remembrance into the hand of Mrs Dean, and disregarding her expostulations at my rudeness, I vanished through the kitchen, as they opened the house-door" (*WH*, p. 367). Lockwood's vanishing act here evokes an earlier show of peeping and disappearing: his retrospective disclosure to the reader of his efforts to avoid the returned gaze of the seaside "goddess." That earlier withdrawal had culminated in his retreat to the country which sets the scene for the telling of the story. It is that withdrawal, moreover, which Lockwood narrates as evidence of the "peculiarity" of his "constitution" (*WH*, p. 47).[11] However, in the final manifestation of Lockwood's peep-and-run tendency, when he "escape[s]" from Cathy and Hareton, he seems to be avoiding something far less inviting than a reciprocating gaze. Well might Lockwood imagine Cathy and Hareton sending his way a pitying or scornful gaze, is even worse, they might utterly fail to reciprocate this gaze, so mutually transfixed are these young lovers in looking at the moon and at each other. The scopophilic pleasure of satisfied curiosity outweighs the pain of frustrating if titillating, envy only when Lockwood watches unseen, from a distance, and preferably through a window.

Watching through windows and abrupt departure are motifs also associated with Coverdale. Appearing in his city clothes at the communal Blithedale dinner table, Coverdale announces his intention of taking "a short visit to the seaside" (*BR*, p. 137), a "leave-taking" occasioned by his falling out with Hollingsworth, and thus with Hollingsworth's devotees, Zenobia and Priscilla. Coverdale does not withdraw from the arena because he has lost the contest, as we might assume about Lockwood's hasty retreat; Coverdale is merely changing seats to regain a view of the show. Installing himself in an urban hotel room, Coverdale reimmerses himself in the dreamy pleasures of solitary bachelor life: fireplace, rocking chair, cigar, novel, and especially the unobstructed view from his window directly onto the windows at the back of a "stylish boarding-house." The boarders at whom he peeps – including Priscilla and Zenobia who unexpectedly materialize in the city just a few days later – are "actors in a drama"; Coverdale's mind is a "mental stage" (*BR*, p. 156); and when Zenobia draws the window curtain to obscure his view, it falls "like the drop-curtain of a theatre, in the interval between the acts" (*BR*, p. 159).

The theatrical connotations of Coverdale's spectatorship forge unmistakable links to the urban performance of spiritualist mediumship, which itself forms a counterpart to the rural performance of utopian communal life. Thus, the "white linen curtain" (*BR*, p. 159) that both frustrates and stimulates Coverdale's desire to watch conspicuously recalls the veil that covers Priscilla in her starring role as "The Veiled Lady." Coverdale sees the performance of "The Veiled Lady" in the city the night before he departs for the simpler pastoral life at the utopian community of Blithedale, modelled, as is well known, on Hawthorne's own experience at Brook Farm. What these two cultural discourses – utopian communalism and spiritualist mediumship – have in common is the rhetoric of the permeability of boundaries between self and other, between self and world, and between this world and the next. Thus Westervelt, the sinister impresario and Svengali-prototype, explains the phenomenon of his mesmerical control over the Veiled Lady/Priscilla in terms that could describe equally well the visionary project of utopian Blithedale: "He spoke of a new era that was dawning upon the world; an era that would link soul to soul, and the present life to what we call futurity, with a closeness that should finally convert both worlds into one great, mutually conscious brotherhood" (*BR*, p. 200). The "new era" of closeness that Westervelt claims to herald is unadulterated by hierarchy. Even more crucially, this new era is distinguished by the crossing or even the removal of boundaries which separate this world from the other world, the private from the public, and ultimately self from other, fundamentally destabilizing or dissolving conventional notions of bourgeois individuality.[12]

The mingling or dissolution of discrete identities associated with spiritualist mediumship and utopian communalism in *Blithedale* has a correlative in *Wuthering Heights*'s discourse of erotic, romantic, and/or supernatural merger.[13] This merging of individuals and spheres is most famously summed up by Catherine when she explains her plan to aid Heathcliff with Edgar Linton's money after marrying him. When Nelly condemns this as "the worst motive you've given yet for being the wife of young Linton," Catherine explodes:

It is not ... it is the best! The others were the satisfaction of my whims; and for Edgar's sake, too, to satisfy him. This is for the sake of one who comprehends in his person my feelings to [*sic*] Edgar and myself. I cannot express it; but surely you and everybody have a notion that there is, or should be an existence of yours beyond you. What were the use of my creation if I were entirely contained here? ... If all else perished, and *he* remained, I should still continue to be; and if all else remained, and he were annihilated, the universe would turn to a mighty stranger ... Nelly, I *am* Heathcliff – he's always, always in my mind – not as a pleasure, any more than I am always a pleasure to myself – but as my own being[.] (*WH*, p. 122)

This merging of self and other in *Wuthering Heights*, as in *Blithedale*, is described in terms of enchantment, suggesting the discourse of the supernatural and the romantic, or in terms of possession, suggesting the discourse of madness and also of private property. Both of these meta-phors for merger, moreover, suggest the tension between competing models of Victorian bourgeois marriage: the cultural fantasy of two halves forming one whole versus the mid-nineteenth-century legal real-ity of the husband's ownership of his wife's goods and body.[14] As many feminist historians and critics have noted, when Victorian "man and wife" are joined as one, that one is legally the man.[15] To the extent that Victorian marriage legally reorganizes the boundaries of individual identity, that reorganization is fundamentally hierarchical and possess-ive.

While *Blithedale* may be more self-conscious about the sexual politics of spiritualist mediumship and utopian communalism than *Wuthering Heights* is about the gendered asymmetries of the merging of Catherine and Heathcliff, the effects of such gendered asymmetries and their sexual politics are palpable in both texts. Both novels offer these radical interminglings of self and other as potential, if not ultimately viable, alternatives to the culturally hegemonic institutions of bourgeois mar-riage, family life, and private property, and to more conventional understandings of the relation of the world of the living to the world that lies on the "other side" of the veil. The damaging effects of conventional gender and sexual relations, particularly for female characters, are shown in these texts, however, to be ultimately replicated, even intensifi-ed, in these seemingly radical alternatives to marital merger. These alternatives to marriage are portrayed as even more hierarchical and possessive than traditional marriage itself.

Conventional relations of property, individuality, and mortality are reinstated by the conclusion of each novel, a restoration of the *status quo* that is both formally and ideologically conservative.[16] Both second-generation heroines, Priscilla and Cathy II, end up prospering within more or less conventional marriages; if conventional femininity is confining to them, it nonetheless allows them certain "powers of the weak," powers enjoyed by wives as well as by invalids. By contrast, both first-generation heroines succumb as a result of their performances of unconventional femininity, or perhaps from their very attempts to conform to the strictures of conventional femininity. Zenobia drowns herself, having lost both Hollingsworth and Priscilla as the consequence of her self-interested ambition;[17] Cathy dies in married childbirth after a pregnancy that is clearly incompatible with her primary bond to Heathcliff. Each novel offers up the uncanny spectacle of the dead first-generation heroine as a kind of gendered object lesson.[18] These displays of female bodily mortality converge, moreover, with the ethereally disembodied figure of the Veiled Lady, that uncanny representative of the living dead who is also *Blithedale's* emblem of the public, career woman.[19] All three female spectacles are located somewhere between the realms of life and death, whether lying peacefully horizontal (Cathy), kneeling erect in *rigor mortis* (Zenobia), or hovering upright slightly above the ground (Priscilla).

These novels' living-dead heroines, heroines who both conform to and transgress conventional boundaries of gendered identity, have their counterparts in the novels' invalid bachelor narrators. Coverdale's description of his illness – "I speedily became a skeleton above ground" (*BR*, p. 41) – explicitly recalls the uncanny spectacle of the Veiled Lady. Lockwood's account of the onset of his illness evokes the uncanny, Gothicized experiences of live burial and return from the dead – he describes himself "sinking up to the neck in snow, a predicament which only those have experienced it can appreciate" (*WH*, p. 73), and notes that "everybody conjectured that I perished last night; and they were wondering how they must set about the search for my remains" (*WH*, p. 73). Thus, in addition to their unreliability as narrators and their conspicuously inaccurate self-portrayal as thwarted suitors, Coverdale and Lockwood share yet another striking set of similarities. Early on in both novels, the bachelor narrators leave a domestic space warmed by the hearth. Both bachelor narrators also leave comfortable urban environs for more rugged rural ones, although this transition occurs before the story time for Lockwood. They both travel through chilling snow and consequently fall ill. Both narrators recover their health only by virtue of assiduous nursing during a protracted convalescence. While illness is a motif common to both novels, its manifestation in the novels' bachelor narrators is all the more conspicuous for its apparent gratuitousness to the plotting, if not the narration, of both novels.

Whereas Coverdale's illness is less than central to the narrative *mise en scène* of *Blithedale*, Lockwood's is the enabling condition of narrative in *Wuthering Heights*. Lockwood's illness is apparently caused by his exposure to the elements during his two-hour struggle back to Thrushcross Grange through the snow, after he has pronounced himself "quite cured [by Heathcliff's inhospitality] of seeking pleasure in society, be it country or town. A sensible man ought to find sufficient company in himself" (*WH*, p. 70). Lockwood almost immediately breaks his vow of "hold[ing] myself independent of all social intercourse" (*WH*, p. 74), and thereafter is repeatedly moved by the boredom and loneliness of his convalescence to seek out Nelly's company: "This is quite an easy interval. I am too weak to read, yet I feel as if I could enjoy something interesting. Why not have up Mrs Dean to finish her tale?" (*WH*, p. 130). Installed in the same room that Nelly set up for Catherine when she was convalescing from brain fever and which also served as a nursery for the motherless baby Cathy, Lockwood undergoes a kind of "listening cure": "Dree, and dreary! I reflected as the good woman descended to receive the doctor; and not exactly of a kind [of story] which I should have chosen to amuse me; but never mind! I'll extract wholesome medicines from Mrs. Dean's bitter herbs" (*WH*, p. 191). Nelly's narrative is represented here as a prescription as much as a pastime for what ails Lockwood.

Meanwhile, back at *Blithedale*, neither Zenobia's burnt gruel nor her desultory story-telling speed Coverdale's convalescence.[20] Indeed, Coverdale suggests that Zenobia's bedside attendance makes him even more "morbidly sensitive" (*BR*, p. 44), exacerbating a major symptom of his illness:

The soul gets the better of the body, after wasting illness, or when a vegetable diet may have mingled too much ether in the blood... The spheres of our companions have, at such periods, a vastly greater influence upon our own, than when robust health gives us a repellent and self-defensive energy. Zenobia's sphere, I imagine, impressed itself powerfully on mine, and transformed me, during this period of my weakness, into something like a mesmerical clairvoyant. (*BR*, pp. 46–7)

The penetrating power of "Zenobia's sphere" transforms the weakened invalid bachelor into a Priscilla-like, spiritualist medium, a prophetic seer capable of reading other people's minds. Hollingsworth's sphere is at least as forceful as Zenobia's, yet it is the muscular philanthropist who becomes Coverdale's nurse ideal. The attentiveness of Hollingsworth's bedside manner encourages Coverdale to believe that he "would have gone with me to the hither verge of life, and have sent his friendly and hopeful accents far over on the other side, while I should be treading the unknown path" (*BR*, p. 42). Coverdale envisions Hollingsworth's nursing as having the power to effect a more perfect union between individuals while bridging the boundaries which divide the earthly sphere from the eternal one. The spiritualist rhetoric Coverdale uses to describe his illness is comparable to that which he uses to describe Hollingsworth's nursing:

My fit of illness had been an avenue between two existences; the low-arched and darksome doorway, through which I crept out of a life of old conventionalisms, on my hands and knees, as it were, and gained admittance into the freer region that lay beyond. In this respect, it was like death. And, as with death, too, it was good . . . In literal and physical truth, I was quite another man. (*BR*, p. 61)

The separate "lives" bridged by illness may be embodied by two different men, as in the intimacy produced when Hollingsworth nurses Coverdale, or by one man over time, as in the case of Coverdale's "lively sense of the exultation with which the spirit will enter on the next stage of its eternal progress" (*BR*, p. 61).

Although the "tenderness" of his nursing seems initally to redeem Hollingsworth from unmeliorated "masculine egotism" (*BR*, p. 241), Coverdale discovers that the redeeming "soft place in his heart" is soon "forgotten" by Hollingsworth (*BR*, p. 41). It is merely a ruse meant to enlist him to Hollingsworth's cause:

But, by-and-by, you missed the tendernesss of yesterday, and grew drearily conscious that Hollingsworth had a closer friend than ever you could be. And this friend was the cold, spectral monster which he had himself conjured up, and on which he was wasting all the warmth of his heart . . . It was his philanthropic theory! (*BR*, p. 55)

Or, in Zenobia's indicting words, Hollingsworth cares for "nothing but self, self, self!" (*BR*, p. 218). Just as Hollingsworth's practice of nursing fails to transcend his own implicitly masculine self-interest, Coverdale's performance of illness, despite its "effeminacy" (*BR*, p. 58), does not exactly mitigate the self-seeking qualities he associates with masculine nature, what he calls "this ugly characteristic of our sex" (*BR*, p. 41). Illness may make Coverdale "quite another man" (*BR*, p. 61), but he

remains a man. While conventional gender can be bent in this novel –
witness Hollingsworth's nursing, Zenobia's intellect and ambition, Priscilla's public appearances – the asymmetries of gender do not permit
simple androgyny in either its male or female gender-benders. The
invalid bachelor, though feminized in certain respects by his illness,
nevertheless retains many of the powers and fears of bourgeois manhood.

While Coverdale's susceptibility to the influence of other people's
spheres recalls Priscilla's clairvoyant "sympathy" with other lives, it also
recalls Westervelt's mesmerical control over her. Indeed, Coverdale
describes his own sensitivity in terms more suggestive of the mesmerist
than of the mesmerical subject when he characterizes himself as "making my prey of people's individualities, as my custom was" (*BR*, p. 84),
and when he observes that the "cold tendency, between instinct and
intellect, which makes me pry with a speculative interest into people's
passions and impulses, appeared to have gone far towards unhumaniz-
ing my heart" (*BR*, p. 154).[21] We can see shades of the Veiled Lady but,
even more, we see the dark shadow of her Svengali in Coverdale's
description of his own tendency "to live in other lives, and to endeavor –
by generous sympathies, by delicate intuitions, by taking note of things
too slight for record, and by bringing my human spirit into manifold
accordance with the companions whom God assigned me – to learn the
secret which was hidden even from themselves" (*BR*, p. 160).[22] While the
twentieth-century reader might hear a foreshadowing of *Dracula* in this
image of vampiristic mind control, and mid nineteenth-century readers
might have heard resonances of one or more of that novel's popular
literary predecessors, Coverdale himself suggests a closer affinity between his habit of mind and the practices portrayed in a different
medical horror story, Mary Shelley's *Frankenstein*:

It is not, I apprehend, a healthy kind of mental occupation, to devote ourselves
too exclusively to the study of individual men and women. If the person under
examination be one's self, the result is pretty certain to be diseased action of the
heart... Or, if we take the freedom to put a friend under our microscope, we
thereby insulate him from many of his true relations, magnify his peculiarities,
inevitably tear him into parts, and, of course, patch him very clumsily together
again. What wonder, then, should we be frightened by the aspect of the
monster, which ... may be said to have been created mainly by ourselves! (*BR*,
p. 69)[23]

The bachelor invalid Coverdale suffers from a "diseased action of the
heart" produced by an egotistic self-fixation associated in this novel with

untempered masculinity. He is also aligned with the scientist or medical doctor, male figures whose fixed gaze is also represented as damaging. The scientific detachment of Coverdale's dissecting gaze through the microscope does an emotional violence to its objects, inflicting damage that cannot be surgically repaired.

The illness of the bachelor is therefore associated with hypermasculine detachment, indifference, and objectivity *as well as* with hyperfeminine attachment, sympathy, and subjectivity. Indeed, the one extreme may be seen as Coverdale's attempt to compensate for the other:

I betook myself away, and wandered up and down, like an exorcised spirit that had been driven from its old haunts, after a mighty struggle. It takes down the solitary pride of man, beyond most other things, to find the impracticability of flinging aside affections that have grown irksome. The bands, that were silken once, are apt to become iron fetters, when we desire to shake them off. Our souls, after all, are not our own. We convey a property in them to those with whom we associate, but to what extent can never be known, until we feel the tug, the agony, of our abortive effort to resume an exclusive sway over ourselves... Hollingsworth, Zenobia, Priscilla! These three had absorbed my life into themselves. (*BR*, p. 194)

Coverdale experiences the permeability of the boundaries of his individuality as threatening: to the rootedness of the living on earth; to the integrity of each human soul in its own body; to the rights of privacy and private property; and to "the solitary pride of man," the pride of masculine autonomy that is shackled by the "iron fetters" of feminine "affections." His "inexpressible longing" for absorption into the triangulated desire which unites Hollingsworth, Zenobia and Priscilla produces in Coverdale an equal and opposite "stubborn reluctance to come again within their sphere" and a "morbid resentment of [his] own pain." Coverdale withdraws to his urban hotel-room-with-a-view for the same reason that he resorts earlier in the novel to his "hermitage," the tree-top hide-out and spying place that he counts as "my one exclusive possession, while I counted myself a brother of the socialists" (*BR*, p. 99). His withdrawals are engendered not by his failure to connect with other people, but by what he experiences as an excessive and overwhelming connection. He feels that "Unless renewed by a yet farther withdrawal towards the inner circle of self-communion, I lost the better part of my individuality" (*BR*, p. 89).

Overwhelmed by his experience of emotional connection and even by his very desire for such connection, Coverdale retreats to a distance. Lockwood's retreat to the countryside from the seaside "goddess" and from society more generally is also an attempt to compensate for what he experiences as his excessive engagement with others. Both bachelors put themselves at a physical distance from others in order to shore up the threateningly permeable boundaries of their individuality, in order to regulate more properly the boundaries within and between selves. Yet their isolation ultimately intensifies, rather than diminishes, the self-projections through which they constitute their identities. Thus when Nelly proposes to abbreviate her narration, Lockwood vehemently objects, describing for her his "tiresomely active mood": "Are you acquainted with the mood of mind in which, if you were seated alone, and the cat licking its kitten on the rug before you, you would watch the operation so intently that puss's neglect of one ear would put you seriously out of temper?" (*WH*, p. 102). Elaborating on this conceit, he brings out the contrast between urban and rural life as well as the visual element of his vicariousness in both worlds: "I perceive that people in these regions acquire over people in towns the value that a spider in a dungeon does over a spider in a cottage, to their various occupants; and yet the deepened attraction is not entirely owing to the situation of the looker-on" (*WH*, p. 102). The vicarious "value" of objects to be visually consumed multiplies with the privations of "sitting alone" or even languishing in a dungeon.

It is not insignificant that the fulfillment of Lockwood's vicarious desire depends upon the proximity of Nelly as a primary source of the narrative which he so avidly consumes, and then relays to the reader. Nelly is the mother cat giving her kittens a thorough going-over; she is the spider who sews or knits while spinning her tale. She thus represents both object and subject of the narrative's gaze; the "situation of the looker-on" is doubled in the double narration of Lockwood and Nelly.[24] This doubling of the narrative perspective represents another version of the mingling of self and other that, as we have seen, is also associated in these two novels with illness, spiritualist mediumship, utopian communalism, and the merger of Cathy and Heathcliff. Though Lockwood's and Nelly's narratives provide separate and different frames for the story, these frames are not impermeable. One might expect a palpable distinction between what Nelly calls her "true gossip's fashion" of orally telling the story and the obfuscatingly pretentious, hyperliterate self-expression that sometimes characterizes Lockwood's voice. However, the narrative is generally undifferentiated in this regard, perhaps reflect-

ing the fact that Nelly is unusually well read for "a poor man's daughter," as she tells Lockwood when he comments on her relative lack of
"provincialisms" and her well cultivated "reflective faculties." (*WH*,
p. 103). The distinction between the voices of the two narrators fully
breaks down when Lockwood announces that he will "continue it in her
own words, only a little condensed. She is, on the whole, a very fair
narrator, and I don't think I could improve her style" (*WH*, p. 192).

Just as the two narrative voices overlap stylistically, the separate
spheres of narration also break down at the level of plot. That is to say,
not all of Lockwood's knowledge comes from Nelly, and each narrator
also separately enters the story as a character, thereby 'breaking the
frame.' This intersection between the narrators' spheres has a correlative in the spatial and social boundary-crossing that each one commits.
Lockwood's violent breaking of the casement window and his brutal, if
terrified, efforts to keep out the child ghost – events that also emblem-
atize the uncertain boundary between dreams and waking, and between
life and death in this novel – are only the most vivid of his transgressions.
If he is "unmistakably out of place in that pleasant family circle" (*WH*,
p. 56) into which he forces himself at Wuthering Heights, then he also
has a distinctly ambiguous status in his role as gentleman tenant – "I'm
Mr Lockwood, the master" (*WH*, p. 337), he announces to the flustered
servants upon his unexpected return to Thrushcross Grange, although
he most clearly does not "belong" there. Nelly transgresses as much as
Lockwood in her role as housekeeper of Wuthering Heights, a role that
requires her to be both family insider and hired outsider, both foster
sister/mother and servant, both *heimlich* and *unheimlich*. Given her ambiguous status in the family, as well as the competing demands of her
different masters and the conflicts between her own needs and those of
others, it is no wonder that Heathcliff describes Nelly's *modus operandi* as
"double dealing" (*WH*, p. 266).

Nelly's double dealing sometimes takes the form of outright lies and
partial truths, but more often it reveals itself in Nelly's oscillation
between sympathy for and detachment from those placed in her care, a
movement reminiscent of the fluctuation between distance and proximity exhibited by the novel's invalid bachelor narrator. This ambivalence
is particularly evident in her attendance first at Catherine's sickbed and
then at her deathbed, revealing Nelly's ambivalence toward the woman
to whom she is surrogate mother, sister, servant, and also a sometime
rival for the affections of Heathcliff and Linton. Nelly initially fails or
refuses to recognize the onset of Catherine's delirium, a lack of sym-

pathy in her role as nurse that is only partly explained by her knowledge that Catherine is, at least at first, only playing sick. Later, when Nelly realizes that Edgar is about to discover Heathcliff's presence at Catherine's bedside, another potentially life-threatening situation for which Nelly herself will bear some part of the blame, she clearly expresses her resentment:

I wrung my hands, and cried out; and Mr Linton hastened his step at the noise. In the midst of my agitation, I was sincerely glad to observe that Catherine's arms had fallen relaxed, and her head hung down.
   "She's fainted or dead," I thought; "so much the better. Far better that she should be dead, than lingering a burden and a misery-maker to all about her." (*WH*, p. 199)

Weary of the "burden" of nursing her, and perhaps also resentful of the "misery" she has inflicted on Linton and Heathcliff, Nelly frankly wishes Catherine dead. The violence of Nelly's death-wish gives way, at the opening of the next chapter, to her tersely affectless, even depersonalized, announcement of Catherine's death: "the mother died" (*WH*, p. 201). This drastically understated notice of death, in turn, cedes almost immediately to Nelly's ostentatiously overstated evocation of the spectacle of Catherine's beautiful dead body and of Nelly herself keeping watch by the deathbed, an intricately elaborated, narrative-halting, verbal and visual caressing of the corpse.[25] Nelly decries the "selfishness" of those, like Edgar Linton, who regret their loved ones' "blessed release," yet one can't help but thinking that she seems a little too "happy while watching in the chamber of death" (*WH*, pp. 201–2), especially because she pronounces herself less than fully confident that Catherine has, in fact, gone to a better place.

   Nelly attempts to represent the difference between her own and Edgar's response to Catherine's death as the difference between masculine self-indulgence and feminine self-renunciation, but her own rhetoric confounds this effect to segregate gendered styles of emotion and relation within correspondingly gendered individuals. The rapid movement from Nelly's passionate death-wish to her affectless announcement of Catherine's death, then from the rapture with which she "gaze[s] on that untroubled image of Divine rest" to the "cold reflection" with which she describes herself later speculating on the unlikelihood of eternal peace for Catherine's soul, reveals her oscillation between extremes of attachment and detachment, of emotional involvement and dispassionate distance. Nelly's coldness does not reveal true distance but, rather, a self-distancing attempt to compensate for, or at least to veil, a range of emotions which are even more transgressively unfeminine: envy, jealousy, resentment, even hatred. Just as they are unbecoming in a Victorian "true woman," the improperly regulated emotions that Nelly displays, often in the very act of covering them up, are equally inappropriate in a sickbed nurse and deathbed watcher.

Nelly's ambivalent feelings toward her charges, and especially towards Catherine, generate a doubling within of her own narrative voice, as well as a doubling of the novel's narrative voice in the dialogism of this female nurse who speaks to, and through, a male invalid narrator. Both kinds of narrative doubling, moreover, correlate with Emily Brontë's own projection of her authorial voice through the assumed identity of "Ellis Bell." Lockwood, we might say, serves as a male medium for Nelly, just as Ellis Bell provides a male medium for Brontë. To the extent that spiritualist mediumship and invalidism were aligned with bourgeois femininity in nineteenth-century culture, both Nelly's and Brontë's projections of self involve a *doubled* inversion of gender: a woman speaking as a man speaking as a woman.[26] In her Biographical Notice to the 1850 edition of *Wuthering Heights*, written after Emily's death, Charlotte Brontë claims that she and her sisters chose their pseudonyms for their gender-neutrality:

Averse to personal publicity, we veiled our own names under those of Currer, Ellis, and Acton Bell; the ambiguous choice being dictated by a sort of conscientious scruple at assuming Christian names positively masculine, while we did not like to declare ourselves women, because – without at that time suspecting that our mode of writing and thinking was not what is called "feminine" – we had a vague impression that authoresses are liable to be looked on with prejudice: we had noticed how critics sometimes use for their chastisement the weapon of personality, and for their reward, a flattery, which is not true praise. (*WH*, p. 31)

The advantage of the "ambiguous choice" is that it avoids the outright lie of claiming to be men while it also avoids the harsher criticism and the patronizing praise meted out to women writers. By assuming an authorial persona neither decisively masculine nor decisively feminine, Emily Brontë attempted to enjoy the advantages of both: to enjoy the expressive and financial benefits of "writ[ing] as a son" while enjoying the social sanction given to a proper, a private or "veiled," Victorian woman.[27]

Whereas Brontë employed a bachelor narrator as well as an "ambiguous" pseudonym to write "as a son," thereby to obtain the so-called "unprejudiced" critical attention that male writers enjoyed on the English literary scene, Hawthorne tried to use a bachelor narrator to get, or at least to hold onto, a piece of the action that women writers were enjoying in the mid-century American literary market. Hawthorne famously portrayed himself as a casualty of the "damned mob of scribbling women," a "melodrama of beset manhood" that reveals this bourgeois man's habituation to male privilege as much as it reveals the male author's perception of a threat in the literary marketplace, in the masses and mass culture, and in women and femininity.[28] Not all mid-century American male fiction writers felt so threatened: witness the spectacular 1850 success of Ik Marvel's unabashedly sentimental *Reveries of a Bachelor*, a success upon which Hawthorne tried to capitalize with his own 1852 bachelor-narrated romance. If his use of the bachelor narrator Coverdale was a device which allowed Hawthorne to "write like an American" and to "write like a man," the twin imperatives that Herman Melville urged in his anti-sentimentalist 1850 review, "Hawthorne and his Mosses," then the feminization of this figure also reveals the dangers of competing with women writers. For Hawthorne, beating women writers also meant joining them. And if the threat of public exposure encouraged Emily Brontë to use a male pseudonym and a bachelor narrator, these male impersonations were also immodest in their own way, like wearing a man's breeches in public. For both of these mid-century novelists, the bachelor narrator was, as Charlotte Brontë suggests, an "ambiguous choice."

The boundary-defying performances of the bachelor as narrator, and especially of the bachelor invalid as narrator, provided a viable solution to the different challenges of gendered authorship faced by Brontë and Hawthorne. The figure of the bachelor invalid narrator also stands as a solution, though a more vexed one, to the problems of hegemonic masculinity and conventional gender relations. It is possible to read the invalid bachelor narrators of *Blithedale* and *Wuthering Heights* as radically revisionary models of bourgeois manhood, as male figures whose susceptibility to the spheres of others enables them not simply to speak for those others, but also to speak in a doubled voice, one which is collaborative rather than preemptive. In this reading, the different voice of the bachelor narrator allows for differences of gender within and between individuals, and even for differences in the ways that individuality itself is constructed. Such a reading highlights the framing of these texts' critiques – of conventional marriage plotting, gender relations, and bourgeois individuality – from the "ex-centric' point of view of the bachelor narrator.

If it were to stop there, however, such a reading would miss the simultaneous critique of marital *alternatives* in these novels' plots. *Blithedale* exposes spiritualist mediumship as an exploitive fraud and utopian communalism as a dilettantish fad; *Wuthering Heights* underscores the inevitable violence associated with otherworldly merger of individualities upon this earth. Just as these plotted alternatives prove to be of limited viability, the alternative masculinity of the bachelor invalid is also limited both in scope and effect. It is crucial to recognize the ways in which these bachelor invalids reiterate, or perhaps rechannel, the hierarchical and possessive patterns of relationship and identity from which they only partially quarantine themselves. Equally problematic is these texts' reliance upon, the hence their reinforcement of, what is an explicitly pathologized alternative to normative masculinity. The fact that Coverdale and Lockwood are only temporarily indisposed does not immunize them or their narratives against the ill effects of pathologized images of "ex-centric" manhood.

Yet the very gratuitousness of these bachelors' invalidism – they don't *have* to get sick for the novels' plots to function, and they maintain their characteristic permeability despite the fact that they recover – is also salutary to our attempts to recuperate these masculine figures. Just as the quadrangulating function of the bachelor narrator is superfluous to the demands of mediated desire, the invalidism of the bachelor character is decidedly in excess of the demands of the novels' plots. We might say that the characterization of these figures is visibly in excess of their invalidism. While the boundary-crossings of these figures are sometimes regulated in ways that reaffirm the *status quo* of proper identity, the surplus value associated with their invalidism offers a challenge to the strict economies of bourgeois manhood, the domestic household, and novelistic fiction. The narratorial negotiations of these bachelor invalids thereby provide readers with a different window onto the domestic worlds of these novels. Their ways of looking and telling provide an opening, however small, for revisionary gender relations in the house of fiction.

SEEING SICKNESS, CONSUMING CONSCIOUSNESS: *THE PORTRAIT OF A LADY*

Just as Hawthorne and Brontë use their vicariously constituted invalid bachelor narrators to provide a window onto the worlds of their respective novels, James uses the figure of the vicarious bachelor invalid to frame his *Portrait of a Lady*. Ralph Touchett is not a first-person narrator, of course, but rather a "reflector," a term that James used synonymously in his critical writings with "register," "mirror," and "center of consciousness." James uses all these terms in two different, though overlapping, senses. They refer primarily to James's method of representing the story by analyzing the inward thoughts and feelings of one or more of the characters involved in the story's action. Used in this sense, "reflector" suggests that the character provides the author and reader with indirect access to the world of the story, "indirect" because the author approximates the character's perspective, but does not ventriloquize his "voice" or even his or her "point of view."[29] But James also uses these terms, and particularly the term "reflector," to describe characters who reflect upon, both by thinking about and responding to, the novel's main characters. Such characters provide an off-center perspective on the novel's main characters and action. They also vicariously center themselves in another character or characters. They are, one might say, "off-centers of consciousness."

In the Preface to *Roderick Hudson*, James describes one of his earliest attempts to use an off-center or, rather, his accidental discovery of this device's utility:

My subject, all blissfully, in face of difficulties, had defined itself – and this in spite of the title of the book – as not directly, in the least, my young sculptor's adventure. This it had been but indirectly, being all the while in essence and in final effect another man's, his friend's and patron's, view and experience of him. One's luck was to have felt one's subject right... The centre of interest throughout "Roderick" is in Rowland Mallet's consciousness, and the drama is the very drama of that consciousness...[30]

If Rowland Mallet's consciousness is the center of the novel, his own consciousness is centered elsewhere, in his "view and experience" of Roderick Hudson. Here, as in "Daisy Miller," the reputation-making *nouvelle* that intervened between *Roderick Hudson* and *The Portrait of a Lady*, James puts the text's center of consciousness in the figure of a bachelor onlooker who fails to understand fully and ultimately loses the unconventional object of his desire to early, unnatural death. Just as *Portrait* incorporates yet also revises these plot elements, it also draws on the narrative configuration of these earlier, eponymously titled, bachelor-reflector fictions, though with a difference. *Portrait* locates its main center of consciousness within the unconventional artist figure herself, rather than in her bachelor onlooker. Nevertheless, the novel retains the bachelor onlooker as a crucial off-center of consciousness, a consciousness that resembles but is not identical to that of the authorial narrator who provides his own responses to the lady of his portrait.

Ralph's engagement with Isabel also resembles but is not identical to that of her other suitors in the novel. Ralph's tubercular consumption requires certain renunciations; as he himself explains, "I haven't many convictions; but I have three or four that I hold strongly. One is that people, on the whole, had better not marry their cousins. Another is that people in an advanced stage of pulmonary disorder had better not marry at all."[31] While his illness may foreclose on certain privileges and pleasures of normative masculinity, it opens up others. Ralph's consumptive subjectivity challenges the integrity of selfhood, lending itself to alternative modes of connection within and between selves. The transgression of boundaries and the merger of identities effected by the bachelor invalid in this novel, as in *Blithedale* and *Wuthering Heights*, evokes an off-center, or "ex-centric," model of manhood and gender relations.

Ralph's function as an off-center also registers the status of *Portrait* as a major step toward the full articulation of James's centers of consciousness technique, the technique which enabled him to avoid the aesthetic compromises that he associated with both first-person narration and "omniscient" authorial narration in longer fiction. In the next chapter, I will analyze James's critical objections to first-person narration, revealing the gendered significance of his reservations, while considering the gendered implications of the epistemological indeterminacies produced by first-person narration and by reflector figures, as embodied by the bachelor figures who appear in his shorter fictions. Here, I will attend to the narrative and thematic role of the consumptive bachelor invalid as narrative reflector in *Portrait*, tracing the gendered and authorial implications of Ralph Touchett's vicarious investments. The vexed relation of *Portrait*'s bachelor invalid to the "great financial house" (I, p. 281) of Touchett gives shape to the novel's "literary form," a form which James famously envisioned as one of "a million – a number of possible windows" in "the house of fiction" (*LC2*, p. 1075).

When James justifies "the idea of making one's protagonist 'sick'" in the Preface to *The Wings of the Dove*, that most emphatically invalid-centered of his fictions, he invokes his earlier use of Ralph Touchett as an "accessory invalid":

Why should a figure be disqualified for a central position by the particular circumstance that might most quicken, that might crown with a fine intensity, its liability to many accidents, its consciousness of all relations? ... One had moreover, as a various chronicler, one's secondary physical weaklings and failures, one's accessory invalids – introduced with a complacency that made light of criticism. To Ralph Touchett in "The Portrait of a Lady," for instance, his deplorable state of health was not only no drawback; I had clearly been right in counting it, for any happy effect he should produce, a positive good mark, a direct aid to pleasantness and vividness. (*LC2*, p. 1288)

James describes Ralph's illness as enhancing his function as a narrative device because illness provides Ralph, and therefore the author and reader, with heightened access to experience. By prohibiting the more mundane events and perceptions of good health, illness "crown[s] with a fine intensity" Ralph's "consciousness of all relations," "quicken[ing]" them both in frequency and quality. When James notes the "pleasant-ness and vividness" produced by Ralph's invalidism, it sounds as if he is describing Ralph's invalidism as a social asset as much as a fictional one. He goes on to describe this dual enhancement of Ralph's character as a gendered conundrum:

The reason of this moreover could never in the world have been his fact of sex; since men, among the mortally afflicted, suffer on the whole more overtly and more grossly than women, and resist with a ruder and an inferior strategy. I had thus to take *that* anomaly for what it was worth, and I give it here but as one of the ambiguities amid which my subject ended by making itself at home and seating itself quite in confidence. (*LC2*, pp. 1288–9)

James identifies as an "anomaly" the salutary effect of this male charac-ter's terminal suffering on other characters and on the novel, if not on himself. The mystery behind this "ambiguity" comes clear in the assess-ment, focalized in *Portrait* through Isabel's consciousness, of the effect of illness on Ralph's character: "He was so charming that her sense of his being ill had hitherto had a sort of comfort in it; the state of his health had seemed not a limitation but a kind of intellectual advantage; it absolved him from all professional and official emotions and left him the luxury of being exclusively personal" (II, pp. 59–60). Isabel judges Ralph's illness a social asset because it "absolve[s]" its masculine subject of normatively bourgeois masculine preoccupations, the "professional and official," and thereby leaves him "the luxury of being exclusively personal." For Isabel as for James, Ralph's illness is an "advantage," recalling Madame Merle's wry estimation of Ralph as "very lucky to have a chronic malady" (I, p. 281).

The corrupt but clear-seeing Madame Merle pinpoints the role of his illness in Ralph's masculine self-constitution:

"Look at poor Ralph Touchett: what sort of a figure do you call that? Fortunately he has a consumption; I say fortunately, because it gives him something to do. His consumption's his *carrière*; it's a kind of position. You can say: 'Oh, Mr Touchett, he takes care of his lungs, he knows a great deal about climates.' But without that who would he be, what would he represent? 'Mr Ralph Touchett: an American who lives in Europe.' That signifies absolutely nothing – it's impossible anything should signify less. 'He's very cultivated,' they say: 'he has a very pretty collection of old snuff-boxes.' The collection is all that's wanted to make it pitiful. I'm tired of the sound of the word; I think it's grotesque. With the poor old father it's different; he has his identity, and it's rather a massive one. He represents a great financial house, and that, in our day, is as good as anything else. For an American, at any rate, that will do very well. But I persist in thinking your cousin very lucky to have a chronic malady so long as he doesn't die of it." (I, pp. 280–1)

Madame Merle describes Ralph's illness as an avocation that, however enervated, sustains a conspicuously leisurely American man abroad. Providing Ralph with "something to do," invalidism also provides him with something or someone to be, with something or someone to "represent." Lacking the professional affiliation that confirms his father's "massive" masculine "identity," Ralph makes do with an alternate career in knowing a great deal about climates and cultivating his health.

Madame Merle's analogy to the collection of snuff-boxes is pointed. It has become a critical commonplace that *Portrait* levels its most stringent criticism at a way of living that depends on the act of collecting, on aesthetic connoisseurship of objects and aesthetic "cultivation" of persons, persons who may include others as well as oneself.[32] Under such an aestheticizing regime, as Madame Merle explains to Isabel, "one's house, one's furniture, one's garments, the books one reads, the company one keeps – these things are all expressive" (I, pp. 287–8). If acquaintances, friends, and even family can be numbered among one's expressive things, then human beings are reduced to a decidedly object-like and material status. They become, in Marx's formulation, "commodity fetishes." The pathologized culture of consumption, the alienated and alienating consumer culture that is the world of James's *Portrait*, is emblematized by Ralph's illness. Ralph's consumption is the very "germ," to use a quintessentially Jamesian metaphor, of the novel. When selves are coextensive with self-presentation, then even one's own body is merely part of the packaging. Ultimately, the individual's most inner self may prove itself to be alienated, heartless, hollow at the core.

Of course, the character in the novel who comes closest to having an utter heart of darkness is Gilbert Osmond, whom Madame Merle describes as being an even more identity-deficient American man abroad than Ralph: "... he lives in Italy; that's all one can say about him or make of him. He's exceedingly clever, a man made to be distinguished; but, as I tell you, you exhaust the description when you say he's Mr Osmond who lives *tout bêtement* in Italy. No career, no name, no position, no fortune, no past, no future, no anything" (I, p. 281). Lacking even the alternate career in invalidism which compensates Ralph for his meagerness of conventionally masculine filiations, Osmond is afflicted with a "worse case" (I, p. 281) of expatriate American manhood than Ralph himself. Osmond's acquisition of Isabel and her fortune is the most ruthless act of unsympathetic detachment and opportunistic exploitation in the novel, a marital merger of individual lives that is clearly a hostile takeover. Yet virtually all of the characters in the novel, from Ned Rosier and Pansy, to Henrietta Stackpole and Lord Warburton, to Isabel herself, display symptoms of the aesthetic possessiveness and exploitiveness that afflict Osmond most virulently, though not as terminally as they afflict Ralph.

While vicariously consumptive self-constitution is limited neither to bourgeois men nor to expatriate Americans, the novel's bourgeois expatriate American men – Osmond, Ralph, and Caspar Goodwood – do seem to suffer more than others from their consumptive self-constitution. While one might expect Caspar Goodwood to be immune to the condition that plagues all the characters in the novel, even this embodiment of seemingly impermeable manhood turns out to be susceptible. Introduced as an ex-Harvard athlete who can "vault and pull and strain" (I, p. 163) intellectually as well as physically, and as the holder of a patent for a mechanical cotton-spinner in that most American of industries, Caspar is characterized in strikingly phallic and aggressive terms, culminating with his name: "There were intricate, bristling things he rejoiced in; he liked to organise, to contend, to administer; he could make people work his will ... there was nothing cottony about Caspar Goodwood" (I, p. 164). This initial character sketch appears to situate Caspar outside, or above, the aesthetic consumption that afflicts the others. But Caspar is merely on the supply side of what is, after all, a consumer culture; the separation of the production of his cotton textiles from their consumption is deceptive. Moreover, Caspar spends the preponderance of the novel on the European side, or consumer side, of the Atlantic. Caspar is an absentee captain of the industry that enables the languorous, expatriate, aestheticizing consumption at which the novel takes its most direct aim.[33]

The metaphors of eating, seeing, and spending that Ralph uses to describe his own terminal condition map out the contours of the consumptive self in this consumer culture. Consider, for example, Ralph's demurral when Isabel asks him point-blank whether he, too, intends to propose to her:

By no means. From the point of view I speak of that would be fatal; I should kill the goose that supplies me with the material of my inimitable omelettes. I use that animal as the symbol of my insane illusions. What I mean is that I shall have the thrill of seeing what a young lady does who won't marry Lord Warburton. (I, p. 212)

Ralph speaks of killing the goose but the fatality at issue is his own. The metaphoric energy of his utterance also seems to put Isabel in danger of extinction – the goose seems as much an emblem for her as it is a "symbol" of Ralph's "insane illusions." Isabel's value for Ralph depends upon her delivery of "the material of his inimitable omelettes," upon a performance that furnishes him with "the thrill of seeing." If Ralph eats his goose, he can't have his golden eggs too.

In the passage cited above, Ralph's metaphor for bodily consumption – eating – is linked to a figure of visual consumption. If life is something to be eaten like an "omelette," then Ralph must take it in through his eyes. By endowing Isabel with the means to fulfill "the requirements of [her] imagination" (I, p. 261), Ralph also enables himself to meet "the requirements of my imagination" (I, p. 265), to live for and through the vicarious "thrill of seeing" (I, p. 212):

What kept Ralph alive was simply the fact that he had not yet seen enough of the person in the world in whom he was most interested: he was not yet satisfied. There was more to come; he couldn't make up his mind to lose that. He wanted to see what she would make of her husband – or what her husband would make of her. This was only the first act of the drama, and he was determined to sit out the performance. (II, pp. 146–7)

If Ralph is literally "kept alive by suspense" (II, p. 147), the suspense of the story results in part from his initial speculative investment *in* the story: "What's the use of being ill and disabled and restricted to mere spectatorship at the game of life if I really can't see the show when I've paid so much for my ticket?" (I, pp. 209–10). Ralph hasn't simply paid the price of his ticket, he has backed the entire show by engineering the elder Mr. Touchett's bequest. Thus, when Isabel brings up her decision to marry Osmond, Ralph tells her, repeating an expression he uses when they first discuss her inheritance, that "if you were to get into trouble I should feel terribly sold" (II, p. 75; see also I, p. 320).

Ralph's fear of "feeling terribly sold" reveals his desire to be the active subject rather than the passive object of economic exchange, to sell rather than to be sold. It suggests his desire to have made a shrewd economic investment, to have proved himself a savvy businessman rather than a sucker, to take rather than to be taken in. These desires suggest Ralph's investment in activity over passivity, and in a market-place ethos in which reciprocity is an illusory ideal at best. They also reveal Ralph's attempt to realign himself with a particular style of marketplace masculinity, despite or even by virtue of his illness. Ralph's illness may require him to "give up work" (I, p. 51), to remove himself from the marketplace as well as from the marriage market, but he reinserts himself into the public, productive, masculine arena of the agora through his speculative investment in Isabel. In the speculative market economy of the late nineteenth century, spending was a part of business as usual: an entrepreneur or venture capitalist had to spend big to earn big. While conspicuous consumption was in many respects associated with bourgeois femininity, expenditure itself was hardly confined to the distaff, the supposedly private and feminine side, of consumer culture. Thus, if Ralph's big spending potentially undermines, or reveals the preexisting fragility, of both his health and his manhood, it also reinforces and even enables his participation in this normatively masculine public arena. Ultimately, the complexities of Ralph's masculine subjectivity, and his narrative function as a reflector, are generated by the competition between different models, or "economies," of economy itself, of the body, and of manhood. I will describe these internally conflicted models and their bearing on Ralph's identity in the order I have listed them here.

A nascent market economy came into existence as early as the twelfth century. But hostility to speculation based on the assumption that "it represents the antithesis of the natural, the productive, household economy," "the birth of money from money," as Aristotle referred to the particular abomination of usury, had been voiced as far back as the seventh century B.C., and probably much further.[34] With the industrial revolution and the rise of industrial capitalism in the eighteenth and nineteenth centuries, suspicions about speculation intensified.[35] These suspicions targeted especially that property which wasn't "real" but "personal," and particularly that category of "personal property" which encompassed "incorporeal" articles such as stocks and bonds.[36] In the nineteenth century, the imaginary alternative *par excellence* to the speculative capitalist marketplace was the sphere of the home, the domestic economy which was nostalgically imagined as divorced from the vagaries, the competitiveness, and the disorder of the modern, public marketplace. Another equally imaginary nineteenth-century alternative was found in the notion of a pre-, non-, or anti-capitalist model of the marketplace: a non-speculative, "closed system" in which economic resources are conceived as finite. In such a closed economy, resources must be hoarded prudently or spent rationally since they cannot be renewed or multiplied through speculation, a practice that can only succeed in a market that is based on irrationality, on "desire and disorder."[37] Ralph has a stake, I would argue, in all these economies: both in the anti-market ideal of the private sphere and in the market ideal of the public sphere; both in domestic economy and in market economy; both in a finite, "closed system" and in an infinite "open system." Each of these pairings reveals the contrast, or contest, between an economy of satiated plenitude and an economy of insatiable demand.

The analogy to these alternative or competing models of economy in nineteenth-century medical discourse is the "closed energy" model of the male body versus the "open energy" model. The closed bodily economy, which was the predominant model until late in the nineteenth century, conceives of unregulated male sexual "spending" as debilitating, depleting to a man's finite "spermatic economy" and hence to the collective "spermatic economy" of a class or a nation, even of mankind as a whole. In contrast, the open bodily economy, a medical view which came into ascendence around the turn of the century but which never completely eradicated the earlier model, encourages male sexual expression, viewing such expenditure as a necessary investment in a man's health.[38] The open model of the body is roughly analogous to the economic system of insatiable demand, based on the idea "that a healthy economy must incessantly expand or grow,"[39] whereas the closed model is predicated on satiated plenitude. Of course, both medical models of the male body promulgate proper regulation of expenditure, whether the regulatory mechanism involves prudent hoarding or prudent spending in appropriate venues, that is, venues which are ideally heterosexual, marital, coital, and reproductive.

Ralph's investment in Isabel raises two sets of questions about his ill health and the vicarious way of being associated with it. Assuming a closed energy system, one might ask: does Ralph's emotional and financial spending constitute a profligate spilling of his seed (money), a reckless, promiscuous, and even "perverted" expenditure of his limited resources, or is it a way for him prudently to make use of his limited physical energies? Assuming an open energy system, one might ask: does Ralph's "spending" constitute a proper, therapeutic expenditure, a necessary, if vicarious, venting of male energies that would otherwise "back up" and hasten his demise, or does his illness itself signal that he is improperly channelling his resources in ways that are overstimulating and themselves pathological? James's text leaves these questions unanswered. The impossibility of adjudicating with any certainty among the possible answers raised by these questions, either separately or taken together, results from the tensions within and between the closed and open economies of the male body in this 1880 novel. When Ralph asserts that "It's impossible for a man in my state of health to spend much money, and enough is as good as a feast" (I, p. 257) and asks his father to "kindly relieve me of my superfluity and make it over to Isabel" (I, p. 261), he indicates that his investment in Isabel is therapeutic, or at least nontoxic, under either bodily economy. But Mr. Touchett's anxiety about the "immoral[ity]" (I, p. 264) of Ralph's way of "tak[ing] an interest" (I, p. 263) in Isabel suggests the possibility that his vicarious investment in her is less than salutary in its effects on Ralph and Isabel alike. Mr. Touchett's perplexed observation that "Young men are very different from what I was. When I cared for a girl – when I was young – I wanted to do more than look at her" (I, p. 262) also indicates a perceived shift in styles of male heterosexual desire, as well as a tension between models of male embodiment that are both chronologically consecutive and simultaneous.

The ambiguities raised by the novel's competing models of the male body are compounded by other, related but not identical, ambiguities raised by two competing models of manhood that bear on Ralph's consumptive masculine subjectivity: civilized manliness versus primitive masculinity. As discussed in chapter 1, Gail Bederman among others has compellingly mapped the incomplete and uneven shift from mid-nineteenth-century civilized manliness characterized by emotional and physical self-restraint, to turn-of-the-century primitive masculin-

ity, a style of bourgeois manhood that partook of behavior and principles including roughness of manner, bodily excess, and sexual unre-
straint. Admittedly, it is difficult to see the primitive man in Ralph, so
firmly does his cultured urbanity seem to place him in the camp of
civilized manliness; his aesthetic sensibility and his riches are more
suggestive of aristocratic than working-class manhood. If any character in the novel is a likely candidate for the new, primitive masculinity,
it would surely be Caspar Goodwood, with his "hard manhood" (II,
p. 436) and his way of "show[ing] his appetites and designs too simply
and artlessly" (I, p. 165). But Ralph's specular and speculative investment in Isabel can nonetheless be understood along the lines of either
of these models of manhood: either as a form of masculine self-regulation, self-restraint, even as self-renunciation, or as a self-indulgent and
self-asserting way of fulfilling his own vicarious desires (a tendency
associated both with the aristocratic libertine and the working-class
tough). While they are often mutually exclusive of each other, primitive and civilized styles of manhood strikingly come together, for
example, in one of Ralph's attempts to see behind Isabel's mask and
thereby to help her:

He had an almost savage desire to hear her complain of her husband – hear her
say that she should be held accountable for Lord Warburton's defection... He
would have liked to warn Isabel of it – to let her see at least how he judged for
her and how he knew. It little mattered that Isabel would know much better; it
was for his own satisfaction more than for hers that he longed to show her he
was not deceived... [H]er cry for help ... was the only thing he was bound to
consider. (II, pp. 251–2)

I would note here, following Bederman's lead, that despite the cultural
fantasy of the essential unregulatedness of primitive masculinity, this
style of manhood is no less culturally mediated than the more patently
regulated, civilized manliness.

   Since both civilized and primitive manhoods, and both open and
closed economies of the male body, are simultaneously at work and in
contention in this 1880 novel, Ralph's economic and emotional investment in Isabel both builds and diminishes his symbolic gender capital.
One plausible net result is that Ralph's imaginary accumulations depend upon and even exacerbate his physical depletion; as Ralph's
body wastes, his fantasmatic masculine "identity," rooted in the visual
vicariousness of his invalidism, becomes correspondingly "massive" (I,
p. 281). Such a reading assumes that Ralph's vicariousness is essentially

vampiristic, that Ralph feeds off others, especially Isabel and even off himself. The process of exchange which saps Ralph's own lifeblood in order to replenish his mental "sacred fount" thus resembles the mutual transfusion between individuals that obsesses the bachelor narrator of *The Sacred Fount*, except that in *Portrait* the trade-off occurs between body and mind and within one individual. Such self-consumption suggests self-cannibalism as much as self-vampirism, evoking a scenario in which the civilized man ingests his primitive counterpart's body, after having cooked it in the mental "stewpot or crucible of the imagination, of the observant and recording and interpreting mind," the organ of consumption that James typically associates in his writings with the figure of the artist.[40] I admit that this scenario of self-cannibalism is never made explicit in James's *Portrait*, though Ralph's odd comparison of himself to Caliban (1, p. 169), that paradigm of primitivism, does suggest the possibility of this type of reverse self-colonization.[41]

Such an interpretation, however, downplays the ways in which Ralph's consumption also engenders his increased sensitivity to and sympathy for others, traits that run counter to his tendency to objectify and consume others. While Ralph's illness makes him the emblem of a way of being that characterizes all of the characters in the novel, it also distinguishes him from those others. As I will argue later, the literalized pathology of Ralph's consumption contributes to his portrayal as a kind of martyr, an innocent whose death symbolically, though not unproblematically, enables others to live. Ralph's consumption allows him to participate in the consciousnesses of others. This participation is not merely pathological but life-giving, not merely terminal but restorative of himself and others. In crossing the line between life and death, and in breaching the boundaries of identity that divide self and other, the bachelor invalid in *Portrait*, as in *Wuthering Heights* and *Blithedale*, stands as a potentially revisionary figure of masculine selfhood.

An example of the self/other divide as reconstituted with a difference by Ralph's consumption can be found within Ralph himself. The description of the onset of Ralph's invalidism suggests his alienated sense of self-difference:

He had caught a violent cold, which fixed itself on his lungs and threw them into dire confusion. He had to give up work and apply, to the letter, the sorry injunction to take care of himself. At first he slighted the task; it appeared to him it was not himself in the least he was taking care of, but an uninteresting and uninterested person with whom he had nothing in common. This person, however, improved on acquaintance, and Ralph grew at least to have a certain grudging tolerance, even an undemonstrative respect, for him. (I, pp. 51–2)

"This person" is, of course, Ralph himself, but the point is that he is a new Ralph with a new identity: Ralph the consumptive invalid. While the narrative describes him as gradually accepting of this "person with whom he had nothing in common," it is an acceptance based on an uneasy sense of his own alterity. This sense of self-difference is at once the sign of pathology and the sign, if not of recovery, then of his learning to live with his disease and his "other self."

Another version of Ralph's self-reconciliation, a self-reconciliation not incompatible with a fundamental sense of self-alienation, appears in the scene of conspicuous invalidism with which the novel opens, the tea party on the lawn at Gardencourt. The narrator obliquely notes that "the persons concerned in it were taking their pleasure quietly, and they were not of the sex which is supposed to furnish the regular votaries of the ceremony I have mentioned" (I, pp. 1–2). The figures composing this tea party are, that is to say, male, an inversion of conventional gender roles that bears on Ralph's conspicuously gender-bending or gender-revising consumption. The conversation of these male figures is, moreover, indistinguishable from the discourse of invalidism and the sick-room: does Mr. Touchett want more tea? is he comfortable? does he need his lap shawl or not? is the tea hot enough? The "Mr. Touchett" here is not Ralph but his elderly and ailing father, a doubling or merging of identities made explicit by the father's praise of Ralph's deft attentiveness: "he's not clumsy – considering that he's an invalid himself. He's a very good nurse – for a sick-nurse. I call him my sick-nurse because he's sick himself" (I, p. 8).

Mr. Touchett's wordplay typifies the arch double-entendre of the opening scene as a whole. Earlier, Mr. Touchett refers to himself and Ralph as "two lame ducks" (I, p. 7): he can't walk and Ralph himself is "not very firm on his legs" (I, p. 6). When Mr. Touchett rubs his own legs in response to Ralph's solicitous inquiry about whether he is cold, he says "I can't tell till I feel." This response prompts Ralph to reply, "Perhaps someone might feel for you," which Mr Touchett playfully caps, "Oh, I hope some one will always feel for me!" (I, p. 6). All of these puns rhetorically amplify the doubling or permeability of self associated with Ralph's illness. The doubling of the "sick-nurse" is particularly evocative of permeability since it suggests the intense identification of nurse and patient which offsets the alienation within the self produced

by Ralph's illness. Just as Ralph feels a certain resentful detachment
from his newly consumptive self, he also feels a certain self-asserting or
self-interested "dis-ease" with his father's illness, especially at first:

Ralph had always taken for granted that his father would survive him – that his
own name would be the first grimly called. The father and son had been close
companions, and the idea of being left alone with the remnant of a tasteless life
on his hands was not gratifying to the young man, who had always and tacitly
counted upon his elder's help in making the best of a poor business.[42] (I, p. 85)

The tenderness for his father that Ralph displays in the novel's opening
vignette suggests that he has come to a sympathetic engagement with his
father's sick self that matches the sympathetic self-respect he has learned
to have for his own invalid "other self." Ralph's performance of the part
of his father's "sick-nurse" is not a self-denying evacuation of identity,
but rather a self-fulfilling identification with another.

Ralph's "other self" also materializes in a moment of bantering with
Henrietta Stackpole. When Henrietta asks Ralph whether he will be yet
another suitor for Isabel's hand, he flirtatiously parries that he is "in love
with Another!" Henrietta responds to his attempt at gallantry, "You're
in love with yourself, that's the Other!" (I, p. 169). What Henrietta sees
in Ralph is not healthy self-love, but self-centered and destructive
narcissism. Like Madame Merle, Henrietta believes that Ralph primarily cultivates himself, that he participates in a closed circuit of desire in
which the self is the sole subject and object. Ralph's spectatorship is not,
however, a hermetically sealed circuit of self-regard in which self-image
encloses an utterly empty center and other people are merely disposable
packaging. His desires are both other-centered and self-centered, disinterested and self-interested, nurturant and self-nurturing. His vicariousness does not completely eliminate or neutralize his sympathy for others;
his role as a reflector does not completely reduce others to objects
paralyzed by the glare of his gaze.

This other effect of Ralph's onlooking is most vivid in his deathbed
scene, a spectacle-in-the-text which inverts the conventionally gendered
Victorian tableau in which a dying woman or child is mourned by a
husband, suitor, son, or father, figures who play supporting roles and
also perform as the audience for the spectacle. Here, the woman is the
spectator, though also a crucial performer in the scene, and the dying
man is the spectacle to be visually consumed. Moreover, the Victorian
"angel in the house" is refigured here as an "angel of death." Ralph tells
Isabel that "You've been like an angel beside my bed. You know they

talk about the angel of death. It's the most beautiful of all. You've been like that; as if you were waiting for me" (II, pp. 412–13). When Isabel denies that she has been waiting for his death, Ralph corrects her: "There's nothing makes us feel so much alive as to see others die. That the sensation of life – the sense that we remain. I've had it – even I. But now I'm of no use but to give it to others. With me it's all over" (II, p. 413). Ralph represents himself as making the ultimate sacrifice, as giving his life so that Isabel may live vicariously through witnessing the spectacle. This donation of self is not only self-abnegating; it is also self-fulfilling in much the same way that we have come to understand a particular style of bourgeois Victorian femininity: as predicated upon a paradoxically self-assertive self-sacrifice. In the Christ-like performance of the "powers of the weak," the weaker one is, the more one has to give.

In other words, the trajectory of the deathbed gaze is bi-directional and ambivalent. If Isabel watches at Ralph's deathbed, then Ralph watches Isabel back. His gaze, like hers, reflects both the differences and the similarities between them. The words accompanying their looks simultaneously acknowledge and deny, simultaneously reinforce and tear down, the boundaries between them and between life and death:

"O Ralph, you've been everything! What have I done for you – what can I do to-day? I would die if you could live. But I don't wish you to live; I would die myself, not to lose you." (II, p. 413)

"You won't lose me – you'll keep me. Keep me in your heart; I shall be nearer to you than I've ever been. Dear Isabel, life is better; for in life there's love. Death is good – but there's no love." (II, pp. 413–14)

The permeability of boundaries extends to the boundaries within individuals as well as those between them: "She felt a passionate need to cry out and accuse herself, to let her sorrow possess her. All her troubles, for the moment, became single and melted together into this present pain" (II, p. 414). The melting together and becoming single occasioned by Isabel's "passionate need" resembles the mingling of Isabel and Ralph occasioned by the spectacular intensity of their specular relations: "nothing mattered now but the only knowledge that was not pure anguish – the knowledge that they were looking at the truth together" (II, p. 414). This mutual looking at a common object, like their gaze at each other, bestows upon Ralph and Isabel an intersubjectivity that makes them one while allowing their differences:

"Yes, he was in love with me. But he wouldn't have married me if I had been poor. I don't hurt you in saying that. How can I? I only want you to understand. I always tried to keep you from understanding; but that's all over."

"I always understood," said Ralph.

"I thought you did, and I didn't like it. But now I like it."

"You don't hurt me – you make me very happy." And as Ralph said this there was an extraordinary gladness in his voice. (II, p. 415)

In this sentimental scene, the mutual understanding of "looking at the truth together" is potentially redemptive. The masochistic self-renunciation which finally joins Ralph and Isabel most closely – "'Oh my brother!' she cried with a movement of still deeper prostration" (II, p. 417) – is pleasurable because painful, a suffering whose comfort lies in the fantasy of putting another's interest before one's own.[43]

In the world of this novel, of course, such a fantasy is always subject to question, since consumer culture, like Ralph's consumption, is notoriously all-consuming; as Michael Gilmore has persuasively argued, "The possibility of genuine deliverance from the commodity world is, nonetheless, an illusion . . . Isabel [is] never more implicated in the value system of advanced capitalism than in [her] renunciation" (p. 73). Thus one would be well justified in pointing out that Ralph benefits as much or more than Isabel in "giving up" his inheritance to her. One might well also note that Ralph doesn't die for Isabel's sake any more than he manages truly to understand her in this scene. The ironizing distance between Ralph's and Isabel's subjectivities that taints this scene of mutual understanding indicates the inexorable boundary-asserting force of the commodity world's possessive, hierarchizing, property-based relations.

But to insist that Isabel suffers *because of* Ralph's gift is to deny her the agency that Ralph as patron, and James as author, are eager to grant her. Similarly, to insist solely upon the inexorability of commodity relations in the world of this novel is to deny the possibility of resistance, however futile, to this all-consuming force. Such insistence misses the possibility of another register in the novel, a shadow world that diverges from the exploitive self-interest which is the novel's dominant note. Such a reading would miss, for example, the differences between the sentimental discourse that characterizes the representation of self-other mingling in Ralph's deathbed scene and the economic discourse used elsewhere in the novel to evoke possessive and hierarchical mergers of individuals. When Ralph comes to Isabel's bedside as a ghost, for example, the narrative gestures toward a different order of connection, between individuals as well as spheres, by shifting into a palpably spiritualist discourse:

> [Ralph] had told [Isabel], the first evening she ever spent at Gardencourt, that if she should live to suffer enough she might some day see the ghost with which the old house was duly provided. She apparently had fulfilled the necessary condition; for the next morning, in the cold, faint dawn, she knew that a spirit was standing by her bed . . . She heard no knock, but at the time the darkness began vaguely to grow grey she started up from her pillow as abruptly as if she had received a summons. It seemed to her for an instant that he was standing there – a vague, hovering figure in the vagueness of the room. She stared a moment; she saw his white face – his kind eyes; then she saw there was nothing. (II, pp. 418–19)

Ralph comes to Isabel as a ghost, summoning her to his bedside, but too late for her to see the last of him. When "[s]he opened the door with a hand as gently as if she were lifting a veil from the face of the dead," Ralph is already gone. The narrative's ghostly representation of this absent presence, its conspicuous non-representation of Ralph's death resembles its conspicuous non-representation of Isabel's return to Osmond. Just as Isabel comes to Ralph's door too late to see him again at the opening of the final chapter, Caspar arrives at Henrietta's door too late to see Isabel again at the chapter's, and the novel's, close. The lady vanishes, and only the bachelor reflector, a role in which Caspar now has replaced Ralph, remains visible to the reader's gaze in the novel's final scene.

Caspar joins, or replaces, Ralph in his identity as an invalid bachelor reflector who is finally unable to see the "person in the world in whom he was most interested" (II, p. 146). It is true that Ralph's "want of seriousness" (II, p. 59) and his "love of conversation" (II, p. 146), traits explicitly linked to his invalidism, initially distinguish him from Caspar. Isabel numbers among Caspar's other "defects" the "collective reproach of his being too serious, or, rather, not of his being so, since one could never be, but certainly of his seeming so," and the fact that "when one was alone with him he talked too much about the same subject, and when other people were present he talked too little about anything" (I, p. 165). Toward the end of the novel, however, Caspar comes to have more in common with Ralph, belying Henrietta's belief that Caspar is "just the opposite of" (I, p. 173) Ralph. When Caspar is charged by Isabel to be Ralph's "caretaker" and by Ralph to "care" for Isabel, he takes on the role of the "sick-nurse" earlier associated with Ralph. And when Caspar learns, belatedly, that Isabel has returned to Rome, he is unable to move and has "added, on the spot, thirty years to his life" (II, p. 438), traits that recall Ralph's illness-associated premature aging and his ultimate immobility on his deathbed. Henrietta's injunction to Caspar, "Look here, Mr Goodwood . . . just you wait!" (II, p. 437), also evokes the suspense that keeps Ralph alive. Thus, the "key to patience" (II, p. 438) that Henrietta believes she has given Caspar with these words resembles the "key to the mystery" (II, p. 146) of what sustains Ralph's life: his desire to see what Isabel will do.

Henrietta's "Look here . . . just you wait!" provides the novel with an open ending that might mean either hope or eternal despair, redemption or hell. Will "patience" give Caspar a chance, or will he be left in eternal suspense? Does Ralph die so that Caspar might live, or is Caspar a zombie-like reincarnation of Ralph, one who undergoes no renewing rebirth but only an eternal death-in-life, a vampiristically vicarious life as the undead? Of course, the open ending of the novel is even more pointed with respect to Isabel: is her self-sacrifice "worth" anything? is it a successful form of resistance to the commodity world or is it just the ultimate expression of subjection to it? The novel leaves these questions unanswered, or perhaps answers them both ways. Here, as in "Daisy Miller," the 1878 *nouvelle* that served as journeywork for James's more fully elaborated 1880 portrait of the American girl abroad, the traditional motif of the redemptive death of the innocent is critiqued even while it is deployed. James overtly participates in this traditionally moralistic plotting, while also covertly sending it up. Even though he "signifies upon" this tradition, he also suggests that there is, in fact, a better world beyond, an aesthetic world of intensely sympathetic vicariousness that transcends the lumpen, commodified fallenness of life on this side of the veil. In James's *Portrait*, this other world beyond the pale is already present on earth in the sentimentalized spectacle of the suffering male body, in the transubstantiation of selves that occurs when Caspar assumes the onlooking though occluded perspective of this suffering male self, and when the reader is invited to do the same.

The performance of these bachelor reflectors as witnesses, vicariously experiencing the suffering of Isabel at several removes, is reiterated not only by the readers of the text but also by its author. Other critics have noted the variable, and gradually increasing, epistemological distance of the authorial narrator from Isabel, a distance that corresponds to the distance of Ralph Touchett from the "person in the world in whom he was most interested" (II, p. 146).[44] This image of the author as limited witness rather than omniscient creator correlates with the one that James famously construes in his Preface to *Portrait*, where he represents his own relation to his characters as an act of vicarious spectatorship, in which the novelist looks out upon his "choice of subject" from within the "house of fiction" (*LC2*, p. 1075). This spectatorship is undeniably tainted by hierarchical and possessive relations – James notoriously describes his "possession" of Isabel, her presence as a "rare little 'piece'" in the "dusky, crowded, heterogeneous back-shop of the mind [of the] wary dealer in precious odds and ends" (*LC2*, p. 1076), aligning himself as author with Osmond as an objectifying aesthetic collector. He also describes himself as having "waked up one morning in possession" of all of the novel's subsidiary characters, whom he likens to the novel's hired help: "They were like the group of attendants and entertainers who come down by train when people in the country give a party; they represented the contract for carrying the party on" (*LC2*, p. 1081).

But James also describes these subsidiary characters as "privileged high officials . . . who ride with the king and queen" and as "true agents" with whom he enjoys relations of "confidence" and "trust," relations that depends upon their autonomy:

It was as if they had simply, by an impulse of their own, floated into my ken, and all in response to my primary question: "Well, what will she *do*?" Their answer seemed to be that if I would trust them they would show me; on which, with an urgent appeal to them to make it at least as interesting as they could, I trusted them. (*LC2*, 1081)

Like Ralph, James is driven by the "primary question" of what Isabel will do; like Ralph, James meets "the requirements of [his] imagination" by proxy; and like Ralph, James declines responsibility for being the "beneficent author of infinite woe" (ii, p. 192–3), a label that gets assigned to the elder Mr. Touchett through the focalized consciousness of Isabel. As "apostles of freedom" (ii, p. 245), neither James nor Ralph are fully disinterested. James himself admits in his *Preface* that the autonomy he invests in his characters is a "trick" of his imagination: "the trick of investing some conceived or encountered individual, some brace or group of individuals, with the germinal property and author-ity" (*LC2*, p. 1073). While factitious, this fiction of autonomy allows James to develop his method for avoiding the authorial intrusions of telling, to show his subject via the mediating consciousnesses of his reflectors. This willful self-dispossession grants the author a privileged, if vicarious, access to experience which resembles that of his bachelor invalid reflector. In taking up residence in the house of fiction, James articulates an authorial identity that draws upon the off-center masculinity of Ralph, a bachelor invalid who represents but also renounces his interest in the House of Touchett.

CHAPTER 3

An artist and a bachelor: Henry James, mastery, and the life of art

London is on the whole the most possible form of life. I take it as an artist and a bachelor; as one who has the passion of observation and whose business is the study of human life ... I had complete liberty, and the prospect of profitable work ... I took possession of London.[1]

Thus wrote Henry James in his first American journal, glancing backward in 1881 to his 1876 arrival in England. In representing himself as an artist and a bachelor, James describes a double life divided between "passion" and "business," yet joined by the single purpose of studious observation. The appositive structure of the second sentence seems to assign "passion" to the artist and "business" to the bachelor, suggesting a constitutive difference, a schism or struggle between two of the many sourc of identity that informed James's sense of himself as an author. Yet the artist and the bachelor seem here to be more compatible than not. They are joined in harmony rather than in conflict: united by the shared object of their gaze and particularly by the intensity that their ways of seeing have in common. The artist and the bachelor share a fascination with and dedication to that encompassing other, London, which is itself a "form of life."

Artistry and bachelorhood were themselves "the most possible form[s] of life" for James, two intricately bound aspects of masculine authorial selfhood that James continually negotiated in his fiction and in his criticism, his notebooks, and his private letters. While these identities sometimes appear in his writings as deviations from bourgeois masculine normativity, at other times they figure as privileged forms of access to hegemonic masculinity and thereby as potentially revisionary models of normative manhood. It is worth noting that in aligning the artist with passion and the bachelor with business, the passage from the American journal does not fully reflect the fact that, in James's historical moment, bachelors were equally often associated with the self-indulgent excesses of passion and artists with the self-denying asceticism of studiousness. But by making artist and bachelor into mutually supplementary embodiments of dedication who counterbalance each other in their self-assertions and self-effacements, James envisions the possibility of attaining or reinventing normative masculinity via these identities.

The coupling of bachelor and artist is informed by a related but more generalized pairing which appears even more frequently in James's writing: the man and the artist. In James's writing, as in that of many nineteenth-century male writers before him and perhaps even more twentieth-century male writers after him, a man's status as an artist is often imagined as disqualifying or excluding him from full, achieved, or dominant manhood. Both his limited commercial potential as a literary author and his private residence in the "house of fiction," his consuming preoccupation with the "inner life," mark the distance of the male artist from the attainments of a more conventionally active and public 'marketplace masculinity.' Yet James and these other writers also imagine artistry, paradoxically, as an alternative way for a man to fulfill the requirements of hegemonic manhood; this alternative means of attaining manhood inevitably revises the manhood which is its end. Both the luxury afforded and the discipline demanded by the aesthetic "life of art" provide alternative models for a properly regulated masculinity. By associating literary mastery with success, often by way of the "complete liberty" and "profitable work" mentioned in my epigraph, James compensates for the masculine renunciations that high art was often thought to exact.[2]

Though it is not apparent from my chosen epigraph, the man/artist pairing for James is not always, or simply, a matter of intrapersonal self-division. Just as often, the man/artist pairing shapes relations between men. Although male self-division and male–male relations were hardly subject to identical meanings or identical regulations in legal, medical, or other discourses of late nineteenth- and early twentieth-century British and American culture, they often serve as figures for each other in literary discourse of this period.[3] Robert Louis Stevenson's *The Strange Case of Dr. Jekyll and Mr. Hyde* (1886), Oscar Wilde's *The Picture of Dorian Gray* (1891) and *The Importance of Being Earnest* (1895), and Conrad's "The Secret Sharer" (1912) (the last text is discussed in the next chapter) are all paradigmatic examples of the mutual figurings of male self-division and homoerotic/homosocial male bonds at the *fin de siècle*. The "double lives" in these texts encompass both the imaginary consolidation of charged relations between men within the figure of a single man and the imaginary distribution of a single man's self, riven by conflict, between two male figures. These and other literary figurings of "double lives" indicate the demand for and the difficulty of the proper regulation of masculine identity and desire in this period. In James's writings, as in these other fictions contemporary with his own, the reflections that the divided self and the male couple mutually cast upon each other are key to our understanding of the narrative use and cultural significance of the figure of the bachelor.

I will argue that the figure of the bachelor, as a paradoxical exemplar of both normative and counternormative masculinities, helped to shape the figure of the high-cultural male artist that James wished to be and, in fact, became. In James's mid-career tales of literary life and in his personal papers and literary criticism, the figure of the bachelor represents the tensions between man and artist as well as the compatibility of these two identities. The relationship between these identities is enacted both within James's bachelor figures and also between these bachelor critics and writers and their "Masters." These Masters are male author figures whom the bachelor critics and writers challenge for dominance and to whom they submit, figures with whom they long to be joined not only in rivalry but in loving fraternity. In intrapsychic dynamics and interpersonal relations alike, the proper regulation of masculine identification and desire is subject to competing ideals of hierarchy/liberty and reciprocity/equality, the constitutive tension that underlies a longstanding tradition of liberal thinking. In the second section of this chapter which discusses the gendered implications of James's negotiations of life and art in his criticism and fiction, and in the last section which explores James's use of bachelor figures in the first-person narrated fictions, "The Aspern Papers" and "The Figure in the Carpet," I argue that James's imagining of the figure of the bachelor registers his response to the requirements of properly regulating gendered relations within and between men.

Bachelors abound in James's fiction. A far from exhaustive list of James's bachelors would include Roger Lawrence in *Watch and Ward*, Rowland Mallet in *Roderick Hudson*, Winterbourne in "Daisy Miller," Ralph Touchett in *The Portrait of a Lady*, the many bachelor-artists and bachelor-critics, some named and some nameless, in his tales of "the literary life" (*LC2*, p. 1228) and fictions of "poor sensitive gentlemen" (*LC2*, p. 1250), the uncle in "The Turn of the Screw," the unnamed narrator of *The Sacred Fount*, and even Lambert Strether in *The Ambassadors* who might be said to epitomize Jamesian bachelorhood even while disqualifying himself from the bachelor ranks on the technicality that he is a widower. Not all of these bachelors are narrators.[4] (Those seeking scrupulous consistency may also object, "Not all of these 'bachelors' are *bachelors!*"). Although James uses first-person narration in many of his shorter pieces, he objects to its use in longer fiction, preferring to employ third-person or heterodiegetic narration with reflector characters or centers of consciousness.[5] The first section of this chapter analyzes James's critical objections to first-person narration in longer pieces, arguing that James conceives of first-person narration as a threat because he associates it both with femininity and popularity, and also with an aggressive style of hypermasculinity and with modernity. For James, first-person narration was also a marker of autobiography and romance, two literary genres whose gendered implications for the male high-cultural author are ambivalent at best and downright threatening at worst. James's multiply and inconsistently gendered readings of this narrative technique give us insight into his attempts to reclaim literary fiction as an arena of fully masculinized endeavor, and into his re-modelling of masculinity via the figure of the bachelor. The figure of the bachelor ultimately enabled James to imagine art and life not as mutually exclusive ways of being but as mutually constitutive.

GENDER, GENRE, AND THE AIRPLANE OF FIRST-PERSON
NARRATION

In my discussion of *The Portrait of a Lady* in the previous chapter, I noted that Jamesian centers of consciousness are not always identical to the main or eponymous characters of his fictions. In some instances, James's reflectors are "off-centers of consciousness," characters who, like Ralph Touchett, center their subjectivities in other characters. In other instances, such "off-centered" characters are themselves at the imaginative center of his fiction. For example, James notes in his New York Edition Prefaces that the "subject" of *Roderick Hudson* is "another man's, his friend's and patron's view and experience of" Roderick Hudson (*LC2*, p. 1049), and that the subject of "The Figure in the Carpet" is located in the perceptions of one who is not the great artist of that story: "Vereker's drama indeed – or I should perhaps say that of the aspiring young analyst whose report we read" (*LC2*, p. 1235). In summing up both "Figure" and *Roderick Hudson*, James redefines his subject as one man's vicarious "view and experience" of another man. But the other-center-ing of these two texts occurs under strikingly different narrative circumstances. Unlike the first-person narrated or homodiegetic "Figure," *Roderick Hudson*, like *Portrait*, is narrated by an "impersonal," third-person, or heterodiegetic narrator.

What is the significance of using one man to tell another man's story when a heterodiegetic authorial narrator, a disembodied third voice, actually tells the story? What is the difference between James's use of the bachelor as a first-person narrative frame in *nouvelles* like "Figure" and "Aspern" and his use of bachelor centers of consciousness in novels like *Roderick Hudson* and *The Portrait of a Lady* or even *The Ambassadors*, and in shorter pieces like "Daisy Miller" and "The Lesson of the Master"? As my discussions of "Lesson" and of "Figure" and "Aspern" in the two last sections of this chapter will make clear, the issues of masculine discipline and indulgence, of epistemological indeterminacy and narrative authority obtain whether James's off-centered bachelors narrate or not. But James's critical objections to the use of first-person narration in longer works of fiction betray a distinctly gendered and generic agenda, whether or not the fictions themselves actually fall into the traps that he anticipates. I will attempt to show here that his critical objections are of a piece with his attempts to construe a fully masculinized "life of art."

In his New York Edition Preface, James estimates *The Ambassadors*, a novel that revisits the terrain of vicarious single manhood common to many of the mid-career tales, "as, frankly, quite the best, 'all round,' of all my productions" (*LC2*, p. 1306). This endorsement is even more striking when we consider that James excluded from the canon-forming New York Edition his simultaneously written *The Sacred Fount*, a novel whose nameless first-person bachelor narrator could be mistaken, at a distance, for Strether's evil twin. This nameless narrator's prurient fascination with the relationships he witnesses bears a distinct family resemblance to Strether's own vicarious self-constitution. While there are surely many reasons that James, and we with him, might prefer *The Ambassadors* and Strether to *The Sacred Fount* and its narrator, it is nevertheless certain that James's exclusion of *The Sacred Fount* was at least partly determined by its use of non-heterodiegetic, first-person narration.

Signally, the Preface to *The Ambassadors* contains some of James's most fully articulated objections to the use of "the first person, in the long piece" (*LC2*, p. 1315). In this Preface, he deplores first-person narration as "the darkest abyss of romance" (*LC2*, p. 1315) and "a form foredoomed to looseness" (*LC2*, p. 1315), censuring its "terrible *fluidity* of self-revelation" (*LC2*, p. 1316). For James, first-person narration is watery, dark, and deep. This bottomless pool of molasses-hued quicksand is even less buoyant than the Conradian "destructive element." By hampering the ability of the author and his readers alike to orient themselves and to maneuver, the medium of first-person narration thwarts all efforts to "make the deep, deep sea keep you up."[6] Less metaphorically speaking, first-person narration threatens epistemological certainty by dispensing with the firm sense of context provided by a heterodiegetic narrator, a narrator who is not a character in the plot. James sees Strether, by contrast, as both "encaged and provided for" by the non-first-person "exhibitional conditions" (*LC2*, p. 1316) of *The Ambassadors*, conditions whose "stiffer and more salutary" "proprieties" supply a sturdier frame of reference for us ... and apparently also for the characters themselves. *The Ambassadors*'s narrative method gives Strether the last word, simultaneously banal and profound – "'Then there we are!' said Strether'" – in a novel that foregrounds the importance of knowing where one stands.[7]

James's description of the disorientation and loss of control occasioned by homodiegetic, first-person narration in longer fiction draws on various images of cultural "otherness" to illustrate the nature of the threat. Thus, the darkness of James's "darkest abyss of romance" (*LC2*, p. 1315) resembles the racialized other of Conrad's *Heart of Darkness*, though without the full measure of ambiguity of Conrad's title which gestures more emphatically towards alterity *within* the self.[8] Moreover, one of the dangers associated with this abyss – "variety, and many other queer matters as well, might have been smuggled in a back door" (*LC2*, p. 1315) – insinuates a homosexual undercurrent in the polymorphous perversity of one man who, as first-person narrator, would enjoy the "double privilege of subject and object" (*LC2*, p. 1316). The danger of the "others" that James associates with first-person narration is not that they are definitively external to the heterosexual white male subject, but that they may already be found within that masculine subject, "smuggled in the back door."

Ultimately, the "looseness" and "fluidity" that James associates with the threat of first-person narration gesture toward what may be the most consistently invoked "others" of male literary modernism, "others" insistently defined as external, but feared as always already within: the feminine and the popular.[9] James frequently links the fluidity of the feminine to the looseness of the popular in his literary criticism, as, for example, in his response to Mrs. Everard Cotes who in 1900 sent James a copy of her novel, *His Honour and a Lady*:

I think your drama lacks a little *line* – bony structure and palpable, as it were, tense cord – on which to string the pearls of detail. It's the frequent fault of women's work – and *I* like a rope (the rope of the direction *and march of the subject*, the action) pulled, like a taut cable between a steamer and tug, from beginning to end. [Your plot] lapses on a trifle too liquidly.[10]

This passage attributes the "liquidness" of a woman's text to its lack of fictional rigor and physical turgor, making it possible to read into James's extended metaphor an authorial "pissing contest" in which the male writer maintains a distinct advantage over the female. The "liquidness" of Mrs. Cotes's plot suggests that part of the threat behind the "terrible fluidity of self-revelation" is the threat of "piddling" in the sense of triviality and indirection though not necessarily of volume. That is to say, James also implies that Mrs. Cotes, in her "liquidness," runs off at the mouth. Thus "fluency," like "fluidity," denotes a too easy prodigiousness of output, as James suggests of Harriet Prescott in his 1864 review of her *Azarian*: "like the majority of female writers, – Mrs. Browning, George Sand, Gail Hamilton, Mrs. Stowe, – she possesses in excess the fatal gift of fluency."[11] In a comparative evaluation of Sand and Flaubert, James's images of fluidity similarly connote both the prolific and the substandard:

Flaubert is at any rate represented by six books, so that he may on that estimate figure as poor, while Madame Sand, falling so little short of a hundred, figures as rich; and yet the fact remains that I can refer the congenial mind to him with confidence and can do nothing of the sort for it in respect to Madame Sand. She is loose and liquid and iridescent, as iridescent as we may undertake to find her; but I can imagine compositions quite without virtue – the virtue I mean, of sticking together – begotten by the impulse to emulate her. She had undoubtedly herself the benefit of her facility, but are we not left wondering to what extent *we* have it?[12] (*LC2*, pp. 343–4)

For James, Sand's "facility" means that she is "facile." The "loose and liquid" productivity of the woman writer might seem to make her writing "rich," but they really make her writing and the writing of those who emulate her slippery, lacking in the "virtue . . . of sticking together." James chooses literary quality over literary quantity, assuming that they must be mutually exclusive. For a writer so prolific as James was, such an assumption must have generated some measure of authorial anxiety.

James does not limit his criticism to his female colleagues and foremothers, although their femininity and the feminine itself, even when attributed to male writers, bear the brunt of his critical bias. While he often shows great generosity to novices, especially to those who pay obeisance to their "Chèr Maître," James could be deeply critical of members of the fictional fraternity, including masters like Hawthorne and Flaubert and his own contemporaries and protégés. The use of first-person narration provides the occasion for some of James's most severe attacks, in part because he sees it as linked to popular literature which is distinctly not within the purview of men's literary work as he envisions it. In a 1911 letter written in thanks for the gift of his *New Machiavelli*, James chides H. G. Wells for the "form" that his fiction takes:

... I make remonstrance ... upon the bad service you have done your cause by riding so hard again that accurst autobiographic form which puts a premium on the loose, the improvised, the cheap and the easy. Save in the fantastic and the romantic (Copperfield, Jane Eyre, that charming thing of Stevenson's with the bad title – "Kidnapped"?) it has no authority, no persuasive and convincing force – its grasp of reality and truth isn't strong and disinterested. R. Crusoe, e.g., isn't a novel at all. There is, to my vision, no authentic, and no really interesting, and no *beautiful*, report of things on the novelist's, the painter's part unless a particular detachment has operated ...[13]

This letter touches on both generic forms with which James associates first-person narration: autobiography and romance. This double generic association is self-contradictory since, for James, the autobiographical reveals an author's actual experience and identity whereas the romantic depicts experience or even *is* an experience that is definitively unknown (I will elaborate on this point further along).[14] In other words, the epistemological crisis that occurs in the "darkest abyss of romance" is at odds with the epistemological certainties of autobiography's "terrible *fluidity* of self-revelation." The fact that James's literary theory contains contradictions is hardly news. What is of interest here are the ways that James's delineations of first-person narration dovetail with his attempts to reconcile his high-cultural identity as a writer of literary fiction with his cultural identity as a bourgeois man.

James demotes autobiography and the first-person form with which he associates it to the ranks of the sub-literary or low-brow. In his letter to Wells, James attributes qualities to autobiography – "the loose, the improvised, the cheap and the easy" – which he deplores because they interfere with those qualities that he values most highly. The valued qualities – the "authentic," the "interesting," and the "beautiful" – can be attained only through "a particular detachment." That is to say, autobiography is not "strong and disinterested" because it lacks the "detachment" that distinguishes the truly literary and high cultural.

James understands first-person narration, moreover, as a quintessentially "autobiographic form" because he presumes that the identity of the narrating speaker or writer is identical to that of the author. While late twentieth-century literary critics might intuitively attribute detachment or even self-alienation to the authorial process of assuming a fictional narrative persona, James sees such a persona as too closely associated with the author himself. In eschewing first-person narration, that "accursed autobiographic form," James preferred to be a more invisible male author than H. G. Wells.

James's preference for a more invisible narrator, one who "focalizes" the subjectivities of centers of consciousness via "impersonal," heterodiegetic narration, also plays a crucial role in his conception of romance as a bubble, delicate and illusory, that must not be pricked by the rude penetration of the author's voice. As Goetz persuasively argues, James sees the intrusions of both a Trollopean omniscient narrator and a Conradian first-person narrator as diverting the reader's attention from the story to the author, thereby destroying the essential dramatic illusion of romance.[15] The illusion created by romance is that, at least temporarily, it *is* real:

The balloon of experience is in fact of course tied to the earth, and under that necessity we swing, thanks to a rope of remarkable length, in the more or less commodious car of the imagination; but it is by the rope we know where we are, and from the moment that cable is cut we are at large and unrelated: we only swing apart from the globe – though remaining as exhilarated, naturally, as we like, especially when all goes well. The art of the romancer is, "for the fun of it," insidiously to cut the cable, to cut it without our detecting him. (*LC2*, p. 1064)

The quintessential experience of romance is not the reader's blithe pleasure in flying high, but the moment of vertigo when he realizes that he has come untethered. To induce this mind-blowing effect, the "romancer" must keep his presence unfelt at least until the crucial moment and preferably not even then.

The romancer's undetected cutting of the cable indicates that the undercutting of epistemological certainty is a crucial feature of Jamesian romance. Although the indeterminate distance of the "balloon of experience" from the ground of reality produces disorientation, the cable-cutting also recreates reality and reorients us to it. Romance creates worlds apart where the usual rules do not apply: a new "real world" of romance. The vertiginously indeterminate distance between the old real world and the new real world of romance may be spatial, as with the balloon image, or it may be geographic or even temporal, as in the examples of "the romantic and the fantastic" in James's letter to Wells. The desert island world in *Robinson Crusoe* is at a geographical distance from a metropolitan center, much as the worlds of childhood in *David Copperfield* and *Jane Eyre* and *Kidnapped* are at a temporal distance from adulthood; *Kidnapped* is at an even further temporal remove from the present in its status as historical fiction. All four of James's cited examples, moreover, join the autobiographical and the romantic to first-person narration.

The creation of a new real world implicit in James's conception of romantic "worlds elsewhere" foregrounds another tellingly paradoxical aspect of his critical theory. On the one hand, James sets romance in opposition to the reality and life associated with realism, and thus conceives of romantic fiction as more fictional than realistic fiction, which would be seen, in turn, as more real. On the other hand, James views romance as more than a fictional or literary mode; romance is itself a type of experience, as the "balloon of experience" implies and as the rest of his commentary on romance in the Preface to *The American* attests: "the only *general* attribute of projected romance that I can see, the only one that fits all its cases, is the fact of the kind of experience with which it deals – experience liberated, so to speak; experience disengaged, disembroiled, disencumbered, exempt from the conditions that we usually know to attach to it" (*LC2*, p. 1064). If romance is a kind of experience, then it is also a form of life, possibly an even more intense and lively sort of life than realism can represent or than reality actually is. (I will return to the notion of an aestheticized and ascetic "art of life" as an alternative model of masculinity in the next section of this chapter.)

James communicates his appreciation for such larger-than-life intensity when, in his 1911 letter, he admires the way H. G. Wells "ride[s] roughshod and triumphant" over those decorous considerations of narrative method that preoccupy James himself. When he lauds "that life and force and temperament, that fulness [sic] of endowment and easy impudence of genius, which makes you extraordinary and which have long claimed my unstinted admiration," James equates Wells's writerly engagement with a romantic and fully masculinized zest for life. James's sketch of the romantic rough rider, however, takes on a less adulatory cast when he professes to admire Wells's "big feeling for life, your capacity for chewing up the thickness of the world in such enor-

mous mouthfuls, while you fairly slobber, so to speak, with the multitud-
inous taste."[16] Although rhetorically posed as a compliment and intended to counterbalance the criticism later in the letter of Wells's use of
"that accurst autobiographic form," this image of Wells eating with his
mouth open seems to betray a certain uneasiness, even disgust, with
such an immoderate, piggish style of authorial engagement. For James,
the violence of Wells's narrative method does not reside in its potential
for cannibalism. Indeed, James himself could easily be indicted for
cannibalistic tendencies: witness his own portrayal of himself in the
Ambassadors's Preface as "bit[ing] into the "thickened motive and accu-
mulated character" (*LC2*, p. 1306) of this novel's mature hero. In this
regard, Mrs. Henry Adams's snide comment that Henry James fastid-
iously "chawed more than he bit off" may not fall so wide of the mark.[17]
It is not *that* Wells eats or *what* Wells eats which James finds crude and
excessive – it is *how* he eats. The male writer as rough rider is envisioned
by James as a brutish ogre or perhaps just as a greedy little boy who bolts
his food without pausing to allow the "great stewpot or crucible of the
imagination" to perform the necessary "chemical transmutation" of life
into art.[18] For James, the inveterate masticator, Wells is too rough
because he seems too ready – at once for eager and too forceful to take a
manageable mouthful.

In his 1914 essay, "The New Novel," originally entitled "The
Younger Generation," James objects to a similarly distasteful
overeagerness and aggressiveness that he sees as animating Conrad's
use of first-person narrators. Elsewhere, James takes exception to Conrad's most famous first-person narrator, the bachelor Marlow, to whom
he disdainfully refers as "that preposterous master mariner."[19] In "The
New Novel," he singles out Conrad's deployment of a series of framing
first-person narrators in *Chance*, which James calls "multiplying his
creators or, as we are now fond of saying producers":

Mr. Conrad's first care ... is to set up a reciter, a definite responsible interven-
ing first person singular, possessed of infinite sources of reference, who immediately proceeds to set up another, to the end that this other may conform again
to the practice, and that even at that point the bridge over to the creature, or in
other words to the situation or the subject, the thing "produced," shall, if the
fancy takes it, once more and yet once more glory in a gap.[20]

Conrad and his crew of narrators may find "glory in a gap," but to James
this "gap" indicates a failed bridge between narration and "subject" and
perhaps also between reader and story. Referring to himself in the

first-person plural, James recommends his own narrative method as a way to avoid such pitfalls: "We usually escape the worst of this difficulty of a tone *about* the tone of our characters, our projected performers, by keeping it single, keeping it 'down' and thereby comparatively impersonal or, as we may say, inscrutable" (*LC1*, 1 p. 149). The self-concealing reticence of the heterodiegetic, non-intrusive Jamesian narrator who neither participates in the plot as a character nor makes much in the way of editorial commentary ultimately reveals the author's artistic mastery. The true artist shows his masculine self-discipline by not showing himself. By "keeping it single" and "keeping it 'down'," James achieves the desired effects of impersonality and inscrutability.

The "inscrutable" quality that James endorses in his own writing differs from the opacity on the brink of which he sees Conrad teetering. Even when Conrad "attempt[s] to clarify," he still flirts with the "danger of steeping his matter in perfect eventual obscuration as we recall no other artist's consenting to with an equal grace" (*LC1*, p. 149). James does admit to a certain "grace" in Conrad's feat, an athletic and intrepid grace that is "Mr. Conrad's gallantry itself":

It literally strikes us that his volume sets in motion more than anything else a drama in which his own system and his combined eccentricities of recital represent the protagonist in face of powers leagued against it, and of which the dénouement gives us the system fighting in triumph, though with its back desperately to the wall, and laying the powers piled up at its feet. This frankly has been *our* spectacle, our suspense and our thrill; with the one flaw on the roundness of it all the fact that the predicament was not imposed rather than invoked, was not the effect of a challenge from without, but that of a mystic impulse from within. (*LC1*, pp. 149–50)

James identifies Conrad's system of narration as the "protagonist," but the antagonistic "powers leagued against it" are intrinsic to the system; these antagonists are "not the effect of a challenge from without, but that of a mystic impulse from within." In suggesting that Conrad's gallant struggle against antagonists is really a struggle against and within himself, James portrays Conrad as fencing, or shadowboxing, with himself. "The one flaw on the roundness of it all," the crack in the golden bowl of Conrad's art is that Conrad is his own worst enemy. Conrad's damning flaw is his over-eager willingness to fight when a more diplomatic avoidance of multiple first-person narrators could have circumvented the violent confrontation in the first place.

Here, as in his critique of Wells, James deplores the gratuitousness of Conrad's election of first-person narration, which he sees as an overly aggressive display whose brute force is impressive but whose prudence is questionable. For James, the seasoned pro who participates at this tourney solely as a spectator, discretion is truly the better part of masculine valor. While it may be pleasurable, and even thrilling, for the spectator to watch this fight, the fact that it *can* be observed is proof of a fatal flaw. Conrad may fight spectacularly well, but in choosing to fight at all, Conrad has made the wrong choice. James condemns both Wells's and Conrad's use of first-person narration as debased and debasing displays of primitive masculinity, alternately childish and animalistic, finally grotesque in their effects. Whereas Wells is left with food on his face, Conrad ends up surrounded by corpses. For James, such crude self-displays betray an unmanly lack of restraint to which his own disciplined and controlled narrative method stands as a more civilized and manly alternative.

Remarkably, James also holds out Edith Wharton, the only woman whom he sees fit to include in his assemblage of literary new-comers and not-so-new-comers in "The Younger Generation," as a manly alternative to Conrad. James contrasts Conrad's "luxuries of looseness" (*LC1*, p. 152) and the "waste of [his] having kept us so dangling on the dark esthetic abyss" (*LC1*, p. 155) with Wharton's unwasteful, "consistently, almost scientifically" "satiric light": "the light that gathers is a dry light, of great intensity, and the effect, if not rather the very essence, of its dryness is a particular fine asperity... A shade of asperity may be in such fashion a security against waste" (*LC1*, p. 155). Wharton's "dry light" is far preferable to both Conrad's "dark esthetic abyss" and Wells's wet "slobbering"; it is controlled, precise, and rational rather than emotional, enigmatic, or physical. James attributes Wharton's talent to "the dry, or call it perhaps even the hard, intellectual touch in the soft, or call it perhaps even the humid, temperamental air" (*LC1*, p. 155), that is, to her combination of masculine and feminine qualities. But James is finally more impressed with Wharton's masculinity than with her femininity or with the gender blending that he sees as constituting her "rare identity": "the masculine conclusion tend[s] so to crown the feminine observation" (*LC1*, p. 155). "Feminine observation" may be a queen, but the crown she wears is "masculine conclusion"; the man remains decisively on top.

James's deprecation of the unmanly lack of restraint in Conrad's narrative method also registers his sense of that method's epistemological shortcomings. In James's view, the reader of *Chance* ends up knowing both too much and too little. He knows too little about the story and its characters because he is confronted with "that baffled relation between the subject-matter and its emergence which we find constituted by the circumvalations of *Chance*" (*LC1*, pp. 154–5). And he knows too much about the author and his narrators because Conrad's method of narration "invites consideration of itself" in ways comparable to the "terrible fluidity of self-revelation" associated with autobiography:

the omniscience, remaining indeed nameless, though constantly active, which sets Marlow's omniscience in motion from the very first page, insisting on a reciprocity with it throughout, this original omniscience invites consideration of itself only in a degree less than that in which Marlow's own invites it; and Marlow's own is a prolonged hovering flight of the subjective over the outstretched ground of the case exposed. (*LC1*, p. 149)

The "prolonged hovering flight of the subjective" in this passage suggests an indeterminate distance from the epistemological ground comparable to the one attained by the romantic "balloon of experience." Conrad's method of narration thus undercuts epistemological certainty in much the same way that romance does:

We make out this ground but through the shadow cast by the flight . . . as if by some tremendous forecast of future applied science, the upper aeroplane causes another, as we have said, to depend from it and that one still another; these dropping shadow after shadow, to the no small menace of intrinsic colour and form and whatever, upon the passive expanse. (*LC1*, p. 149)

If romance is a balloon, then first-person narration is an airplane. The epistemological indeterminacy occasioned by the indeterminate altitude of the balloon is multiplied by the sequential "drops" of each successive narrator's airplane. The shadows cast by the airplanes induce in the reader an unpleasant sensation – airsickness? – comparable to the vertigo induced by the heights scaled by the balloon. The reader of *Chance* can only approximate the various narrators' positions, and hence his own position, by looking at the shadows cast by their successive airplanes. The shadows' distortions of the "intrinsic color and form" of the "passive expanse" pose an active and aggressive "menace."

James's satiric description of the "tremendous forecast of future applied science" represented by Conrad's narrative method is consonant with his view of the needless heroics of Conrad's authorial display of technical skill. This invention of "applied science," moreover, stands in James's essay not merely as a sign of the times but also as a portent of the future. In 1914, the image of the airplane was an image of modernity, a prediction of the futuristic "world elsewhere" that James's own world was becoming. A key attribute of the airplane of first-person narration is its spatial liminality, its hovering at an unknown altitude between ground and sky. The modernity of the airplane also suggests a kind of historical liminality and, with it, James's uneasy historical situation between the Victorian and modern worlds. Nor can we forget the uneasiness of the world in 1914, hovering as it was on the brink of war.[21]

The epistemological uncertainties of Conrad's first-person technique thus represent no single or simple threat for James. The "loose and liquid" fluidity of feminine and popular writing, and the "terrible *fluidity* of self-revelation" of autobiographical writing, reappear in the "luxuries of looseness" (*LC1*, p. 152) of Conrad's masculine and modernist narrative method. The "dark abyss of romance" reemerges in the "waste [of Conrad's] having kept us so dangling on the dark esthetic abyss" (*LC1*, p. 155). James's imagery also anticipates the emblems that stood for the anxieties and enthusiasms of his younger contemporaries and successors. His lamentation of "waste" forecasts Eliot's "Waste Land" as well as the "waste land" that crumbles beneath the eyes of Dr. T. J. Eckleburg in *The Great Gatsby*; his fear of the "abyss" prefigures Wyndham Lewis's and Ezra Pound's celebration of the awe-inspiring Vortex. In fact, the explosive avant-gardism of this even younger "younger generation" was well under way when James's "Younger Generation" came out, only two months before the publication of the first issue of Lewis's *Blast: The Review of the Great English Vortex*. James perceived both the attractions and the dangers of modernist pyrotechnics.[22]

James aligns Conrad's first-person narrative technique with the modernist imperative that exceeded the aesthetic valorization of art for art's sake in order to champion difficulty for difficulty's sake. Indeed, the corollary of Pound's modernist slogan, "Make it new!" might well have been "Make it difficult!" While James disapproves of Conrad's gratuitously difficult narrative method, he nevertheless shows his appreciation for those methods whose difficulties are properly regulated: "the claim for method in itself, method in this very sense of attention applied, would be somehow less lighted [sic] if the difficulties struck us as less consciously, or call it even less wantonly, invoked" (*LC1*, p. 148). Defining "method" here as "attention applied," James makes "the exemplary value of attention, attention given by the author and asked of the reader" (*LC1*, p. 148) into an end in itself, its own source of value. James's self-reflexive attention to "attention" prefigures the modernist attention to form and the New Critical attention to attentive "close reading." Yet what James alludes to as a "blest method" (LIC p. 147) is a decidedly mixed blessing. The "consciously" and "wantonly invoked" difficulty that James discerns in Conrad's first-person narrative method is always on the verge of falling from a masculinizing performance into a demasculinizing self-display, from self-discipline into self-indulgence, from restraint into debauchery. James's attribution of femininity *and* hyper-virility to first-person narration marks his ambivalent response both to the literary past and to the literary future. Poised uncomfortably between popular writers of the nineteenth-century (who as a group were far from being all-female but with whom he associated a threatening femininity) and high-cultural modernists of the twentieth century (who as a group were far from being all-male but with whom he associated a threatening hyper-virility), James was truly living in an awkward age. In the next section, I shall argue that the figure of the bachelor represented a potential solution to these difficulties for the male high-cultural author, as a "possible form of life" whose indulgences and renunciations, luxuries and deprivations, were compatible with a manly "life of art."

"THE LESSON OF THE MASTER" AND OTHER VICISSITUDES OF THE LITERARY LIFE

James's "The Lesson of the Master" (1888), one of his mid-career "tales of literary life," makes explicit that the "life of art" must depend upon the proper regulation of relations within and between men. This story is less explicit, however, about what constitutes proper regulation. The main enigma of "The Lesson of the Master" – a reading trap that puts the reader in a position comparable to that of the bachelor disciple of the Master – concerns the nature of the "lesson" of the title. Does Henry St. George, the successful writer, send the neophyte Paul Overt to Europe to save Overt's art from the corruption engendered by married life, or does he send him away in order to keep the female object of Overt's affections for himself? Must an artist renounce "the full, rich, masculine, human, general life, with all the responsibilities and duties and burdens and sorrows and joys – all the domestic and social initiations and complications," or is this a false imperative endorsed by St. George as a means of retaining his superior position, of preventing Overt from unseating him?[23] Responding to Overt's agitated question – "The artist – the artist! Isn't he a man all the same?" – St. George avers, perhaps genuinely, perhaps calculatingly, that "sometimes I really think not" (*CT*, vii, p. 268). St. George's manifest, or "overt," lesson is that one person cannot be both man and artist since a man must live in the world and an artist must live in his art. He thus implies, as does the story more generally, that the worldly pleasures of sexual indulgence are reserved for married men whereas the artist's portion is celibacy and asceticism, which are in this story exclusively associated with bachelorhood. The story nevertheless reveals that intimate, intense, and eroticized male-male bonds between master and disciple make the "initiations and complications" associated with married life central to the life of the bachelor artist as well.

What is less clear is whether the master–disciple bond is exempt from the plays of power that characterize worldly manhood, whether these supposedly other-worldly male–male bonds are constituted on the basis of equality rather than hierarchy, reciprocity rather than coercion, sympathy rather than hostility and violence. Does the master–disciple relation, a relation paradoxically necessary to and disruptive of the development of artistic mastery, invariably involve mastery over another man? Or does the self-mastery inherent in the life of art afford away out of this bind? Does the internalized mastery of the man/artist coupling within one individual provide a reprieve from the externalized mastery associated with relations between men in public arenas such as the marketplace? Or is the mastery of one's self and the self-discipline of artistic production contingent upon mastery over another man?[24]

To put the question somewhat differently: does the realm of art share the values of the world to which it is ostensibly set in opposition, or is it ultimately just a subset or a reflection of that world? This is, of course, the quintessential question of modern aesthetics, the question of the autonomy of art. James's story, not surprisingly, does not propose a definitive answer. By shifting into the present tense in the last lines of his story, James turns to the reader and the future to supply the answer:

St George's words were still in his ears, "You're very strong – wonderfully strong." Was he really? Certainly, he would have to be; and it would be a sort of revenge. *Is* he? the reader may ask in turn, if his interest has followed the perplexed young man so far. The best answer to that perhaps is that he is doing his best but that it is too soon to say. When the new book came out in the autumn Mr and Mrs St George found it really magnificent. The former still has published nothing, but Paul Overt does not even yet feel safe. I may say for him, however, that if this event were to befall he would really be the very first to appreciate it: which is perhaps a proof that St George was essentially right and that Nature dedicated him to intellectual, not to personal passion. (*CT*, vii, p. 284)

Given the way the authorial narrator poses the question, even the future will be hard put to resolve the paradox of the relation between man and artist. Should St. George publish a magnificent book of his own and Overt be the very first to appreciate it, then St. George would have been right after all: man and artist cannot exist within one individual, or at least not within Overt who would be artist enough, that is sufficiently "dedicated ... to intellectual, not to personal passion," to applaud St. George's artistic triumph. But were St. George to publish a magnificent book, that in itself would demonstrate that man and artist *can* coexist within the same man, that is, within St. George himself. Just as man and artist both *can* and *cannot* exist within a single individual, the world of art sustains a similarly paradoxical relation to the larger world. The world of art, as engendered by the relationship of master and disciple, seems to be founded both on domination, manipulation, and hierarchical relations between and within men and also, paradoxically, on supportive, altruistic and reciprocal relations.

James's private letters deliver a similarly mixed message about the vexed relation between life and art, particularly as these realms are defined via gendered relations between men and via the masculine self-constitution of the figures of bachelor and artist. His letters to his married brother William generally sound a wistful note, linking bachelorhood to an exclusion from wider experience: "How large your life swings compared to mine, and how much – beside the lone bachelor's – it takes in!"[25] But when James refers in another letter to his own comparatively "wifeless, childless, houseless, classless, mother- and sister-in-lawless, horseless, cowless, and useless state," it is ambiguous whether his tone is self-pitying and self-effacing or, as Philip Horne suggests, self-congratulatory and self-vaunting. Horne highlights James's emphatic portrayal of marital renunciation as an enabling condition, citing James's 1884 explanation to Grace Norton of the reason that he will "to a dead certainty never change my free unhoused condition... [S]ince definitely and *positively* (from a merely negative state) making up my mind not to marry, I feel that I have advanced in happiness and power to *do* something in the world."[26] Being "unhoused" as a bachelor is here imagined as a condition of "freedom" and "happiness," a positive choice rather than a "negative state." Absenting himself from the world of marriage empowers James "to do something in the world," his literary endeavors conceived as active and worldly, as masculine in a hegemonic, bourgeois sense. Notably, the world is a public sphere that James can inhabit by virtue of, not despite, his residence in the house of fiction.

In many of his manifestoes on fiction, including some of the ones discussed in the previous section of this chapter, James claims art in general and fiction in particular as masculine realms of endeavor, remasculinizing the "life of art" by means of counterposing rhetorics of ascetic self-discipline and luxurious self-indulgence. In his Preface to *The American*, for example, James glowingly, if self-righteously, endorses Robert Louis Stevenson's vision of art as its own reward:

[T]he partaker of the "life of art" who repines at the absence of the rewards, as they are called, of the pursuit might surely be better occupied. Much rather should he endlessly wonder at his not having to pay half his substance for his luxurious immersion. He enjoys it, so to speak, without a tax; the effort of labour involved, the torment of expression, of which we have heard in our time so much, being after all but the last refinement of his privilege. It may leave him weary and worn; but how, after his fashion, he will have lived! (*LC2*, p. 1061)

Rather than endorsing a view that focuses upon the "absence of the rewards," James here metaphorically immerses the male artist in a luxurious medium in which he may take his hedonistic pleasure without suffering any luxury tax. They may leave him "weary and worn," but the artist's "torment" and "effort" are ultimately envisioned more as "refinement" than coarseness, more as leisurely "privilege" than hard labor. The "life of art" is imagined as an exquisite pleasure-in-pain, something that is worthwhile not despite the fact that it hurts, but *because* it hurts.[27] Such untaxed pleasures are, of course, predicated on a normalizing counterdiscourse of rigorous, or taxing, masculine self-discipline. Renunciation of the conventional attainments of masculine privilege paradoxically remasculinize the life of art, enabling James to recuperate such an aesthetic and ascetic life as more intense, vibrant, and transcendent than any life of conventionally taxing labor or conventionally taxed luxury.

James thus redefines art as work worthy of men, work of which men can strive to be worthy. In his 1884 critical treatise, "The Art of Fiction," James also uses the example of Stevenson to formulate art as an adventure. Here, the Paterian and Stretherian imperative to "live all you can" becomes a way for a man to be all that he can be.[28] James compares Stevenson's *Treasure Island* to de Goncourt's *Chérie* in order to rebut Walter Besant's claim that adventure is the key ingredient necessary to literary fiction: "One of these works treats of murders, mysteries, islands of dreadful renown, hairbreadth escapes, miraculous coincidences and buried doubloons. The other treats of a little French flirt who lived in a fine house in Paris, and died of wounded sensibility because no one would marry her" (*LC1*, p. 61).[29] James challenges the assumption that fiction is impossible without adventure by taking this opportunity to redefine what counts as adventure. In doing so, he refers back to the recently composed *The Portrait of a Lady*:

> Mr. Besant does not, to my sense, light up the subject by intimating that a story must, under penalty of not being a story, consist of "adventures." Why of adventures more than of green spectacles? . . . Why without adventure, more than without matrimony, or celibacy, or parturition, or cholera, or hydropathy, or Jansenism? This seems to me to bring the novel back to the hapless little *rôle* of being an artificial, ingenious thing – bring it down from its large free character of an immense and exquisite correspondence with life. And what *is* adventure, when it comes to that, and by what sign is the listening pupil to recognise it? It is an adventure – an immense one – for me to write this little article; and for a Bostonian nymph to reject an English duke is an adventure only less stirring, I should say, than for an English duke to be rejected by a Bostonian nymph. (*LC1*, p. 61)

In illustrating the idiosyncrasy of singling out adventure, James moves from the mundane to the ridiculous. But his choice of examples under-lines this essay's redefinition of the purviews of both fictional art and adventure. The heterogeneity of the items on his list would seem to open the field to all comers, yet the emotional, relational, and domestic cast of certain of his examples, especially matrimony and parturition though also celibacy, suggest the potential dangers of such inclusiveness. If the emotional challenges of failed courtship are as much an adventure as the intellectual activity of writing, it would seem that literary art could be drawn into the debased realms of the familiar, the sentimental, the feminine, and the popular, "bring[ing] the novel back to the hapless, little *rôle* of being an artificial, ingenious thing" (*LC1*, p. 61). But James redresses these threats to high-cultural masculine authorship by chemi-cally transmuting the dross of such subject matter in the white-hot crucible of the artist's disciplined and profound imagination. Indeed, the true artist overcomes the challenges to mastery posed by his absorp-tion with the inner life by making that life, however mundane or banal, the preferred arena of literary endeavor. Hence for the most part James's fictions situate themselves in what looks like the world of de Goncourt's *Chérie*, finding true adventure not in Stevenson's exotic "worlds elsewhere" but in the relational, emotional, and psychological worlds within.

I have already noted how James uses Stevenson to take the measure of de Goncourt and to measure his own artistic progress. In "converting admired authors into Masters,"[30] James converts himself into a contender. James's famous essay on Hawthorne substantiates the idea that identification with a master also means competition with him, or, in a different idiom, that influence elicits anxiety. James did not serve a single master; many of his other critical pieces betray the same literary one-upmanship of his Hawthorne essay. For example, "The Art of Fiction" arrogantly appropriates its title from the 1884 Walter Besant lecture that it rebuts. His late career essay on *The Tempest* (1907), too, depicts the work of a master as a challenge, particularly with regard to the relation between the man and the artist. The essay begins on the note of a contest of wills:

If the effect of the Plays and Poems, taken in their mass, be most of all to appear often to mock our persistent ignorance of so many of the conditions of their birth, and thereby to place on the rack again our strained and aching wonder, this character has always struck me as more particularly kept up for them by The Tempest. (*LC1*, p. 1205)

Competition is here eroticized as sadistic domination on the part of the master, whom James imagines as subjecting his reader and disciple to a painfully humiliating torture comparable to the "torment" of the writer as an exquisite and luxurious pleasure discussed earlier. James significantly figures the reader/disciple as "ignorant of so many of the conditions of [the plays' and poems'] birth," thereby portraying this reader/disciple as the male child of a father who deliberately withholds knowledge of the primal scene, who refuses him access to the mysteries associated with dominant, here explicitly heterosexual, manhood.

What literally baffles James is the fact that, having written this masterpiece "in easy middle life" and seemingly in mid-career, Shakespeare simply stopped writing. This topic had particular resonance for James at the time of this essay's writing, since he had recently completed his major novelistic achievements and was embarking on the retrospective critical and autobiographical works of his later years. James professes himself unable to imagine what could have motivated Shakespeare, like Prospero, to relinquish his work at the height of his powers. Although he speculates on Shakepeare's desire for financial security as a possible motive, James appears to find this explanation less than satisfactory because it reduces the great man of letters to the mere man of business.[31] The irreconcilable discrepancy that James insists upon between the art and the business of writing is at least partly based on his sense of an unbridgeable gap between Shakespeare the artist and Shakespeare the man: "The eternal mystery, the most insoluble that ever was, the complete rupture, for our understanding, between the Poet and the Man ... the complexity arises from our suffering our imagination to meddle with the Man at all... The Poet is *there* [in the plays and sonnets], and the Man is outside" (*LC1*, pp. 1215–16). In this passage, the man is a base entrepreneur, the "man of exemplary business-method" (*LC1*, p. 1217) with whom the reader should not concern himself, who threatens to infiltrate the sacrosanct arena of art. Yet elsewhere in the essay the man/artist dichotomy displays a different face: "The man himself, in the Plays, we directly touch, to my consciousness, positively nowhere: we are dealing too perpetually with the artist, the monster and magician of a thousand masks... The man everywhere, in Shakespeare's work, is so effectually locked up and imprisoned in the artist" (*LC1*, p. 1209). In this passage, the artist is not besmirched by the petty intrusions of the businessman. Rather, the artist is seen here as a monster or magician, a Caliban or a Prospero, who subjects the man to his powers.[32] What these two versions of the relationship between the man and the artist have in common is their emphasis on an antagonism, a conflict between these two masculine identities or two components of a single masculine identity. Such antagonism is evident in James's portrayal of the man as the essential, true self "locked up and imprisoned in the artist." This portrayal conceives of the artist with his "thousand masks" as a cage or jail constraining the man, not as a performative identity offering adventure or freedom.

In the passage cited above, the man is *within* the powerful artist but later in the essay James attributes interiority to the figure of the artist:

It is true of the poet in general – in nine examples out of ten – that his life is mainly inward, that its events and revolutions are his great impressions and deep vibrations, and that his "personality" is all pictured in the publication of his verse. Shakespeare, we essentially feel, is the tenth, is the millionth example; not the sleek bachelor of music, the sensitive harp set once for all in the window to catch the air, but the spirit in hungry quest of every possible experience and adventure of the spirit, and which, betimes, with the boldest of all intellectual movements, was to leap from the window into the street. (*LC1*, p. 1218)

The external movement that James attributes to Shakespeare as a "spirit in hungry quest" is used oddly here to describe the interiority of the artist. That is to say, James strangely typifies the "inward life" of the poet, whose being consists in "great impressions and deep vibrations," by his "leap from the window into the street." Going inward is apparently compatible with going out the window. However, neither the penetrating movement inward nor the bold movement outward is available to "the sleek bachelor of music," James's figure for nine out of ten artists. Poised on the threshold, the Aeolian harp is "sensitive" yet immobilized, responsive to breezes but unable to initiate movement, fixed between two worlds but belonging fully to neither. The liminality of this bachelor connotes limitation rather than possibility, dispossession rather possession. The bachelor of the "sleek bachelor of music" thus differs from the bachelor whom James describes as "an artist and a bachelor." The latter bachelor, like Shakespeare, actively takes "possession" of "human life" via his "passion of observation"; for this bachelor, art and life are mutually constitutive rather than mutually exclusive. In his deployment of the image of the "sleek bachelor of music" to describe the Aeolian harp, then, James reclaims life for the artist at the expense of the bachelor.

The liminality of the bachelor as Aeolian harp nevertheless suggests a connection between outer and inner experience and between man and artist, not merely a rupture between these realms and identities. James denies a rupture, for example, when he insists that man and artist are one: "In greatness as much as in mediocrity the man is, under examination, *one*, and the elements of character melt into each other. The genius is a part of the mind, and the mind a part of the behaviour, so . . . where does one of these provinces end and the other begin?" (*LC1*, p. 1217). Here, ostensibly disparate "elements of character" merge by "melt[ing] into each other." Elsewhere in the essay, the mingling of man and artist occurs via images of plunging and sinking: "the great primary plunge, made once for all, of the man into the artist . . . [Into his characters] he sinks as deep as we like, but what he sinks into, beyond all else, is the lucid stillness of his style" (*LC1*, p. 1209). In these passages and in the essay more generally, there are two sets of connections, or relations, at issue: the intrapsychic dynamics *within* Shakespeare between his identity as man and his identity as artist, and the intersubjective dynamics *between* James as desiring male reader and Shakespeare as desired male artist. That the "lucid stillness of his style" could screen the artist from the reader is hardly an inconceivable notion for James, a writer of sometimes stunning opacity, to have entertained. But style also gives the reader access to the man behind the artist: "The secret that baffles us being the secret of the Man, we know, as I have granted, that we shall never touch the Man *directly* in the Artist. We stake our hopes thus on indirectness, which may contain possibilities" (*LC1*, p. 1220). The "indirectness" mentioned here is style or the literary text itself. James suggests that the master's opus, or perhaps his entire *oeuvre*, is the proper key to the mystery of the man behind the master. Although James deplores the "morbid and monstrous curiosity" (*LC1*, p. 1216) that drives those seekers of the man behind the artist, the man is nevertheless what most interests James.

Who, then, is the man behind the artist? If the powerful artist is comparable to Prospero or Caliban, the elusive man resembles a different character from *The Tempest*: "In front of the tapestry sits the immitigably respectable person [the artist] ... while the undetermined figure [the man] ... the figure who supremely interests us, remains as unseen of us as our Ariel, on the enchanted island, remains of the bewildered visitors" (*LC1*, p. 1216). James compares the figure behind the tapestry neither to the masterful father nor to the brutish slave, but rather to the indeterminately sexed Ariel, the spirit who appears as often in the feminine, yet powerful, guise of nymph and harpy as he does in his own apparently masculine, though conspicuously immaterial, character. While subject to the dominion of others, Ariel nevertheless retains certain powers; while his powers are not fully his own, they nevertheless enable him to gain his liberty and to own himself. Ariel retains a certain measure of agency, for example, when he gains early release from his servitude to Prospero by the uncomplaining and efficient way he performs his admittedly required duties. He also retains a certain measure of will, if not agency, in his earlier refusal to perform the witch Sycorax's commands. As a figure of the artist in James's text, Ariel is both a proxy for another man *and* his own man. Moreover, the invisible Ariel is a figure of representation in two different senses: he represents another man and he represents the "magic" of artistic representation itself, an unseen something that simultaneously transfixes and frees, that paradoxically frees its audience by transfixing it. In choosing Ariel, James imagines a figure behind the tapestry of art whose gendered and sexual ambiguities mesh nicely with the ambivalence James expresses throughout his essay about the proper regulation of intra- and interpersonal relations between the man and the artist.

James mixes his Shakespearean metaphors with another allusion to the figure behind the tapestry which appears in the final sentence of the essay: "The figured tapestry, the long arras that hides him, is always there, with its immensity of surface and its proportionate underside. May it not then be but a question, for the fulness [*sic*] of time, of the finer weapon, the sharper point, the stronger arm, the more extended lunge?" (*LC1*, p. 1220). James pictures himself here as Hamlet, stabbing through the arras at a "rat" who turns out to be Polonius, a different figure behind the figured tapestry. Hamlet gets his man all right, but it turns out, tragically, to be the wrong man, the wrong father. Although misdirection is built into this literary model, "getting at" the master here suggests an attempt to master the literary father by killing him off. Patricide is thus an important model for the reader's epistemological endeavors and for the writer's attempt at literary mastery. James portrays reading and writing as arenas of competitive struggle, as contests between men that are aggressive to the point of violence.

For James, the desire to penetrate the man behind the carpet also has a homoerotic signification that cannot be simply reduced to or collapsed into the desire to murder him. Knowing a man does not necessarily mean killing him; penetration in James's writing has an erotic signification that is not limited to its violent or aggressive meanings. While at the *fin de siècle* homoerotic desire posed an obvious threat to properly regulated homosocial relations, James shows little or no concern here about the same-sex identities of the subject and the object of desire. Rather he concentrates on the *ways* that past attempts at knowing the man behind the artist have been conducted, finding the "morbid and monstrous curiosity" of past critics "infantile" (*LC1*, p. 1220), that is, as deviating from properly regulated masculinity in the directions of boyishness, neurasthenia, or beastliness. In particular, James criticizes the assumption of past criticism that penetration, or perhaps penetration conceived as a form of aggression, is the only or best way to know the master:

We know enough ... when we admire enough, and as difficulties would appear to abound on our attempting to push further, this is an obvious lesson to us to stand as still as possible. Not difficulties – those of penetration, exploration, interpretation, those, in the word that says everything, of appreciation – are the approved field of criticism, but the very forefront of the obvious and the palpable, where we may go round and round, like holiday-makers on hobby-horses, at the turning of a crank. (*LC1*, p. 1216)

James suggests that a subdued "admiration" is the proper alternative to the "difficulties" attendant upon "attempting to push further." While difficulties might seem to be associated with the adventurous masculine realms of "penetration, exploration, interpretation," they prove to be mere child's play, trivial and futile. Only by "stand[ing] as still as possible," by inducing in himself a state of passive alertness and engaged receptivity, may the disciple/reader enter into communion with the master and hence avoid the "rebuke to a morbid and monstrous curiosity" (*LCi*, p. 1216) that more active probing would elicit. Self-discipline is here the "obvious lesson" that the disciple must learn.

While such vigilantly passive immobility makes the disciple/reader properly receptive to the master, it also runs the risk of seeming to invite penetration by the master and therefore represents a new position of danger. While penetration might be seen as a collaborative or reciprocal act, in this essay the alertly passive position that the reader of Shakespeare must assume verges on a masochistic, and potentially unmanning, submission. James acknowledges the danger of being overmastered, but he never comes up with a fully satisfying solution to the problem: "forever met by a locked door flanked with a sentinel who merely invites us to take it for edifying... We take it ourselves for attaching – which is the very essence of mysteries – and profess ourself doomed forever to hang yearningly about it" (*LCi*, p. 1217). Eternal but unfulfilled admiration leaves the disciple doomed to be a "victim of unappeased desire," the fate that the bachelor narrator of James's "The Figure in the Carpet" describes himself as sharing with another man who also fails to learn the master's secret. The bachelor narrators of "Figure" and "The Aspern Papers," an earlier *nouvelle* in a similar register, attempt to remodel the deprivations attendant upon a life of art by recasting discipleship as manly self-discipline. Their attempts are comparable to, but finally less successful than, the revisions of normative masculinity performed by James himself as a "bachelor and an artist."

BACHELOR NARRATION IN "THE ASPERN PAPERS" AND "THE FIGURE IN THE CARPET"

The "undetermined figure" behind the "figured arras" in James's *Tempest* essay makes a powerful Jamesian allusion as well as the Shakespearean ones discussed above. James's "The Figure in the Carpet" (1896) hinges on its bachelor narrator's compulsion to know the secret the man asserts is there but that his art does not divulge: "For God's sake, try to get *at* him" (*CT*, IX, p. 274), George Corvick urges the unnamed narrator, his proxy reviewer of the master's latest book.[33] In this story, as in the *Tempest* essay, the unfulfilled desire of a reader to know the secret associated with the master's art overlaps with the disciple's equally ungratified desire to know the man behind the artist:

"Not only had I lost the books, but I had lost the man himself: they and their author had been alike spoiled for me. I knew too which was the loss I most regretted. I had liked the man still better than I had liked the books" (*CT*, IX, p. 294). The bachelor narrator of "The Aspern Papers" (1888) similarly pursues a literary secret explicitly connected with the man behind the artist. The eponymous "papers" that this bachelor critic so powerfully desires to read and possess are, signally, not the master's poetical works but his love letters. The man, and particularly the man as he is represented by his written and sexual past, is the object of this bachelor's urgent desires, as well as the master to whom he submits himself.

Both "The Aspern Papers" and "The Figure in the Carpet" can be read in terms of competing plots: competing past and present plots, competing masculine and feminine plots, and competing heterosexual and homosexual plots. Eve Kosofsky Sedgwick's category of male homosocial desire provides a point of contact among these various plots, showing how heterosexual male–female relations may be productively understood as promoting homosocial bonds between men. For example, the attempts of the bachelor narrator of "Aspern" to "make love" to Miss Tina and to pay off Juliana in order to gain access to Aspern's papers fit this model of classic homosocial plotting. So do the bachelor narrator's admittedly feeble inroads on Gwendolen in "Figure": he considers proposing marriage to her in order to learn the secret that her husband has transmitted to her, the secret of the Master's art verified by the Master himself.

In both texts, the bachelor narrators attempt to make women into conduits by which they can gain access to the master, into means through which they can attain the end of both having and becoming the master. In both texts, the bachelor narrators ultimately do not follow through on the marriage plots designed to transform into conduits the female obstacles they perceive as blocking their path to the male objects of their desire and identification. For each, the failure to follow through on the marriage plot does not result from any moral qualm, but rather from an apparently insurmountable distaste for the notion of marriage and/or the proximity of women. The narrator of "Aspern," for example, can only imagine marrying, and can barely imagine it at that, when it becomes clear that this step alone can bring him in touch with Aspern's papers, the ultimate object of his ardor. His temporary willingness to "pay the price" of marriage to Miss Tina manifests itself in her transfiguration before his eyes into a conventional vision of feminine beauty – "her look of forgiveness, of absolution, made her angelic. It beautified her; she was younger; she was not a ridiculous old woman." Tellingly, he sees her revert to "a plain, dingy, elderly person" (*CT*, VI, pp. 381–2) when he learns that she has destroyed the papers.[34]

The narrator's twice-revised vision of Miss Tina suggests that his narrative perspective is conspicuously unreliable. It also invites us to revise our own initial interpretation of the story. Indeed, the story encourages us to ask whether the "problem" with this narrator's vision is not that it is too variable, but that it is too fixed: that the narrator keeps his eyes too obsessively glued to the prize, or perhaps too fixedly searching for a prize which remains conspicuously out of view. In this regard, James's text seems to offer a harsh if unspoken critique of the narrator's way of looking, a critique which targets not so much the chosen object of his vision, but the ineffectiveness of his style of looking and, indeed, the isolation produced by his entire *modus operandi*. The compulsive quality of his fetishistic quest for the letters ultimately cuts him off from, rather than connecting him to, the male object of his desire and the female subject who desires him.[35]

Moreover, alternatives to the narrator's relentlessly probing yet apparently unseeing vision are represented within the text in the "patient eyes" (*CT*, VI, p. 295) of Miss Tina and the green eyeshade of Juliana. Though represented in the text only obliquely, these female characters' ways of looking encourage us to question the narrator's version of the story. After all, who really deploys the marriage plot in "The Aspern Papers"? Juliana masterminds and Miss Tina executes a feminine plot to maintain control over Aspern's private papers and the heterosexual romances, both Juliana's romance with Aspern and Miss Tina's romance with the narrator, they represent. They set in motion a juggernaut that eventually rolls over the narrator's comparatively insubstantial strategizing. Indeed, this plot might even be seen as Juliana's attempt to rewrite her illicit romance with Aspern by using the "relics" of the former plot to garner for her niece the marital prize that she herself never obtained. Although the narrator cannot be induced to take the bait, their collaborative plotting nevertheless triumphs over his scheming, potentially defusing or at least subverting the bid for dominance in the narrator's Master-plot.

These competing masculine and feminine plots are epitomized by two different subnarratives of the myth of Orpheus which resonates in "The Aspern Papers." Laurence Holland notes the Orphic strain in the story, elaborating upon the narrator's view of Orpheus as a prototype for Aspern, who "immortalize[s] and victimize[s] his Juliana in betraying or giving her away to posterity." Holland also sees the narrator in the guise of Orpheus when he undertakes the "Orphic task of retrieving the papers from their tomb and resurrecting the dead."[36] By this analogy, the papers, and Aspern by association with them, are feminized as the objects of the narrator's Orphic desire, desire that in this context is masculine and heterosexual. However, the final backward glance that Miss Tina gives the narrator before separating from him puts a different spin on the myth's gender roles. When Miss Tina looks back at the narrator, *she* takes on the role of Orpheus, who sends the narrator, cast here in the part of Eurydice, back to a hell of his own making. She has already determined her own fate by destroying the letters, thereby asserting a dignity that distinguishes her from both the narrator's and Miss Juliana's graspingness. Admittedly, Miss Tina's choices are limited to either being exploited or renouncing the marriage plot; her destruction of the papers is the most positive action that her circumstances permit. Although the scope of her agency is limited, Miss Tina's choice of non-marriage marks her as belonging to a later generation of New Woman than Juliana, who seeks financial security for her niece through marriage rather than beyond it.

The only explicit reference to Orpheus in "The Aspern Papers," however, alludes to a component of the myth different from the one Holland emphasizes:

Half the women of his time, to speak liberally, had flung themselves at his head, and out of this pernicious fashion many complications, some of them grave, had not failed to arise. He was not a woman's poet, as I had said to Mrs Prest, in the modern phase of his reputation; but the situation had been different when the man's own voice was mingled with his song. That voice, by every testimony, was one of the sweetest ever heard. "Orpheus and the Maenads!" was the exclamation that rose to my lips when I first turned over his correspondence. Almost all the Maenads were unreasonable and many of them insupportable; it struck me in short that he was kinder, more considerate than, in his place (if I could imagine myself in such a place!) I should have been. (*CT*, VI, p. 278)

In both components of the myth, that is, both the backward-glance-of-Orpheus component and the Orpheus-and-the-Maenads component, the power of desire causes the death of its object. Whereas Orpheus's desirous gaze ultimately sends Eurydice back to Hell, it is the awesomely powerful desire of the Maenads which leads them to dismember Orpheus. In the myth of the Maenads, the object of the gaze is male and the gazers, also auditors, are female and powerful. Aspern as Orpheus is thus the victim of the wild passion that he arouses in his female admirers but cannot control.[37] Furthermore, the heterosexual pairing of female subject and male object aligns the narrator himself with the crazed fans of the "woman's poet." The narrator is at once feminized and also profoundly dangerous: a kind of male hysteric who constantly verges on doing violence, if not directly to the body of the poet he worships, then to that poet's relics.

The narrator defends his idol against the charge of being a "woman's poet" to save the master from the linked threats of popularization and feminization, but he is also trying to protect himself from contamination by this double threat. Actually, it is a triple threat; the myth of the Maenads has variants which further complicate the meaning of the gendered and sexual relation between the bachelor narrator and the male object of his desire and identification, of his literary and erotic passion. One variant takes the Maenads' frenzy as induced by their jealousy over Orpheus's supposed preference for men over women, not simply by the beauty of his music. The Orpheus on whom the "woman's poet" of "The Aspern Papers" is modeled may not have been a consummate ladies' man but rather a practitioner of Greek love. The legacy of the fictional Aspern thus derives additionally from a different model of the master poet, an historical rather than mythic Don Juan, who is invested with some of the same sexual ambiguities as Orpheus: Byron.

It is well known from James's New York Edition Preface that the "germ" of "The Aspern Papers" was an anecdote about an "ardent Shelleyite" who took lodgings with the elderly Mary Jane Clairmont – the one-time mistress of Byron, mother of his daughter Allegra and half-sister of Mary Godwin – and her "younger female relative" in order to gain access to some "Shelley documents" (*LC2*, pp. 1175–6). In one of his notebooks, James identifies the source of the anecdote, Eugene Lee-Hamilton, and its real-life hero, "Captain Edward Silsbee – the Boston art-critic and Shelley-worshipper," and specifies further that the "interesting papers" were "letters of Shelley's and Byron's."[38] In the Preface, James describes his attempts to obscure his fiction's reliance on the notorious historical past:

Delicacy had demanded, I felt, that my appropriation of the Florentine legend should purge it, first of all, of references too obvious; so that, to begin with, I shifted the scene of the adventure ... It was a question, in fine, of covering one's tracks ... I felt I couldn't cover mine more than in postulating a comparative American Byron to match an American Miss Clairmont. (*LC2*, p. 1179)

The demands of "delicacy" notwithstanding, here and in the story itself James stresses the Byron connection: "Juliana, as I saw her, was thinkable only in Byronic and more or less immediately post-Byronic Italy" (*LC2*, p. 1179).

The Byronic overtones are palpable throughout "Aspern": in its fascination with the "man of 1820"; in its naming of "Juliana" which echoes the Julia of "Don Juan"; and above all in the narrator's stated intention of defending Aspern against "an impression about 1825 that he had 'treated her badly'" (*CT*, VI, p. 278).[39] This bad behavior is left unspecified – it is arguably the very secret of the man, the primary object of the narrator's epistemological quest. When James wrote "Aspern" in 1887 it was common knowledge, or at least a commonly known allegation thanks to Harriet Beecher Stowe's sensational and iconoclastic *Lady Byron Vindicated* (1870), that the real-life Byron had engaged in adulterous incest with his half-sister.[40] Interestingly, in his 1879 review of the "Memoir of the Rev. Francis Hodgson, B. D., with Numerous Letters from Lord Byron and Others," James declines to name Byron's "unforgiveable sin," insisting instead upon an epistemological blank: "Even if the inference we speak of were valid, it would be very profitless to inquire further as regards Byron's unforgiveable sin; we are convinced that, if it were ascertained, it would be, to ingenuous minds, a great disappointment" (*LC1*, p. 819). James's jaded prediction that this sin would disappoint "ingenuous minds" partakes of the same cynicism that he earlier attributes to Byron, a "cynicism ... half natural and half affected" (*LC1*, p. 817). When he predicts disappointment, James assumes the ultimate aesthetic pose: he leaves Byron's sin unspecified not because he dares not speak its name, but because it is entirely too boring to bother. James's reluctance to specify the sexual misdeeds of Byron, like the narrator's vagueness about the "shabby behaviour" (*CT*, VI, p. 278) of his Byronic hero, unites the different sexual transgressions of heterosexual adultery, heterosexual incest, and homosexuality under the sign of the blank, possibly even placing all sexuality under the aegis of the unspeakable or the unknowable.

The epistemological blank of the sexual in "The Aspern Papers" is connected to the problem of knowing and representing the past, and particularly of knowing and representing another man's sexual past. In this *nouvelle*, "having a history" means having a sexual history that will be problematic for future men to know and to represent. The distance between Aspern's sexual past and the narrator's present interest in it resembles the configuration of James's unfinished novel, *The Sense of the*

Past, which he began in 1899. In this novel, the frame of a portrait separates "the man of 1820" – James's label of choice for the Byronic man of action – from "the man of 1910," but this frame also provides a point of connection, or rather transubstantiation, between them. By comparison, the narrator of "Aspern" imagines himself as communing with Aspern when he gazes at his miniature portrait of him, but it is this very picture which, in the story's closing frame, reminds him of his "intolerable" loss (*CT*, VI, p. 382), his unbridgeable separation from the master. While it is less rigidly symmetrical than *The Sense of the Past*, "Aspern" shares with this later fiction the unmerged, parallel activity of two different plots, past and present, that center on two different men. Thus, the present plot in which the narrator's attempts to use Miss Tina to advance his goals frames the historically distanced plot in which Aspern uses Juliana for his own aesthetic ends. The present plot, moreover, is deployed specifically to effect a point of contact with the past, to effect a connection with the man of the past.

The double plot of "Aspern" thus resembles the classic double plotting of detective fiction in the way that the story of the crime and the story of its detection are simultaneously reconstructed by the detective himself as the first-person narrator.[41] "Aspern" also resembles classic detective fiction in the way that the detective comes increasingly to resemble the criminal. The detective has to think like the criminal, to follow figuratively and sometimes literally in the criminal's footsteps, even to *become* a criminal in order to "get" his man. Aspern as criminal and the bachelor narrator as detective are thus united by the desire of the man who comes after his predecessor in order to "get" him, even if, or perhaps especially if, it means becoming him.[42] The narrator of "Aspern" thereby frames himself in more ways than one. His vicarious interest allies him with a man who is under suspicion of sexual indiscretions, crimes of the heart if not actual crimes, and his first-person narration of the story becomes the focus of our interest, the ineluctable subject of our interpretation. The very title, "The Aspern Papers," evokes this self-reflexive doubling: are the "papers" Aspern's love letters, or are they the pages that we read when we read the document supposedly generated by the narrator as a record of his own exploits? The possibility lurks in the narrative that those other papers do not exist at all, since the narrator and therefore we, as readers, never actually "see" them. All we have is the narrator's belief that they exist. If the pages we read are the papers themselves, then the distinction between "the story of one's hero" and "the story of one's story" (*LC2*, p. 1309) becomes murky indeed, resulting in what might well be called the "darkest abyss of romance."

A similar self-reflexive ambiguity undercuts "The Figure in the Carpet." It is possible that the secret of the Master is that there is no secret. The secret is never disclosed to the narrator and the dangers of naming it are made clear to us from the fatalities suffered by the readers in the text.[43] The first-person narration of this story also provides a self-reflexive frame – the "figure" may be the narrator's own desire to figure out the mystery. This frame is literalized in the structure of the story which opens and closes with vignettes of homosocial competition and communion between men, intimate and rivalrous partnerships that refract the narrator's own desire to penetrate the Master's mystery. The story begins with the narrator's competitive self-definition in relation to the intellectual and financial attainments of another critic:

> I had done a few things and earned a few pence – I had perhaps even had time to begin to think I was finer than was perceived by the patronising; but when I take the little measure of my course (a fidgety habit, for it's none of the longest yet) I count my real start from the evening George Corvick, breathless and worried, came in to ask me a service. He had done more things than I, and earned more pence, though there were chances for cleverness I thought he sometimes missed. (*CT*, ix, p. 273)

The story ends with the narrator's description of his relation to Drayton Deane, the critic who marries Gwendolen after Corvick's untimely death:

> So abrupt an experience of her want of trust had an agitating effect on him, but I saw that immediate shock throb away little by little and then gather again into waves of wonder and curiosity – waves that promised, I could perfectly judge, to break in the end with the fury of my own highest tides. I may say that to-day [sic] as victims of unappeased desire there isn't a pin to choose between us. The poor man's state is almost my consolation; there are indeed moments when I feel it to be almost my revenge. (*CT*, ix, p. 315)

Although Deane has enjoyed marital "possession" of Gwendolen, the narrator reveals to him that he has missed out on a more profound union with the Master, thus transforming Deane into another "victim of unappeased desire." The narrator's proof that Drayton has missed his true "chance at cleverness" is his continued "want of voice, want of form" (*CT*, ix, p. 312). Although the narrator believes that the widow is "bravely dowered" by her first husband with the secret of the Master, her second husband never displays "the fruit of the affair," the outward signs of intellectual impregnation with the Master's seed.

These homosocial vignettes bracket the body of the narrative, but in "Figure," as in "Aspern," the plot of male–male consummation is supplanted or challenged, not enabled, by a woman and her feminine plot. The enigmatic "figure" whose discovery seems to require male collaboration with a woman, ideally with a wife – the narrator worries that Corvick and Gwendolen "together would puzzle something out" and Vereker allows that marriage "may help them" (*CT*, IX, p. 289) – inevitably comes to be appropriated and hoarded by Gwendolen in her capacity as a woman writer: "'I heard everything,' she replied, 'and I mean to keep it to myself!'" (*CT*, IX, p. 305). Despite Vereker's initial conviction that a "woman will never find out" the secret (*CT*, IX, p. 288), Gwendolen obscurely but emphatically contends, "It's my *life!*" (*CT*, IX p. 307), and publishes her second and better novel, "Overmastered," a year and a half later. Thus, the alluring yet imposing figure behind the carpet is not only a male figure, an envied and desired father figure, but also a female figure or a mother figure, whose re-productive capacity as an artist the narrator also envies and desires. Gwendolen's death in childbirth while at work on her third novel, however, suggests an incompatibility between her maternal and authorial roles. It would be interesting, though beyond the aims of the present chapter, to investigate the comparable challenges to masculine high-cultural authorship presented by the woman writer of James's historical present and recent past, and by the "woman's poet" of his more distant historical past.[44] For our purposes here, it is sufficient to note that James represents these two different models of gendered authorship as enjoying access to both experience and popular success. Popular success was particularly unavailable to the high-cultural male writer of fiction as James himself performed the role, while access to experience was necessarily routed through the aesthetic "form of life" which James most often associates with visual vicariousness. The visual vicariousness of the bachelor narrator as James represents him in "Figure" and "Aspern" thus links this character to the male author and critic that James himself was in the process of becoming.

The narrator of "Figure," however, describes himself as a passive and unwitting victim of circumstances, a hapless voyeur whose gaze is shaped by the performers far more than it is able to shape them: "Pen in hand, this way, I live the time over, and it brings back the oddest sense of my having been for months and in spite of myself a kind of coerced spectator. All my life had taken refuge in my eyes, which the procession of events appeared to have committed itself to keep astare" (*CT*, IX,

p. 303). This image of "coerced spectatorship" is supported by the narrator's account of Corvick's (stage) directions: "He did me the honour to declare that, putting aside the great sitter [Vereker] himself, I was individually the connoisseur he was most working for. I was therefore to be a good boy and not try to peep under the curtain before the show was ready; I should enjoy it all the more if I sat very still" (*CT*, IX, p. 303). This language recalls the passive yet alert critical receptivity espoused in the *Tempest* essay, a style of critical reception which resembles the high-brow audience's respectfully composed appreciation, a cultural stance described by Lawrence Levine as emerging in the second half of the nineteenth century.[45] But when Corvick tries to induce the narrator to assume this receptive position, it is unclear whether he is really trying to help him to see the show or to keep him away from it. It seems more likely than not that Corvick is trying to exclude the narrator from the arena rather than trying to enhance his aesthetic pleasure. In this scenario, the true disciple, Corvick, approaches the inner sanctum of art by "overmastering" another man: by reducing the lesser disciple, the narrator, to a "good boy" who must merely watch, or perhaps just imagine, the thrilling exploits of the man behind the curtain, a "real man" who is either Vereker or Corvick, now a Master himself. Implicit in this understanding of the story is the assumption, one that this narrator himself seems to hold, that Corvick attains mastery at the expense of another disciple. Rather than following the more conventional Oedipal trajectory of collaborating to kill their father, here two brothers war against each other in their competition to commune lovingly with, and thereby to become, the father.

The narrator tries to cut his losses by reenvisioning his unmanning "coerced spectatorship" as the bourgeois masculine virtue of self-discipline. He does so by portraying his relations with Corvick, and later Drayton Deane, as loving fraternal bonds which are ultimately in service of a higher principle:

There are doubtless people to whom torments of such an order appear hardly more natural than the contortions of disease; but I don't after all know why I should in this connexion so much as mention them. For the few persons, at any rate, abnormal or not, with whom my anecdote is concerned, literature was a game of skill, and skill meant courage, and courage meant honour, and honour meant passion, meant life. (*CT*, IX, p. 296)

The "torment" that this critic endures, like the exquisite torture James associates with the life of art in his Preface to *The American* and in his essay on *The Tempest*, is potentially "abnormal," even unnatural or diseased. Yet the bachelor critic recuperates this aesthetic torment for normative masculinity by taking the critical reception of literature as an emblem of valor and authenticity. In this passage, literature is equated with life by means of a metonymic train that passes through the realms of skill, courage, honour, and passion, thus linking aesthetic passion to the military disciplines of skill, courage and honor. The associative train in "Figure" does work comparable to that done by a metonymic sequence which appears in "The Art of Fiction": "*One perceives* in that case – by the light of a heavenly ray – that the province of art is all life, all feeling, all observation, *all vision*" (*LC1*, p. 159, emphasis mine). In equating life with art, James begins and ends with visual perception, suggesting that life is no longer the referent but merely the sign of vision. Seeing thus becomes a quintessentially masculine way of being, an access to experience whose intensity depends upon its very vicariousness. Redefining adventure as that which encompasses the emotional and the intellectual, the familiar and the domestic, the visual and the literary, James brings the life of art into the purview of adventure and hence into the realm of hegemonic masculinity.

James finally differs from more than he resembles the bachelor critics and artists who narrate his tales of literary life. These bachelor disciples ultimately have more in common with the "sleek bachelor of music," the Aeolian harp whose pretty noise is inferior to the masterful appropriations and transformations of "the spirit in hungry quest." James, by contrast, was able to leap "from the window into the street" while also retaining his place at what he described in his Preface to *Portrait* as one of "a million – a number of possible windows not to be reckoned." Like Fitzgerald's bachelor narrator in *The Great Gatsby*, who projects himself onto "the casual watcher in the street" looking up at "our line of yellow windows" and yet insists that "life is much more successfully looked at from a single window," James was both "within and without." A permanent resident of the house of fiction, James was also a man of the streets, a flâneur who took visual possession of the "biggest aggregation of human life – the most complete compendium of the world."[46] The double life of "an artist and a bachelor" enabled James to live a life of art whose indulgences and renunciations were compatible with work and liberty.

In his performance as a Master, James did not want for disciples. He did, however, lack a popular audience. When it finally became undeniably evident that such popularity would not be forthcoming, he resolved to renounce mass appreciation.[47] Vowing to "take up my *own* old pen again – the pen of all my old unforgettable efforts and sacred struggles ... that I may do the work of my life," James made the work of high culture do the work of gender, remasculinizing the life of art and in the process redefining the realm of normative bourgeois masculinity.[48] James shared with many other male writers of modernist fiction an anxiety about popular success or, rather, about their lack of it. In the next chapter, I will analyze how Conrad's use of a bachelor narrator registers his own ambivalent relation to popular success, as well as his gendered relation to his reading subjects and to the subjects of his fiction.

CHAPTER 4

A way of looking on: bachelor narration in Conrad's Under Western Eyes

Joseph Conrad acknowledged a change in focus when he changed the title of his 1911 novel-in-progress from "Razumov" to *Under Western Eyes*.[1] The title change reflects Conrad's recognition that the focus of his novel had shifted from its Russian protagonist, the student Razumov, to the point of view of the English bachelor and language-teacher who narrates the story. The story, as told by Conrad's narrator, ultimately focuses less on Razumov than on the female object of his desire, the Russian expatriate, Natalia Haldin. This bachelor narrator can't keep his Western eyes off her.

The focus of the narrator's eyes on the novel's heroine reflects Conrad's attempt to write something recognizably along the lines of the English novel of sensibility, a tradition of the novel marked not only by its national affiliation but also by its courtship and marriage plotting.[2] *Under Western Eyes* was Conrad's first serious attempt to capture that segment of the English reading public for whom his earlier sea-faring novels had little appeal: women readers. By centrally featuring a female character and by addressing parts of this novel to the Woman Question, Conrad was responding to the popularity of "women's fiction" – fiction written by and for women – as well as to the gender politics at issue in the popular New Woman novels of the *fin de siècle*. In this regard, *Under Western Eyes* represents a clear departure from Conrad's turn-of-the-century Marlow tales which, for many of their contemporary readers, exemplified the male-oriented tradition of adventure romance.[3]

But Conrad does not depart so far from this male-oriented tradition as to allow his New Womanly heroine to tell her story in her own words. He uses instead a bachelor narrator to "translate" Natalia's experience. Indeed, the novel is marked thematically and structurally by the conceit of translation: by the pretext that the English teacher of languages perceives the events of the story through his Western eyes, and that he translates the manuscript written by Razumov and handed over to him by Natalia for the Western eyes of his readers. While it has long been assumed that the difference between East and West is *the* primary signifier of difference in *Under Western Eyes*, the novel's bachelor narrator stands at a cultural interface that is marked by gender difference as much as by national, racial and linguistic difference; as Conrad wrote in a 1903 letter, "Homo duplex has in my case more than one meaning."[4]

The gendered divides across which the narrator attempts to signify are not limited to the differences between masculine and feminine, but encompass the range of masculine subject positions delineated in the novel. The masculine subject position from which Conrad's English bachelor narrator tells the heroine's story differs in certain vital ways from the masculine subject positions of the novel's self-exiled counter-revolutionary Russian protagonist, Razumov, and of its expatriate Russian revolutionary who is Razumov's chief foil, Peter Ivanovitch. Although Peter Ivanovitch explicitly styles himself a feminist, this "burly celebrity" (p. 157) ultimately has only his own political ends at heart; his self-serving principles and ruthless methods prove to be more than a match for Razumov's own.[5] While the narrator's "way of looking on" *does* distinguish him in certain respects from Peter Ivanovitch and Razumov, it also aligns him with these two male characters who count themselves as "inspired" by the sight of Natalia Haldin.[6] His spectatorial self-constitution is both the enabling mechanism and the stumbling block of the narrator's revisionary gender relations.

This double bind of male specularity, and finally of male feminism itself, reflects the related gendered double bind that Conrad himself experienced in writing the novel. While he was moving towards subject matter that he hoped would ultimately garner him a larger female readership and financial reward (his next novel, *Chance*, would be his first truly popular success[7]), Conrad felt a conflicting need to keep his distance from femininity and popularity alike. In a letter to John Galsworthy outlining his early plan for "Razumov," he lamented that "there's nothing more cruel than to be caught between one's impulse, one's art and that question [of saleability] which for me simply is a question of life and death."[8] Later, in the midst of struggling to write *Under Western Eyes*, a novel initially intended to be a short story which took him over two years to finish and whose completion was punctuated by a nervous breakdown, Conrad dashed off with surprising ease one of his sparest and most complex short fictions. Its cast of characters was, notably, all-male. Conrad shared his own sense of its artistic achievement in a letter to Edward Garnett: "'The Secret Sharer,' between you and me, is *it*. Eh? No damned tricks with girls there. Eh? Every word fits and there's not a single uncertain note. Luck my boy. Pure luck. I knew you would spot the thing at sight."[9] While "damned tricks with girls" might earn him badly needed financial compensation, Conrad equally craved recognition as a high-cultural artist, recognition that he believed was antithetical to the success that a broader audience, an audience which included women readers, would mean.

Conrad employed the English bachelor who narrates *Under Western Eyes* as a means of simultaneously getting closer to and yet backing off from his Russian subject matter and his female reading audience. This ambivalent movement is apparent both in the rhetorical doublings of this bachelor's narration and in Conrad's own treatment of his narrator in his 1920 Author's Note to *Under Western Eyes*. It is instructive to compare Conrad's rather cool retrospective appraisal of the narrator of *Under Western Eyes* with his palpably affectionate backward glance in 1917 at Marlow:

The man Marlow and I came together in the casual manner of those health-resort acquaintances which sometimes ripen into friendships. This one has ripened. For all his assertiveness in matters of opinion he is not an intrusive person. He haunts my hours of solitude, when, in silence, we lay our heads together in great comfort and harmony; but as we part at the end of a tale I am never sure that it may not be for the last time. Yet I don't think that either of us would care much to survive the other . . . Of all my people he's the one that has never been a vexation to my spirit.[10]

What I was concerned with mainly was the aspect, the character, and the fate of the individuals as they appeared to the Western Eyes of the old teacher of language. He himself has been much criticized; but I will not at this late hour undertake to justify his existence. He was useful to me and therefore I think that he must be useful to the reader both in the way of comment and by the part he plays in the development of the story. In my desire to produce the effect of actuality it seemed to me indispensable to have an eyewitness of the transactions in Geneva. I needed also a sympathetic friend for Miss Haldin, who otherwise would have been too much alone and unsupported to be perfectly credible. (p. 50)

Conrad describes Marlow as *his* secret sharer, as a man with whom he shares a vitalizing intimacy imagined in terms of physical and spiritual closeness. Conrad and Marlow "lay [their] heads together" in a way reminiscent of the homoeroticized pillow talk of Leggatt and the narrator of "The Secret Sharer." Conrad's description of those "health-resort acquaintances which sometimes ripen into friendships" also recalls the health-resort association of Ford Madox Ford's first-person narrator with the "other man" of his narration, Edward Ashburnham, in *The Good Soldier*. It conjures as well the secret-sharing intimacy that Conrad himself had once shared with Ford in their literary collaborations.[11] In contrast, Conrad describes the nameless bachelor narrator of *Under Western Eyes* in more workmanlike terms, in terms of the narrator's "usefulness" rather than terms of endearment. Although he estimates the teacher of languages as having been "indispensable" in producing credible effects, effects that depend on his role as an eyewitness and a sympathetic friend, Conrad stolidly, though contradictorily, maintains that he will not "undertake to justify his existence."[12] In this way, Conrad rhetorically distances himself from, even while declaring his allegiance to, the narrator of *Under Western Eyes*, a narrator who himself struggles with conflicting imperatives of distance and proximity.

NATIONAL LOYALTY, FAITHFUL TRANSLATION, AND BETRAYING NARRATION

In his 1920 Author's Note, Conrad describes his writing of *Under Western Eyes* as a complex act of negotiation among conflicting demands:

My greatest anxiety was in being able to strike and sustain the note of scrupulous impartiality. The obligation of absolute fairness was imposed on me historically and hereditarily, by the peculiar experience of race and family, in addition to my primary conviction that truth alone is the justification of any fiction which makes the least claim to the quality of art or may hope to take its place in the culture of men and women of its time. (pp. 49–50)

"[T]he peculiar experience of race and family" is Conrad's allusion to Russian rule in Poland, Czarist persecution of his Polish parents, and his own decision to emigrate in 1874. If this "peculiar experience" demands scrupulous impartiality, it also makes such "absolute fairness" difficult: "I had never been called before to a greater effort of detachment: detachment from all passions, prejudices, and even from personal memories" (p. 50).[13] Conrad attributes both the book's "failure" and its success to this authorial detachment: "*Under Western Eyes* on its first appearance in England was a failure with the public, perhaps because of that very detachment. I obtained my reward some six years later when I first heard that the book had found universal recognition in Russia and had been re-published there in many editions" (p. 50). The "truth alone" that justifies "any fiction which makes the least claim to the quality of art" is here measured by the "universal recognition" of the novel's Russian reception. In a novel that is "as a whole an attempt to render not so much the political state as the psychology of Russia" (p. 49), the reward of recognition depends upon the self-recognition the novel afforded to its Russian readers.

Such a "reward" almost surely would have been ambivalently received by Conrad, since representing Russianness accurately required, according to the theory of fiction he espouses here, detachment from his Polish past, a detachment even more extreme than that achieved by his expatriation.[14] Yet such success clearly would have gratified the naturalized English author who longed for a wider audience and for the financial solvency that would accompany it. This desire would, in turn, have brought him into conflict with his dedication to high art, to the "truth alone [that] is the justification of any fiction which makes the least claim to the quality of art" (p. 50). The conflicts between authorial and national identity, between artistic detachment and historical bias, and between uncompromised art and good sales, made self-betrayal, or at least ambivalence, unavoidable for Conrad.[15] Conrad's dilemmas about nationality and literary representation described in the Author's Note are replayed in Razumov's inexorable repetitions of betrayal in the novel's plot. Razumov's betrayal of Haldin, or of himself, as he comes to see it, in order to write the "prize essay" (p. 61) can be understood in the context of Conrad's own vexed relation to success as a writer about Russia and, later, as a writer for Russian readers. But his English narrator too refigures these authorial conflicts, embodying the split between detachment and involvement, between objectivity and subjectivity, in his role as translator in and of an Eastern story for Western eyes.

Throughout the novel, the narrator insists upon his limited function as translator, claiming that the story he tells "is based on a document; all I have brought to it is my knowledge of the Russian language, which is sufficient for what is attempted here" (p. 55). He also repeatedly "disclaim[s] the possession of those high gifts of imagination and expression" (p. 55):

Wonder may be expressed at a man in the position of a teacher of languages knowing all this with such definiteness. A novelist says this and that of his personages, and if only he knows how to say it earnestly enough he may not be questioned upon the inventions of his brain in which his own belief is made sufficiently manifest by a telling phrase, a poetic image, the accent of emotion. Art is great! But I have no art, and not having invented Madame de S-, I feel bound to explain how I came to know so much about her. (p. 179)

The narrator's insistence here on the historical reality as opposed to novelistic realism of his narrative resembles Conrad's emphasis in his Author's Note on the psychological "truth" of his "historical novel" (p. 49).[16] But, unlike Conrad, the narrator denies any deeper understanding that would suit him for his task:

Yet I confess that I have no comprehension of the Russian character. The illogicality of their attitude, the arbitrariness of their conclusions, the frequency of the exceptional, should present no difficulty to a student of many grammars; but there must be something else in the way, some special human trait – one of those subtle differences that are beyond the ken of mere professors. (p. 56)

Despite his emphasis on the illogical, arbitrary, and exceptional nature of Russian character, on the differences that make Russians incomprehensible to Westerners, the English narrator nevertheless gives it his best shot:

What must remain striking to a teacher of languages is the Russians' extraordinary love of words. They gather them up; they cherish them, but they don't hoard them in their breasts; on the contrary, they are always ready to pour them out by the hour or by the night with an enthusiasm, a sweeping abundance, with such an aptness of application sometimes that, as in the case of very accomplished parrots, one can't defend oneself from the suspicion that they really understand what they say. There is a generosity in their ardour of speech which removes it as far as possible from common loquacity; and it is ever too disconnected to be classed as eloquence… But I must apologize for this digression. (p. 56)

Expanding here on the grim reckoning of the novel's second paragraph – "To a teacher of languages there comes a time when the world is but a place of many words and man appears a mere talking animal not much more wonderful than a parrot" (p. 55) – the narrator homes in on a feature of Russianness that just might unlock the mystery of Russian character. The key he offers, the Russian "love of words," locates meaning just where he suggests that there is a radical absence of signification. To compound the indeterminacy of this self-contradictory definition of the essence of Russianness, the narrator then apologizes for his digression, indicating that his speculations are tangential to the real story.

The opening passage of the next section of Book I again foregrounds the narrator's sense of his own inadequacy at translating Russian experience: "On looking through the pages of Mr Razumov's diary I own that a 'rush of thoughts' is not an adequate image. The more adequate description would be a tumult of thoughts – the faithful reflection of the state of his feelings" (pp. 71–2). The faithfulness in question here is not Razumov's divided loyalty, but the narrator's representation of it. He locates the problem of adequate description in the radically "different conditions of Western thought":

It is unthinkable that any young Englishman should find himself in Razumov's situation. This being so it would be a vain enterprise to imagine what he would think... He would not have an hereditary and personal knowledge of the means by which a historical autocracy represses ideas, guards its power, and defends its existence. (p. 72)

The "hereditary and personal knowledge" necessary to imagine Razumov's situation recalls Conrad's own "peculiar experience of race and family" which he describes in the Author's Note as having been imposed upon him "historically and hereditarily" (pp. 49–50). While it may be impossible for a Westerner to imagine an Eastern subjectivity conditioned as it is by historical circumstance, this is precisely the task that Conrad assigns his English narrator. The inevitability of failure and the consequent sense of inadequacy built into the narrator's situation reflect Conrad's experience as a Pole writing about Russia for an English audience – both Easterner and Westerner, both inside and outside Russia as a Pole, both inside and outside the East as an expatriate Pole writing and living in England.[17]

The narrative pattern of disclaiming comprehension of Russianness, then offering a "key-word" (p. 105) to Russian character or naming the "psychological secret of the profound difference of that people" (p. 134), followed by an apology for the "digression," recurs at the opening of each of the three subsections of the Russian part of the novel (Book I), as well as at the opening of the longer Geneva part (Book II) which comprises the rest of the novel. I will not argue here about whether the narrator's proposed "key-word" – "cynicism" (p. 105) – is the right key word, or whether his account of the "secret" of Russian difference – "they detest life, the irremediable life of the earth as it is, whereas we westerners cherish it with perhaps an equal exaggeration of its sentimental value" (p. 134) – is borne out by the story, although one could conceivably test the narrator's reliability in this way. Instead, I want to emphasize the rhetorical effect of the pattern itself. The disclaimers with which he begins these early sections of the novel all take the form of defining the East as mysterious, defining himself as unable to comprehend the mystery, and then plunging ahead to offer us a solution to the mystery. With each repetition of the formula, the reader must choose between the claim and the disclaimer. (This interpretive conundrum is only slightly less insoluble than the one generated in James's "The Lesson of the Master," where the two potential interpretations of the lesson are fundamentally incompatible and yet mutually contingent.) The narrator further destabilizes his meaning by following his offers to solve the mystery of Russianness with apologies for digressing. The destabilization of signification in this case does not divide readers' interpretations between a found and an unfindable solution, or between the narrator's genuine and performed naïveté, but rather between the essential story and what is supplementary to it.

While ostensibly reaffirming the centrality of the story of Razumov and Natalia's ill-fated courtship and the primacy of Razumov's original manuscript, the narrator's apologies inexorably redirect our attention to his interventions in the novel's love plotting and his translation of the Russian manuscript into English. The digression-as-supplement is as much a substitute or replacement for, as it is an addition to, Razumov's Russian document and love story. By drawing attention to the narrator himself while ostensibly directing our attention away from him, the paradoxically self-effacing assertions or self-asserting effacements of the narrator – his repetitions of "But I digress" – thus make a latent challenge for dominance beneath their manifest submissiveness. The double edge of this rhetorical maneuvering is not simply the inevitable double logic of writing itself. Rather, this doubling can be read into and through the conflicts that define this narrator's subjectivity. These conflicts are found not simply in his position as a Western translator, but also in his role as a bachelor who witnesses and relays this novel's plots of love and betrayal.

DOUBLE LIVES, SECRET SHARING, AND MARRIAGE PLOTTING

The rhetorical doubleness of the narration is perhaps most pronounced in the bachelor's representations of Natalia Haldin and his own feelings for her. These representations resonate with his conflicting desires, particularly the conflict between his sexual desire for her and his desire to protect her and himself from such desire. The rhetorical maneuverings by which the narrator negotiates – both defends against and enacts – these conflicts strikingly resemble those by which he negotiates the problems of representing Russia. Just as he repeatedly gestures toward the unknowability of the East, he also foregrounds the difficulty of knowing Natalia Haldin: "It may be that she thought I understood her much better than I was able to do. The most precise of her sayings seemed always to me to have enigmatical prolongations vanishing somewhere beyond my reach" (p. 145). Though the narrator's desire to grasp Natalia may exceed his reach, he also feels a need to keep her at a safe distance:

We became excellent friends in the course of our reading. It was very pleasant. Without fear of provoking a smile, I shall confess that I became very much attached to that young girl. At the end of four months I told her that now she could very well go on reading English by herself. It was time for the teacher to depart. (p. 133)

He "confesses" here his attachment to Natalia Haldin just as elsewhere he "confess[es] that I have no comprehension of the Russian character" (p. 56). The rhetorical gesture of confessing invests the content of his utterance with an illicit charge, particularly in the context of Razumov's dramatic confessions at the end of the novel. In claiming to be "without fear of provoking a smile," moreover, the narrator betrays his consciousness of having sinned or committed a crime in the very process of denying it. The suggestion that his confessed transgression would provoke a (contemptuous? accepting? sympathetic?) smile diminishes his offense to the status of an embarrassing foible. Thus, the narrator's confession is at once self-aggrandizing and self-deprecating, placing him on the novel's larger stage of emotional and political treason while simultaneously disclosing the diminutive scale of his self-betrayal.

One facet of the narrator's conflict comes clearer in another of his unelicited "confessions":

Such thoughts as these seasoned my modest, lonely bachelor's meal. If anybody wishes to remark that this was a roundabout way of thinking of Natalia Haldin, I can only retort that she was well worth some concern. She had all her life before her. Let it be admitted, then, that I was thinking about Natalia Haldin's life in terms of her mother's character, a manner of thinking about a girl permissible for an old man, not too old yet to have become a stranger to pity. (pp. 300–1)

Clearly, his defensiveness is meant to ward off, or at least to preempt, charges that his thoughts and feelings are not socially "permissible for an old man," especially with respect to a woman young enough to be his daughter. In defending himself against the imaginary charges of lecherous and (metaphorical if not actual) incestuous desire, this "lonely bachelor" thereby inculpates himself. Yet, his shamefaced confession of a lack of proper manly self-restraint also stands as a boast about his masculine virility: "She directed upon me her grey eyes shaded by black eyelashes, and I became aware, notwithstanding my years, how attractive physically her personality could be to a man capable of appreciating in a woman something else than the mere grace of femininity" (pp. 132–3). His use of the phrase "notwithstanding my years" suggests the impropriety of cross-generational sexual desire, although the remainder of the sentence counters the disreputable implications with the reputable maturity and sophistication of "a man capable of appreciating in a woman something else than the mere grace of femininity."

Similar rhetorical complexities inform a passage which echoes the "without fear of provoking a smile" formulation cited above:

I intended to leave [Razumov and Miss Haldin] to themselves, but Miss Haldin touched me lightly on the forearm with a significant contact, conveying a distinct wish. Let him smile who likes, but I was only too ready to stay near Nathalie Haldin, and I am not ashamed to say that it was no smiling matter to me. I stayed, not as a youth would have stayed, uplifted, as it were poised in the air, but soberly, with my feet on the ground and my mind trying to penetrate her intention. (p. 193)

By brazening out actual or imagined humiliating judgements on his motivations and actions with respect to Miss Haldin, the bachelor narrator displays conduct most becoming. While he initially intends to cede the field to the young woman's proper suitor, he is "only too ready to stay near," his readiness as well as his soberness and gravity flesh out his self-portrait as a chivalrous champion, as a bachelor knight whose chastity emblematizes his selfless devotion. In distinguishing his conduct from that of "a youth," he denies that he is, or even wishes to be, a rival suitor, painting himself as a mature defender rather than a youthful aggressor. Yet his attempt to "penetrate her intention" hints at a protest against a desexualized paternal or avuncular role that he elsewhere accepts with greater resignation.

The doublings of the narration enable the bachelor narrator to play both suitor and guardian to Natalia Haldin, two masculine subject positions that are mutually exclusive in the world of this novel because the suitor wants to initiate the female object of his desire into sexual knowledge and the guardian wants to defend her against such initiation. Divergence along these lines is not inevitable in marriage plotting *per se*, but such a split is unavoidable because, in this novel, sexual knowledge amounts to betrayal, an equation suggested by one of the narrator's duplicitously desirous descriptions of Natalia Haldin:

She had reflected already (in Russia the young begin to think early), but she had never known deception as yet because obviously she had never yet fallen under the sway of passion. She was – to look at her was enough – very capable of being roused by an idea or simply by a person. At least, so I judged with I believe an unbiased mind; for clearly my person could not be the person – and as to my ideas! . . . (p. 133)

The very claim to an "unbiased mind" reveals the subjective bias in this representation and, with it, the narrator's disavowed desire to be the one to arouse Natalia. By transparently dismissing the fantasy of himself as a plausible object of Natalia's desire, the narrator rhetorically casts himself in the role of seductive deceiver. This rhetorical effect hinges, tellingly, upon the passage's equation of passion and deception.

The linkage between deception and passion in *Under Western Eyes* might better be said to end rather than to begin with the narrator's rhetorical doublings, since this connection is grounded in Razumov's story. Razumov literally lives a "double life" in his mutually exclusive roles of revolutionary co-conspirator and government informer. The rhetorical self-betrayals within the novel's narration can be understood as a translation, a repetition with a difference, of the conflicts that animate the love story of the novel's male protagonist. But even the marriage plot at the heart of the novel must itself be understood as a repetition and revision, a translation, of a prior plot of love and betrayal. Razumov's scheme to betray Natalia Haldin repeats his earlier betrayal of her brother, Victor Haldin, who seeks help from Razumov after confessing his own "original sin," his involvement in a bloody bomb-throwing attack on the government official, "de P-." If the initial Russian plot of assassination is initially homoeroticized by its confession in a scene of bedroom intimacy between two men, then it is ultimately heterosexualized by the Geneva plot.

Razumov reimagines his initial conflict between loyalty to and betrayal of another man through a plot of heterosexual union with, and thus a plot against, that man's sister. Thus, in his confession to Natalia, he writes:

Victor Haldin had stolen the truth of my life from me, who had nothing else in the world, and he boasted of living on through you on this earth where I had no place to lay my head. She will marry some day, he had said – and your eyes were trustful. And do you know what I said to myself? I shall steal his sister's soul from her. (p. 331)

By "stealing his sister's soul," Razumov hopes to repossess what he feels Haldin has stolen from him. At the same time, his union with Natalia would enact the "incredible fellowship of souls" with Haldin that Razumov fantasizes – "a full confession in passionate words that would stir the whole being of that man to its innermost depths; that would end in embraces and tears" (p. 83) – but quickly repudiates.[18] This fellowship is threatening to Razumov because of both the potentially feminizing effects of male–male desire conceived as gender transitive, and the potentially feminizing effects of sentiment and affiliation, anathema to a style of masculinity imagined as anti-sentimental and autonomous. Having Natalia would enable Razumov to unite with Haldin . . . but also to dominate him; he would "have" him in two different ways at once. Moreover, by having Natalia, Razumov would recreate the originary, male–male double self that he feels he has lost at least as much through his own self-alienating betrayal of Haldin as through Haldin's alienating confession to him.

The homosocial triangulation of masculine identity and desire in the Razumov–Victor–Natalia plot can better be understood with reference to the plotting of "The Secret Sharer," which Conrad wrote in the midst of composing *Under Western Eyes*. Conrad had finished writing the Russian section, and was struggling to finish the second and longer Geneva section of *Under Western Eyes*, when he dashed off "The Secret Sharer" in just over two weeks.[19] "The Secret Sharer" works through in highly distilled form issues that Conrad elaborated in *Under Western Eyes*. Both texts feature doubled "primal scenes": a homoerotic primal scene of two men sharing secrets in bed, and an even more primal scene, a scene-behind-the-scenes, of murder which is not directly represented in either text but is intradiegetically narrated by the murderer to his confidant. While murder may be the common figure in the carpet, or the ultimate ground against which the male figures in these texts stand out, the motive and ultimate signification of murder is neither simple or single.

In "The Secret Sharer," Leggatt, the chief mate on the *Sephora*, had strangled a shirking crewmember when a wave broke over the ship during a violent storm. This act cannot be resolved as simply signifying either passion or duty, either the failure of discipline or the apotheosis of discipline. His crime represents, as he does himself, both the failure and the quintessence of properly regulated masculine desire and, thus, of properly regulated masculinity. The narrator's complicity with Leggatt, like Leggatt's original sin itself, has antithetical meanings. The bond between these men is at once anathema and a necessity to the authority of the captain narrator; the presence of the stowaway both undermines the narrator's command and enables him to achieve full command. Thus, Leggatt is both the narrator's main problem, or the main symptom of his problem, and also the solution to his problem. In each of these positions, Leggatt is doubled: in his roles as the narrator's super-ego and his libido, as the emblem of the narrator's law-abiding conscience and his law-breaking desire. Leggatt's fleshly embodiment as an "other man," a man whom the narrator may physically or imaginatively internalize or incorporate but cannot be summarily reduced to an externalized projection of the narrator's psyche, produces the radical indeterminacy of Leggatt's status in the text. He is at once a literal and metaphorical presence, preventing any simple or single reading of his relation to the narrator.

The multiple and self-contradictory nature of Leggatt's status in the text also reveals the competition within and among styles of manhood, styles that are differently and often incompatibly inflected by the competing demands of autonomy and reciprocity, equality and hierarchy, passion and discipline, and the demands of devotion to oneself, to others, and to a higher principle or cause. These competing demands, and the competing models of manhood they inflect, are at stake in the captain narrator's anguished negotiation of his relations to his older and more experienced "subordinates," as well as in his own self-relation. But if multiple versions and sources of manhood are in contention in the plotting of this all-male, shipboard story, then it is all the more striking that the resolution of the story ultimately depends upon a symbolic feminine presence. Despite Conrad's insistence that "No damned tricks with girls" contaminate this story, it is ultimately the threat of the feminine, the "feminine within" that infiltrates the ship along with the illicit stowaway, that raises the stakes of the contest within and between men.[20]

At the story's climax, the captain narrator steers perilously close to the land in order to give the stowaway a chance to swim to safety, a move whereby he both eliminates and rescues the hidden murderer. In this monumental game of "chicken," the captain redeems his authority by mastering his ship:

And now I forgot the secret stranger ready to depart, and remembered only that I was a total stranger to the ship. I did not know her. Would she do it? How was she to be handled? ...

[The maneuver is successfully executed.] Already the ship was drawing ahead. And I was alone with her. Nothing! no one in the world should stand now between us, throwing a shadow on the way of silent knowledge and mute affection, the perfect communion of a seaman with his first command.[21]

"She" who is the ship replaces the significant other who is another man; in mastering "her," the captain gains full control over himself. His successful maneuver of the ship signifies the masculine authority associated with his internalized self-regulation and his autonomy. In mastering this feminine other, the captain makes himself appear autonomous and undivided; he now displays an apparently unified selfhood that had been undermined by the presence of his "Other Self" or "Secret Self," both early titles for the story.[22] I emphasize his monolithic *appearance* rather than any actual attainment of singularity since one can read the "disappearance" of Leggatt in terms of an internalization of discipline, a concealment of counternormative excesses or displays of passion. In other words, the performance of discipline exemplified by the removal of Leggatt from the ship paradoxically indicates the agonistic struggle that the captain endures. If the story ends with "a free man, a proud swimmer striking out for a new destiny," it also ends with a man who "take[s] his punishment," a performance of internalized discipline upon which his masculine normativity depends.[23]

The heterosexual "communion" of the captain with his feminine ship, then, does not compromise his autonomy and predominance but rather epitomizes and enables them. The symbolic presence of the feminine thus occasions masculine singularity and hegemony, symbolizing the need for them and providing a means to them. The feminine ship as an object to be regulated also stands for the pervasive hierarchical order by which the captain commands his crew, and the order by which he regulates his own manhood. His control over "her" metonymically expresses the captain's now unquestionable authority over his men and himself. Thus, the naturalized hierarchy of the sex/gender system obscures yet enforces the differences between men – here, not of race or class, but of rank – that undergird the captain's command. The introduction and mastery of the feminine conceals the ways in which men are subject to other men by naturalizing this hierarchy as a male/female binary, that is, as gender difference.

Razumov's plot to betray Natalia by marrying her does comparable double duty. It enacts his assertion of dominance over, as well as his desire for union with, another man by displacing both onto a woman. Razumov initially conceives of his marriage plot as a way to fulfill his longing for revenge, but also for communion – "I want to be understood" (p. 83) – and for self-reintegration – "In giving Victor Haldin up, it was myself, after all, whom I have betrayed most basely" (p. 333). However, he eventually comes to see this plot as the consummation of duplicity and his "ultimate undoing." It is his burgeoning love for Natalia that awakens him to the utter damnation that marriage to her would mean:

It was as if your pure brow bore a light which fell on me, searched my heart and saved me from ignominy, from ultimate undoing. And it saved you too. Pardon my presumption. But there was that in your glances which seemed to tell me that you . . . Your light! your truth! I felt that I must tell you that I had ended by loving you. And to tell you that I must first confess. Confess, go out – and perish. (p. 333)

In *Under Western Eyes*, true love means having to say you're sorry even though forgiveness is impossible; true love necessitates the truth, even though the truth is so terrible that it will extinguish love. Razumov ultimately does the right thing under the influence of his love for Natalia – "You fascinated me – you have freed me from the blindness of anger and hate – the truth shining in you drew the truth out of me" (p. 333). Heterosexual love is portrayed here as a kind of romantic antivenin that deactivates the poisonous humors of self-serving and violent feelings, and also of the betrayals associated with male–male desire.

Razumov's revision of the marriage plot against Natalia reflects Conrad's own revision of the novel's plot. By January of 1908, Conrad had finished the Russian section and had planned, but not yet written, a second section in which Razumov marries Natalia and confesses to her only after the birth of their child.[24] The completed manuscript, however, reveals a plot of marriage only in Razumov's *ex post facto* written confession to Natalia. I have found no external evidence explaining what motivated Conrad to alter his plans for the novel's plot. But the effects of this plot change, if not the authorial intentions behind it, are clear. In the revised plot, Razumov saves Natalia, along with the love that she generates and represents, by renouncing his marriage plot and sacrificing his life. He chooses to remain a bachelor in order to save Natalia from the trauma of marrying her brother's betrayer, and in order to preserve what little integrity he has left.

MASCULINE AFFILIATION, MALE FEMINISM, AND THE
BACHELOR'S "WAY OF LOOKING ON"

Ironically, it is Razumov's very isolation, his exclusion from the patro-
nymic and the property that would have been his birthright had his
parents' union been legitimate, that inspires Victor Haldin to choose
him for a confidant: "you have no one belonging to you – no ties, no one
to suffer for it if this came out by some means. There have been enough
ruined Russian homes as it is" (p. 67), explains Haldin to the resentful
Razumov. And it is also this lack of what Razumov bitterly calls
Haldin's "domestic tradition – your fireside prejudices" (p. 100) that
inclines him to betray Haldin to the authorities:

Razumov thought: "I am being crushed – and I can't even run away." Other
men had somewhere a corner of the earth – some little house in the provinces
where they had a right to take their troubles… Razumov stamped his foot –
and under the soft carpet of snow felt the hard ground of Russia, inanimate,
cold, inert, like a sullen and tragic mother hiding her face under a winding sheet
– his native soil! – his very own – without a fireside, without a heart! (p. 78)

Conrad elaborates on the connection for Razumov between the dead
mother and mother Russia in his Author's Note: "Being nobody's child
he feels rather more keenly than another would that he is a Russian – or
he is nothing" (p. 50). Razumov explains himself even more succinctly to
Natalia: "I am independent – and therefore perdition is my lot" (p. 333).
    But in the world of this novel, the Russian illegitimate son is no more
utterly "independent" than the English bachelor. Bachelorhood, like
illegitimacy, does not signify absolute autonomy from marriage or
family, those privileged markers of the private, the domestic, and the
emotional. Rather, in this novel bachelorhood and illegitimacy alike
require delicate and sometimes torturous negotiations of the conflicting
imperatives of proximity and distance, of intimacy and disengagement,
of affiliation and autonomy. Thus in substantiating his "very real sympathy" for the Haldin women, the bachelor narrator affirms that "the
anguish of irreparable loss is familiar to us all. There is no life so lonely
as to be safe against that experience" (p. 140). This mournful reflection
sounds very much like that standard of the popular bachelor tradition,
the bachelor's gesture toward a love lost long ago to death or marriage, a
gesture that sometimes explains and sometimes provides an alibi for his
non-marriage. The narrator's gesture toward loss may also, or alternately, indicate the loss of his parents or family of origin either through death

or distance, or perhaps a more generalized sense of loss associated with his expatriate status.

As the examples of Razumov and the narrator make clear, bachelors, like illegitimate sons, are no more "safe" from loss than anyone else; their plight signifies the inevitability rather than the avoidability of loss. As I will argue at greater length in the final section of this chapter, a primary sense of loss precedes the narrator's fixation on Natalia, just as it precedes both Razumov's conception of the marriage plot against her and, later, his renunciation of that plot. While Razumov's confession traumatizes Natalia, it is intended to avert the worse trauma of marriage; the damage inflicted by Razumov's experience of loss, a primary loss that Razumov's betrayal of Haldin repeats rather than causes, cannot be completely undone by revising the marriage plot.

Although the proceedings of this novel are represented from the perspective of a bachelor, marriage *per se* is not the principal target of the novel's criticism. Indeed, this bachelor narrator idealizes marriage: in a passage canceled in the typescript (that is, canceled much later than Conrad's revisions of Razumov's marriage plot) in which he criticizes the "modern" marriage plans of his niece;[25] in Sophia Antonovna's failed romance with the Americanized Yaklovitch; in Tekla's unfailing devotion to her dying Andrei. In these examples, heterosexual romance, love, and marriage are potentially ideal sources of meaning and mutuality, but the world of politics fatally adulterates them. The bourgeois bachelor narrator views the sphere of the private/personal as potentially redemptive, but as not fully enough separated from the public/political realm. Marriage is thus corrupted, in his eyes, by the exploitation and violence that he associates with the public and the masculine. The novel's chief representative of these twin evils is Peter Ivanovitch. Thus, the novel's "epilogue," in which Sophia Antonovna announces and defends Peter Ivanovitch's marriage to a peasant girl, reads as a grim travesty of the closure device closely associated with the marriage tradition of the novel.[26] The only character rewarded with wedded bliss at the end of this novel is one of its worst villains.

For the narrator, Peter Ivanovitch's villainy resides in his exploitation of women under the cover of revolutionary feminism. His "symbolic" autobiography and his other books are "written with the declared purpose of elevating humanity" and they set forth "the cult of the woman," but their popular and financial success only promotes the cause of the "burly celebrity" (pp. 156–7) himself. Just as he attends the horrific Madame de S- in pursuit of her fortune, he is motivated to marry the peasant girl by his hypocritical opportunism. Peter Ivanovitch's identity as the "great feminist" (pp. 182, 218) is finally a front for his true identity as the "great man." Tekla, the abused *dame de compagnie*, clarifies the stakes of "great man"-hood when she warns Razumov against bringing Natalia to Peter Ivanovitch: "He is a great man. Great men are horrible" (p. 234).[27] She makes things even more explicit in her parting words to Razumov: "Don't you understand that Peter Ivanovitch must direct, inspire, influence? It is the breath of his life. There can never be too many disciples. He can't bear thinking of anyone escaping him. And a woman, too! There is nothing to be done without women, he says. He has written it" (p. 238). For the "great feminist," marriage is just another way of enhancing his own power in the world.

In his representation of the "great feminist," the narrator establishes a rivalry between himself and Peter Ivanovitch, an explicit rivalry over Natalia Haldin and an implicit competition over who is the better man ... and the real male feminist. A confrontation in a cafe between Peter Ivanovitch and the narrator – in an episode excised from the typescript, probably to refocus attention on the Natalia/Razumov plot – dramatizes their rivalry and encapsulates their respective positions on the Woman Question:

[Peter Ivanovitch:] "I know your inherited prejudices. Charity, good works, gentleness, compassion and all that. Now, I think that women are quite fit to take the highest line of action. You hereditarily don't think so. For the self-effacement under whatever disguise it has been forced upon them is not women's part. Their very nature revolts against it. It is they who are created for freedom – not the men."

[Narrator:] "Which in other words amounts to saying that you want to subject to your influence a young girl chance has thrown in your way. What do you want her for? For an active revolutionist? Or is it simply that you must get hold of her to make her your disciple."[28]

Each man is essentially right about the other; Peter Ivanovitch's defence of women's rights *is* self-serving and the narrator *does* want to shelter Natalia from the world of politics and "action," a public sphere that extends beyond the acceptably limited interventions of "charity" and "good works." While this showdown exposes the differences between their two versions of male feminism, between paternalistic protectiveness and opportunistic exploitiveness, it also suggests the similarities between the narrator and Peter Ivanovitch. That is, the rivalry between two men over a woman fits a more conventional model of gender relations than either Peter Ivanovitch or the narrator care to admit. Both versions of male feminism, moreover, fall short of envisioning women as full agents and conscious subjects; the paternalistic model denies women consciousness, whereas the opportunistic model grants them only the agency necessary to serve its own ends.

Nevertheless, the novel does hold out some hope for the bachelor as the representative of an alternative style of masculine identity, a style of manhood that revises, even while it partakes of, traditional models of masculine identity and gender relations. This argument differs from humanist readings that champion the narrator as the novel's true male feminist without recognizing the complicity of his "way of looking on" (p. 157). Such readings overemphasize the potential, if not the longing, for redemption that Conrad's bleakly modernist fiction offers, whether that redemption is sought in the realm of global politics or domestic/sexual politics.[29] By contrast, I argue that the narrator's "way of looking on" – his spectatorship – casts him as an masculine alternative even while occasioning his complicity in the spectacle that he witnesses.

In a portion of the Author's Note cited earlier in this chapter, Conrad attributes the narrator's usefulness to his performance as an "eyewitness" and as a "sympathetic friend" (p. 50). Reconciling these potentially contradictory roles, Natalia locates the value of the narrator's friendship precisely *in* his spectatorial way of being: "There is a way of looking on which is valuable. I have felt less lonely because of it. It is difficult to explain" (p. 157). The narrator's "male gaze" is not necessarily, or solely, objectifying, alienating, and disempowering to its female object, since she herself experiences it as beneficent. Indeed, it may be the disempowerment and marginality associated with his spectatorial stance that make Natalia feel less lonely since that is her position too. Natalia's tribute thus mitigates the narrator's frequent deprecations of his spectatorship as "helpless" and "out of it."

Implicit in her tribute to his "way of looking" is the notion that Natalia reciprocates this look, that his gaze allows or perhaps even enables her to look back, if not directly at him, then at herself. Because of the narrator's desirous and/or identificatory gaze at Natalia, she is able to see herself, to experience a comforting or consoling sense of identification with and desire for herself. This circuit of identification and desire – she sees herself by seeing him seeing her – is finally not self-alienating, or even "narcissistic" in any negative sense of that term.[30] Despite the fact that it is the self who is brought into focus by this circuit of looks, it is necessarily her awareness of the other *as other* that enables this self-relation. Natalia experiences not a simple or damaging incorporation of the other, but a complex self-identification through watching another identify with and desire her.

If his spectatorship is not omnipotent, then neither is it entirely impotent. The exploitation and violence often associated with normative heterosexual gender relations and particularly with the performance of conventional masculinity in this novel are implicated in the bachelor narrator's "way of looking on." This complicity of his gaze is particularly visible in the framing of the novel's climactic scene of love and betrayal as a spectacular tableau, a set piece that combines aspects of the painterly still life, the modelled statue, and the theatrical performance. The narrator is painfully aware of the superfluousness of his presence at this final, "dramatic" interview between Razumov and Natalia, displaying his abjected sense of extraneousness as part of the *mise en scène*:

And I observed them. There was nothing else to do. My existence seemed so utterly forgotten by these two that I dared not now make a movement . . . It was the second time that I saw them together, and I knew that next time they met I would not be there, either remembered or forgotten. I would have virtually ceased to exist for both these young people. (p. 322)

What he looks at is them looking at each other:

To me, the silent spectator, they looked like two people becoming conscious of a spell which had been lying on them ever since they first set eyes on each other. Had either of them cast a glance then in my direction, I would have opened the door quietly and gone out. But neither did; and I remained, every fear of indiscretion lost in the sense of enormous remoteness from their captivity within the sombre horizon of Russian problems, the boundary of their eyes, of their feelings – the prison of their souls. (p. 320)

The way that his fascinated gaze mirrors their mutually transfixing gazes suggests the narrator's identification with the figures at whom he looks. In his spectatorship he shares their experience of being visually captivated. "Every fear of indiscretion lost" suggests that he too is spell-bound, but it is his sense of "enormous remoteness from their captivity" that produces this effect, a phrase that emphasizes the distance of his experience from theirs, rather than its proximity. Thus the passage highlights the spectatorly experience of exclusion, separation, or withdrawal at the same time that it accents the potential for identification in spectatorship.

This scene of doubled visual captivation – further multiplied by the narrator's written representation of the scene of spectacle – distorts space and perspective. His "remoteness" from the lives of the Russian pair is "enormous," but so, implicitly, is the "horizon" that nevertheless holds them captive. If their Russianness is a space of captivity, then it is a space too huge for Western comprehension. The perspectival distortion produced by the simultaneous expansiveness and containment, the boundlessness and boundedness of the "horizon of Russian problems, the boundary of their eyes, of their feelings – the prison of their souls," effectively locates the narrator at once inside and outside the space of the spectacle. His doubling as a spell-bound spectator within the scene thus makes him both object and subject of the multiple gazes that constitute the scene, a proxy for the gazing lovers and a stand-in for the gazing readers. This doubling epitomizes the multiplicity of specular subject positions that the bachelor narrator of this novel assumes.

VEILED SPECTACLES, MALE FETISHISM, AND THE STANDARD OF THE MEDUSA'S HEAD

Even those scenes and figures that the narrator might prefer to relegate to the sphere of the private are as much constituted by spectacular display as explicitly public scenes and figures. If the claim is made that the private/public distinction itself is constituted by the notion of the gaze, with the private imagined as an arena shielded from the gaze, an arena into which the gaze cannot enter, spectacular displays are particularly charged when they cross the imaginary lines demarcating the public and the private spheres. These transgressions demonstrate the actual nonseparation between these spheres. The boundary-crossing trajectory of the narrator's gaze also illuminates his voyeuristic habit of mind, his tendency to make a spectacle of the private even as he avows his horror at such an indiscretion.

The spectacle of the private is emphasized in the two episodes that immediately precede the novel's climax. When the narrator accompanies Natalia to Peter Ivanovitch's hotel in search of Razumov, he is privy to a tableau of revolutionary conspiracy, his "glance leaving them [the gathered revolutionists] all motionless in their varied poses." He explains to readers that he later learned about their abortive plot from newspaper articles: "And while my eyes scanned the imperfect disclosures (in which the world was not much interested) I thought that the old, settled Europe had been given in my person attending that Russian girl something like a *glimpse behind the scenes*" (p. 309; emphasis mine). When they arrive back at the Haldin apartment, the narrator gets a second, different glimpse:

The thought that the real drama of autocracy is not played on the great stage of politics came to me as, fated to be a spectator, I had this other *glimpse behind the scenes*, something more profound than the words and gestures of the *public play*. I had the certitude that this mother refused in her heart to give her son up after all. It was more than Rachel's inconsolable mourning, it was something deeper, more inaccessible in its frightful tranquillity. Lost in the ill-defined mass of the high-backed chair, her white, inclined profile suggested the contemplation of something in her lap, as though a beloved head were resting there.

I had this *glimpse behind the scenes*, and then Miss Haldin, passing by the young man, shut the door. (p. 316; emphasis mine)

The figures in these *tableaux vivants* – the revolutionists plotting in their hotel room, the mother grieving in her armchair, the lovers locked in each other's gaze – are not in a "public play" yet they are still performing, even "behind the scenes." The realm of the private is the locus of authenticity, but the real is still a "real drama," and thus depends upon the gaze of a spectator. In "play[ing] [the] part of helpless spectator," in his "character of a mute witness" (p. 314), the narrator participates in the drama that plays out the private truth behind the public performance.[31]

The narrator's setting of the climactic scene heightens our sense of the private apartment as a realm of theatrical performance:

The ante-room had a row of books on the wall nearest to the outer door, while against the wall opposite there stood a dark table and one chair. The paper, bearing a very faint design, was all but white. The light of an electric bulb high up under the ceiling searched that clear square box into its four bare corners, crudely, without shadows – a strange stage for an obscure drama. (pp. 318–19)

The narrator describes the room as if he were a playwright providing directions for a play's setting, then self-reflexively comments on his rhetorical mimicry. His behind-the-scenes glimpse of Mrs. Haldin in her armchair also contributes to his construction of the scene as a kind of stage set. Mrs. Haldin, while concealed from sight throughout the climactic scene, is not sitting in the wings, off-stage. Rather, her placement in the drawing-room, concealed behind the door to the ante-room, corresponds to the use of "discovery" scenes in Elizabethan and Restoration drama. The drop curtain at the back of the stage would be lifted at the play's climax, "discovering," for example, a pair of illicit lovers *in flagrante delicto* or the supposedly dead heroine resurrected as a living statue.[32] The "discovery" is a spectacular scene-behind-the-scenes, hiding what is private but nevertheless destined for a spectacular dénouement that may bring either comic justice or romantic reunion.

The narrator leads Natalia into the hidden drawing-room just after Razumov has confessed his betrayal to her in the anteroom. Again we get a glimpse of the grieving mother at the far end of the room – "the profile of Mrs. Haldin, her hands, her whole figure had the stillness of a sombre painting" (p. 329) – her "stillness" making her into a sort of uncanny still life. A shift of perspective follows Razumov's self-denunciation, with the movement of the narrator and Natalia from the anteroom to the drawing-room. The narrator now looks downstage from within the "discovery" scene rather than looking upstage into this hidden chamber:

After assisting Miss Haldin to the sofa, I turned round to go back and shut the door. Framed in the opening, in the searching glare of the white ante-room, my eyes fell on Razumov, still there, standing before the empty chair, as if rooted for ever to the spot of his atrocious confession . . . I stared at the broad line of his shoulders, his dark head, the amazing immobility of his limbs. (pp. 328–9)

The behind-the-scenes scene has become the site of the spectator, a place from which the narrator looks, rather than the ultimate sight, the ultimate object of this spectator's gaze. If the narrator shares the "immobility" of the betrayer, he also shares the perspective of the traumatized woman who gazes out from within the "discovery" of betrayal. At this moment, "looking on" is hardly a position of power, but rather one of helpless, incapacitated shock. The onlooker participates in this horrifying drama but is unable to interrupt it, unable to stop the show or to walk out. It is a scene that conjures up horror movies or nightmares – appalling yet irresistible, at once paralyzing and transfixing: "And I observed them. There was nothing else to do" (p. 322).[33]

This scene had begun with Natalia removing, then dropping, her veil. After his devastating confession, Razumov takes Natalia's veil and flees, an act that departs from the traditional curtain call but nevertheless effectively concludes his performance of the private scene:

At his feet the veil dropped by Miss Haldin looked intensely black in the white crudity of the light. He was gazing at it spell-bound. Next moment, stooping with an incredible, savage swiftness, he snatched it up and pressed it to his face with both hands. Something, extreme astonishment perhaps, dimmed my eyes, so that he seemed to vanish before he moved.

The slamming of the outer door restored my sight, and I went on contemplating the empty chair in the empty ante-room. The meaning of what I had seen reached my mind with a staggering shock. (p. 329)

While the veil may contribute to the "staging" of the climax, its meaning is more complex, even though the narrator's spoken response to the "meaning of what I had seen" belies such complexity: "'That miserable wretch has carried off your veil!' I cried, in the scared deadened voice of an awful discovery. 'He...'" (p. 329). This ejaculation is ludicrously insufficient to the paralyzing scene that has just taken place before his eyes. The narrator functions here as a Chorus figure, as a representative of the audience who stands on stage and reacts expressively and instructively to the tragedy he has witnessed, but his response reveals his unsuitability for the part. Of course, his inarticulate, off-target reaction to the crisis of this tragedy may indicate his identification with the heroine's horror and shock rather than simply demonstrating his obtuseness.[34] But his exclamation has a metaphorical signification that resonates with meaning, even if it does not fully redeem the narrator's acuteness of insight or his facility with language. Quite transparently, Natalia's purloined veil is a symbol, an explicit symbol of symbolic figuration, a signifier of artistic or linguistic signification.

The status of the veil as a signifier of signification is suggested when Razumov wraps Natalia's veil around his completed manuscript, the manuscript that forms the basis of the narrative, after the language teacher receives it from Natalia, its original recipient. This textual relay literalizes the notion of a chain or play of signification characterizing textual transmission. Implicit in Razumov's "veiling" of his manuscript is also the notion of language, or narrative, as a veil that simultaneously conceals and reveals the truth or the true story, the "word that could stand at the back of all the words covering the pages" (p. 105). Language or narrative as a veil is further suggested by the narrator's description of the dropped veil as "intensely black in the white crudity of the light" (p. 329), like black print on a white page. The veil wrapping Razumov's manuscript metonymically suggests that the narrator serves as a kind of veil for Razumov, as a filter or lens that transmits, however dimly, this Eastern drama to Western eyes.

The rhetorical doublings of the narration described in the previous section of the chapter suggest the uncanniness of the narration-as-veil, an uncanniness that Marjorie Garber seems to be describing in her account of the "permeable boundary" of the veil as "a borderline between denial or repression on the one hand and sexual fantasy on the other, projecting both desire and its interdiction in the same figure."[35] As this description of the antithetical or paradoxical significations of narration-as-veil suggests, this figure of figuration, this Ur-symbol cannot be fully separated from its gendered and sexual meanings. As Garber emphasizes in her *Vested Interests*, "the veil as a sign of the female or the feminine has a long history in Western culture, whether its context is religious chastity (the nun, the bride, the orthodox Muslim woman) or erotic play (the Dance of the Seven Veils)." Garber's caveat about the dangers of reductive presuppositions about the gendered functions of the veil – "that it is worn to mystify, to tantalize, to sacralize, to protect, or put out of bounds"[36] – is well worth keeping in mind when we consider that, in *Under Western Eyes*, the unveiling of the truth of Razumov's betrayal coincides with the literal unveiling of the heroine:

While speaking she raised her hands above her head to untie her veil, and that movement displayed for an instant the seductive grace of her youthful figure, clad in the simplest of mourning. In the transparent shadow the hat rim threw on her face her grey eyes had an enticing lustre. Her voice, with its unfeminine yet exquisite timbre, was steady, and she spoke quickly, frank, unembarrassed. As she justified her action by the mental state of her mother, a spasm of pain marred the generously confiding harmony of her features. (pp. 322–3)

It may seem odd that this scene of confession is punctuated by Natalia's unveiling since it is Razumov who discloses his true identity as betrayer behind his mask of loyal friend. Yet it is easy – perhaps too easy – to account for the significance of Natalia's unveiling. She, like Razumov, undergoes a major change in this climactic scene of dénouement: her experience can be compared to the passage from the naïveté of girlhood to the sexualized knowledge of womanhood. The veil and its lifting mark a threshold or *limen*, her initiation into a new phase of life; in a related idiom, her veil would be a symbolic *hymen* penetrated by Razumov's disclosure, and discarded because of her new, more complete knowledge. Thus Razumov's grand finale – in which he gazes "spell-bound" at the veil, kisses it, then "steals" it--consummates the conventional plot of seduction in which the seducer steals the heroine's virtue – represented by the hymen/veil – and abandons her to her fate. Here, the twist on the seduction plot is that the seducer attempts to save, rather than to ruin, the heroine by abandoning her; he runs off with her veil instead of with her. In this consummation, the veil is as much a replacement for as it is a representation of Natalia herself. The veil, we might say, serves as Natalia's "body double," protecting her from dangerous stunts and possibly also from indecent exposure.

While the interchangeability of Natalia and the veil can be justified in the logic of Razumov's attempt to revise the seduction plot, this very justification obscures what nevertheless remains troubling about the unveiling of the heroine: the self-disclosure of the hero coincides with an exposure of the heroine. This double exposure is compulsory because Razumov's last-minute revision of his plot fails. His attempt to substitute the veil for Natalia herself, and to run off with it rather than her, is doomed because he has already stolen her innocence, initiated her into a knowledge that is concomitant with betrayal. A related explanation can be found in the narrator's "way of looking on." Although at the climax of the scene he looks out from within the Haldin women's private chamber upon Razumov in the anteroom, for the most part the narrator shares Razumov's perspective, turning his gaze upon Natalia and the spectacle of her disabusement. In other words, the narrator's description of Natalia removing her veil is typical of his attention to her. In his description of her, she is fragmented, catalogued into a collection of attributes: her figure, her eyes, her voice. His awareness of "the generously confiding harmony of her features," and even the disfiguring "spasm of pain" that "marred" this harmony suggests his aestheticizing appraisal of the total effect, as well as his fetishizing attention to her parts. The narrator's attention to Natalia's "parts" transforms the removal of her veil into a virtual striptease, an archetypal dance of the seven veils. The "transparent shadow" cast by her yet unremoved hat gives her eyes their "enticing lustre"; the gesture of unveiling displays the "seductive grace" of her figure. His characterization of her voice in the passage as "unfeminine, yet exquisite" – like his emphasis elsewhere on the "exquisite virility" (p. 145) of her grip – also contributes to his fetishization of her.

The narrator's eroticized fixation on Natalia's body parts and his conception of her as "unfeminine" or "masculine" signal her status as a fetish. There is a connection, moreover, between his fetishization of her and the rhetorical "doubling" characteristic of his narration: his way of simultaneously knowing and not-knowing the object of his desire, his way of avowing and disavowing his very desire. The narrator's portrayal of Natalia as a "phallic woman," his representation of her as having phallic qualities or even as being herself a phallus, can be understood both as a performance of self-reassurance and as a display of anxiety, a simultaneous denial and confirmation of the inevitability of loss.[37] For

Freud, of course, the fetish is an anxiety-reducing representation of the maternal phallus, although even for Freud castration was not the only loss warded off by the fetish. Hal Foster reminds us that "many losses or separations (from the womb, the breast, the feces...) precede the hypothetical sighting of castration – even if they are understood as such only retrospectively through this optic."[38] Even when this sighting of castration is "hypothetical," imaginary, or merely metaphorical, the visual or spectacular has a privileged, if ambivalent, status in Freudian and Freudian-influenced accounts of fetishism. Most prominent among these is Lacan's reading of the gaze and his theory that "[the phallus] can play its role only when veiled."[39] This emphasis on occluded specularity provides a framework for understanding the narrator's momentary blindness when Razumov steals Natalia's veil: "Something, extreme astonishment perhaps, dimmed my eyes, so that he seemed to vanish before he moved. The slamming of the outer door restored my sight" (p. 329). If Natalia is imagined by the narrator as a kind of Salome figure, a phallic woman or even a boy in woman's clothing performing an erotic striptease, then the removal of her last veil must remain undescribed, undescribable.[40]

The fetishistic demand for perfection in the object of the gaze, a demand that compels the fetishist both to look and also to avert his eyes, provides us with a window onto the narrator's aestheticizing "way of looking" and also onto Razumov's way of looking.[41] Although Razumov is described as "looking down" during this scene of unveiling, he nevertheless listens to Natalia's voice with the "air of a man who is listening to a strain of music rather than to articulated speech" (p. 323), an aesthetic appreciation similar to the narrator's aestheticizing visual delectation of the "harmony" of her features. Razumov's fetishistic appreciation of Natalia as an art object is further delineated in the "translated" fragment of his written confession which is imbedded in the narrative:

You were defenceless – and soon, very soon, you would be alone . . . I thought of you. Defenceless. For days you have talked with me – opening your heart. I remembered the shadow of your eyelashes over your grey trustful eyes. And your pure forehead! It is low like the forehead of statues – calm, unstained. It was as if your pure brow bore a light which fell on me, searched my heart and saved me from ignominy, from ultimate undoing. And it saved you too. (p. 333)

Razumov's attention to the "shadow of your eyelashes over your grey trustful eyes" recalls the narrator's own fixation on the veiling effect on

Natalia's eyes produced by "the transparent shadow the hat rim threw on her face." Razumov's simile, moreover, unveils Natalia as a kind of statue, figuratively putting her up on a pedestal as a monument of truth, goodness, inspiration. He envisions her "light" as having an instructive character-building influence, presumably like the influence of classical statuary on its viewers. Her radiant energy powers his conversion narrative; Razumov exposes himself to art – the highest art that is no art but sheer artlessness, sheer truth – and its influence compels him to expose the truth about himself. In this sequence, the hero's self-exposure does not cause the exposure of the heroine, but vice versa: with her "pure brow" shining out in the darkness like a searchlight or a light-house, the heroine must be seen in order that the hero can be inspired to save himself by confessing the truth.

In his written confession, Razumov envisions Natalia as a statue; his spoken confession which immediately precedes the placement in the text of the "translated" fragment of his manuscript also metamorphoses her, first into stone and then into ice. In the early part of the confession scene, it is Razumov who "look[s] as if his heart were lying as heavy as a stone in that unwarmed breast of which he spoke" (p. 320), and who speaks with "strangely lifeless" (p. 326) and "colourless lips" (p. 327). Yet as Natalia gradually becomes aware that something is gravely wrong with the scene that Razumov is making, "she seemed turned into stone" (p. 327) and in the final words of the scene she reports that she "feel[s] my heart becoming like ice" (p. 329). The petrifying effect of his confession to her, a confession spurred by his aestheticizing view of her, is apparent in this narrative sequence.

Razumov's petrification of Natalia has more than a little in common with the narrator's way of looking at her. Indeed, the freezing-over of the heroine before Razumov's eyes recalls an earlier episode in which the narrator rhetorically indicts himself for a "crime" of disclosure, thereby aligning himself with Razumov and his crime. Having discovered the arrest of Victor Haldin in an English newspaper, the narrator feels torn between concealing and revealing the bad news, between the moral and emotional ramifications that either action must have:

It was quite enough to give me a sleepless night. I perceived that it would have been a sort of treason to let Miss Haldin come without preparation upon the journalistic discovery which would infallibly be reproduced on the morrow by French and Swiss newspapers. I had a very bad time of it till the morning, wakeful with nervous worry and nightmarish with the feeling of being mixed up with something theatrical and morbidly affected. The incongruity of such a complication in those two women's lives was sensible to me all night in the form of absolute anguish. It seemed due to their refined simplicity that it should remain concealed from them for ever. Arriving at an unconscionably early hour at the door of their apartment, I felt as if I were about to commit an act of vandalism ... (p. 139)

Breaking the bad news to the Haldin women, however gently, feels like "vandalism," but forestalling their discovery of it indefinitely would be "treason." As Razumov does later on, the narrator tries to spare Natalia by disclosing the truth before she discovers it under more traumatic circumstances, but he also wants to be the one to penetrate her veil of ignorance. The narrator's chivalrously protective strategy, like Razumov's attempt to save Natalia from himself, inevitably contributes to the plot that transforms the heroine into stone: "I pulled the paper out of my pocket. I did not imagine that a number of the *Standard* could have the effect of Medusa's head. Her face went stony – her eyes – her limbs. The most terrible thing was that being stony she remained alive. One was conscious of her palpitating heart" (p. 140). Like Razumov's silent pressing of his "denunciatory finger to his breast" (p. 328), the narrator's gesture with the newspaper signifies the true story to Natalia without words. When no news is good news, the mere sight of the newspaper is enough to produce horror in the viewer. Here the newspaper, like Natalia's veil, is a symbol not only of truth, but also a symbol that stands for representation itself, the very mediation or dissemination of "the news."

But why is the Medusa's head the "Standard" that this narrator bares/bears? The Medusa's head, like the newspaper in this passage, is a complex symbol associated with artistic representation and with spectacular visual representation in particular. For example, the winged horse, Pegasus, is said to have sprung from the Medusa's severed neck and with his hoof to have opened the Pierian Spring, the haunt of the muses; the shield of Perseus, as discussed further below, is considered a prototype of image-making, the mirror of art which allows one to look on the terrible through a displaced image, or reflection, and live.[42] And like the symbol of the veil discussed earlier, the Medusa's head is also a symbol that resonates with multiple, heterogenous, and self-contradictory gendered and sexual connotations: the phallic, snaky locks on the female, severed head both confirm and deny the threat of castration. Donatello vividly renders this ambiguity or doubleness by giving his Perseus and his Medusa's head the same face, as does Caravaggio who makes his Medusa a young boy.[43]

Freud's 1922 interpretation of the Medusa's head also elucidates the uncanny elements of the myth and their significance for gender identity and sexuality.[44] For Freud, the snakes signify both penises and the pubic hair surrounding the vagina, both male and female genitalia. For Freud and for his hypothetical little boy, female genitalia are tellingly imaginable only as an absence or a lack, as the castrated and castrating sex of the mother. These snakes, he posits, are horrifying because they suggest castration, but they also mitigate the horror of castration because they replace the penis. Similarly, the stiffness produced in the observer of the Medusa's head reveals to Freud the viewer's horror of castration, but also stands as a reassurance of potency and thus uncastratedness.[45] For Freud, the viewer's transformation into stone paradoxically confirms both his castration/lack/deadness and his potency/non-lack/aliveness, an uncanny death-in-life or life-in-death that meshes compellingly with Conrad's narrator's horrified response to Natalia's horror: "The most terrible thing was that being stony she remained alive."

This uncanny death-in-life aligns Natalia herself with Medusa. In some versions of the myth, it is the Medusa's return of the spectator's gaze, not just the mere sight of her, that is the source of horror. This version, remythologized by Hélène Cixous in her well-known "The Laugh of the Medusa," suggests that it is female subjectivity and female desire that paralyze the male spectator who expects, or demands, only female "objectivity."[46] But the scenario specifically evoked by the passage in *Under Western Eyes*, the image of the narrator pulling the newspaper out of his pocket like Perseus pulling Medusa's head out of his wallet, aligns Natalia primarily with the petrified male opponents whom Perseus conquers by brandishing his secret weapon, the head of Medusa. The narrator may wish to envision Natalia as Andromeda, the maiden in chains whom Perseus valiantly rescues and later marries, but here he portrays her as an adversary, even a rival, one whose enforced spectatorship is her doom. Like Perseus, the narrator plays the part of a spectator too, but a spectator who safely witnesses *someone else* witnessing a horrifying spectacle, a spectator who, in fact, sets up the scene and then looks on at its deadly effects.[47] His spectatorship does not rule out the possibility of identification – without his shield, he too would be petrified – but his spectatorship nonetheless makes him into a figure of violent aggression. His aggression is concomitant with his chivalrous protectiveness, even though it also conflicts with it.

The narrator's unveiling of the Medusa's head *to* Natalia and his unveiling *of* Natalia thus occur simultaneously; simultaneously, he makes her an abjected spectator and a fetishized spectacle. The figure of the Medusa's head in *Under Western Eyes* thus encapsulates the disavowed similarities between competing versions of male feminism as much as it recapitulates the avowed play of differences between male and female. The narrator's "way of looking on" simultaneously enables him and us to see and not to see, to be horrified and to be reassured, to come thrillingly close but also to keep a safe distance. His gaze transforms Natalia into stone, petrifies her, fetishizes her even while it also provides the occasion for identifying with her. But the woman with whom he can identify is only or almost only imaginable for him as a castrated man, hence his sympathetic, even hysterical, blindness when Razumov steals Natalia's veil.[48] The alternatives of protective paternalism and exploitive voyeurism thus leave a space, but a very small one, for a third mode, a masculinity that can truly imagine, that can at once identify with and desire, a feminine subjectivity.

The notion of the Medusa's head as a figure that denotes visual spectacle or even representation *per se* can also be brought to bear on the complex of conflicts that Conrad experienced as a Pole attempting to prove himself as an English author by writing about Russia, and as a male author known for his all-male ship-board stories attempting to write a popular novel centering on a heterosexual romance for an audience of female readers, all the while craving recognition as a high-cultural male artist among other male artists. The conflicts within and among sexual and national politics and aesthetics come together in the uncanny figure of the Medusa's head, a figure whose long-standing associations with artistic representation, with unruly women, and with revolution, were not lost on Conrad. Just as Natalia herself, more than Peter Ivanovitch or even Razumov, may be considered the bachelor narrator's truly uncanny double, so can we see the bachelor narrator as Conrad's own uncanny double, at once similar to and different from him in his expatriate, national, marital and gender identities: at once *heimlich* and *unheimlich*. Not only does the bachelor narrator represent the author's eyes and voice, but he also functions as the author's translucent veil and his polished shield. The bachelor narrator of *Under Western Eyes* represents Conrad's anxiety that something would be lost in translation.

CHAPTER 5

The necessary melancholy of bachelors: melancholy, manhood, and modernist narrative

This chapter is not about bachelor uncles, although it could have been. The bachelor uncle is a stock character in popular and literary writing of the nineteenth and twentieth centuries, a figure so prevalent that the 1850s *Harper's* story "Why My Uncle Was a Bachelor" might almost as plausibly have been entitled "Why My Bachelor Was an Uncle."[1] In fictional plots of inheritance and education, adoption and guardianship, illegitimate fatherhood and incest, the figure of the bachelor uncle registers the boundaries of normative bourgeois familial and sexual relations, as well as the permeability of those boundaries.[2] The function of the bachelor uncle as a threshold figure who marks by crossing the boundaries of familial and sexual normativity is evident, for example, in a 1908 *Putnam's Magazine* piece, entitled "The Necessary Melancholy of Bachelors." While the essay is amply substantiated with melancholy bachelors from history and literature – Shakespeare's Antonio, Lord Macaulay, Robert Burton, Thomas Gray, Oliver Goldsmith, and Charles Lamb are all brought forward as evidence – the narrative *mise en scène* also testifies to the essay's premise. It is no coincidence that the melancholy bachelor who narrates this essay is also a bachelor uncle.

The essay's narration is framed by a reported exchange between the bachelor uncle and his niece, who initiates the conversation by observing that money is necessary to bachelor comfort and therefore to bachelor happiness. Her uncle disagrees, maintaining that despite the fact that "[b]achelors ... are the most comfortable people in the world," they feel "a fundamental lack in the lack of responsible love ... [which] shows itself in a mild melancholy that may not be deeply marked, but that is persistent and clear enough."[3] The body of the essay does not, however, consist of their debate on this topic: when his niece "choos[es] not to follow my lead" on this "unpleasant" subject, the bachelor contines to speak "but in soliloquy, for she had turned to the piano. I did not choose ... to let her soft music woo me from my thoughts" (p. 695). His resistance to her "woo[ing]," musical and otherwise, is not absolute: he does momentarily "yield ... to the thoughts of the days she had made pleasant for me" and, in his closing lines, allows himself to be led back to happier thoughts:

Let us be charitable, therefore, and say that most men drift into bachelorhood, and that many have it thrust upon them. There are many, yes, very many causes. It is seldom the deliberate choice of any man – for which God be thanked.
    To which happy conclusion I was led by my gentle niece, who had sat down by my chair, and slipped her hand into mine. (p. 697)

The bachelor's "happy conclusion," illustrated with a drawing of the melancholy-miened bachelor uncle with his equally sober-faced niece seated by his knee, manifestly denies the possibility of adequate alternatives to marriage, that is, of styles of domesticity that are equal to yet different from married life. But in its evocation of the marital coupling of husband and wife or perhaps the familial dyad of father and daughter, the concluding vignette also tells a more complex story. By allowing himself to be led away from his morbid reveries in this moment of domestic affirmation, the narrating bachelor uncle complicates his claim that lack, and hence melancholy, is the inevitable and unmitigated portion of bachelors.

Although the narrator contends that the possession of "real, vital affection, and its responsibilities" (p. 696) distinguishes the lot of the married man from that of the bachelor, affection and responsibility seem equally intrinsic to bachelor life in this essay. For instance, the uncle instructs his niece that "[a] real bachelor ... needs a sympathetic little niece ... two maiden aunts to advise regarding investments, and a nephew whom he can advise regarding the conduct of his college course, and some married friends of his youth, the patronage of whose wives will teach him humility" (p. 695). As portrayed here, bachelorhood is sustained by a range of familial and quasi-familial affiliations, varying in their degree and kinds of reciprocity, dominance, even voluntariness. The emotional and relational variety *within* just one of the bachelor's non-marital affiliations is exemplified by the minuette of leading and being lead executed by the uncle and his niece in the narrative frame of the essay. Their domestic partnership is characterized by indulgences and renunciations, intimacies and distances, happy endings and melancholy moods. Their alliance is, moreover, familial but not nuclear; domestic but not marital; conducted between adults but not intragenerational; eroticized but not explicitly sexual. The uncle/niece pairing stands in this essay as an alternative to more conventional marital and familial domesticity, and also signifies the depressing "lack" of such alternatives: "To the elemental demand for simple and first-hand affection, the best possible response is a strong friendship or two that may be sincere, even beautiful, but that is lacking in a certain necessary vitality" (pp. 695–6). In short, the bachelor may accept certain substitutes for wife and marriage, but he must also reconcile himself to lack.

This essay's manifest connection of bachelorhood with lack, and of lack with melancholy, together with its ambivalent presentation of the bachelor uncle's and his niece's domestic coupling as a legitimate alternative to marital domesticity, inform our understanding of the popular and literary figure of the bachelor more generally. Of course, the "necessary melancholy" described in this essay is limited neither to fictional bachelor uncles nor even to bachelor figures more generally. It is one of the defining moods of a familiar strand of modernist writing. This modernist melancholia, a self-defining sense of pervasive loss coupled with a refusal to recognize that loss, different from the experience of grief and acceptance associated with normal mourning, is perhaps most famously articulated in Eliot's "The Lovesong of J. Alfred Prufrock." The vexed object relations of melancholia also shape the two-protagonist form which is a staple of modernist fiction. While double protagonists appear in a wide range of modernist novels – *Ulysses*'s Leopold Bloom and Stephen Daedalus, *Mrs. Dalloway*'s Mrs. Dalloway and Septimus Smith, even the double–voiced "I" of Gertrude Stein's *The Autobiography of Alice B. Toklas* come to mind – this configuration is particularly notable, and particularly melancholic, in three first-person bachelor-narrated modernist novels that bear the name of another man: *Lord Jim, The Good Soldier*, and *The Great Gatsby*.[4]

Much of the energy of these "off-centered" or ex-centric first-person narratives is expended in negotiating the honorific modifier: the greatness, goodness, or lordliness of the cipher-like antiheroes at the heart of these novels. Indeed, the primary anxiety of these novels' bachelor narrators is that their exemplars of authentic manhood may prove to be "hollow men," men whose outward form hides inward emptiness, or worse, a heart of darkness. The fear of a moral vacuum behind the facade is a preoccupation of modern life and modernist literature, but in these texts it insistently expresses itself, or is formed by, these bachelors' identification with and desire for other men. In these bachelor-narrated stories of the other man, gender trouble and epistemological trouble go hand in hand. The fragmentation, temporal displacements, and other formal elements that foreground the problem of interpretation register the ambivalent relation of the bachelor narrators to the men of their dreams. These male objects of the bachelors' identification and desire are all men with "soft spots"; the failure of these figures to live up to an heroic ideal ultimately reveals competing, and ultimately incompatible, models of manhood against which the narrators measure them. In *The Good Soldier* and *The Great Gatsby*, the desires of the titular heroes both invite and confound the narrators' attempts to canonize them, producing fault lines within their narratives. The narrators' repudiation of the sentimentality of their idols reveals the melancholic sense of masculine lack that inspires their narratives.

The unrealizable desire for oneness with the male other in Ford's and Fitzgerald's novels is prefigured in the quasi-familial affiliations that drive Conrad's *Chance* and *Lord Jim*. These Marlow-narrated texts influentially demonstrate the gap between idealized heroism and the realities of a modern world barren of adventures, a gap revealed in conflicts between men and between incompatible styles of manhood within individual male figures. Like Dowell's narration of Edward Ashburnham's story and like Nick Carraway's narration of Gatsby's story, Marlow's narration of Jim's story is fissured by the irreconciliability of vindication and indictment, commemoration and forgetting, intimacy and distance, and of homoerotic desire and its homophobic disavowal. Quasi-familial mentor figures in *Chance* contribute to our understanding of Marlow's performance as "good uncle" to Jim, a performance which figures within the novel's more pervasive reinvention of family and home life in terms of the racist and sexist evolutionary model of the "Family of Man." Anxiety about modern and male lack, and the melancholic response of incorporating, and hence failing to relinquish, the lost and abjected male object of identificatory desire, animates all of these bachelor narratives. The marking and crossing of boundaries between individuals and spheres characteristic of the bachelor narrator tradition thus engenders the more familiar tensions of modernist fiction, especially those between alienated subjectivity and intersubjective bonds.

THE BACHELOR NARRATOR AND THE "GOOD UNCLE":
CHANCE AND *LORD JIM*

Not until *Chance*, when Conrad revived Marlow for his swan song thirteen years after *Lord Jim*, is this most famous of Conrad's narrators explicitly identified as a bachelor. It is Marlow, in fact, who calls himself a "careless bachelor in farmhouse lodgings," a characterization that links him to such bachelor predecessors as Ik Marvel's comfortable yet slovenly bachelor-in-the-country in *Reveries*, Brontë's Lockwood as rural gentleman tenant, and Hawthorne's Coverdale as temporary farmhouse boarder and hotel-room habitué.[5] In describing himself with reference to his rented lodgings, Marlow evokes the uncertain status of the bachelor in relation to conventional married domesticity.

Tellingly, this moment of naming occurs at "The Tea Party" (the title of chapter 5), to which Marlow invites the married couple, Mr. and Mrs. Fyne. He issues the invitation in response to Mrs. Fyne's request for his advice on the delicate matter of how to prevent the marriage of her brother, Captain Roderick Anthony, to Flora, the novel's heroine and the daughter of the convicted bankrupt financier de Barral. Marlow explains the oddity of Mrs. Fyne's asking for his guidance in such family matters:

She had formed a very favourable opinion of my practical sagacity . . . This was the first I ever heard of it. I had never suspected that Mrs Fyne had taken the trouble to distinguish in me the signs of sagacity or folly . . . I prepared myself for the afternoon's hospitalities, calling in the farmer's wife and reviewing with her the resources of the house and the village. She was a helpful woman. But the resources of my sagacity I did not review. Except in the gross material sense of the afternoon tea I made no preparations for Mrs Fyne . . . It was impossible for me to make any such preparations. I could not tell what sort of sustenance she would look for from my sagacity. (*C*, pp. 118–20)

Continuing to lean heavily on the word "sagacity," Marlow sarcastically denies credit when Mrs. Fyne compliments him on the comfort of his lodgings:

"I engaged these rooms by letter without asking any questions. It might have been an abominable hole," I explained to her. "I always do things like that. I don't like to be bothered. This is no great proof of sagacity – is it? Sagacious people, I believe, like to exercise that faculty. I have heard that they can't even help showing it in the veriest trifles. It must be very delightful. But I know nothing of it. I think that I have no sagacity – no practical sagacity." (*C*, p. 121)

Marlow's emphatic denial of his own "practical sagacity" amounts to a verbal assault on Mrs. Fyne. Marlow's hostility towards Mrs. Fyne is based in part on his antipathy towards feminists; elsewhere in the novel he suggests his preference for the fine "privilege" of "femininity" over the coarse "attitude" of "feminism" (*C*, p. 127). His hostility towards her also reveals his resentment towards women more generally: "[f]or myself it's towards women that I feel vindictive mostly... Mainly I resent that pretence of winding us round their dear little fingers, as of right" (*C*, p. 131). But Marlow's attack stems most directly from his dislike of her snobbishly hypocritical wish to prevent a convict's daughter from marrying into her family. So intense is Mrs. Fyne's desire to exclude Flora that it drives her to the drastic measure of inviting Marlow into her domestic circle. Under normal circumstances, the Fynes would be no more likely to allow a "careless bachelor" a place of authority within the familial sanctum than they would be to allow a dog indoors.

The Fynes' dog – a recurrent motif in the novel that Henry James found particularly ludicrous[6] – serves here and throughout the text as an emblem of the exclusions of conventional domesticity, and particularly of Marlow's own uncertain place at the domestic tea table. The Fynes bring their dog to Marlow's tea party, but then tie him outside the house where he barks incessantly, making a noise "like stabs through one's brain."[7] Having "bribed the Fyne dog into some sort of self-control" with a piece of cake, Marlow asks Mr. Fyne "Why don't you let him come inside?":

Oh dear no! He couldn't think of it! I might indeed have saved my breath, I knew it was one of the Fynes' rules of life, part of their solemnity and responsibility, one of those things that were part of their unassertive but ever present superiority, that their dog must not be allowed in. It was most improper to intrude their dog into the houses of the people they were calling on – if it were only a careless bachelor in farmhouse lodgings and a personal friend of the dog. (*C*, p. 125)

The Fynes' bourgeois "rule of life" is a home rule that bars undesirables including dogs, bachelors, and convicts' daughters. In paying lip service to Mrs. Fyne's higher domestic authority – "[s]he was familiar and olympian, fenced in by the tea-table, that excellent symbol of domestic life in its lighter hour and its perfect security" (*C*, p. 132) – Marlow challenges both Mrs. Fyne and the "perfect security" she represents. Marlow resents her conventional domesticity not so much because it "fence[s]" her in, but because she hypocritically uses it to fence others out.

It is another "careless bachelor" who, with an apparent lack of self-control and a seeming disregard for propriety, casts Flora in the role of Mrs. Fyne's sister-in-law. Like Marlow himself, Mrs. Fyne's brother strikingly resembles the bachelor on the *Reveries* model, a likeness apparent in Marlow's description of him as "a man of long and ardent reverie wherein the faculty of sincere passion matures slowly in the unexplored recesses of the heart" (*C*, p. 273). Marlow's own *Reveries*-esque preference for sitting "feet up on the sill of an open window, a book in my hands and the murmured harmonies of wind and sun in my heart making an accompaniment to the rhythms of my author" (*C*, p. 63) is matched by Captain Anthony's habit of lying in the grass, smoking his pipe, and daydreaming away the hot summer days, a habit which provokes his nieces to "exchang[e] jeering remarks about 'lazy Uncle Roderick'" (*C*, p. 135). While Mrs. Fyne abhors the vice of Roderick's "amazing indolence" (*C*, p. 134), Marlow defends it as "the force of a contemplative temperament" (*C*, p. 135). His sedentary ways notwithstanding, this bachelor uncle acts swiftly when confronted with the suffering of the young woman described by Mrs. Fyne as "an orphan 'to a certain extent'" (*C*, p. 60). Although "he [is] actually too shy to get on terms with his own nieces" (*C*, p. 134), Uncle Roderick essentially adopts Flora de Barral, thereby enacting a version of that perennially favorite motif: "the bachelor and the baby."[8] Living up to his billing as "The Knight" (the title of part II of the novel), Roderick chivalrously rescues Flora first by marrying her and then by renouncing the sexual aspect of their relationship as a sign of his courtly devotion.

Marlow plays more of a supporting role in the drama of "The Damsel" (the title of part I) in distress. While Marlow is more vicarious in his engagement *with* Flora than Roderick is in his engagement *to* her, Marlow's performance as Flora's bachelor confidant is not without effect. Marlow is useful to Flora much as the bachelor narrator of *Under Western Eyes* is useful to Natalia Haldin: in his "way of looking on." Like the narrator of *Under Western Eyes*, Marlow is "a little ashamed" of his interest in the heroine's intimate disclosures, "as if listening to her I had taken advantage of having seen her poor, bewildered, scared soul without its veils" (*C*, p. 195). Also like the *Under Western Eyes* narrator, he indicts his own voyeurism – "to render myself justice without false modesty – I was anxious; anxious to know a little more" (*C*, p. 195) – yet also offers evidence in defense of this tendency. While he uses Flora's suffering for his vicarious pleasure, his proclivity for onlooking also saves her life: Flora abandons her suicide attempt when she sees that Marlow is watching her. Only after the event does Marlow discover, and in the next chapter does he reveal to the reader, that it is the Fynes' dog, not himself, whom Flora views as her true savior: "You see, she imagined the dog had become extremely attached to her. She took it into her head that he might fall over or jump down after her" (*C*, p. 172). The ironic deflation caused by this discovery does not, however, disrupt Marlow's aggrandizing self-image as a maiden-rescuing bachelor knight. Rhetorically distancing himself from damsel-eating dragons – "You needn't stare as though I were breathing fire and smoke out of my nostrils. I am not a woman-devouring monster" (*C*, p. 131), he tells the novel's unnamed external narrator – and also from the dog who is so "unchivalrous" (*C*, p. 47) as to desert Flora, Marlow tries to remain true to his assumed chivalrous role.

Driven both by his sense of moral obligation to Flora and by a vicarious interest in her suffering, Marlow appears two other times in the role of Flora's "chance confidant" (*C*, p. 201). The second occurrence is when Marlow keeps Flora company on the sidewalk while Mr. Fyne confronts Captain Anthony in his hotel room:

[O]f all the individuals who passed by none appeared to me or the moment so pathetic in unconscious patience as the girl standing before me; none more difficult to understand . . . but we two, strangers, as we really were to each other, had dealt with the most intimate and final of subjects, the subject of death. It had created a sort of bond between us. It made our silence weighty and uneasy. I ought to have left her there and then; but, as I think I've told you before, the fact of having shouted her away from the edge of a precipice seemed somehow to have engaged my responsibility as to this other leap. (*C*, pp. 177–8)

Marlow describes the "subject of [her intended] marriage" to Captain Anthony as another "intimate subject between us to lend more weight and more uneasiness to our silence" (*C*, p. 178). "This other leap," which literally refers to Flora's decision to elope, part of a pattern of "jumps" and "leaps" culminating in her ascension by rope from the deck of the sinking *Ferndale*, also recalls the leaps that mark the progress of the young protagonist of *Lord Jim*. Of course, Flora's "fine adventures" (*C*, p. 365) are rather different from Jim's: whereas Flora is abandoned by her guardians, Jim abandons ship; whereas Flora elopes with Captain Anthony, Jim leaps into a new life as Lord Jim. Each protagonist's misfortunes and opportunities are shaped by historically based gender differences. Just as the spectacular suffering of each protagonist takes place in differently gendered arenas, Marlow's performances as the "looker-on at a game" (*C*, p. 39) also vary according to gendered differences. For instance, Marlow observes that "you can't buttonhole familiarly a young girl as you would a young fellow" (*C*, p. 178), a comment which suggests that confidential male–female relations of the sort he shares with Flora are less simple, both less candid and less comfortable, than male-male ones of the kind he has with Jim.

Yet the dynamics of intimacy between older men and younger men in these novels are far from simple. We see the complexities of intimacy between older and younger men in the cross-generational relationships of "Young Powell," Jim's other counterpart, beside Flora, in *Chance*. The novel begins with Powell's lengthy retrospective narration to Marlow and the frame narrator of how he got his "real start in life" (*C*, p. 30). Unable to obtain an officer's berth after passing the arduous seamanship examination, Young Powell turns for help to a "Mr Powell in the Shipping Office" (*C*, p. 18), a stranger who coincidentally bears the same name as himself. When Captain Anthony suddenly appears at the Shipping Office in urgent need of a replacement for his injured second mate, Old Powell coolly offers him the young man standing by, referring to him familiarly as "Charles." After Anthony signs him on and leaves, Young Powell scrupulously attempts to clear up what he thinks has been Old Powell's, and not just Captain Anthony's, misunderstanding: "I believe the captain of the *Ferndale* was thinking all the time that I was a relation of yours."

"Did he?" says he. "That's funny, because it seems to me too that I've been a sort of *good uncle* to several of you young fellows lately. Don't you think so yourself? However, if you don't like it you may put him right – when you get out to sea." At this I felt a bit queer. Mr Powell had rendered me a very good service – because it's a fact that with us merchant sailors the first voyage as officer is the real start in life. He had given me no less than that. I told him warmly that he had done more for me that day than all my relations put together ever did. (*C*, p. 30; emphasis mine)

As his "good uncle," Old Powell initiates Young Powell into his new life as an officer. Nepotism is the familial sign under which Old Powell advances Young Powell's career, but the defining trait of their relationship is its quasi-familiality or even its non-familiality.

Young Powell tells Old Powell that he has done more for him "than all my relations put together ever did," yet Young Powell has not been entirely without familial support. He mentions to Marlow that the only living relation he had at that time, the only person he needs to visit before shipping out, was an aunt "who quarrelled with poor father as long as he lived about some silly matter that had neither right nor wrong to it. She left her money to me when she died. I used always to go and see her for decency's sake" (*C*, p. 32). His aunt gratuitously helped him in the past as his "good uncle" does now, yet Powell emphasizes the difference between intercessions on his behalf by his family of origin and those performed by his new, adoptive family of choice: the all-male, quasi-family of the Mercantile Marine. The figure of the newly appointed officer who must visit his aunt before shipping out recalls Marlow at the beginning of *Heart of Darkness*. In that novel, however, it is the aunt herself who provides the nepotistic connection. Marlow is dismayed to find himself turning for help to a family member, and a female relative to boot: "Then – would you believe it – I tried the women. I, Charlie Marlow, set the women to work – to get a job! Heavens!"[9]

The Shipping Office episode of *Chance* thus provides Young Charles Powell with more than one quasi-familial "namesake" (*C*, p. 31): Powell the elder *and* Charles (Marlow) the elder.[10] Powell undergoes initiation by a good uncle not once, but twice in the novel: in the first chapter Old Powell gives him a needed leg up into his officer's berth, and in the last chapter Old Charlie pushes him to propose marriage to the widowed Flora. Of course, Marlow is more a peer of Powell's than his mentor – this confirmed bachelor can hardly initiate another old bachelor into the mysteries of marriage. Marlow does return in this final episode as Flora's confidant and domestic advisor, urging her to encourage Powell to propose and to accept him. This act of intercession is relatively unambivalent, although there is a suggestion in the external narrator's "sarcastic manner" of grinning that Marlow is visiting upon these two just what he wouldn't want for himself. Without question, he is promoting the institution of marriage while avoiding it himself. Yet, in doing this service for Powell and Flora, Marlow seems motivated by the vicarious pleasure of generosity, not sadism.

Greater ambivalence is apparent in Old Powell's mentoring of Young Powell, or at least Marlow suggests that one might interpret his actions this way. When Powell retrospectively describes Old Powell's intercession on his behalf as an "uncommonly kind" act, Marlow retorts:

He did what he could ... and on his own showing that was not a very great deal. I cannot help thinking that there was some malice in the way he seized the opportunity to serve you. He managed to make you uncomfortable. You wanted to go to sea, but he jumped at the chance of accommodating your desire with a vengeance. I am inclined to think your cheek alarmed him. And this was an excellent occasion to suppress you altogether. (*C*, pp. 31–2)

Marlow suspects "some malice" in Old Powell's seeming lack of fore-thought. In so precipitously fulfilling Young Powell's desire for initi-ation, Old Powell may have been motivated by a desire "to suppress" an alarmingly aggressive neophyte. "[A]ccommodating your desire with a vengeance," Marlow suggests, is a covertly hostile act; it is a way, just short of refusing him, to dispose of this young upstart. Young Powell rejects this interpretation, although he does "admit it was something like telling a man that you would like a bath, and in consequence being instantly knocked overboard to sink or swim" (*C*, pp. 31–2).

As Young Powell's comment suggests, professional initiation into the "secret society" (*C*, p. 45) of the Mercantile Marine, and particularly into that inner circle of officers who have "got a ship" (*C*, p. 18), creates quasi-fraternal and quasi-filial bonds which encompass both affection and hostility, dependence and self-reliance, equality and hierarchy. The intimate bond between initiator and initiate both binds *and* liberates, a paradox vividly exemplified by Conrad's "The Secret Sharer," as dis-cussed in the previous chapter. Part of the danger of male–male inti-macy, of course, resides in its association with homoerotic desire, a danger that grew more intense with the late nineteenth-century illegaliz-ation of homosexual activities and the pathologizing and popularizing of homosexuality as a cultural identity. The longstanding association of the pedagogue with the pederast, and later with the emergent nineteenth-century type of the pedophile, only compounded the threat of ho-moerotic desire in quasi-avuncular relations.[11]

For all of these reasons, it is not surprising that Marlow equates the desire to get a job for a young man with the desire to get rid of him. But in *Chance*, as in *Lord Jim* where Marlow himself takes responsibility for getting a younger man a position, such intercessional acts enable the mentor both to get rid of his young man and also to keep him. The bond of intimacy between initiator and initiate is paradoxically predicated on the initiate's attainment, whether gradual or sudden, of greater author-ity and ultimately of greater independence from the initiator. Thus, as much as Marlow wishes to help Jim to get and keep a position, Marlow also wants

to get him out of the way; out of his own way, be it understood. That was our main purpose, though, I own, I might have had another motive which had influenced me a little. I was about to go home for a time; and it may be I desired, more than I was aware of myself, to dispose of him – to dispose of him, you understand – before I left. (*LJ*, pp. 205–6)

The literal distance between them, however, enables rather than precludes their bond. Thus Marlow experiences his most "real and profound intimacy" with Jim at the moment that he thinks they are parting company forever:

Jim and I, alone as it were, to leeward of the mainsail, clasped each other's hands and exchanged the last hurried words. My heart was freed from that dull resentment which had existed side by side with interest in his fate ... On that occasion the sort of formality that had been always present in our intercourse vanished from our speech; I believe I called him "dear boy," and he tacked on the words "old man" to some half-uttered expression of gratitude, as though his risk set off against my years had made us more equal in age and in feeling ... He exerted himself to soothe me as though he had been the more mature of the two. (*LJ*, p. 220)

Having been identified by Marlow several pages earlier as "my very young brother" (*LJ*, p. 207), Jim undergoes an accelerated rhetorical maturation in this passage, rapidly progressing from being a "dear boy," to "equal in age," to "the more mature of the two." The new maturity that Marlow attributes to Jim signals the easing of the "resentment" that Marlow feels against Jim. Marlow is able to feel closer to a Jim who can take care of himself, a Jim who is on the verge of going away for good.

The distant intimacies of Marlow's role as "good uncle" to Jim are reinforced by Marlow's sharing with other men the open secret of Jim's past and the responsibility for finding him employment. The first in this series of secret sharers is an unnamed friend whom Marlow describes as "a cynical, more than middle-aged bachelor, with a reputation for eccentricity" (*LJ*, p. 179). This bachelor takes Jim on, first as an employee in his rice-mill and then as a housemate:

"Not having been able so far to find more in my heart than a resigned toleration for any individual of my kind, I have lived till now alone in a house that even in this steaming climate could be considered as too big for one man. I have had him to live with me for some time past. It seems I haven't made a mistake." It seemed to me on reading this letter that my friend had found in his heart more than tolerance for Jim ... (*LJ*, p. 180)

Like Captain Anthony with Flora, this bachelor virtually adopts Jim as he would a child; as Jim tells Marlow later, "I was called Mr. James there as if I had been the son" (*LJ*, p. 182). The bachelor also takes Jim as a kind of child bride, at least in a metaphorical sense. This enactment of the "bachelor and the baby" plot is suggested by the bachelor's comparison of Jim to a girl: "Had he been a girl – my friend wrote – one could have said he was blooming – blooming modestly – like a violet, not like some of these blatant tropical flowers" (*LJ*, p. 180). Whether as a son or a lover, Jim and his youthful "freshness" (*LJ*, p. 180) rejuvenate this old bachelor:

> He had been in the house for six weeks, and had not as yet attempted to slap him on the back, or address him as "old boy," or try to make him feel a superannuated fossil... "The dew is yet on him, and since I had the bright idea of giving him a room in the house and having him at meals I feel less withered myself. The other day he took it into his head to cross the room with no other purpose but to open a door for me; and I felt more in touch with mankind than I had for years. Ridiculous isn't it?" (*LJ*, p. 180)

While Jim's respectful solicitude puts the old bachelor back "in touch with mankind," his sudden departure breaks the spell and returns the bachelor to his characteristic cynicism, a reversion to type indicated in his next letter to Marlow: "Allow me to say, lest you should have some more mysterious young men in reserve, that I have shut up shop, definitely and for ever" (*LJ*, p. 181). "Shutting up shop" nicely captures the emotional and professional nuances of the bachelor's disappointment in both Jim and Marlow.

The last "good uncle" with whom Marlow shares the open secret of Jim's past and consults about his future is Stein, a "solitary, but not misanthropic" (*LJ*, p. 195) widower who, like Marlow's bachelor friend before him, takes Jim into his house. But Stein's house is, as Marlow points out, really his business: "[h]is 'house' (because it was a house, Stein & Co.)" (*LJ*, p. 191). In helping Marlow to help Jim, Stein revisits his own past and thereby fulfills his own sense of filial and professional obligation: "Stein characteristically enough had a sentimental motive. He had a notion of paying off (in kind, I suppose) the old debt he had never forgotten ... [of] passing on to a young man the help he had received in his own young days" (*LJ*, pp. 212–13). Marlow recounts the story of how Stein had gotten his start in Patusan from an "old Scotsman, the only white man allowed to reside in the country at the time":

> I often heard Stein relate how that chap, who was slightly paralysed on one side, had introduced him to the native court a short time before another stroke carried him off... He dragged his leg, thumping with his stick, and grasped Stein's arm, leading him right up to the couch. "Look, queen, and you rajahs,

this is my son," he proclaimed in a stentorian voice. "I have traded with your fathers, and when I die he shall trade with you and your sons."

By means of this simple formality Stein inherited the Scotsman's privileged position and all his stock-in-trade, together with a fortified house on the banks of the only navigable river in the country. (*LJ*, pp. 193–4)

Filial succession is rather less simple among the people of Patusan themselves. In the outbreak of civil unrest after the queen's death, Stein "join[s] the party of a younger son," Mohammed Bonso, and fights to defend the sovereignty of this ally who is also, once Stein marries his princess sister, a brother-in-law. And comparable "wonderful adventures" (*LJ*, p. 194) of war are replayed in the next generation by Jim and Dain Waris, his own native ally and counterpart.

The advent of fratricidal war in Patusan suggestively coincides with the flowering of brotherly love between individual native leaders and the European men who come as colonialists to live among and trade with them. Predictably, Marlow emphasizes the opportunities for equality and reciprocity, not just for hierarchy and exploitation, presented by these interracial bonds. He tellingly characterizes the quasi-fraternal camaraderie that unites Jim to Dain Waris as "one of those strange, profound, rare friendships between brown and white, in which the very difference of race seems to draw two human beings closer by some mystic element of sympathy." He explains that "mystic element": "I seemed to behold the very origin of friendship. If Jim took the lead, the other had captivated his leader. In fact, Jim the leader was a captive in every sense. The land, the people, the friendship, the love, were like the jealous guardians of his body. Every day added a link to the fetters of that strange freedom" (*LJ*, p. 236). The oxymoronically fettered freedom of Jim's attachment to his adopted homeland evokes the distant intimacies of the quasi-familial, good uncle guardians, and the paradoxical status of home more generally in this novel.

In describing Jim and Dain Waris's quasi-fraternal bond, Marlow rhetorically makes their friendship into the "origin of friendship" itself, into a kind of missing link to an imaginary prehistorical past. He also sees Dain Waris himself as a missing link or simply as an atavism: "Such beings open to the Western eye, so often concerned with mere surfaces, the hidden possibility of races and lands over which hangs the mystery of unrecorded ages" (*LJ*, p. 232). In other words, when Jim emerges from the "soft and sticky mudbank" in Patusan, the new life into which he is symbolically reborn is, in fact, timelessly old: not merely traditional in its family orientation, but primeval. As Dain Waris's brother, Jim is reaffiliated with a new family which is the "primitive" Family of Man. Such a reinvention of home life via the social Darwinist evolutionary and anthropological model of the Family of Man is a staple of late nineteenth- and early twentieth-century male adventure romance.

Despite the shift, persuasively described by Edward Said, in late Victorian and modern European culture from "filiation" (familial relations) to "affiliation" (non-familial relations), filiation persists in adventure romance and in colonialist fictions more generally as "a metaphoric afterimage." Anne McClintock uses this evocative term to characterize the insistent projection of the anachronistic, naturalized image of the family onto emerging affiliative institutions of the late nineteenth-century, a projection that served to naturalize the policy and practices of "new orders of industrial bureaucracy, nationalism, and colonialism."[12] McClintock elucidates the ways that the naturalized image of the Family of Man suppresses the role of women, and particularly mothers, either by excluding them altogether or abstracting them as nature or as "dark continents." This reading gives point to *Lord Jim*'s use of quasi-fraternal and quasi-filial figures in its reconstitution of an effectively all-male family.[13] In her analysis of the imaginary constitution of an all-male family in the authorship, narration, and plotting of Rider Haggard's 1885 *King Solomon's Mines*, McClintock draws upon Macherey's insight that the trope of the journey to origins is "not a way of showing the absolute or beginning but a way of determining the genesis of order, of succession," a way of justifying the gendered and racial hierarchy of the Family of Man which is also operant in *Lord Jim*'s plotting and narration.[14] In *Lord Jim*, as in the adventure romance tradition more generally, home is not the literal point of origin but an imaginary vanishing point from which the ordering of the present and the justification of the future must be extrapolated.

The primeval origin, or home, to which Jim returns is uncanny, both *heimlich* and *unheimlich*. Patusan is *unheimlich* because it is not Jim's literal place of origin. Jim's sojourn in Patusan epitomizes, in fact, the "transcendental homelessness" that Georg Lukács describes as the defining condition of the modern Western mind. If going to Patusan is like being transported backwards in time, to "the original dusk of ... being" (*LJ*, p. 204), then it is also tantamount to being launched into outer space: "had Stein arranged to send him into a star of the fifth magnitude the change could not have been greater" (*LJ*, p. 203–4). A spatial and temporal remove of this magnitude is necessary for Jim to escape from what Marlow calls the "earthly failings" (*LJ*, p. 204) of his past.

Marianna Torgovnick contextualizes Lukács's theory by noting that it is no coincidence that "a state of exile – literal or metaphoric – often accompanies an interest in the primitive": "Whatever form the primitive's hominess takes, its strangeness salves our estrangement from ourselves and our culture."[15] One can too easily make the leap from this observation to Conrad's own exilic, expatriate, colonialist, and modernist subjectivity, finding in the novel's author a source, or origin, of his characters' transcendental homelessness.

The *unheimlich*, however, is only half of the uncanny – Patusan is also *heimlich*, strange in its very familiarity. Following Macherey's observation that the trope of the journey to origins "cannot be an exploration in the strict sense of the word but only discovery, retrieval of a knowledge already complete," McClintock notes that in *King Solomon's Mines* "the return to prehistory is not a moment of origin but rather the beginning of a historical return and regression for the journey has already been made."[16] If Jim discovers a new life of heroism in Patusan, it is because this new life resembles – repeats, but also revises – the old life he is trying to leave behind. Marlow, too, attempts to recover from the alienation of the present by returning to his own past, to the home which is England. For Marlow, as for Jim, home is uncanny, located both distantly beyond and intimately within:[17]

And then, I repeat, I was going home – to that home distant enough for all its hearthstones to be like one hearthstone, by which the humblest of us has the right to sit... [E]ven those for whom home holds no dear face, no familiar voice, – even they have to meet the spirit that dwells within the land, under its sky, in its air, in its valleys, and on its rises, in its field, in its waters and its trees – a mute friend, judge, and inspirer... I think it is the lonely, without a fireside or an affection they may call their own, those who return not to a dwelling but to the land itself, to meet its disembodied, eternal, and unchangeable spirit – it is those who understand best its severity, its saving power, the grace of its secular right to our fidelity, to our obedience. (*LJ*, p. 206)

Marlow envisions home both as a place and a person, but most importantly as an intangible yet inspiring "spirit," both within and beyond the lone wanderer. The paradoxical status of home for these "thousands" of wanderers is epitomized by Jim's affiliation with the "house" of Stein. In acknowledging Jim as "one of us," Marlow and Stein provide a quasifamilial source of non-abjected male selfhood whose effectiveness depends upon its ability to take Jim light-years away.

The "spirit" of home in the passage cited above bears a striking rhetorical resemblance to another "spirit" that Marlow describes earlier:

It is when we try to grapple with another man's intimate need that we perceive how incomprehensible, wavering and misty are the beings that share with us the sight of the stars and the warmth of the sun. It is as if loneliness were a hard and absolute condition of existence; the envelope of flesh and blood on which our eyes are fixed melts before the outstretched hand, and there remains only the capricious, unconsolable, and elusive spirit that no eye can follow, no hand can grasp. (*LJ*, p. 136)

The "disembodied, eternal, and unchangeable spirit" (*LJ*, p. 206) is the spirit of home and the "capricious, unconsolable, and elusive spirit" (*LJ*, p. 136) is the spirit of "another man." Both of these spirits are forceful yet ethereal, proximate but also definitively out of reach, self-defining yet located within an "incomprehensible" and untouchable other. The existential alienation evoked by both of these passages is grounded in an unrelieved and essentially unrelievable nostalgia for an imaginary past, a past associated with the concretely knowable, with domestic certainty, and with masculine integrity. Marlow's sense of an intolerable epistemological indeterminacy coincides with his recognition of "another man's intimate need" and the masculine lack that it signifies. Precisely because he is "fated never to see him clearly" (*LJ*, p. 221), Marlow is driven to tell the story of this other man: "I cannot say I had ever seen him distinctly – not even to this day, after I had my last view of him; but it seemed to me that the less I understood the more I was bound to him in the name of that doubt which is the inseparable part of our knowledge" (*LJ*, p. 206). Marlow contends that "for each of us going home must be like going to render an account" (*LJ*, p. 206), but his own fragmented and disrupted narrative account bears witness to the impossibility of a coherent rendering and an authentic return to origins.

Believing in Jim allows Marlow to retain membership, however tenuously, in a masculine community of belief, "an obscure body of men held together by a community of inglorious toil and by fidelity to a certain standard of conduct" (*LJ*, p. 80), a community whose very standards Jim's dishonor disrupts. The indiscernable yet "infernal alloy in [Jim's] metal" (*LJ*, p. 76) affronts the manly standard of conduct that Marlow wants to believe is absolute, non-negotiable, definitively not open to interpretation. It threatens the stability of the system of belief, and ultimately of signification or meaning, that Marlow assumes or quasi-inherits. Marlow's own affiliative self-definition as a "good uncle," as one who knows the right stuff when he sees it, is thereby undermined:

I liked his appearance; I knew his appearance; he came from the right place; he was one of us... He was the kind of fellow you would, on the strength of his looks, leave in charge of the deck – figuratively and professionally speaking. I say I would, and I ought to know. Haven't I turned out youngsters enough in my time, for the service of the Red Rag, to the craft of the sea... I would have trusted the deck to that youngster on the strength of a single glance... and it wouldn't have been safe. (*LJ*, pp. 74–6)

The undetected "soft spot, the place of decay" (*LJ*, p. 52) in Jim blights Marlow's manhood as well as Jim's: "If he had not enlisted my sympathies he had done better for himself – he had gone to the very fount and origin of that sentiment, he had reached the secret sensibility of my egoism" (*LJ*, p. 155). Motivated by a desire for self-preservation as much as by a sense of "jealous guardian"-ship (*LJ*, p. 236), Marlow affirms that Jim "achieved greatness," much as in *Heart of Darkness* he affirms that Kurtz was a "remarkable man": valiantly or perhaps desperately maintaining as true what he has seen and shown to be patently false.

The "sheer sentimentalism" (*LJ*, p. 206) of Marlow's affirmations is finally comparable to Jim's romanticism.[18] Where Jim fails to relinquish his faith in the realism of romance, Marlow doggedly maintains the fiction of masculine plenitude in the face of obvious masculine lack. Marlow fetishizes the suffering of his other men in the novels he narrates, simultaneously avowing and disavowing the loss to which his telling repeatedly returns. This bachelor's melancholy testimony insists upon the sovereignty of Lord Jim while exposing him as a pretender to the throne. Understanding the impossibility of "full utterance" and the fragmentary effect of his "stammerings," and recognizing that "there is never time to say our last word," Marlow pronounces his "last words about Jim" (*LJ*, pp. 208–9).

THE PENDULUM OF THE OTHER MAN: *THE GOOD SOLDIER* AND *THE GREAT GATSBY*

The ambivalent oscillation between avowing and disavowing another man's goodness, or even his greatness, links Conrad's turn-of-the-century *Lord Jim* to Ford's *The Good Soldier* (1915) and Fitzgerald's *The Great Gatsby* (1925). Critics have long noted the affinities among these writers and their novels; Ford and Fitzgerald themselves made a point of their indebtedness to Conrad.[19] My purpose here is not to trace the borrowings, obvious and obscure, among these writers although sometimes I will not be able to resist this temptation. Rather, my aim is to elucidate the striking similarities among these novels' articulations of melancholic longing for non-abjected manhood from the perspective of a bachelor narrator. These narrators and their narratives are melancholic, first, because the non-abjected, or heroic, manhood that they interminably lament never existed in the first place and hence can never come again. Melancholia is also their lot because their imaginary attempts to exalt an idealized manhood are confounded by their ambivalent repudiation of the other men whom they interminably mourn. Their ambivalence towards these other men is organized around the sentimentality they attribute to their lost male objects, a sentimentality that is at once the imaginary source and, paradoxically, the compromising affront to a whole and non-abjected manhood. The sentimental nostalgia of these narrators reveals their melancholic incorporation of their sentimental other men, an imaginary relation to these male figures which spurs their melancholic dreams of a return home and yet ensures these bachelor narrators' "transcendental homelessness."

The quasi-familial persists as a "metaphoric afterimage" projected onto the male-male affiliations in these bachelor-narrated novels as in Conrad's Marlow-narrated ones. John Dowell and Nick Carraway are less "bachelor uncles" to the other men of their narratives than metaphorical little brothers, who feel themselves both imposed upon and elevated by their responsibility for preserving the memory of their other men. In fact, Dowell explicitly compares his narrative's other man to "a large elder brother," though his erotic identification with Edward Ashburnham crosses over from filiation into the realm of shared identity:

> For I can't conceal from myself the fact that I loved Edward Ashburnham – and that I love him because he was just myself. If I had the courage and the virility and possibly also the physique of Edward Ashburnham I should, I fancy, have done much what he did. He seems to me like a large elder brother who took me out on excursions and did many dashing things whilst I just watched him robbing the orchards, from a distance.[20]

"Robbing the orchards" is an episode recounted in St. Augustine's *Confessions*, but Ford lifts this image directly from the passage in *Lord Jim* in which his bachelor friend writes to Marlow: "I declare I am unable to imagine [Jim] guilty of anything much worse than robbing an orchard" (*LJ*, p. 180).[21] As Dowell describes his own deviations from the ideal of married male sexuality, these deviations mirror yet also revise those of his other man:

> In my fainter sort of way I seem to perceive myself following the lines of Edward Ashburnham. I suppose that I should really like to be a polygamist; with Nancy,

and with Leonora, and with Maisie Maidan, and possibly even with Florence. I am no doubt like every other man; only, probably because of my American origin, I am fainter. At the same time I am able to assure you that I am a strictly respectable person. I have never done anything that the most anxious mother of a daughter or the most careful dean of a cathedral would object to. I have only followed, faintly, and in my unconscious desires, Edward Ashburnham. (*GS*, p. 237)

Dowell, I note here, is no more a bachelor than James's Strether is, but I am according him the honorary title of bachelor narrator here partly in recognition of his unconsummated marriage, a state of married celibacy which, he hints in places, might really be married virginity. Nick Carraway gives an equally psychological-sounding explanation for his own sexual reticence: "I am slow thinking and full of interior rules that act as brakes on my desires."[22] Nick's automotive metaphor reflects his own ambivalence towards the dangerously reckless drivers, including Gatsby, who people the world of his narrative. While both bachelor narrators claim to have distinctly muted sexual appetites, the intensity of their retrospective recounting of the sexual adventures of their other men surely complicates, though it may not utterly refute, these claims.

Both *The Good Soldier* and *The Great Gatsby* pivot on multiple, interwoven plots of transgressive sexual desire, plots that veer wildly from the idealized image of marital domesticity which is operant, if compromised, in these early twentieth-century novels. In both novels, the titular heroes are propelled by adulterous desires which teeter between the profound and the banal. Both heroes are imagined or imagine themselves as martyrs for love, yet their violent deaths verge on the pathetic, even the grotesque: the "good soldier" slits his own throat; the "great Gatsby" is shot in a case of mistaken identity. Just as violent death disrupts the lives, not to mention the marriages, of these novels' eponymous heroes, their improperly regulated sexual desires threaten to disrupt the idealized manhood they are enlisted to represent. The very adulterous desires and actions that threaten to undermine their heroic standing also, paradoxically, reinforce that standing. Gatsby's and Dowell's desires and actions may break the law, but they also potentially define these male figures as beyond the law, or perhaps more accurately as bound to a higher law.

The paradoxical effects of adulterous desire upon the status of these men results from the novels' bachelor narrators' reliance upon competing models of manhood – civilized manliness and primitive masculinity – to understand their heroes. The narrators construe the transgressive desires of their other men both as unmanning violations of bourgeois morality and also as remasculinizing expressions of uncontainable sexual or romantic nature. The incompatibility of these interpretations, and of the competing models of manhood upon which they are based, produces the incoherence of these narrators' celebrations and condemnations of their other men. Dowell and Nick are finally subject to an irreconcilable set of desires and judgments, "simultaneously enchanted and repelled" (*GG*, p. 40) by what they see in the men whose stories they are driven to retell.

On one level, Dowell attempts to distance himself in his narrative from the sexual rapacity of his other man. He does so by aligning his own sexual "faintness" with the idealized manhood of the courtly love tradition – "[Florence] would wish me goodnight as if she were a *cinque cento* Italian lady saying good-bye to her lover" (*GS*, p. 89) – and of the somewhat later tradition of chivalric romance: "I hardly believe that I cared for her in the way of love after a year or two of it. She became for me a rare and fragile object … as it were, the subject of a bet – the trophy of an athlete's … soberness, his abstentions, and of his inflexible will" (*GS*, p. 91). Both traditions involve elaborate and stylized codes of male conduct intended to bring glory to the man's objects of desire and identification, positions shared by the lady and by the king. This is an erotics that is always already triangulated, with further mediations supplied when the knight is a "bachelor knight" who serves under the aegis of a more senior knight. Both traditions, moreover, valorize male chastity.[23]

Dowell's rhetorical attempts to stand in the shoes of chaste courtly lovers and bachelor knights are not entirely becoming to him. His retrospective portrayal of his own "soberness" and "will" reveals the debased, even parodic, nature of his performance of the part of the chaste poet or champion. In his enactment of this role, Dowell exposes what one critic has called "the masochistic underside of the medieval archetype of passionate love," an archetype which idealizes the pain of love. If masochism has a place within the idealized manhood of the courtly lover and bachelor knight, then Dowell's unfulfilled desires, not to mention his self-flagellating narrative account of his abjection, have paradoxical effects.[24] They simultaneously emasculate and remasculinize him. Like Ralph Touchett's consumption, an alternative *carrière* which marks his distance from and his proximity to normative manhood, Dowell's "profession … of keeping heart patients alive" (*GS*, p. 47) serves a comparably paradoxical function.[25] His nursing career begins with his wife, Florence, who is afflicted with a factitious though meta-phorically apt bad heart: "For in Florence I had at once a wife and an unattained mistress – that is what it comes to – and in the retaining of her in this world I had my occupation, my career, my ambition" (*GS*, p. 49). And it culminates in his devotion to the insane Nancy Rufford: "So here I am very much where I started thirteen years ago. I am the attendant, not the husband, of a beautiful girl, who pays no attention to me" (*GS*, p. 236). "The attendant, not the husband" is both an emas-culated male sick-nurse and a remanned bachelor knight.

If on one level Dowell's compulsory chastity distinguishes him from Edward and his sexual excesses, on another level Dowell's chastity also proves to be a point of similarity between the two men. Edward operates according to his own version of ideal male chastity which Dowell sums up as "his intense optimistic belief that the woman he was making love to at the moment was the one he was destined, at last, to be eternally constant to" (*GS*, p. 27). Dowell identifies "constancy" as a key word in Edward's vocabulary of masculine integrity: "the big words – 'courage,' 'loyalty,' 'honor,' 'constancy' ... he would say that constancy was the finest of the virtues. He said it very stiffly, of course, but still as if the statement admitted of no doubt" (*GS*, p. 27). Edward's contingent code of masculine conduct, which I would call serial monogamous chastity, coincides with his chaste treatment of his wife, for which Dowell supplies this justification: "you may not believe it, but he really had such a sort of respect for the chastity of Leonora's imagination that he hated – he was positively revolted – at the thought that she should know the sort of thing he did existed in the world" (*GS*, p. 57). Edward tries to "preserve the virginity of his wife's thoughts," because, according to Dowell, "he had not wished to sully her mind with the idea that there was such a thing as a brother officer who could be a blackmailer – and he had wanted to protect the credit of his old light of love" (*GS*, p. 64). When Edward defends the reputation of the lady who is his former mistress, he also champions the honor of an officer and a gentleman, and also a blackmailer, thus burnishing the apparent integrity of his identity by virtue of his affiliation with his "brother officer."[26]

Clearly, Edward's practical application of this chaste masculine ideal is as debased in its own way as Dowell's version of masculine chastity. Edward's self-righteous endorsement of chaste masculinity is certainly hypocritical, either a consciously deceitful or an unconsciously self-deluding attempt to mask his own failure to live up to this ideal. The discrepancy between Edward's avowed code of honor and the way he actually comports himself can be understood in terms of a conflict between the more sexually expressive and aggressive style of primitive masculinity ascendant in the late nineteenth and early twentieth centuries, and the more restrained style of civilized manliness of the early to mid-Victorian period. The sexually performative stallion was coming to seem a more manly man than the self-regulating gentleman who, as Dowell worries, was starting to look distinctly emasculated: "Am I no better than a eunuch or is the proper man – the man with the right to existence – a raging stallion forever neighing after his neighbor's womenkind?" (*GS*, p. 12). The stallion was a problematic model of the proper man, however, since he violated laws of propriety which remained intact in Edwardian society.

Edward's divided self-constitution need not be understood as reflecting a timeless or ahistorical clash between passion and convention.[27] Rather, the division within Edward, like the conflict between him and Dowell, reveals a clash between historically based discourses of masculinity. The uneven development of new norms of manhood is visible, for example, in the neochivalrism practiced by the mid nineteenth-century "Pre-Raphaelite Brotherhood," to which Ford himself was affiliated through his mother, the daughter of Pre-Raphaelite painter, Ford Madox Brown. But neochivalrism really hit its stride in the Edwardian period, a period of which *Edward* Ashburnham may be considered a representative man.[28] Edward's violations of his chaste ideal dramatize the conflict between an outmoded standard and modern contingency. The compromise formation of Edward's serial monogamous chastity creates a double standard that lets him play two kinds of "proper man" (*GS*, p. 12) at once, but at the considerable cost of being two-faced.

The two faces of Edward pose an epistemological challenge to Dowell, whose categories of interpretation are not quite up to the task of interpreting Edward's character:

It is impossible of me to think of Edward Ashburnham as anything but straight, upright, and honourable. That, I mean, is, in spite of everything, my permanent view of him. I try at times by dwelling on some of the things that he did to push that image away, as you might try to push aside a large pendulum. But it always comes back – the memory of his innumerable acts of kindness, of his efficiency, of his unspiteful tongue. He was such a fine fellow.

So I feel myself forced to attempt to excuse him in this as in so many other things. It is, I have no doubt, a most monstrous thing to attempt to corrupt a young girl just out of a convent. But I think Edward had no idea at all of corrupting her. (*GS*, p. 113)

The pendulum of the other man, oscillating between comrade and enemy, ally and rival, hero and villain, inexorably impinges upon the bachelor narrator's memory. The figure of the pendulum neatly evokes the ambivalence of Dowell's response to Edward, as much as it evokes the bifurcated extremes of Edward's own masculine self-fashioning. The two incompatible versions of manhood – the monstrous libertine and the fine fellow – divide the masculine subject (Dowell) as well as the masculine object (Edward) that Dowell attempts, but is finally unable, to know. Defense and accusation are ways in which Dowell attempts to reconcile Edward's standards with his actions. Together they are mutually contradictory yet neither one alone sufficiently accounts for Edward or for Dowell's relationship to him.

Faced with the enigma of Edward, Dowell acknowledges the difficulty, even the impossibility, of knowing a man's character at all:

For who in this world can give anyone a character? Who in this world knows anything of any other heart – or his own? I don't mean to say one cannot form an average estimate of the way a person will behave. But one cannot be certain of the way any man will behave in every case – and until one can do that a "character" is of no use to anyone. (*GS*, pp. 155–6)

Dowell's plaintive lament makes visible the difference between Victorian and modernist conceptions of character, a distinction that is different from, though conceivably related to, the Victorian and modern models of manhood discussed above. Michael Levenson compellingly argues that

Dowell's disillusionment follows the arc of modernism. He begins with presuppositions typical of much Victorian characterization: the individual conditioned by circumstance, composed of intelligible motives, susceptible to moral analysis – the justified self. Then, confronted with the singularity of desire, his "generalizations" totter and fall. He moves to a conception of character that will become predominant in modernist narrative: the self estranged from circumstance and no longer comprehensible in its terms, confounding familiar motives, beyond the reach of social explanation.[29]

Thus Levenson contrasts the Victorian conception of character as integrated, representable by a compendium of traits, with the fragmented modernist character whose enumerated traits do not add up to a unitary whole. He also points to the identification of types – "the reassuring impersonalities of cultural generalizations" – as a method of characterization used by the characters in this novel, but which proves insufficient for justifying themselves or their actions.[30]

The insufficiency of social typing as a way of knowing individuals is one of Dowell's own preoccupations, one that is closely related to his fixation upon Edward: "After forty-five years of mixing with one's kind, one ought to have acquired the habit of being able to know something about one's fellow beings. But one doesn't. I think the modern civilized habit – the modern English habit – of taking everyone for granted is a good deal to blame for this" (*GS*, p. 36). "Taking everyone for granted" is the primary mode of typing that occurs in the novel, the primary way of distinguishing between "good people" and "those who won't do":

And the odd, queer thing is that the whole collection of rules applies to anybody – to the anybodies that you meet in hotels, in railway trains, to a less degree, perhaps, in steamers, but even in the end, upon steamers. You meet a man or a woman and, from tiny and intimate sounds, from the slightest of movements, you know at once whether you are concerned with good people or with those who won't do. You know, that is to say, whether they will go rigidly through with the whole programme from the underdone beef to the Anglicanism. It won't matter whether they be short or tall; whether the voice squeak like a marionette or rumble like a town bull's; it won't matter whether they are Germans, Austrians, French, Spanish, or even Brazilians – they will be the Germans or Brazilians who take a cold bath every morning and who move, roughly speaking, in diplomatic circles.

But the inconvenient – well, hang it all, I will say it – the damnable nuisance of the whole thing is, that with all the taking for granted, you never really get an inch deeper than the things I have catalogued. (*GS*, p. 37)

(Shades of Marlow's frustration with the insufficiency of "the right kind of looks" for determining who qualifies as "one of us"!) Here, "good people" apparently means people of a certain social class, although in this democratized new world, high birth is not an absolute requirement for proper English gentlemanliness. Apparently, one does not even have to be English to be a proper English gentleman, since Germans and Brazilians are eligible, or even have to be a man, since high-voiced puppets and low-voiced animals can also qualify. Yet this way of knowing, or classing, people does not sufficiently account for character. It fails to bring character to account not simply because of the superficiality of the method that Dowell bemoans here, but also because character is a category that has been emptied of meaning.

The emptying-out of meaning that troubles the concept of character in this novel is generated, in part, by the incongruities among several different meanings or interpretations of "character": character as personality; character as a figure in a work of literary fiction; character as moral rectitude; and character as a symbol, a sign, a cipher. In his attempts to give Edward a character, Dowell tries to reconcile the first three meanings and ends up with the cipher:

Have I conveyed to you the splendid fellow that he was – the fine soldier, the excellent landlord, the extraordinarily kind, careful, and industrious magistrate, the upright, honest, fair-dealing, fair-thinking public character? ... I can remember a thousand little acts of kindliness, of thoughtfulness for his inferiors, even on the Continent... But, although I liked him so intensely, I was rather apt to take these things for granted. They made me feel comfortable with him, good towards him; they made me trust him. But I guess I thought it was part of the character of any English gentleman... I thought it was only the duty of his rank and station. (*GS*, pp. 93–4)

Dowell's catalogue of nouns – soldier, landlord, magistrate – and of adjectives – upright, honest, fair-dealing, fair-thinking – do not add up, any more than do Edward's "thousand little acts of kindliness," in accounting for "the character of any English gentleman."[31] Edward is inexplicable as a moral character and unjustifiable as a literary character – he is a cipher, in fact *the* cipher, of Dowell's narrative. The proper English gentleman is both a standard for character in the novel and an emblem of the meaninglessness, or the conflicted meanings, of character.

I note here, in passing, that in *The Great Gatsby*, a novel written ten years after *The Good Soldier* and on the other side of the Atlantic, the proper English gentleman also stands as an archetype of ideal manhood.[32] Oddly enough, Gatsby's recipe for self-made American manhood includes such ingredients as alluding to his Oxford days, calling people "old sport," and inhabiting a vague approximation of an ancestral English country house, described as a "factual imitation of some Hôtel de Ville in Normandy" (*GG*, p. 9), although the "high Gothic library, panelled with carved English oak, and probably transported complete from some ruin overseas" (*GG*, p. 49) is more in keeping with his fictitious pedigree. The fact that Gatsby only affects what is Edward's birthright, masking his ethnic and class identity as the son of poor central European immigrants, might seem to provide a ready explanation for the lack of substance beneath his assumed character: "He hurried the phrase 'educated at Oxford,' or swallowed it, or choked on it, as though it had bothered him before. And with this doubt, his whole statement fell to pieces and I wondered if there wasn't something a little sinister about him after all" (*GG*, p. 69). Even after Gatsby presents Nick with the "proof" of his wartime valor and his English education – his

Montenegro medal and the photograph of himself at Oxford – the coherence of Gatsby's character remains shattered. Nick, like Dowell, tries a mock-epic catalogue to account for his other man:

> Once I wrote down on the empty spaces of a time-table the names of those who came to Gatsby's house that summer . . . I can still read the gray names and they will give you a better impression than my generalities of those who accepted Gatsby's hospitality and paid him the subtle tribute of knowing nothing whatever about him. (*GG*, p. 65)

But the list of names that follows – the names of people who "know nothing whatever about" Gatsby – does not add up to the man, any more than Dowell's catalogue adds up to Edward. In the "character" of the "figure of the host" (*GG*, p. 60), Gatsby inspires "romantic speculation" (*GG*, p. 48) among his guests because of the very blankness of the surface he presents.

In *The Good Soldier*, the face of the proper English gentleman is remarkable for its cipher-like blankness: "His face hitherto had, in the wonderful English fashion, expressed nothing whatever. Nothing. There was in it neither joy nor despair; neither hope nor fear; neither boredom nor satisfaction. He seemed to perceive no soul in that crowded room; he might have been walking in a jungle. I never came across such a perfect expression before and I never shall again" (*GS*, p. 25). (One can hear an echo, especially in the last two sentences, of the fascination and regret that Marlow experiences in his scrutiny of both Kurtz and Jim.) The perfection of Edward's utter impassiveness nonetheless registers a complex range of cultural identifications; its very neutrality is a sign of upper-class and English restraint, of imperialist self-possession and masculine reserve. Similarly, Dowell's detailed list of "the sort of thing [Edward] thought about" – "Martingales, Chiffney bits, boots; where you got the best soap, the best brandy, the name of the chap who rode a plater down the Khyber cliffs; the spreading power of number-three shot before a charge of number-four powder" (*GS*, p. 26) – speaks everything about the type of man Edward is, and yet it tells Dowell nothing of what he wants to know.[33]

Dowell attempts another way to account for Edward's character. Taking Edward as the key to the past history of the "four-square coterie" (*GS*, p. 5) consisting of Dowell and Edward, Florence and Leonora – it is actually a five-square coterie, if one includes Nancy Rufford – Dowell proposes a key to Edward: "Good God, what did they all see in him? . . . Ah, well, suddenly, as if by a flash of inspiration, I know. For all good soldiers are sentimentalists – all good soldiers of this type" (*GS*, p. 26). Having seized upon this possible key to Edward, Dowell runs with it: "I trust I have not, in talking of his liabilities, given the impression that poor Edward was a promiscuous libertine. He was not. He was a sentimentalist" (*GS*, p. 57). And: "I hope I have not given you the idea that Edward Ashburnham was a pathological case. He wasn't. He was just a normal man and very much of a sentimentalist" (*GS*, p. 152). And his penultimate word on Edward: "Well, Edward was the English gentleman; but he was also, to the last, a sentimentalist" (*GS*, p. 255). Dowell's formulation, "Well, he was a sentimentalist" (*GS*, p. 241), carries the same totalizing weight as his more general refrain of "Well, that was Edward Ashburnham" (*GS*, p. 28). The incantation of this answer to the question of Edward reveals the utter unanswerability of the question, or at least the emptiness of this answer. The formulaic repetition of "he was a sentimentalist" ultimately reveals only the unbridged gap between signifier and signified, the discrepancy between character as cipher and character as moral rectitude, rather than tapping into the essence of the man. Dowell's "flash of inspiration" proves to be a rhetorical tic.

This ticcing effect is heightened by Dowell's use of the word "type" to categorize Edward and his sentimentalism. The clanging repetition of "type" immediately after Dowell's assessment of "all good soldiers of this type" (*GS*, p. 26) compounds the stereotyped nature of Edward's sentimentalism: "he would pass hours lost in novels of a sentimental *type* – novels in which *type*writer girls married marquises and governesses earls . . . And he was fond of poetry, of a certain *type* – and he could even read a perfectly sad love story" (*GS*, p. 27; emphasis mine). The clattering type that the typewriter puts on the page here drowns out the referential resonances of the sentimental type. Like "character," "type" starts to ring hollow, becoming a signifier emptied of meaning, a cipher. Just as the disruption of unitary, knowable character is an element of modernist fiction, the foregrounding of language as a thing, of words as objects or images on the page, is a feature of modernist form. At this moment in Dowell's narrative, these two markers of modernist aesthetics go together.

While the potential for thoroughly destabilizing both conventional character and conventional signification is palpable in *The Good Soldier*, the novel does not go all the way. Indeed, Edward's sentimentalism has certain distinct meanings for Dowell, even though his rhetorical insistence upon it verges on outright Dadaism. It stands, for example, as a marker of relative literary value when Dowell asserts that Edward "talked like quite a good book – a book not in the least cheaply sentimental" (*GS*, p. 28). Dowell's ambivalent critical judgment of Edward – "But the fellow talked like a cheap novelist. – Or like a very good novelist for the matter of that, if it's the business of a novelist to make you see things clearly" (*GS*, p. 109) – echoes Conrad's 1897 definition of the novelist's task: "My task which I am trying to achieve is, by the power of the written word to make you hear, to make you feel – it is, before all, to make you *see*!"[34] This echo reinforces the high cultural imperative by which Ford and Conrad valorized their literary efforts. Yet Dowell's uncertainty about the difference between a "cheap novelist" and a "very good novelist" also undermines such cultural distinctions, especially considering that Ford's early title for the novel was *The Saddest Story*. Sentimentalism is both cheap and not cheap, both distinct from and aligned with good books, both an occlusion of vision and a way of seeing things clearly.

Sentimentalism is crucial to Dowell's identification with Edward, despite his disparagement of Edward as "a sentimental ass": "For I can't conceal from myself the fact that I loved Edward Ashburnham – and that I love him because he was just myself . . . And, you see, I am just as much of a sentimentalist as he was" (*GS*, pp. 253–4). The transgression or dissolution of boundaries between selves that Dowell describes here recalls Adam Smith's seminal account of sentimentalism itself. According to Smith, moral sentiment depends upon an imaginative identification with another: "it is by the imagination only that we can form any conception of what are [the] sensations [of our brother on the rack] . . . By the imagination we place ourselves in his situation, we conceive ourselves enduring all the same torments, we enter as it were into his body, and become in some measure the same person with him."[35] As a discourse which foregrounds emotional fulfillment as part of a process of identification and a facet of refamilialization, the sentimental is a particularly apt discursive rubric for the imaginary merger of masculine selves in this narrative. If the generational hierarchy suggested in Dowell's image of Edward as a "large elder brother" keeps Dowell watching him "from a distance," this quasi-fraternal relation nevertheless affords an undeniable intimacy between them. The hierarchical distance that threatens to separate them is closed, or at least foreshortened, when Dowell counts himself, with Edward, among the ranks of the sentimentalists.

The disruption of stable, unitary selfhood effected by Dowell's deployment of the "sentimental type" to characterize both himself and Edward reveals a point of commonality between sentimental discourse and modernist discourse. Suzanne Clark describes the "shatter[ing of] the pure, proper, inviolable 'I' in modernist literature," noting that this disruption was "confined to the text" as a way of insulating the critical intelligence of the author from the questioning of identity that implicated his fictional characters. She exposes an unacknowledged tension in the writings of those modernists and "modernist new critics" who "wrote with a longing and sense of loss that suggested utopian critical perspectives, not a rejection of the sentimental. Even *The Waste Land* gains power from its melancholy nostalgia. But T. S. Eliot, taking up Hulme's severity, wrote insistently about the priority of form over content in judgements about art . . . This *formalism* connects Eliot to the new critics."[36] The dismissal of literary and cultural others as merely sentimental was hardly invented by the New Critics, but they refined this exclusionary technique, making a virtual science of what had formerly been a mere art.[37] The repudiation of sentimentality was a stock gesture of self-legitimization which many male modernist writers shared with the New Critics who canonized them. It enabled these writers to make distinctions between their own manly arts and the debased products of women and mass culture.

This characteristic gesture of exclusion disguised the fact that high-cultural writers and their literary critic champions sometimes had more in common with their popular literary predecessors and contemporaries than they wanted to admit. Thus, in *Chance*, the external narrator jokes that "[t]his is like one of those Redskin stories where the noble savages carry off a girl and the honest backwoodsman with his incomparable knowledge follows the track," leading Marlow to reply "indulgently" that "It is not exactly a story for boys" (*C*, p. 259). Yet when Conrad was targeting a readership that would include women with a novel that finally garnered him the popular audience and financial success he had long desired. And *Lord Jim* links Jim's fatal flaw to his taste for "light literature" (*LJ*, p. 47) while the novel's Patusan episode reads as a rough approximation of Jim's favorite genre: adventure romance.[38] Ford shared Conrad's manifest disdain for the debased products of mass culture, singling out for opprobrium the mid-Victorian "novel of commerce" which he scathingly called "the nuvvel."[39] Yet Ford was not above promoting "The Commercial Value of Literature" in a radio address of 1938, a foray into mass media which he undertook to publicize his own recently published *The March of Literature*. This guide to literature through the ages was meant to encourage the culturally *and* commercially beneficial "habit of reading something more lasting" in those more accustomed to reading the "sports columns of the newspapers... [and] detective or mystery stories."[40]

In contrast to Ford, Fitzgerald did not espouse the notion that popularity and high-cultural status must be antithetical, at least not initially. Although he supported himself by magazine-writing and some Hollywood script-writing, Fitzgerald at first expected his novels to be both critical and financial successes. His first novel, *This Side of Paradise* (1920), garnered both critical acclaim and high profits, but his next one, *The Beautiful and the Damned* (1922), did less well on both scores. *The Great Gatsby*, his third novel, actually sold poorly, even though it had very strong reviews and later ascended to its seemingly timeless place in the canonical firmament on the wings of the New Criticism.[41] Before *Gatsby* came out, Fitzgerald worried in a letter to his editor, Maxwell Perkins, that "it may hurt the book's popularity that it's *a man's book*." By this, Fitzgerald alluded to his and Perkins's shared feeling that the male characters in *Gatsby* were more fully developed than the female ones. When his fears about poor sales were confirmed, he reiterated his interpretation of the situation: "...the book contains no important woman character and women control the fiction market at present."[42]

Female producers certainly had no monopoly on the popular literary market. It is true that in the same year that *Gatsby* died in the marketplace, one of the ten best-selling novels was Anne Parish's *The Perennial Bachelor*, a family romance about three self-sacrificing sisters and one self-satisfied bachelor brother. But at least half the ten best-selling novels of 1925 were written by men, a statistic that undercuts the "melodrama of beset manhood" that Fitzgerald rhetorically stages in his letters to his editor.[43] High-cultural modernists were not all men; best-selling popular and sentimental writers were not all women. And while women readers may have played a vital role as consumers of contemporary fiction, their tastes were neither entirely different from those of male readers, nor did their consumption entirely cancel out the market for whatever different preferences male readers may have had. Significantly, modernist fiction and sentimental fiction were not so profoundly opposed, either in their aesthetics or their values, as the literary practitioners and critical proponents of modernism may have wished to believe.

The ambivalent repudiation and recuperation of the sentimental is palpable in *The Great Gatsby*, just as it is in the other modernist bachelor-narrated fictions discussed in this chapter.[44] This ambivalence is particularly visible, for example, when Gatsby tells his "life story" – it *is* a story, to be sure – to Nick, a passage in which the voice of the novel is effectively doubled. Gatsby's story is given as direct discourse but it is obviously mediated through Nick whose recounting is shaped by an aesthetic sensibility both distinctive and familiar. We are presented here with a narrative that alternates between Gatsby's sensationalist story and Nick's cynical reception of it, creating a kind of collaborative, or even dialogic, utterance in which Gatsby's mass-cultural telling sounds the call and Nick's high-cultural gloss provides the response:

[Gatsby:] "My family all died and I came into a good deal of money."

[Nick:] His voice was solemn, as if the memory of that sudden extinction of a clan still haunted him. For a moment I suspected that he was pulling my leg, but a glance at him convinced me otherwise.

[Gatsby:] "After that I lived like a young rajah in all the capitals of Europe – Paris, Venice, Rome – collecting jewels, chiefly rubies, hunting big game, painting a little, things for myself only, and trying to forget something very sad that had happened to me long ago."

[Nick:] With an effort I managed to restrain my incredulous laughter. The very phrases were worn so threadbare that they evoked no image except that of a turbaned "character" leaking sawdust at every pore as he pursued a tiger through the Bois de Boulogne.

[Gatsby:] "Then came the war, old sport. It was a great relief, and I tried very hard to die, but I seemed to bear an enchanted life ... I was promoted to be a major, and every Allied government gave me a decoration – even Montenegro, little Montenegro down on the Adriatic Sea!"

[Nick:] ... [m]y incredulity was submerged in fascination now; it was like skimming hastily through a dozen magazines. (*GG*, pp. 70–1)

Nick's cynical commentary calls attention to Gatsby's sensationalist implausibility and sentimental clichés, the "threadbare" covering which fails to contain the sawdust, the stuffing that fills out this hollow man's "character." Nick's criticism betrays not so much his moral objection to Gatsby's whoppers, but rather his disgusted fascination with the medium of Gatsby's message. Although Nick disdainfully compares Gatsby's narrative to "skimming ... through a dozen magazines," the novel in which he makes these distinctions is itself a pastiche of mass-cultural icons and ephemera, its narrative studded with advertising slogans, the lyrics to Broadway songs, the names of producers and starlets, and the titles of popular novels.

Self-conscious irony informs Nick's allusion to the "dozen magazines" since Fitzgerald himself wrote more than 160 magazine stories to subsidize his extravagant lifestyle and his novel-writing. Indeed, irony is the preferred modernist antidote to the dreaded sentimental. While Nick ironically undercuts the romanticized idealism of Gatsby's "life story," that is, both his actual life and the story he tells about it, he fosters a sentimental nostalgia for this supposedly empty ideal under cover of that irony. With the "intense personal interest" (*GG*, p. 165) that prompts him to take responsibility for Gatsby's funeral and his legacy, Nick makes an emotional investment in his narration that short-circuits any purely ironic reading, either his own or ours.[45] If we temporarily suspend our own tendency to read ironically, suspending not our belief but our modernist, or postmodern, disbelief, we can see an archetypally sentimental plot behind this story of failed marriage, banal sexual infatuation, and grotesque death: the affirming death of the innocent. Like little Eva and little Nell, and also like Ralph Touchett, Gatsby suffers and dies for the moral benefit of his earthly survivors, in the text and beyond. Because Gatsby is too good for this world, his death potentially redeems those few who devote themselves to his remembrance. Of course, the irony of such a debased or parodic recasting of sentimental suffering and death here, as in James's *Portrait*, disrupts any straightforward portrayal, whether in his own telling or in my critical reading, of Nick as an effective custodian of an authentic cultural ideal.

We feel the tension between authenticity and inauthenticity, between presence and absence, even between meaning and meaninglessness, particularly at those moments when the narrator of *The Great Gatsby* affirms his belief in, and yet disavows the sentimentality of, his hero:

> Through all he said, even through his appalling sentimentality, I was reminded of something – an elusive rhythm, a fragment of lost words, that I had heard somewhere a long time ago. For a moment a phrase tried to take shape in my mouth and my lips parted like a dumb man's, as though there was more struggling upon them than a wisp of startled air. But they made no sound, and what I had almost remembered was uncommunicable forever. (*GG*, p. 118)

Nick's near-return of the repressed signals the uncanny status of his memory of the past, a past which is itself both *heimlich* and *unheimlich*. This uncanny past is irretrievable, I would argue, because it is associated with disavowed sentimentality. The ineffable phrase that rises to Nick's lips recalls the ecstatic oral communion in the preceding paragraphs where he describes Gatsby's vision of climbing alone to a "secret place above the trees" to "suck on the pap of life, gulp down the incomparable milk of wonder" (*GG*, p. 117), a vision that kissing Daisy's lips fulfills and thus destroys. Nick's elegiac longing for reunion with Gatsby, like Gatsby's nostalgic longing for reunion with Daisy, is not an experience of mourning but of melancholia. Gatsby's and Nick's idealization of their respective love objects requires them to reject the reality not only of the present, but also of the past. It requires them imaginatively to incorporate the other, absent and debased, or perhaps absent and merely real, as opposed to idealized and imaginary, into themselves and to attempt to reenvision that internalized other as both exalted and present. Committing themselves to unrequitable love means committing themselves to melancholic grief.

The past which Nick sentimentally craves and yet ironically disavows is figured in his narrative in terms of a pre-Oedipal oneness with the maternal breast. The melancholic fantasy of oral communion suggested by the parting of Nick's lips as "a phrase tried to take shape in my mouth" and by the sucking of "the milk of wonder" anticipates the famous imagery of the novel's penultimate passages in which Nick imaginatively looks backward to the "fresh green breast of the new world" whose "vanished trees . . . had once pandered in whispers to the last and greatest of all human dreams" (*GG*, p. 189). Yet these images also forecast Nick's imagery when he describes Myrtle's grotesquely mutilated body after the car accident: "her left breast was swinging loose like a flap and there was no need to listen for the heart beneath. The mouth was wide open and ripped at the corners as though she had choked a little in giving up the tremendous vitality she had stored so long" (*GG*, p. 145). If the breast and the mouth, particularly when taken together, are emblems of physical and emotional "vitality," then they are also the material residue, the "waste" of the violent destruction committed by "careless people . . . [who] smashed up things and creatures and then retreated back into their money or their vast carelessness or whatever it was that kept them together, and let other people clean up the mess they had made" (*GG*, pp. 187–8).[46] The breast/mouth imagery of these passages reveals a tension between nourishing communion and alienating separation, a separation that divides individuals from each other and even tears individuals apart, as, for example, in the sundering of Myrtle's body from her spirit. The image of her mouth "ripped" in "giving up the tremendous vitality she had stored so long" suggests violent regurgitation, a self-destroying expulsion of the "milk of wonder," or even parturition as a shattering of the maternal symbiosis of pregnancy.

The "milk of wonder" figures within what we might well call a "spermatic economy" as well as within a maternalized domestic economy. That is to say, the fantasy of sucking the "milk of wonder," which signals sentimental longing for pre-Oedipal oneness with the mother and the ironic disavowal of that longing, also suggests an equally disavowed subtext of homoerotic communion between men. This homoerotic/homophobic subtext is buoyed up by the dream-like sequence in which Nick follows Mr. McKee out the door in retreat from the sordid scene at Tom Buchanan and Myrtle Wilson's party:

> "Come to lunch some day," he suggested as we groaned down in the elevator.
> "Where?"
> "Anywhere."
> "Keep your hands off the lever," snapped the elevator boy.
> "I beg your pardon," said Mr. McKee with dignity. "I didn't know I was touching it."
> "All right," I agreed, "I'll be glad to."
> ... I was standing beside his bed and he was sitting up between the sheets, clad in his underwear, and with a great portfolio in his hands.
> "Beauty and the Beast ... Loneliness ... Old Grocery Horse ... Brook'n Bridge..."
> Then I was lying half asleep in the cold lower level of the Pennsylvania Station, staring at the morning "Tribune" and waiting for the four o'clock train. (*GG*, p. 42)

The unconscious fantasy that breaches the surface of Nick's narrative has not just homoerotic connotations but also autoerotic and voyeuristic ones, all of which are reinforced by Mr. McKee's inability to "keep [his] hands off the lever" and his drunken thumbing through (or fingering of?) his "great portfolio" for his own pleasure and for Nick's delectation.[47] The few other narrative details that Nick gives concerning Mr. McKee – he is a "pale feminine man" in the "artistic game" (*GG*, p. 34); he has a spot of dried shaving cream on his cheek that Nick wipes away when McKee falls asleep (*GG*, p. 41) – suggest a certain gendered and/or sexual "queerness" to this character, or at least to Nick's thoughts about him.

The eruption of queer fantasy triggered by Nick's elevator encounter with Mr. McKee is also striking for its ambiguous, or mixed, cultural status. Mr. McKee's "great portfolio" contains works of art whose titles indicate their conventionality and sentimentality. The only photograph of Mr. McKee's that actually appears within the manifest narration – as opposed to the titles enumerated in Nick's unconscious fantasy, discussed above – shares those other pictures' relatively low cultural status. "The only picture was an over-enlarged photograph, apparently a hen sitting on a blurred rock. Looked at from a distance however the hen resolved itself into a bonnet and the countenance of a stout old lady beamed down into the room" (*GG*, p. 33). The subject of the photograph – the beaming old lady in a bonnet is Myrtle's mother – contributes to the debased parody of domesticity which occurs in Tom's and Myrtle's hotel room. Although its subject is domestic and its treatment is sentimental, the formal aspects of the photograph – the image is blurred up close, but resolves when viewed from a distance – recalls the daubs of Impressionism and the dots of pointillism, two decidedly highbrow styles of early modernist painting. Yet the optical irresolution of this enlarged photograph equally suggests the half-tone method of photographic reproduction associated with mass-market newspapers and magazines.[48] The hybridity of the photograph's cultural status does not end here. The photograph seems to verge upon a Surrealist experiment – "I gathered later that he was a photographer and had made the dim enlargment of Mrs. Wilson's mother which hovered like an ectoplasm on the wall" (*GG*, p. 34) – yet the reference to ectoplasm, the supposed emanation from the body of a spiritualist medium, also places this photograph within the decidedly popular and commercial tradition of spirit photography, further compromising the artistic integrity of Mr. McKee's work. Like Gatsby's fundamentally incoherent narrative of his lifestory, Mr. McKee's photograph does not fully resolve itself into a single cultural image. Nick, moreover, finally disdains Mr. McKee's artistic endeavors on much the same grounds that he discounts Gatsby and his story. Mr. McKee's "great portfolio" and Nick Carraway's great Gatsby are both devastatingly, even mortifyingly, sentimental.

Yet, as I have suggested, the sentimental is Nick's own medium, a fluid essence much like the "destructive element" to which Stein advises Marlow to "submit yourself, and with the exertions of your hands and feet in the water make the deep, deep sea keep you up." Like Marlow and Dowell before him, Nick keeps himself up by "stretch[ing] out [his] arms," reaching ever backwards toward what Marlow describes as "the capricious, unconsolable, and elusive spirit that no eye can follow, no hand can grasp." These bachelor narrators are twice-removed from the sentimental dreams pursued by the other men of their narratives. Gatsby, like Edward and Jim, is once removed from his dream, a "dream [that] must have seemed so close that he could hardly fail to grasp it" (*GG*, p. 189). If the other man of each narrative does not know that his dream "was already behind him," then the bachelor narrator who tells his story is painfully aware that this past never really existed, that it was always just a dream. The bachelor narrator displays a modernist skepticism about the reality and integrity of this imaginary past, yet he is unable to divest himself of faith in it. The melancholy narrator of modernist fiction submits himself to this "last and greatest of all human dreams," a sentimental bachelor's reverie of masculine plenitude that can only bear him "back ceaselessly into the past."

As should already be evident, Nick Carraway descends from a long line of bachelor narrators, a quasi-lineage that is reinforced by Nick's disclosure of his identity as a bachelor great-nephew:

> The Carraways are something of a clan, and we have a tradition that we're descended from the Dukes of Buccleuch, but the actual founder of my line was my grand-father's brother, who came here in fifty-one, sent a substitute to the Civil War, and started the wholesale hardware business that my father carries on to-day.
> I never saw this great-uncle, but I'm supposed to look like him. (*GG*, p. 7)

While it is unclear whether Nick's great-uncle is himself a bachelor, Nick's resemblance to this ancestor tellingly places him at once within and beyond a domestic world, a world of the family reenvisioned here as all-male. Like his uncle before him, Nick defines himself first in relation to the world of war and then to the world of business, although Nick's war is "the Great War" and his business is "the bond business." As the very phrase "bond business" suggests, Nick's bachelor self-constitution combines self-made manhood with familial and quasi-familial inheritance, autonomy with affiliation. These ingredients are not fully compatible. His desire for autonomy – "Almost any exhibition of complete self sufficiency draws a stunned tribute from me" (*GG*, p. 13) – conflicts with the premium he places on sentiment, on the physical and emotional feelings that locate him in his own body and in relation to others. Nick may claim to want "no more riotous excursions with privileged glimpses into the human heart," but the place that he chooses for his retreat from "the secret griefs of wild, unknown men" (*GG*, p. 5) tellingly confounds this aim: "I decided to come back home" (*GG*, p. 185). Nick tells his story after returning to what had once appeared to be "the warm centre of the world," but which comes to seem "like the ragged edge of the universe" (*GG*, p. 7). This warm center will not hold, but the melancholy bachelor narrator of this modernist yet sentimental book of the heart finds himself "borne back ceaselessly into the past" (*GG*, p. 189).

Dowell shares Nick's profound sense of alienation from both domestic hearth and masculine fraternity: "No hearthstone will ever again witness, for me, friendly intercourse. No smoking-room will ever be other than peopled with incalculable simulacra amidst smoke wreaths" (*GS*, p. 8). Neither hearthstones nor smoke wreaths can mitigate his melancholic conclusion that "I know nothing – nothing in the world – of the hearts of men. I only know that I am alone – horribly alone" (*GS*, p. 8). Yet, in telling the story of his spiritual exile, Dowell envisions for himself an ideal listener, an auditor to whom he imaginatively addresses his written text:

So I shall just imagine myself for a fortnight or so at one side of the fireplace of a country cottage, with a sympathetic soul opposite me. And I shall go on talking, in a low voice while the sea sounds in the distance and overhead the great black flood of wind polishes the bright stars. From time to time we shall get up and go to the door and look out at the great moon and say: "Why, it is nearly as bright as in Provence!" And then we shall come back to the fireside, with just the touch of a sigh because we are not in that Provence where even the saddest stories are gay. (*GS*, pp. 12–13)

This listener resembles the "privileged man" to whom Marlow addresses the last, written installment of Jim's story, an addressee-in-the-text whom Marlow describes as living "in the highest flat of a lofty building," and as "alone hav[ing] showed an interest in [Jim] that survived the telling of his story" (*LJ*, p. 292). Dowell's imagined auditor resembles as well the "silent listener ... the *homo bonae voluntatis* – man of goodwill" that Ford imagined as his own ideal audience in his essay "On Impressionism," published while he was completing *The Good Soldier.*[49]

There is an undeniable irony, or perhaps self-delusion, in Dowell's vision of fireside communion with a "sympathetic soul" and his nostalgic evocation of a place where "even the saddest stories are gay," especially in a novel which Ford originally entitled *The Saddest Story.* As Dowell imagines it, his "low voice" is not exactly drowned out by the voice of the sea, but it does reverberate with that distant sound, intensifying rather than mitigating the imponderable immensity of "the great black flood of the wind polish[ing] the bright stars."[50] In the presence of this great black flood, Dowell cannot help but feel his isolation even from his imaginary listener, whom he castigates several pages later for his inscrutable silence: "You, the listener, sit opposite me. But you are so silent. You don't tell me anything" (*GS*, p. 15). This listener is thus another "lost object" whom Dowell melancholically denigrates, a projection rather than an incorporation of a cipher-like other whom Dowell takes in and takes on. Yet, Dowell's fantasized scene of narration cleaves, however desperately, to the notion of redemptive communion with this sympathetic soul. If nothing else, they are united in their common nostalgic melancholy, their sense of bereaved alienation from an imaginary past in Provence. Both together and apart, teller and listener are also within and beyond the realm of the domestic. The bachelor narrator and his imaginary other share a hearth that symbolizes a redeeming knowledge of "the hearts of men" (*GS*, p. 7), however dark, or empty, or merely banal those hearts may be. Even in the ragged wastes of the twentieth century, home is where the bachelor's heart is.

Afterword

Dowell's imaginary fireside *tête-à-tête* brings us full circle to the imaginary hearthside communion of the mid-century bachelor in his reveries. However ironic Ford's revision of this scene of domestic intimacy may be, it nonetheless forges a link to an earlier sentimental tradition in which the exchange of feelings and words is valued as a source of moral and spiritual redemption. The high-cultural tradition of canonical male modernism has roots, albeit disavowed ones, in sentimental traditions of nineteenth-century fiction. Indeed, the redemptive ethos of this earlier tradition stands as a forerunner of the modernist valuation of the aesthetic imagination, of words themselves, as a bulwark shored against the ruins of the twentieth century. To put it another way, the cult of domesticity retains its salience in an age of transcendental homelessness. Indeed, its salience may even by intensified by its imaginary status.

The intersections between the sentimental and the modernist belie notions of an impermeable divide between highbrow and lowbrow modes, forms, texts, and authors. The bachelor as a literary figure, and particularly as figure of narration, reveals the connections among these supposedly separate spheres. The definitional ambiguity of the figure of the bachelor confounds critical attempts to distinguish between the intellectual and emotional vigor of true manhood and the feminized debility of abjected manhoods, gendered discriminations which are typically used to draw a *cordon sanitaire* between classics and trash. Bachelor narratives are the very stuff on which a conservatively modelled male modernist canon is formed, yet the queer excesses of bachelor narratives mark the threshold of cultural norms, situating these figures and their fictions at once within and beyond the pale.

In this book, I have attempted to show how the use of bachelor figures contributed to, but also complicated, the distinctions which have shaped our inherited notions of literary authorship. Central to my critical enterprise has been to defamiliarize the bachelor narrator's gendered subject position, to mark what has long stood as an unmarked category. When Fitzgerald, for example, in an interview with the author of *The Men Who Make Our Novels*, commented that *The Great Gatsby* had been "an attempt at form," he rhetorically erased the gendered, bodily, and political specificity of the bachelor as a historical, cultural, and literary type, and of the bachelor narrator as a site through which gendered subjectivity is constructed.[1] In claiming a truly impersonal impersonality for his text, Fitzgerald contributed to the invisibility of the bachelor as an embodied and gendered source of narrative utterance. And when T. S. Eliot wrote that *Gatsby* "seems to me to be the first step that American fiction has taken since Henry James," and Fitzgerald proudly reported this compliment in a letter in which he also lamented the weak sales of his books in comparison with his "trash," that is, his money-making magazine stories, their distinctions reinforced the notion that classics transcend historical specificities of market, taste, and meaning.[2]

In challenging these intertwined notions – that the first-person masculine singular is a neutral voice, a voice that says "I" effortlessly and without political ramifications, and that classics can be empirically and apolitically distinguished from trash – I am participating in a much larger critical project, or set of projects, concerned to reassess the critical making and the literary and cultural materials of our academic and popular canons. In this assumption-challenging project, I am not without assumptions of my own, assumptions which are partly imbedded within the ideological matrix of the texts and authors I have analyzed. For instance, my own readings are invested to a certain extent in the same dialectic of disillusionment and redemption that I disclose in the modernist and pre-modernist texts I read here. I hope to recuperate bachelor narrators as figures of alternative masculinity, even while conscious of the limited potential of such figures for radical political purposes. For one thing, while there well may be theoretical limits to the effectiveness of championing *any* model of masculinity, I am unconvinced that the scuttling of gender is a possible or even a desirable end. Gender may be a mask, but it is not necessarily one that we can remove; if it is performative, that does not mean we can choose to stop performing. Rather, I think our best bet is to rethink and expand the possibilities of gender: by moving the boundaries to permit a wider compass of gendered identities and relations and by demonstrating more fully the permeability of the boundaries as they stand.

Another limit to the potential of the bachelor as a figure of alternative masculinity may arise from the bourgeois, individualist contexts – the domestic and familial spheres; the novel as a commodity – within which the fictional characters that I discuss are constructed and within which I have situated them. One could well argue that these figures and texts reinforce gendered and cultural norms as much as they challenge them, that their containments overshadow their subversions. Aware of the conservative dimensions of these figures and their narratives, I have nonetheless chosen to attend to their gendered and cultural counternarratives. Although I am much more skeptical than a James or a Conrad about the value of art for art's sake, I finally share their belief that art does matter, that "the power of the written word to make you hear, to make you feel ... before all, to make you *see*," as Conrad so powerfully put it, can make a difference. I believe, with the writers discussed in this book, in the cultural work that writing can do. These singular fictions of bachelorhood, a phrase which describes my own project as well as the texts discussed in this book, do the gendered work of culture in more than one sense of the phrase, creating new understandings, new imaginings, and new stories of manhood.

Notes

1 Percival Pollard, "The Bachelor in Fiction," *The Bookman* 12, no. 2 (October 1900), 146. Further page references will be given in the body of the text.

2 Max Nordau published *Degeneration* in 1892; it was translated into English in 1895. The founder of the most influential forensic psychiatric system in the nineteenth century, Cesare Lombroso, theorized that the "criminal type" was an atavistic throwback; in *The Man of Genius* (1888; English edn. 1891), he argued that genius was a form of madness.

3 Ian Watt's *The Rise of the Novel* (Berkeley: University of California Press, 1957) is generally recognized as a seminal moment in the critical enterprise of tracing the intertwined histories of the novel, marriage, and bourgeois domesticity. Other key studies include Raymond Williams, *The English Novel from Dickens to Lawrence* (New York: Oxford University Press, 1970); Sandra Gilbert and Susan Gubar, *The Madwoman in the Attic: The Woman Writer and the Nineteenth-Century Literary Imagination* (New Haven: Yale University Press, 1979); Nancy Armstrong, *Desire and Domestic Fiction: A Political History of the Novel* (New York: Oxford University Press, 1987); and Joseph Allen Boone, *Tradition Counter Tradition: Love and the Form of Fiction* (University of Chicago Press, 1987). In my view of the novel and domesticity as regulatory practices and institutions, I am following a well-trodden Foucauldian path, a trail which has been perhaps most vividly blazed by D. A. Miller, *The Novel and the Police* (Berkeley: University of California Press, 1987). I depart from Miller's emphasis on the novel's ideological containments, however, in my attention to the revisionary and subversive potential of the bachelor narrator, a figure whom I see as intrinsic, not external, to the worlds of the novel and domesticity.

4 This double sense of "figure" depends on Barthes's distinction between representation – in which desire circulates within the text – and figuration – in which desire circulates not only within the text, but also between text and reader; see *The Pleasure of the Text*, trans. Richard Miller (New York: Hill and Wang, 1975), p. 58.

5 "High art" and "modernist art" do not constitute identical discursive fields, but their contiguity and coextensivity in this period is remarkable. For theoretical and historical accounts of these intersecting cultural formations, see Andreas Huyssen, *After the Great Divide: Modernism, Mass Culture, Post-*

modernism (Bloomington: Indiana University Press, 1986); James Naremore and Patrick Brantlinger (eds.), *Modernity and Mass Culture* (Bloomington: Indiana University Press, 1991); Thomas Strychacz, *Modernism, Mass Culture, and Professionalism* (Cambridge University Press, 1993); and Maria DiBattista, "Introduction," *High and Low Moderns: Literature and Culture, 1889–1939,* ed. Maria DiBattista and Lucy McDiarmid (Oxford University Press, 1996).

6 Accounts of the gendering of modernism and of the high/low divide which I have found particularly useful include Ann Ardis, *New Women, New Novels: Feminism and Early Modernism* (New Brunswick: Rutgers University Press, 1990), and Marianne DeKoven, *Rich and Strange: Gender, History, and Modernism* (Princeton University Press, 1991).

7 Like the "long eighteenth century," which designates the period in English history from 1688 to 1832, the "long nineteenth century" has been used by historians to describe an era extending from the early 1790s to 1918 or 1928; for example, see James Vernon (ed.), *Re-reading the Constitution: New Narratives in the Political History of England's Long Nineteenth Century* (New York: Cambridge University Press, 1996).

8 This explosion of bachelor discourse was itself part of the dramatic increase in the production and consumption of printed material in the nineteenth century, culminating in what has been called the "Magazine Revolution" of the 1890s. It would be naïve to think that periodical writings provide a transparent window onto or a direct influence upon the historical scene, but they nevertheless illuminate the fears, desires, and interests of the era's writers, editors, publishers, and readers. I consider them a valuable source of insight into the attitudes and beliefs that intersected with more material aspects of cultural change. There is a rapidly growing body of work on periodical publication; for several examples, see Christopher Wilson, "The Rhetoric of Consumption: Mass-Market Magazines and the Demise of the Gentle Reader, 1880–1920," *The Culture of Consumption: Critical Essays in American History, 1880–1980,* ed. Richard Wightman Fox and T. J. Jackson Lears (New York: Pantheon, 1983); Helen Damon-Moore, *Magazines for the Millions: Gender and Commerce in the* Ladies' Home Journal *and the* Saturday Evening Post, *1880–1910* (Albany: State University of New York Press, 1994); Matthew Schneirov, *The Dream of a New Social Order: Popular Magazines in America, 1893–1914* (New York: Columbia University Press, 1994); and Richard Ohmann, *Selling Culture: Magazines, Markets, and Class at the Turn of the Century* (London: Verso, 1996).

9 "Uneven developments" is Mary Poovey's phrase; see *Uneven Developments: The Ideological Work of Gender in Mid-Victorian England* (University of Chicago Press, 1988).

10 "Gender trouble" is the term Judith Butler uses to critique the notion that fixed gender identities are grounded in nature, bodies, or in heterosexuality; see *Gender Trouble: Feminism and the Subversion of Identity* (New York: Routledge, 1990).

11 Eve Kosofsky Sedgwick, *Epistemology of the Closet* (Berkeley: University of California Press, 1990), p. 194. Sedgwick addresses the figure of the bachelor in her 1985 English Institute essay, "The Beast in the Closet: James and the Writing of Homosexual Panic," reprinted in *Epistemology*, pp. 182–212.

12 See "Introduction: Axiomatic," in Sedgwick, *Epistemology*, pp. 1–63.

13 Sedgwick, *Epistemology*, p. 188.

14 Of course, an attachment to youth also signifies within Victorian and Freudian developmental models of male desire which posit an evolution from immature homoeroticism to mature heterosexuality. My point is not that the bachelor's investment in the girl's youth is not homosexual or should not be read as such, but rather that gender differences may be less salient than other differences or, for that matter, than points of similarity, between the subject and the object(s) whom he desires.

15 Jonothan Dollimore, *Sexual Dissidence: Augustine to Wilde, Freud to Foucault* (Oxford: Clarendon Press, 1991) and Teresa DeLauretis, *The Practice of Love: Lesbian Sexuality and Perverse Desire* (Bloomington: Indiana University Press, 1994) who have elucidated the political and poetic activity of so-called "deviance" and "perversity" within cultural norms. For an account of the theortical benefits and pitfalls of a poetics and politics of the perverse, see Joseph Allen Boone, *Libidinal Currents: Sexuality and the Shaping of Modernism* (University of Chicago Press, 1998), a brilliant study which I encountered just as my own book was going to press.

16 On the permeability of the boundaries between modernist and non-modernist writing, see Raymond Williams, "Beyond Cambridge English" in *Writing in Society* (London: Verso, 1985) and "Distance" in *What I Came To Say* (London: Hutchinson, 1989); Louis Menand, *Discovering Modernism: T. S. Eliot and His Context* (Oxford University Press, 1987); Thomas Strychacz, *Modernism, Professionalism, and Mass Culture*; and Bruce Robbins, *Secular Vocations: Intellectuals, Professionalism, Culture* (London: Verso, 1993).

17 In "Melodramas of Beset Manhood: How Theories of American Fiction Exclude Women Authors," *American Quarterly* 33, no. 2 (Summer 1981), Nina Baym describes the canon-making practices of twentieth-century male New Critics who portrayed nineteenth-century male writers as beleaguered by a mass market for fiction dominated by female writers and readers. Baym exempts writers such as Howells and James from the sexist bias of the New Critical champions of male writers, yet many nineteenth-century male writers, including James, are aptly described by Baym's paradigm.

18 For a seminal account of melodrama, from which has developed a rich body of work in feminist, queer, and film theory, see Peter Brooks, *The Melodramatic Imagination: Balzac, Henry James, Melodrama, and the Mode of Excess* (1976; New Haven: Yale University Press, 1995).

19 The governess is a comparable threshold figure who marks by transgressing the classed, gendered, and sexual boundaries of the nuclear family, and also of bourgeois femininity. For readings of the figure of the governess which bring out these issues, see Jane Gallop, *The Daughter's Seduction: Feminism and*

Psychoanalysis (Ithaca: Cornell University Press, 1982), pp. 141–8; and Poovey, "The Anathematized Race: The Governess and *Jane Eyre*," *Uneven Developments*, pp. 126–63.

20 Genette coins these terms to counteract the imprecision he discerns in the more traditional categories of first-person and third-person narration. As Genette rightly observes, *someone* – whether real or imagined, specified or unspecified, omniscient or epistemologically limited – is always speaking or writing in the first person, even in what we call third-person narration. In *Narrative Discourse: An Essay in Method*, trans. Jane E. Lewin (Ithaca: Cornell University Press, 1980), Genette distinguishes between "the character whose point of view orients the narrative perspective" and "the character who is the narrator," that is: between "who sees" and "who speaks" (p. 186). But in *Narrative Discourse Revisited*, trans. Jane E. Lewin (Ithaca: Cornell University Press, 1988), Genette observes that "it would be better to ask . . . where is the focus of perception" (p. 64). The question that Genette refocuses for us, then, is not the number, voice, or mood of persons speaking or writing, but the *placement* of the perceiving consciousness with respect to the narrative *mis en scène*.

21 Genette, *Narrative Discourse*, p. 245.

22 "Dominant fiction" is Kaja Silverman's formulation; see *Male Subjectivity at the Margins* (New York: Routledge, 1992), pp. 15–51.

23 Eve Kosofsky Sedgwick, *Between Men: English Literature and Male Homosocial Desire* (New York: Columbia University Press, 1985), see pp. 1–20. See also Gayle Rubin, "The Traffic in Women: Notes Toward a Political Economy of Sex," *Toward an Anthropology of Women*, ed. Rayna Reiter (New York: Monthly Review Press, 1975).

24 My account of the "other Oedipus" is indebted to Christopher Newfield's reading of Freud's *Group Psychology and the Analysis of the Ego* (1921); see "Democracy and Male Homoeroticism," *The Yale Journal of Criticism* 6, no. 2 (Fall 1993), 48–54. See also Newfield's *The Emerson Effect: Individualism and Submission in America* (University of Chicago Press, 1996).

25 For a radical critique of psychoanalytic methodologies, see Gilles Deleuze and Félix Guattari, *Anti-Oedipus: Capitalism and Schizophrenia*, trans. Robert Hurley, Mark Seem, and Helen R. Lane (Minneapolis: University of Minnesota Press, 1983).

26 On the mutual imbrication of identification and desire, see Sedgwick, *Between Men*, pp. 24–7 and *Epistemology*, pp. 61–2 and pp. 159–60; Silverman, *Male Subjectivity at the Margins*, p. 317; and Judith Butler, *Bodies That Matter: On the Discursive Limits of "Sex"* (New York: Routledge, 1993), pp. 95–111.

27 Butler, *Bodies That Matter*, p. 105.

28 Critical treatments of narrative in relation to its ideological contexts include Peter Brooks, *Reading for the Plot: Design and Intention in Narrative* (New York: Vintage-Random House, 1985) and *Body Work: Objects of Desire in Modern Narrative* (Cambridge, MA: Harvard University Press, 1993); Robyn Warhol, *Gendered Interventions: Narrative Discourse in the Victorian Novel* (New Brun-

swick, NJ: Rutgers University Press, 1989); and Michal Peled Ginsburg, *Economies of Change: Form and Transformation in the Nineteenth-Century Novel* (Stanford University Press, 1996). For an overview of the question of a feminist narratology, see the dialogue between Gerald Prince, "On Narratology: Criteria, Corpus, Context," and Susan S. Lanser, "Sexing the Narrative: Propriety, Desire and the Engendering of Narratology," both in *Narrative* 3, no. 1 (January 1995).

29 Edith Wharton, for one, self-consciously alludes to two influential mid-century bachelor narratives in her only first-person narrated novel, *Ethan Frome* (1911; Harmondsworth: Penguin, 1987). Wharton's naming of "Zeena" recalls Zenobia of *The Blithedale Romance*; her introductory defense of her novel's form – "I might have sat [the narrator] down before a village gossip who would have poured out the whole affair to him" (pp. xx–xxi) – gestures towards what Nelly Dean calls her "gossip's fashion" of telling the story to Lockwood, the bachelor narrator of *Wuthering Heights*.

I   TROUBLE IN PARADISE

1 "The Bachelor Bedroom," *All the Year Round* 1, no. 15 (August 6, 1859), 355. Further page references from this text will be given in the body of the chapter. This piece is attributed to Wilkie Collins in Ella Ann Oppenlander, *Dickens' All the Year Round: Descriptive Index and Contributor List* (Troy, NY: Whitson Publishing Co., 1984).

2 This phrase entitles Mary Ryan's *The Empire of the Mother: American Writing about Domesticity, 1830–1860* (New York: Haworth Press in association with the Institute for Research in History, 1982). My discussion of nineteenth-century domesticity is indebted to Ryan's groundbreaking work, especially *Cradle of the Middle Class: The Family in Oneida County, New York, 1790–1865* (New York: Cambridge University Press, 1981).

3 *Oxford English Dictionary*, s.v. "bachelor." The *OED* also notes that bachelor was latinized as "baccalauris," subsequently by wordplay to "baccalaureus," as if connected to "bacca lauri," laurel berry, which has sometimes been incorrectly given as the etymology. This false etymology is given, for example, in T. S. M., "Bachelors and Spinsters," *Leisure Hour* 24 (1875); however, this article's playful presentation of other patently bogus etymological cognates – including "battalarius," "battelarius," and "bottle-arius" – makes it uncertain whether the incorrect etymology is given in earnest.

4 Leonore Davidoff and Catherine Hall, *Family Fortunes: Men and Women of the English Middle Class, 1780–1850* (University of Chicago Press, 1987), note that in the late eighteenth and early nineteenth centuries "[m]asculine identity was equated with an emerging concept of occupation, while women remained within a familial framework" (p. 30). My account of the contradictions of bourgeois masculine identity is indebted to Davidoff and Hall, and to Catherine Hall, *White, Male, and Middle Class: Explorations in Feminism and History* (New York: Routledge, 1988).

5 W. R. Greg, "Why Are Women Redundant?" *National Review* 14, no. 28 (April 1862), 452.

6 How to define "middle class" has long been, and continues to be, subject to debate. Possible parameters include income, home ownership, the employment of domestic servants, and respectability itself as an ideal or aspiration. In what follows, I use the term "middle class" to refer to the writers, audiences, and subjects of representation whose world view seems to have been deeply informed by domestic and separate spheres ideologies, a circular definition perhaps, but sufficient for my purposes here.

7 Linda Kerber addresses the history and limitations of "woman's sphere" as a metaphor within cultural analysis; see "Separate Spheres, Female Worlds, Woman's Place: The Rhetoric of Women's History," *Journal of American History* 75, no. 1 (June 1988).

8 Degler argues that an increasing proportion of women in the United States did not marry, and Jacobson's and Monahan's data shows that for both men and women, the marriage rate bottomed out in the mid-1890s and began rising, though slowly, after that. See Carl N. Degler, *At Odds: Women and the Family in America from the Revolution to the Present* (New York: Oxford University Press, 1980), p. 160; Paul H. Jacobson, *American Marriage and Divorce* (New York: Rinehart, 1959), pp. 21–3; Thomas Monahan, *The Pattern of Age at Marriage in the United States*, 2 vols. (Philadelphia: Stephenson Bros, 1951), vol. I, p. 92.

9 Greg estimates the discrepancy at 440,000 more men than women in the colonies and the United States, a figure that may account for immigrants from countries besides England. Helsinger *et al.* observe that Greg understates the problem of the financial support of unmarried women, since the 1851 census puts the total number of unmarried women at 2.5 million, including 795,194 widows; see Elizabeth K. Helsinger, Robin Lauterbach Sheets, and William Veeder, *The Woman Question: Society and Literature in Britain and America, 1837–1883*, 2 vols. (New York: Garland, 1983), vol. II, pp. 134–9. The sex ratio in Wales, by contrast, was virtually even and unchanging; see Donald Read, *The Age of Urban Democracy: England 1868–1914*, rev. ed. (London: Longman, 1994), p. 40.

10 For an intensive treatment of the demographics of American bachelorhood, see Howard Chudacoff, *The Age of the Bachelor: Creating an American Subculture* (Princeton University Press, forthcoming). My thanks to Professor Chudacoff for allowing me to present his findings.

11 In "Why Are Women Redundant?" W. R. Greg proposed female emigration, as did "A Plea for the Men," *The Spectator* 67, no. 3, 309 (November 28, 1891): "After all, why should not women emigrate to seek a husband, in the same way as men emigrate to seek a fortune? Emigration is to a certain degree responsible for the want of marriageable men in England; therefore let it form an escape for the superfluity of marriageable women" (p. 757).
The anxiety about the falling marriage rate was not only, or even primarily, generated by fears that women would go hungry; a more immediate evil was

the unwelcome competition with men that the increasing presence of unmarried women in the workforce was thought to create.

12 "Why Bachelors Should Not be Taxed," *The North American Review* 184, no. 607 (February 1, 1907), 333 and 334.

13 James Robertson, "Some Pleas for a Special Tax on the Bachelor," *The Westminster Review* 170, no. 5 (November 1908), 531–5; 533 and 534.

14 Robertson, "Some Pleas for a Special Tax," 531.

15 See F. M. L. Thompson, *The Rise of Respectable Society: A Social History of Victorian Britain, 1830–1900* (Cambridge, MA: Harvard University Press, 1988), pp. 51–5; John R. Gillis, *For Better, for Worse: British Marriages, 1600 to the Present* (New York: Oxford University Press, 1985), p. 232; J. A. Banks and Olive Banks, *Feminism and Family Planning in Victorian England* (University of Liverpool Press, 1965), p. 45.

16 See Monahan, *The Pattern of Age*, pp. 104 and 112; see also Elaine Tyler May, *Great Expectations: Marriage and Divorce in Post-Victorian America* (University of Chicago Press, 1980), pp. 62 and 169.

17 In *The Woman Question*, Helsinger *et al.* observe that "between 1800 and 1900 the birthrate fell dramatically in America and substantially in Britain" (p. 72). According to Stephanie Coontz, *The Social Origins of Private Life* (London: Verso, 1988), "American fertility ... fell by nearly 40 percent between 1855 and 1915" (p. 260). Degler, *At Odds*, pp. 178–209, argues that this major shift, called the "demographic transition," had already substantially occurred in America by 1830, and had in fact begun in the early 1700s.

18 In *Country House Life: Family and Servants, 1815–1914* (London: Blackwell, 1994), Jessica Gerard argues that the effects of primogeniture among the landed gentry in the second half of the nineteenth century could be seen in the fact that "many younger sons ... elected to remain bachelors, while those who did go courting were often discouraged as ineligible by match-making mamas" (p. 32). Although "primogeniture ... encourag[ed] heirs to marry," Gerard notes the surprising fact that one in ten male landowners in her research sample remained unmarried. To explain this unexpectedly high figure, she argues that the law of primogeniture paradoxically encouraged – or at least was compatible with – nonmarriage for eldest sons as well as younger sons: "The greater value placed on individualism permitted heirs to make a personal choice [of nonmarriage], bolstered by primogeniture, which secured the inheritance by entail on a brother or nephew" (p. 23).

19 See E. Anthony Rotundo, *American Manhood: Transformations in Masculinity from the Revolution to the Modern Age* (New York: Basic Books, 1993), pp. 114–15; and Richard Sennett, *Families Against the City: Middle Class Homes of Industrial Chicago, 1872–1890* (Cambridge, MA: Harvard University Press, 1970), p. 206. Ethnic differences offset these trends; for example, see George Chauncey, *Gay New York: Gender, Urban Culture, and the Making of the Gay Male World, 1890–1940* (New York: Basic Books, 1994), p. 77, on Irish-American marriage patterns, and Thompson, *The Rise of Respectable Society*, p. 54, on the

marriage patterns of the Irish in Ireland. Read, *The Age of Urban Democracy*, indicates the correlation between class and marriage age for English men: "In 1871 the mean age of marriage among manual workers stood about 24.0 years, whereas among shopkeepers and farmers it was 27.0 and among professional men and managers it reached nearly 30.0" (p. 7); the mean age of marriage for brides varied much less between classes. In *Feminism and Family Planning*, pp. 29–30, Banks and Banks note that while the marriage age was actually lower in the general population than earlier in the nineteenth century, writers of the period portrayed it as higher, an exaggeration that reflects their perception of later marriage age; they also note that *rich* men did, in fact, marry later.

20 See Caroll Smith-Rosenberg, *Disorderly Conduct: Visions of Gender in Victorian America* (New York: Oxford University Press, 1986), pp. 247–54; and Lillian Faderman, *Odd Girls and Twilight Lovers: A History of Lesbian Life in Twentieth-Century America* (New York: Penguin, 1992), pp. 12–16.

21 This statement is attributed to "an English scientist" in the "Live Questions" column in *The Cosmopolitan*, which in November and December of 1888 featured selected "representative" responses to the question, "Is Marriage a Failure?", *The Cosmopolitan* 6, no. 1 (November 1888), 93. Earlier that year, this question had provoked a lively correspondence debate consisting of over 27,000 letters in the English newspaper, the *Daily Telegraph*. Twenty years earlier, the *Telegraph* had aired, or manufactured, a comparable correspondence debate over the choice, "Marriage or Celibacy?"; see John M. Robson, *Marriage or Celibacy?: The* Daily Telegraph *on a Victorian Dilemma* (University of Toronto Press, 1995), pp. 26–43.

22 For a theoretical and historical overview of "race suicide" in turn-of-the-century popular discourse, see Gail Bederman, *Manliness and Civilization: A Cultural History of Gender and Race in the United States, 1880–1917* (University of Chicago Press, 1995), pp. 196–206.

23 Read, *The Age of Urban Democracy*, cites as evidence for these shifts the difference between the 1857 and the 1873 editions of J. H. Walsh's *Manual of Domestic Economy*, noting that "middle-class outlay on food, drink, domestic service and household goods seems to have increased ... by one-half" (pp. 9–10).

24 John Burnett dates the emergence of this concept in the 1840s, just before the rise in marriage age began; see *A Social History of Housing, 1815–1985*, 2nd ed. (London: Methuen, 1986), p. 100.

25 "Bachelors – Why?: Views of Five Hundred of Them on the Income Needed for Matrimony and the Fitness of the Girls for Household Management," *Good Housekeeping* 50, no. 3 (March 1910) and no. 4 (April 1910); "On the Excessive Influence of Women," *Temple Bar* 49 (February 1877); "Single Life Among Us," *Harper's New Monthly Magazine* 18, no. 106 (March 1859), 501. In "I Have No Genius for Marriage: Bachelorhood in Urban America, 1870–1930," PhD thesis, University of Michigan (in progress), Peter Laipson argues that after 1870 the burden of blame for the rise of bachelorhood was

shifted to the shoulders of women; I have not, however, been able to find evidence of this pattern in the popular magazine representations. I am grateful to Peter Laipson for allowing me to read his work-in-progress.

26 Mrs. Alfred [Alice] Pollard, "Why Men Don't Marry: An Eighteenth-Century Answer," *Longman's Magazine* 23, no. 134 (November 1893), 156.

27 Medical student bachelors appear, for example, in "A Bachelor's Story," *Chamber's Journal of Popular Literature, Science, and Arts* 56, no. 808 (June 21, 1879); Clement Bird, "A Bachelor's Bedroom," *Belgravia* 62, no. 245 (March 1887); and Pauline Hopkins, "Talma Gordon," *Colored American Magazine* 1 (October 1900), which opens with its doctor narrator asserting that "I was a bachelor, then, without ties" (p. 271). Stevenson's *The Strange Case of Dr. Jekyll and Mr. Hyde* (1886) famously features a bachelor community consisting largely of lawyers and doctors. In the nineteenth century, the term "professions" expanded from its earlier denotation of medicine, law, the clergy, and the military to include engineering, architecture, accounting and a number of other occupations, sometimes including the arts and authorship; see Magali S. Larson, *The Rise of Professionalism: A Sociological Analysis* (Berkeley: University of California Press, 1977), pp. 2–8.

28 "Marriage of a Medical Man Not Advisable," *British Medical Journal* (November 23, 1861), 570.

29 See Lynne Segal, *Slow Motion: Changing Masculinities, Changing Men* (New Brunswick, NJ: Rutgers University Press, 1990), p. 105. See also Donald E. Hall (ed.), *Muscular Christianity: Embodying the Victorian Age*, (Cambridge University Press, 1994); Claudia Nelson, "Sex and the Single Boy: Ideals of Manliness and Sexuality in Victorian Literature for Boys," *Victorian Studies* 32, no. 4 (Summer 1989), 525–50, especially 525–6 and 547; Norman Vance, *Sinews of the Spirit: The Ideal of Christian Manliness in Victorian Literature and Religious Thought* (New York: Cambridge University Press, 1985); and Bruce Haley, *The Healthy Body and Victorian Culture* (Cambridge, MA: Harvard University Press, 1978), pp. 123–60.

30 On this shift, see Bederman, *Manliness and Civilization*. See also Maurizia Boscagli, *Eye on the Flesh: Fashions of Masculinity in the Early Twentieth Century* (Boulder, CO: Westview Press, 1996), pp. 172–4; Mark C. Carnes and Clyde Griffen (eds.), *Meanings for Manhood: Constructions of Masculinity in Victorian America* (Chicago: University of Chicago Press, 1990), pp. 2–3; John D'Emilio and Estelle B. Freedman, *Intimate Matters: A History of Sexuality in America* (New York: Harper and Row, 1988), p. 179; and J. A. Mangan and James Walvin (eds.), *Manliness and Morality: Middle-Class Masculinity in Britain and America 1800–1940* (New York: St. Martin's Press, 1987).

31 Timothy Gilfoyle, *City of Eros: New York City, Prostitution, and the Commercialization of Sex, 1790–1920* (New York: Norton, 1992), pp. 102 and 98.

32 Chauncey, *Gay New York*, p. 79. Compare Elliott Gorn, *The Manly Art: Bare-Knuckle Prize Fighting in America* (Ithaca: Cornell University Press, 1986): "Sociologists have talked of a 'bachelor subculture' to capture a phenomenon so common to nineteenth- and early twentieth-century cities: large

numbers of unmarried males finding their primary human contact in one another's company... Here, implicitly, was a rejection of the cult of domesticity so characteristic of bourgeois Victorian life" (pp. 141–2); and Gilfoyle, *City of Eros*: "the bachelor attack[ed] ... the feminized family and the trappings of domestic life" (p. 104).

33 Gilfoyle, *City of Eros*, p. 104.

34 Chauncey, *Gay New York*, pp. 76–9, and Gorn, *The Manly Art*, pp. 141–2, themselves note that the nomenclature is misleading.

35 See Rotundo, *American Manhood*, pp. 143–4 on clubs as alternatives to domesticity, and Laipson, "I Have No Genius For Marriage," chapter 2, pp. 13–19, on clubs as quasi-domestic institutions. On nineteenth-century fraternal orders as counterparts to domesticity, see Mary Ann Clawson, *Constructing Brotherhood: Class, Gender, and Fraternalism* (Princeton University Press, 1989), especially p. 175; and Mark C. Carnes, *Secret Ritual and Manhood in Victorian America* (New Haven: Yale University Press, 1989), pp. 39–150.

36 In *Subduing Satan: Religion, Recreation, and Manhood in the Rural South, 1865–1920* (Chapel Hill: University of North Carolina Press, 1990), Ted Ownby employs the geographical description of "male quarters ... a few blocks normally provided the settings for exclusively male professions, services, and recreations" (p. 39), a spatial conceptualization which might provide a useful alternate grid for understanding the multiple subcultures within which bourgeois men interacted and defined themselves.

37 Greg, "Why Are Women Redundant?" p. 452.

38 Jeff Nunokawa emphasizes the sinister aspects of this comment, seeing such rhetoric "in a novel that helped transform the Victorian bachelor into the suspected homosexual" (p. 161) as having a sexually disenfranchising effect; see "The Importance of Being Bored: The Dividends of Ennui in *The Picture of Dorian Gray*," *Novel Gazing: Queer Readings in Fiction*, Eve Kosofsky Sedgwick (ed.), (Durham: Duke University Press, 1997).

39 Coontz, *The Social Origins of Private Life*, p. 227.

40 See David Leverenz, *Manhood and the American Renaissance: The Subversive Imagination in the Age of Emerson and Melville* (Ithaca: Cornell University Press, 1989), pp. 227–58, for a discussion of the conflicts that "entrepreneurial masculinity" entailed for antebellum male writers. See also Cynthia Griffin Wolff, "Masculinity in *Uncle Tom's Cabin*," *American Quarterly*, 47, no. 4 (December 1995), for an account of alternative styles of masculinity among antebellum abolitionists and other social reformers.

41 For an overview of the image and ideology of Victorian fatherhood, see Claudia Nelson, *Invisible Men: Fatherhood in Victorian Periodicals, 1850–1910* (Athens: University of Georgia Press, 1995).

42 See Kevin J. Mumford, "'Lost Manhood' Found: Male Sexual Impotence and Victorian Culture in the United States," *Journal of the History of Sexuality* 3, no. 1 (July 1992), 33–57, for a summary of the use of the crisis paradigm in histories of American culture and Anglo-American manhood. Mumford himself argues that the late nineteenth century was characterized by a

"sexual – more than a gender – crisis" (p. 48).

43 Bederman, *Manliness and Civilization*, pp. 10–11 and p. 7.

44 Frederick W. Shelton, "On Old Bachelors," *Southern Literary Messenger* 19, no. 4 (April 1853); Sarah Tooley, "Famous Bachelors," *The Woman at Home* 6 (February 1898); Dorothy Dix, "Bachelors," *Good Housekeeping* 57, no. 5 (November 1913). "Dorothy Dix" was the *nom de plume* of Elizabeth Gilmer, a reporter who wrote an advice-for-the-lovelorn column in the New Orleans *Times-Picayune*.

45 "Marriage Not à-la-Mode," *Temple Bar* 9 (November 1863), 507; "Alarming Increase of Old Maids and Bachelors in New England," *Literary Digest* 65, no. 2 (April 10, 1920), 66.

46 *The Bachelor Married; or the Biter Bit* (Leeds: Webb and Millington, 1830); "Bachelors – Why?", *Good Housekeeping*, p. 335.

47 Mrs. Ross, *The Bachelor and the Married Man; or The Equilibrium and the "Balance of Comfort"* (London: 1817); *The Old Bachelor, After Southey's "Cataract of Lodore," Described and Dedicated to Bachelors and Bazaars* (Tamworth: J. Thompson, 1839); Frank Chaffee, *Bachelor Buttons* (New York: George M. Allen Co., 1892), pp. 10–11; Deshler Welch, *The Bachelor and the Chafing Dish* (New York: F. Tennyson Neely, 1896), p. 123.

48 "Why We Men Do Not Marry, By One of Us," *Temple Bar* 84 (October 1888), 220–1.

49 Shelton, "On Old Bachelors," pp. 227–8.

50 T. S. M., "Bachelors and Spinsters," *Leisure Hour* (1875), 662–3; *The Old Bachelor, After Southey's "Cataract of Lodore"* (1839).

51 "The Bachelor: A Modern Idyll," *Temple Bar* 25 (February 1869), 362–3.

52 "Single Life Among Us," p. 502. Compare the internal contradiction between idleness and avariciousness perceived in *The Bachelor Married; or the Biter Bit*: "as in the case of most bachelors, there was a kind of inconsistency in the character of Mr. Rhodes; for notwithstanding his anxious desire of amassing wealth, he was incumbered by a certain indolence and sluggishness that prevailed over every consideration" (p. 5).

53 See Herbert L. Sussman, *Victorian Masculinities: Manhood and Masculine Poetics in Early Victorian Literature and Art* (Cambridge University Press, 1995), pp. 10–11, on the nineteenth-century notion of "male energy" that included but was not limited to sexual energy. Earlier studies along comparable lines include Carol Christ, "Victorian Masculinity and the Angel in the House," *A Widening Sphere: Changing Roles of Victorian Women*, Martha Vicinus (ed.), (Bloomington: Indiana University Press, 1977), and G. J. Barker-Benfield, *The Horrors of the Half-Known Life: Male Attitudes Toward Women and Sexuality in Nineteenth-Century America* (New York: Harper and Row, 1976), pp. 72–5 and pp. 179–90.

54 Helsinger *et al.*, *The Woman Question*, p. 72 and p. 280. In "Forbidden by God, Despised by Men: Masturbation, Medical Warnings, Moral Panic, and Manhood in Great Britain, 1850–1950," *Forbidden History: The State, Society, and the Regulation of Sexuality in Modern Europe*, ed. John C. Fout (University of

Chicago Press, 1992), Lesley A. Hall argues that while "homosexuality sometimes might be attributed to a continued habit of masturbation . . . the prime danger of self-abuse was perceived as the establishment of a habit of dangerous indulgence in sensual pleasure, eroding self-discipline and leading to a career of self-gratification likely to involve fornication with harlots, ending in venereal disease" (p. 302).

55 My main source on spermatorrhea is John S. Haller, Jr., and Robin M. Haller, *The Physician and Sexuality in Victorian America* (Urbana: University of Illinois Press, 1976), pp. 190–234.

56 Barker-Benfield coins the term "spermatic economy" to describe the closed energy, or hydraulic, model; see *Horrors of the Half-Known Life*, p. 181. See also David J. Pivar, *Purity Crusade: Sexual Morality and Social Control, 1868–1900* (Westport, CT: Greenwood Press, 1973); Haller, Jr., and Haller, *The Physician and Sexuality in Victorian America*, pp. 211–25; and Charles Rosenberg, "Sexuality, Class, and Role in Nineteenth-Century America," *American Quarterly*, 35, no. 2 (May 1973).

57 Christopher Craft, *Another Kind of Love: Male Homosexual Desire in English Discourse, 1850–1920* (Berkeley: University of California Press, 1994), p. 5.

58 Jeffrey Weeks describes the conceptual linkage among prostitution, homosexuality, and deviance via the infamous Labouchère Amendment to the Criminal Law Amendment Act of 1885, a connection that was further heightened by late nineteenth-century scandals such as the Cleveland Street brothel scandal in 1889–90 and the Oscar Wilde scandal; see *Sex, Politics and Society; the Regulation of Sexuality since 1800* (London: Longman, 1981), pp. 86–9; and Weeks, "Inverts, Perverts, and Mary-Annes: Male Prostitution and the Regulation of Homosexuality in England in the Nineteenth and Early Twentieth Centuries," *Hidden from History: Reclaiming the Gay and Lesbian Past*, Martin Bauml Duberman, Martha Vicinus, and George Chauncey, Jr. (eds.), (New York: New American Library, 1989), p. 200.

59 Sedgwick, *Epistemology*, pp. 9 and 8.

60 Eric Partridge, *A Dictionary of Slang and Unconventional English*, ed. Paul Beale 8th ed. (New York: Macmillan, 1984). Also, "chambre" is the given derivation for "chum," suggesting shared residency as a basis for male friendship.

61 "The Bachelor Bedroom," (see chapter 1, n. 1); "Bachelor's Hall," *Harper's New Monthly Magazine* 31, no. 124 (September 1860); "Bachelor's Hall," *All The Year Round* 133, no. 799 (March 22, 1884), no. 800 (March 29, 1884); Clement Bird, "A Bachelor's Bedroom," (see chapter 1, n. 27); and "The Bachelors' Wing," *Living Age* 249, no. 3222 (April 7, 1906).

62 The nineteenth-century rise of consumer culture has been treated extensively; several of the most influential studies are Alan Trachtenberg, *The Incorporation of America: Culture and Society in the Gilded Age* (New York: Hill and Wang, 1982); Richard Wightman Fox and T. J. Jackson Lears, *The Culture of Consumption: Critical Essays in American History, 1880–1980* (New York: Pantheon, 1983); and Daniel Horowitz, *The Morality of Spending: Attitudes Toward*

the Consumer Society in America, 1875–1940 (Baltimore: Johns Hopkins University Press, 1985).

63 For her theorization of "masculine domesticity" as practiced by married men in American suburbs, I am indebted to Margaret Marsh, "Suburban Men and Masculine Domesticity, 1870–1915," *American Quarterly* 40, no. 2 (June 1988); see also Marsh, *Suburban Lives* (New Brunswick, NJ: Rutgers University Press, 1990), pp. 74–83.

64 "The Bachelor's Christmas," *Blackwood's Edinburgh Magazine* 23, no. 134 (January 1828), 25 and 14.

65 Sharon Marcus, *Apartment Stories: City and Home in Nineteenth-Century Paris and London* (Berkeley: University of California Press, 1999, ch. 3, n. 19. During the Renaissance, chambers were granted for life to members of the Inns of Court, but gradually the modern practice of renting chambers by the year replaced this earlier system; see W. C. Richardson, *A History of the Inns of Court: With Special Reference to the Period of the Renaissance* (Baton Rouge, LA: Claitor's Publishing Division, 1975), pp. 28–9.

66 Charles Dickens, *The Old Curiosity Shop* (1840–1; London: Penguin, 1985), chapter 7, p. 101.

67 The single gentlemen's "cooking apparatus" resembles Alexis Soyer's "Magic Stove" and Thomas Tozer's "Bachelor Kettle," devices that began to be marketed in the 1850s; see Sarah Freeman, *Muttons and Oysters: the Victorians and their Food* (London: V. Gollancz, 1989), pp. 114–15. It is a forerunner of the turn-of-the-century chafing dish, a household appliance associated with bachelors, and also of the somewhat earlier "patent bachelor's kitchen" described in the bachelor-narrated sketch, "The Wife for Me," *Once A Week* (May 26, 1860).

68 Herman Melville, "The Paradise of Bachelors" and "The Tartarus of Maids" (1855), *The Complete Stories of Herman Melville*, ed. Jay Leyda (New York: Random House, 1949), p. 204.

69 Letter to the editor, *The Builder* 34, no. 1720 (Jan. 22, 1876), p. 82.

70 Burnett, *A Social History of Housing*, p. 209. Marmion Savage's *The Bachelor of the Albany* (1848) uses this classic bachelor residence as its setting. The Albany is also the in-town address of Jack/Earnest, a bachelor who epitomizes the pleasures of a double life, in Oscar Wilde's *The Importance of Being Earnest* (1895).

71 Dolores Hayden, *The Grand Domestic Revolution: A History of Feminist Designs for American Homes, Neighborhoods, and Cities* (Cambridge, MA: MIT Press, 1981), p. 72; Hayden quotes here from Andrew Alpern, *Apartments for the Affluent: A Historical Survey of Buildings in New York* (New York: McGraw-Hill, 1975), p. 1.

72 Thompson, *The Rise of Respectable Society*, p. 172; see also Marcus, *Apartment Stories*, ch. 3.

73 In "Nobody's Angels: Domestic Ideology and Middle-Class Women in the Victorian Novel," *PMLA* 107, no. 2 (March 1992), Elizabeth Langland discusses "the increasing demand for the segregation and privacy of sexes and classes in Victorian houses" (pp. 294–5). The division of space by sex

and class is not identical to the understood need of *individuals* for privacy.

74 Elizabeth C. Cromley, *Alone Together: A History of New York's Early Apartments* (Ithaca: Cornell University Press, 1990), pp. 1–15.

75 Cromley, *Alone Together*, pp. 24–5.

76 See Mark Girouard, *The Victorian Country House* (New Haven: Yale University Press, 1979), pp. 20–1, on the propriety of separating "bachelors quarters" from family spaces.

77 "A Bachelor's Christmas," *Harper's New Monthly Magazine* 2, no. 9 (February 1851); page references to be given in the body of the chapter. The bachelor's Christmas is one of the most frequent motifs in popular representations of bachelorhood, reflected in such titles as William Gilmore Simms's compellingly named *Castle Dismal: Or the Bachelor's Christmas; a Domestic Legend* (New York: Burgess, Stringer, 1844); Robert Grant's "The Bachelor's Christmas," *Scribner's Magazine* 14, no. 6 (December 1893); and Tom Masson's "The Bachelor's Christmas Baby," *The Ladies' Home Journal* 22, no. 1 (December 1904).

78 I discuss the association of bachelors with chafing-dish cookery and interior decoration in "A Paradise of Bachelors: Remodeling Domesticity and Masculinity in the Turn-of-the-Century New York Bachelor Apartment," *Prospects: An Annual Journal of American Cultural Studies* 23 (1998).

79 "Scenes in Bachelor Life," *Harper's New Monthly Magazine* 8, no. 43 (December 1853), 142.

80 Oliver Bell Bunce, *Bachelor Bluff: His Opinions, Sentiments, and Disputations* (New York: Appleton, 1881), p. 13. Further page references given in the body of the chapter.

81 "Public mothers" is Carroll Smith-Rosenberg's phrase; see *Disorderly Conduct*, p. 263.

82 On the history the "House Beautiful" trope and the rise of interior decoration as a male profession, see Jonathan Freedman, *Professions of Taste: Henry James, British Aestheticism, and Commodity Culture* (Stanford University Press, 1990), pp. 105–10.

83 On utopian communities and residential reform, see Hayden, *The Grand Domestic Revolution*. For an overview of the settlement house movement in England and America, see Anthony Sutcliffe, *Towards the Planned City: Germany, Britain, the United States, and France, 1780–1914* (New York: St. Martin's Press, 1981), pp. 94–101; Martha Vicinus, *Independent Women: Work and Community for Single Women, 1850–1920* (University of Chicago Press, 1985), pp. 211–46; and Judith Walkowitz, *City of Dreadful Delight: Narratives of Sexual Danger in Late-Victorian London* (University of Chicago Press, 1992), pp. 59–61.

84 "Why We Men Do Not Marry, By One of Us," pp. 219–20. This article's emphasis on the annoying and even life-threatening provisions of available housing for middle-class families – "the jerry-built house . . . is prone rather to inspire typhoid than attachment" (p. 219) – echoes the great housing and environmental debate of the early 1880s which focused on the problems of

high rents, overcrowding, and unsanitary housing in the central districts of large towns, and principally of London. While the objects of greatest concern in that debate were the poor and working classes, this writer suggests that the problems extend up the socio-economic scale: "Will Mr. Besant take the idea, and do something for the middle classes in their turn?" (p. 219).

85 John Seymour Wood, "The Story of an Old Beau," *Scribner's Magazine* 9, no. 2 (February 1891), 199.

86 At least as many new clubs were formed in the 1880s and 90s as during the early 1870s; see Anthony Lejeune, *The Gentlemen's Clubs of London* (London: Bracken, 1984), p. 15; and Anne Henry, *The Building of a Club: Social Institution and Architectural Type, 1870–1905* (Princeton University Press, 1976), p. 3. According to Freeman, *Muttons and Oysters*, p. 187, the late nineteenth-century apogee of the club was predated by a smaller, but nevertheless significant, proliferation of clubs in London during the first half of the century, when the number of clubs rose from three or four to about twenty-five, in effect replacing restaurants.

87 While there were some actual bachelors' clubs on both continents, the most well-known fictional example may have been Israel Zangwill's *The Bachelors' Club* (1891). Brian Harrison, *Separate Spheres: The Opposition to Women's Suffrage in Britain* (London: Croom Helm, 1978) emphasizes the centrality of same-sex institutions for middle- and upper-class London men, both married and single, in the late nineteenth century: "this was an age of bachelors, or of married men who spent a large part of their lives as though they were bachelors: the London clubs – recruited from a number of ancillary male institutions in the public schools, Oxford and Cambridge colleges and professional institutions – catered amply for their needs" (p. 97).

88 Junius Henri Browne's "Are Women Companionable to Men?" *The Cosmopolitan* 4, no. 6 (February 1888), 452–5, claims that "[f]ar more husbands than bachelors are members of clubs, and those are the regular frequenters" (p. 454). Henry's *The Building of a Club* substantiates this anecdotal claim, p. 4.

89 Ralph Nevill, *London Clubs, Their History and Treasures* (London: Chatto and Windus, 1911), pp. 152–3; Nevill lifts this passage virtually verbatim from an 1877 article, "Clubs," *Temple Bar* 51 (October 1877); see 189 and 194.

90 Henry, *The Building of a Club*, p. 34; see also pp. 31–4.

91 E. S. Nadal, "London and American Clubs," *Scribner's Magazine* 9, no. 3 (March 1891), 303.

92 Arthur Conan Doyle, "The Greek Interpreter" (1894), *The Complete Sherlock Holmes* (Garden City, NY: Doubleday, 1930), p. 436.

93 Flora Tristan, *Promenades Dans Londres, Flora Tristan: Utopian Feminist*, eds. Doris and Paul Beik (Bloomington: Indiana University Press, 1993), p. 102.

94 "Bachelors – Why?", *Good Housekeeping*, p. 463.

95 John Timbs, *Clubs and Club Life in London* (1866; London: Chatto and Windus, 1908), p. 211.

96 Henry L. Nelson, "Some New York Clubs," *Harper's Weekly* 34, no. 1 (March 8, 1890), 195. Henry, *The Building of a Club* confirms that "[t]he American city club was designedly social rather than residential. Like a large home, it did provide those bachelors who could not afford or had no desire to maintain quarters for themselves with extensive facilities for entertainment and relaxation, but such men rarely lived in the club" (p. 4). However, in "I Have No Genius for Marriage" (chapter 2, pp. 13–14), Laipson notes that "residence at clubs was sufficiently common that etiquette books provided for it. A bachelor who belonged to a club might engrave or write its name on the lower-left hand corner of a visiting card; if he lived there, on the right hand corner."

97 Cromley, *Alone Together*, gives plans and elevations published in contemporary architectural journals for massive buildings such as the Ansonia, which featured both housekeeping and nonhousekeeping apartments, and also for middle-size and smaller bachelor apartment houses such as the Carlyle Chambers and the Century; see pp. 189–99. See also Elizabeth Hawes, *New York, New York: How the Apartment House Transformed the Life of the City, (1869–1930)* (New York: Knopf, 1993), p. 45 and pp. 146–59. In the same period, comparable new housing options became available, though much less extensively, for New York's "bachelor women"; see Mary Gay Humphreys, "Women Bachelors in New York," *Scribner's* 20, no. 5 (November 1896), and Eulalie Andreas, "Apartments for Bachelor Girls," *House Beautiful* 32, no. 6 (November 1912).

98 Edith Wharton, *The House of Mirth* (New York: Scribner, 1905), p. 9.

99 Of course, there is much one might say about houses and housing in *The House of Mirth* and in Wharton's writing more generally. For example, her first published book was *The Decoration of Houses* (1897). For more on spatial and imaginative structures in Wharton's writing, see Judith Fryer, *Felicitous Space: The Imaginative Structures of Edith Wharton and Willa Cather* (Chapel Hill: University of North Carolina Press, 1986); and Sarah Luria, "The Architecture of Manners: Henry James, Edith Wharton, and The Mount," *American Quarterly*, 49, no. 2 (June 1997).

100 Chaffee, *Bachelor Buttons*, p. 10.

101 According to William Charvat's landmark study, *The Profession of Authorship in America* (Columbus: Ohio State University Press, 1968), p. 241, a novel had to sell at least 5,000 copies to be considered a success in this period. Although the sales of *Reveries* may seem modest when compared with the so-called "decided hits" of the antebellum decade, Geary notes that "whenever figures were mentioned, they represented the extreme rather than the mean"; see Susan Geary, "The Domestic Novel as a Commercial Commodity: Making a Best Seller in the 1850s," *Papers of the Bibliographical Society of America* 70, no. 3 (July–September 1976), 366–9.

102 The reception of *Reveries* is described in Waldo H. Dunn's hagiography, *The Life of Donald G. Mitchell (Ik Marvel)* (New York: Scribner's, 1922), p. 230. See also Wayne R. Kime, *Donald G. Mitchell* (Boston: Twayne Publishers,

1985), pp. 13–14; and Allan Peskin and Arnold G. Tew, "The Disappearance of Ik Marvel," *American Studies* 33, no. 2 (Fall 1992).

103 See Kathryn Whitford, "*The Blithedale Romance*: Hawthorne's *Reveries of a Bachelor*," *Thoth* 15, no. 1 (Winter 1974).

104 Donald Grant Mitchell, *Reveries of a Bachelor, or A Book of the Heart (by Ik Marvel)* (1850; New York: Scribner's, 1851), p. 15. Further page references will be cited in the body of the chapter.

105 On the concept of sentimental ownership, or spiritually redemptive property relations in antebellum culture, see Lori Merish, "Sentimental Consumption: Harriet Beecher Stowe and the Aesthetics of Middle-Class Ownership," *American Literary History* 8, no. 1 (Spring 1996).

106 The decayed dwelling as signifier of inaccessible authenticity is a common motif in sentimental discourse. One precedent that may have directly influenced Mitchell's sentimental representation of selling-off his home is the description of the sale of the old school in Henry MacKenzie's *The Man of Feeling* (1771). The nostalgic backward glances in *Reveries* also connect Mitchell to Washington Irving and the nostalgic vision of an American rural past in *The Sketchbook of Geoffrey Crayon, Gentleman* (1820–2). Mitchell dedicated *Dream Life* to Irving, and also followed Irving in taking up residence in a country home designed along explicitly anachronistic lines to commemorate a vanishing rural life. See Adam W. Sweeting, "'A Very Pleasant Patriarchal Life': Professional Authors and Amateur Architects in the Hudson Valley, 1835–1870," *Journal of American Studies* 29, no. 1 (Spring 1995).

107 Zenobia tells Coverdale, "You are a poet – at least, as poets go, now-a-days – and must be allowed to make an opera-glass of your imagination, when you look at women" (p. 170); *The Blithedale Romance* (1852), *The Centenary Edition of the Works of Nathaniel Hawthorne*, 23 vols. (Columbus: Ohio State University Press, 1964), III. Mitchell himself deployed a comparable metaphor in the title of his satirical publication, *The Lorgnette; or, Studies of the Town* (New York: H. Kernot, 1850). Mitchell attempted to preserve the anonymity of his authorship of *The Lorgnette* by simultaneously publishing "A Bachelor's Reverie" under his own name.

108 With respect to Mitchell and other mid-century American male sketch writers, Ann Douglas notes that the sketch is "perfectly adapted to commercial periodical publication": "it makes no claim to last; it is ultimately dispensable. It concerns itself with the small, the 'picturesque'" (p. 238); *The Feminization of American Culture* (1977; New York: Anchor-Doubleday, 1988). For a more nuanced reading of the disavowal of labor typical of mid-century professional writers, see Sandra Tomc, "An Idle Industry: Nathaniel Parker Willis and the Workings of Literary Leisure," *American Quarterly* 49, no. 4 (December 1997).

109 On the fetishized and reified language of the heart, the highly conventionalized metonymy which connects soul to body and the spiritual to the

material, in Mitchell's text and in sentimental discourse more generally, see Samuel Otter, *Melville's Anatomies: Bodies, Discourse, and Ideology in Antebellum America* (Berkeley: University of California Press, 1999).

110 Both Vincent J. Bertolini, "Fireside Chastity: The Erotics of Sentimental Bachelorhood," *American Literature* 68, no. 4 (December 1996), 719, and Otter, *Melville's Anatomies*, pp. 223, note the mid-nineteenth-century association of reverie with masturbation.

111 Bertolini, "Fireside Chastity," pp. 720–1.

112 The association of bachelorhood with tobacco smoking in popular discourse is ubiquitous; perhaps the quintessential example is J. M. Barrie, *My Lady Nicotine: A Study in Smoke* (1890).

113 One version of bachelor domesticity takes the form of bachelors setting up house with their unmarried aunts, nieces, and/or sisters. On the domestic and quasi-domestic relations of bachelor uncles, see chapter 5. For a fine account of the complex relation of bachelor brothers to the Victorian household and novelistic plotting, see "Domestic Contracts in *The Tenant of Wildfell Hall*," in Cheri Larsen Hoeckley, "Literary Ladies in Anomalous Positions: Victorian Women Writers and the Married Women's Property Movement," PhD thesis, University of California at Berkeley (1997).

114 Walter Pater, *The Renaissance* (1868), ed. Donald L. Hill (Berkeley: University of California Press, 1980), p. 189. For a reading of Pater's "Conclusion" as revising Victorian discourses of normative masculinity, see Sussman, *Victorian Masculinities*, pp. 193–202.

115 Matthew Arnold, *Culture and Anarchy: An Essay in Political and Social Criticism,* (London: Smith, Elder and Co., 1869), p. viii; Pater, *The Renaissance*, p. 190.

116 Otter, *Melville's Anatomies*, p. 225. In "The Disappearance of Ik. Marvel," Peskin and Tew note that "[d]espite the repeated assumption in our time that Mitchell's readers were women, all the evidence from the 1850s through the early years of this century suggests that many of Mitchell's most devoted readers were in fact young men" (p. 15).

117 Otter, *Melville's Anatomies*, p. 225. Otter speculates that "[t]his omission may result from the lack of such letters (thus proving the necessity for his sensitizing literary project) or from the privacy of such correspondence".

118 Leverenz, *Manhood and the American Renaissance*, pp. 9–41, especially 17–18.

119 "Our Young Authors," *Putnam's Monthly Magazine* 1, no. 1 (January 1853), 74. Peskin and Tew, "The Disappearance of Ik Marvel," pp. 16–17, give a sampling of *Reveries*'s contemporary critical reception.

120 The famous images of containing multitudes and the merge are from Whitman's *Leaves of Grass* (1855). Whitman uses the phrases "fervid comradeship" and "adhesive love" in *Democratic Vistas* (1870), though "adhesiveness" appears in his writing from the mid-1850s on; see Robert K. Martin, *The Homosexual Tradition in American Poetry* (Austin: University of Texas Press, 1979), pp. 33–47.

2 SUSCEPTIBILITY AND THE SINGLE MAN

1 "Bachelor Invalids and Male Nurses," *Once a Week* 8, no. 3 (October 7, 1871), 318. Further page references will be cited in the body of the chapter.

2 There have been numerous recent studies of nineteenth-century represen- tations of illness, bodies, sexuality, and gender. Several of the most useful are Elaine Showalter, *The Female Malady: Women, Madness, and English Culture, 1830–1980* (New York: Pantheon, 1985); Catherine Gallagher and Thomas Laqueur (eds.), *The Making of the Modern Body: Sexuality and Society in the Nineteenth Century* (Berkeley: University of California Press, 1987); Sander Gilman, *Disease and Representation: Images of Illness from Madness to AIDS* (Ithaca: Cornell University Press, 1988); Diane Price Herndl, *Invalid Women: Figuring Feminine Illness in American Fiction and Culture, 1840–1940* (Chapel Hill: University of North Carolina Press, 1993); Athena Vrettos, *Somatic Fictions: Imagining Illness in Victorian Culture* (Stanford University Press, 1995); and Peter M. Logan, *Nerves and Narratives: A Cultural History of Hysteria in Nineteenth-Century British Prose* (Berkeley: University of California Press, 1997).

3 I am quoting here from Jeff Nunokawa's illuminating "'All the Sad Young Men': AIDS and the Work of Mourning," *The Yale Journal of Criticism* 4, no. 2 (1991), 1–2. For an exemplary resistant reading of the sort I describe here, see Leo Bersani, "Is The Rectum a Grave?", *AIDS: Cultural Analysis, Cultural Activism*, ed. Douglas Crimp (Cambridge, MA: MIT Press, 1988).

4 Terence McCarthy identifies and contributes to the tradition of reading Lockwood and Nelly as unreliable narrators in "The Incompetent Narrator of *Wuthering Heights*," *Modern Language Quarterly* 42, no. 1 (March 1981), 48–64. Critical treatment of the unreliable narrator in *Blithedale* has shaped itself into two opposing camps: "pro-Coverdale" and "anti-Coverdale"; on this bifurcation, see Keith Carabine, "'Bitter Honey': Miles Coverdale as Narrator of *The Blithedale Romance*," *Nathaniel Hawthorne: New Critical Essays*, ed. A. Robert Lee (London: Vision Press, 1982).

5 Self-portrayal as a thwarted suitor is a stock motif of popular nineteenth- century bachelor discourse. Thus Coverdale's sentiment that "[a] bachelor always feels himself defrauded, when he knows, or suspects, that any woman of his acquaintance has given herself away" (p. 48), is echoed almost verbatim by the bachelor narrator of "My Wife and My Theory about Wives," *Harper's New Monthly Magazine* 11, no. 66 (November 1855): "My pulse sank ... for the good and sufficient reason (which authors have but lately had the honesty to avow) that every bachelor feels himself defrauded when a pretty woman marries" (p. 781). This echo indicates the currency of the bachelor figure in American popular culture of the 1850s as well as the familiarity of *Harper's* writers and readers with Hawthorne's novel. Further references to *The Blithedale Romance* will be cited in the body of the chapter with "*BR*."

6 Making a spectacle of oneself does not always mean abjecting oneself or displaying one's preexisting condition of abjection. The paradoxical status of self-display for Victorian men is addressed in James Eli Adams's *Dandies*

and Desert Saints: Styles of Victorian Masculinity (Ithaca: Cornell University Press, 1995); I return to the issue of self-display as normative and counter-normative, and to its connection with questions of discipline, asceticism, and artistry, in chapter 3.

7 Nina Baym cites Philip Rahv's 1941 *Partisan Review* essay, "The Dark Lady of Salem," as the source of this interpretation, which she herself endorses; see *"The Blithedale Romance*: A Radical Reading," *The Norton Critical Edition of The Blithedale Romance*, ed. Seymour Gross and Rosalie Murphy (New York: Norton, 1978).

8 Gillian Brown notes the homoerotics of the Coverdale-Hollingsworth relation in *Domestic Individualism: Imagining Self in Nineteenth-Century America* (Berkeley: University of California Press, 1990), pp. 111–14 and p. 233, n. 3. A more extensive reading of these homoerotics, which connects them to the novel's representations of free love and utopianism, and also considers the homoerotic/homosocial bond between Priscilla and Zenobia, can be found in Lauren Berlant, "Fantasies of Utopia in *The Blithedale Romance*," *American Literary History* 1, no. 1 (Spring 1989), 36–8.

9 Many critical readers have emphasized the Oedipal dynamics of this love triangle; a classic example is Frederick Crews, *The Sins of the Fathers: Hawthorne's Psychological Themes* (New York: Oxford University Press, 1966), pp. 200–12.

10 I am stressing here the more conventional aspect of the Oedipus myth which implies violence and hierarchical relations between fathers and sons rather than loving bonds of fraternity; for a reading of the Oedipus myth that emphasizes the latter, see Newfield, "Democracy and Male Homoeroticism," especially 48–54. Lockwood's erotic identification with Heathcliff might be seen to encompass both kinds of relations, as for example when he "pairs" himself with Heathcliff as fellow misanthropists: "In all England, I do not believe that I could have fixed on a situation so completely removed from the stir of society. A perfect misanthropist's Heaven – and Mr Heathcliff and I are such a suitable pair to divide the desolation between us ... I felt interested in a man who seemed more exaggeratedly reserved than myself"; Emily Brontë, *Wuthering Heights* (1847; London: Penguin, 1986), p. 45. Further pages references to be cited in the body of the chapter with *"WH."*

11 Many readers of the novel have pointed to Lockwood's anecdote about his flirtation with and subsequent withdrawal from the "fascinating creature" at the sea coast as evidence for his voyeuristic self-constitution. I emphasize here the complex, even self-contradictory, meanings of his narration of this anecdote: the paradoxical self-aggrandizement and self-denigration that his telling itself enacts. Lockwood's confession of his retreat from the reciprocating gaze of the seaside "goddess" – "[W]hat did I do? I confess it with shame – shrunk icily into myself, like a snail, at every glance retired colder and farther" (*WH*, p. 48) – seems more self-flagellating than self-flattering, more masochistically honest than self-protectively unreliable. One wonders, how-

ever, whether he is surreptitiously promoting the rakish "reputation of deliberate heartlessness" that he ostensibly disclaims here as "undeserved" (*WH*, p. 48). This possibility is reinforced by Lockwood's explicitly unreliable characterization of Heathcliff in the immediately preceding passage. Here, Lockwood attempts to masculinize his own snail-like shrinking from reciprocation by aligning it with the more manly and bourgeois "reserve," the "aversion to showy displays of feeling" (*WH*, p. 47) which he attributes first to Heathcliff, and then to himself.

12 My understanding of the gendered politics of nineteenth-century spiritualism owes a great deal to Ann Braude, *Radical Spirits: Spiritualism and Women's Rights in Nineteenth-Century America* (Boston: Beacon Press, 1989). See also Janet Oppenheim, *The Other World: Spiritualism and Psychical Research in England, 1850–1914* (Cambridge University Press, 1985); Alex Owen, *The Darkened Room: Women, Power, and Spiritualism in Late Nineteenth-Century England* (London: Virago, 1989); and Judith Walkowitz, "Science and the Séance: Transgressions of Gender and Genre," *City of Dreadful Delight: Narratives of Sexual Danger in Late-Victorian London* (University of Chicago Press, 1992).

13 Dorothy Van Ghent was among the first to write of the "dark otherness" of the characters in *Wuthering Heights*; see *The English Novel: Form and Function* (New York: Rinehart, 1953), p. 165. For other discussions of self/other relations and narrative boundaries, see J. Hillis Miller, *The Disappearance of God; Five Nineteenth-Century Writers* (Cambridge, MA: Belknap-Harvard University Press, 1963), pp. 169–211; Elizabeth Napier, "The Problem of Boundaries in *Wuthering Heights*," *Philological Quarterly* 63, no. 1 (Winter 1984); John T. Matthews, "Framing in *Wuthering Heights*," *Texas Studies in Literature and Language* 27, no. 1 (Spring 1985); Naomi Jacobs, "Gender and Layered Narrative in *Wuthering Heights* and *The Tenant of Wildfell Hall*," *Journal of Narrative Technique* 16, no. 3 (Fall 1986); and John Allen Stevenson, "'Heathcliff is Me!': *Wuthering Heights* and the Question of Likeness," *Nineteenth-Century Literature* 43 (1988).

14 In *Tradition Counter Tradition*, Boone traces "the emergence of a literary ideal of romantic marriage" (p. 31) from the courtly love tradition of the late eleventh century through to the nineteenth-century novel. His history of literary love plotting has influenced my understanding of fictional manifestations of the construct of gendered and sexual complementarity, that is, my understanding of the long-standing notion that women and men are fundamentally different but that their heterosexual pairing creates a single whole, two as one. Kevin Kopelson offers a corrective to the "compulsory heterosexuality" that pervades even this demystifying analytical tool, noting the suppressed presence of a figure of male–male identification/desire, in addition to the figuring of male–female complementarity, in Plato's originary emblem of the divided self; see *Love's Litany: The Writing of Modern Homoerotics* (Stanford University Press, 1994), especially pp. 5–6.

15 For example, see Mary Lyndon Shanley, *Feminism, Marriage, and the Law in Victorian England* (Princeton University Press, 1989); and Lee Holcombe,

Wives and Property: Reform of the Married Women's Property Law in Nineteenth-Century England (University of Toronto Press, 1983).

16 Some critics have taken the union of Cathy II and Hareton as an improvement over the marriages that precede it in the chronology of *Wuthering Heights*. Patricia Parker, however, theorizes that "[t]he endless debate over whether the novel's second generation constitutes a progress or decline in relation to the first may be precisely endless because the two sides are simply the opposite faces of a single coin – two possibilities within the model of the line," *Literary Fat Ladies; Rhetoric, Gender, Property* (London: Methuen, 1987), p. 175.

17 Certain critics in the unreliable narrator tradition have glimpsed a psychokiller behind the facade of the more-or-less mild-mannered bachelor narrator of *Blithedale*, taking Coverdale's account of Zenobia's drowned corpse as evidence implicating him in her murder. John McElroy and Edward McDonald, "The Coverdale Romance," *Studies in the Novel* 14, no. 1 (Spring 1982), were the first to catch a discrepancy in Coverdale's knowledge of the water's depth and to suggest foul play. Beverly Hume, "Restructuring the Case Against Hawthorne's Coverdale," *Nineteenth-Century Fiction* 40 (1986), "uses the scientific illogic" (p. 390) of Zenobia's *rigor mortis* to prove Coverdale's madness and crime.

18 The uncanniness of Zenobia's rigid and vertical corpse, together with the rumored Medusa-like aspect of the lady beneath the veil in "Zenobia's Legend," contributes to an understanding of Coverdale's sensibility as fetishistic as well as voyeuristic. For a reading of Coverdale's voyeurism and fetishism, see Brown, *Domestic Individualism*, pp. 114–20; for an account of Hawthorne's use of Medusa imagery in *Blithedale* and elsewhere in his fiction, see Joel Pfister, *The Production of Personal Life: Class, Gender, and the Psychological in Hawthorne's Fiction* (Stanford University Press, 1991), pp. 87–103. In chapter 4, I pursue in greater detail the fetishistic implications of the veiled lady and the Medusa's head, two figures which also appear in Conrad's *Lord Jim* and *Under Western Eyes*.

19 For an influential account of nineteenth-century American women in the public sphere, see Mary Kelley, *Private Woman, Public Stage: Literary Domesticity in Nineteenth-Century America* (New York: Oxford University Press, 1984). My understanding of Priscilla's career owes much to Richard Brodhead's "Veiled Ladies: Toward a History of Antebellum Entertainment," *Cultures of Letters: Scenes of Reading and Writing in Nineteenth-Century America* (University of Chicago Press, 1993), pp. 48–68.

20 Certain parallels to Nelly and her intradiegetic story-telling can be discerned in Zenobia's attempts to entertain Coverdale during his convalescence, especially in the interpolated tale which Zenobia narrates to the assembled company at Blithedale and in her supposed talent as a "stump-oratress." However, Zenobia's legend of "The Silvery Veil," like Moodie's story of "Fauntleroy," never attains a status in *Blithedale* comparable to Nelly's history in *Wuthering Heights*. Instead, these imbedded narratives remain

discrete, framed romances within Coverdale's encompassing Romance.

21 In "'Bitter Honey'," Carabine maintains a resolutely pro-Coverdalean stance by contrasting the narrator's "sympathy" with the "old humbugs" of Westervelt's mesmerism and Blithedale's Utopianism, even though he observes that Coverdale's retreat to his hermitage can be linked to a fear that "his own clairvoyance may be demonic" (p. 182). Thomas F. Strychacz similarly sets Coverdale and Westervelt in opposition to each other; see "Coverdale and Women: Feverish Fantasies in *The Blithedale Romance*," *American Transcendental Quarterly* 62 (December 1986), 31.

22 In *Cultures of Letters*, Brodhead describes the dynamics of Coverdale's vicarious self-constitution: "Life as Coverdale understands it is not what he has or does but something presumed to be lodged in someone else. Watching that someone, inhabiting that other through spectatorial self-projection and consuming it through visual appropriation, becomes accordingly a means to live *into his* life some part of that vitality that always first appears as 'other life'" (p. 61).

23 Beth Newman touches on the formal, narrative, and ideological intersections between this concentrically narrated novel and the frame narration of *Wuthering Heights* in "Narratives of Seduction and the Seductions of Narrative: The Frame Structure of *Frankenstein, ELH* 53, no. 1 (Spring 1986), 141–3.

24 For a powerful reading of gender and the gaze, and of visual metaphors for narration in *Wuthering Heights*, see Beth Newman, "'The Situation of the Looker-On': Gender, Narration, and Gaze in *Wuthering Heights*," *PMLA* 105, no. 5 (October 1990).

25 In his 1983 "Masculinity as Spectacle," *Screening the Male: Exploring Masculinities in Hollywood Cinema*, ed. Steven Cohan and Ina Rae Hark (New York: Routledge, 1993), Steve Neale critiques the distinction, posited by Laura Mulvey in her groundbreaking 1975 essay "Visual Pleasure and Narrative Cinema" and by others following her, between voyeuristic gaze's narrative-halting effects and the fetishistic gaze's narrative-generating effects. Neale notes that, in Westerns, cinematic moments of spectacular masculinity do not simply interrupt the development of the story but contribute to it, complicating the assumption that spectacle and narrative must be opposed. One could make a similar argument about the plot-furthering functions of the spectacle of the deathbed scene in *Wuthering Heights*, though I emphasize here the ways in which Nelly's narrative caressing of the corpse does, in fact, seem to interrupt or slow the progress of the story.

26 Not all mediums were women, nor were all invalids. But the cultural connection among these identities contributes to the assumed "femininity" of figures who can also be identified by the "unmarked" categories such as (white) race and (middle) class. In *Domestic Individualism*, Brown notes the analogous dynamics of the overlapping cultural phenomenon of hysteria, particularly with respect to its implications for labor and leisure identities; see especially p. 65. We might therefore compare the physical housekeeping work that Nelly does as a working-class woman with the intellectual literary

work that Emily Brontë does as a bourgeois woman. The gender and class connotations of each woman's labor are ambiguous, although differently ambiguous, suggesting a play between normative and counternormative identities for both.

27 I am indebted here to Margaret Homans's analysis of *Wuthering Heights*'s double narration in *Bearing the Word: Language and Female Experience in Nine-teenth-Century Women's Writing* (University of Chicago Press, 1986), pp. 68–83. Homans also treats the larger range of strategies used by the Brontës and other Victorian women writers to reconcile authorship and motherhood. See Kelley, *Private Woman, Public Stage*, pp. 124–8, for a discussion of the differences between English women writers' use of what were typically male pseudonyms and American women writers' typically female pseudonyms.

28 Baym, "Melodramas of Beset Manhood" (see my Introduction, n. 17). For other accounts of Hawthorne's response to women writers, see Raymona E. Hull, "'Scribbling Females' and Serious Males," *Nathaniel Hawthorne Journal* 5 (1975), 35–9; Nina Baym, *The Shape of Hawthorne's Career* (Ithaca: Cornell University Press, 1976), pp. 108–10 and pp. 191–200; Leland S. Person, Jr., *Aesthetic Headaches: Women and a Masculinist Poetics in Poe, Melville and Hawthorne* (Athens, University of Georgia Press, 1988), pp. 146–72; and James D. Wallace, "Hawthorne and The Scribbling Women Reconsidered," *American Literature* 62, no. 2 (June 1990).

29 On the differences between "centers of consciousness" as a narrative technique and other narrative techniques including first-person narration, free indirect discourse, and stream of consciousness or interior monologue, see William R. Goetz, *Henry James and the Darkest Abyss of Romance* (Baton Rouge: Louisiana State University Press, 1986), pp. 27–31, and Manfred Jahn, "Windows of Focalization: Deconstructing and Reconstructing a Narratological Concept," *Style* 30, no. 2 (1996).

30 Henry James, Preface to *Roderick Hudson* in *Henry James: Literary Criticism*, vol. II *French Writers, Other European Writers, The Prefaces to the New York Edition* (New York: Library of America, 1984), pp. 1049–50. Further quotations from this edition will be cited in the body of the text with the abbreviation "*LC2*."

31 Henry James, *The Portrait of a Lady* (1880), 2 vols. (Fairfield, NJ: Augustus M. Kelley, Publishers, 1976), I, p. 259. Further page numbers quoted in the body of the text with relevant volume number.

32 The vicissitudes of consumer culture in James's fiction have been sounded by New Critics such as Laurence Holland, *The Expense of Vision: Essays on the Craft of Henry James* (1964; Baltimore: Johns Hopkins University Press, 1982), and more recently by Carolyn Porter, *Seeing and Being: The Plight of the Participant Observer in Emerson, James, Adams, and Faulkner* (Middletown, CT: Wesleyan University Press, 1981); Jean-Christophe Agnew, "The Consuming Vision of Henry James," *The Culture of Consumption: Critical Essays in American History, 1880–1980*, ed. Richard W. Fox and T. J. Jackson Lears (New York: Pantheon, 1983); Michael Gilmore, "The Commodity World of

238   *Notes to pages 90–95*

      The Portrait of a Lady," *New England Quarterly* 3, no. 1 (1986); Jonathan Freedman, *Professions of Taste: Henry James, British Aestheticism, and Commodity Culture* (Stanford University Press, 1990); Craig Howard White, "The House of Interest: A Keyword in *The Portrait of a Lady*," *Modern Language Quarterly* 52, no. 2 (1991); and Peter Donahue, "Collecting as Ethos and Technique in *The Portrait of a Lady*," *Studies in American Fiction* 25, no. 1 (1997).

33 Caspar's geographical distance from the American site of industrial production resembles Lambert Strether's and Chad Newsome's disengagement from the family business in Woollett, Massachusetts, and *The Ambassadors*'s own rhetorical distance from the unnamed commodity produced there.

34 Thomas Laqueur, *Making Sex: Body and Gender From the Greeks to Freud* (Cambridge, MA: Harvard University Press, 1990), p. 232.

35 See Karen Halttunen, *Confidence Men and Painted Women: A Study of Middle-Class Culture in America, 1830–1870* (New Haven: Yale University Press, 1982) for a discussion of responses to the panic of 1837 and the spectre of the gambler/speculator, especially pp. 16–20. See also Ann Fabian, *Card Sharps, Dream Books, and Bucket Shops: Gambling in Nineteenth-Century America* (Ithaca: Cornell University Press, 1990), pp. 33–8.

36 Walter Benn Michaels argues that the United States' adoption of the monometallic gold standard in the 1870s, like the gold standard first put into operation by Great Britain in 1821, contributed to anxieties over economic regulation and monetary representation as well as to the rise of the system of literary representation known as naturalism); see *The Gold Standard and the Logic of Naturalism: American Literature at the Turn of the Century* (Berkeley: University of California Press, 1987), pp. 172–80.

37 Brown, *Domestic Individualism*, p. 15.

38 On "closed"/"open" paradigms of male bodily economy, see Kevin J. Mumford, "'Lost Manhood' Found: Male Sexual Impotence and Victorian Culture in the United States," *Journal of the History of Sexuality* 3, no. 1 (July 1992); Lesley A. Hall, "Forbidden by God, Despised by Men: Masturbation, Medical Warnings, Moral Panic, and Manhood in Great Britain, 1850–1950," *Forbidden History: The State, Society, and the Regulation of Sexuality in Modern Europe*, ed. John C. Fout (University of Chicago Press, 1992), especially pp. 295–6; Lesley A. Hall, *Hidden Anxieties: Male Sexuality, 1900–1950* (Cambridge: Polity Press, 1991), pp. 26–32; and Smith-Rosenberg, *Disorderly Conduct*, pp. 261–2. The shift in paradigms of male bodily economy resemble the historically coincident shift from the "closed energy" model of illness, "which held that all illnesses were the result of an imbalance of energy in the body," to the more recent "specific etiology" theory of disease; on the shift in models of illness, see Herndl, *Invalid Women*, p. 234, n. 4.

39 White, "The House of Interest," p. 193.

40 Henry James, "To H. G. Wells," March 3, 1911, *Letters of Henry James*, ed. Percy Lubbock, 2 vols. (New York: Scribner's, 1920), II, p. 181.

41 In "The Commodity World," Gilmore puts Ralph's response – "I'll be Caliban and you shall be Ariel" (I, p. 169) – to Henrietta's attempt to enlist

his help in uniting Isabel and Caspar Goodwood in the context of the divide between mental and manual labor in this period of American history, arguing that the novel abounds in managers and is deficient in workers (pp. 64–65). I would note that the class division suggested here also bears upon the divide between bourgeois and working-class styles of manhood, as indicated by Henrietta's retort: "You're not at all like Caliban, because you're sophisticated, and Caliban was not" (I, p. 169).

42 The "old bachelor" who is still a young man recalls a Jamesian bachelor reflector who seems comparably prematurely aged: Winterbourne in "Daisy Miller." The mirror image produced by the initial meeting between Winterbourne and Randolph, Daisy's precocious little brother with rotten teeth, suggests a weird agedness-in-youth; together, they generate an image of manhood that is at once historically belated and also stunted in growth.

43 My discussion of the sentimental spectacle of male suffering is influenced by Sedgwick's readings of *Billy Budd*, Wilde, and Nietzche; see especially *Epistemology*, pp. 141–50 and 178–81. Sedgwick's treatment of sentimentalism is part of a wider reassessment of the political uses of sentimental discourse; for an overview of this critical reassessment, see the Introductions to *The Culture of Sentiment: Race, Gender, and Sentimentality in Nineteenth-Century America*, ed. Shirley Samuels (New York: Oxford University Press, 1992), and to *Sentimental Men: Masculinity and the Politics of Affect in American Culture*, ed. Mary Chapman and Glenn Hendler (Berkeley: University of California Press, forthcoming).

44 Ora Segal, *The Lucid Reflector: The Observer in Henry James's Fiction* (New Haven: Yale University Press, 1969), pp. 40, 49, and 54; Gilmore, "The Commodity World," pp. 69–71.

3 "AN ARTIST AND A BACHELOR"

1 November 25, 1881 entry from James's first American journal, *The Complete Notebooks of Henry James*, ed. Leon Edel and Lyall H. Powers (New York: Oxford University Press, 1987), p. 218.

2 My argument here is indebted to Richard H. Brodhead, *The School of Hawthorne* (New York: Oxford University Press, 1986); especially pp. 112–20.

3 I discuss the late nineteenth-century medicalization and illegalization of homosexual practices and the formation of homosexual subcultures and cultural identities in chapter 1. On literary figurations of "double lives," see Ed Cohen, "The Double Lives of Man: Narration and Identification in Late Nineteenth-Century Representation of Ec-centric Masculinities," *Victorian Studies* 36, no. 3 (1993); and Wayne Koestenbaum, *Double Talk: The Erotics of Male Literary Collaboration* (New York: Routledge, 1989), especially pp. 143–77.

4 In *The Romance of Failure: First Person Fictions in Poe, Hawthorne, and James* (New York: Oxford University Press, 1989), p. 190, n. 16, Jonathan Auerbach constructs a four-part taxonomy of Jamesian first-person narration, ident-

ifying unmarried "analytic men-of-letters" as one type of Jamesian first-person narrator, in addition to "Gothic," "miscellaneous experiments in point of view," and first-person autobiographical and travel writing. Rather than deploying such a taxonomy, I intend here to explore James's own understanding of his narrative method, particularly as it informs his use of bachelor figures.

5 One of the first major, proto-narratological studies to focus on this formal technique in James's fiction is Segal, *The Lucid Reflector*. Gérard Genette coined the term "external focalization" to describe the use of an authorial narrator in concert with characters who function as centers of subjectivity or consciousness; see *Narrative Discourse*, p. 190.

6 Joseph Conrad, *Lord Jim* (1900; New York: Penguin, 1989), p. 200. Further page references from this edition will be given in the body of the text with "*LJ.*"

7 Henry James, *The Ambassadors* (1903; New York: Penguin, 1986), p. 512.

8 For an elegant reading of the multiple resonances of Conrad's title, as well as an insightful comparison of Conrad's Marlow and James's Strether, see Michael H. Levenson, "Two Cultures and an Individual: *Heart of Darkness* and *The Ambassadors*," *Modernism and the Fate of Individuality: Character and Novelistic Form from Conrad to Woolf* (Cambridge University Press, 1991), pp. 1–77. An influential earlier essay on James's view of Conrad's use of first-person narration is Ian Watt, "Marlow, Henry James, and *Heart of Darkness*," *Nineteenth-Century Fiction* 33, no. 2 (September 1978).

9 In *After the Great Divide*, Huyssen argues that the other of male modernism is mass culture represented as feminine; see especially pp. 47–55. In *New Women, New Novels*, Ardis contends that because "modernism's antagonism toward mass culture is itself motivated by an antagonism to the feminization of all culture" (p. 174), the female subject is modernism's primary other. The intersections among the variously gendered, sexed, sexually oriented, and "queer" others of modernism are addressed in Sedgwick, *Epistemology*; Boone, *Libidinal Currents*; and Andrew Hewitt, *Political Inversions: Homosexuality, Fascism, and the Modernist Imaginary* (Stanford University Press, 1996).

10 Susan Winnet, "Women, Men, Narrative, and Principles of Pleasure," *PMLA* 105, no. 3 (May 1990), 505.

11 Sandra Corse, "Henry James on George Eliot and George Sand," *South Atlantic Review*, 51, no. 1 (January 1986), 60.

12 On the construction of masculinity in James's extensive critical commentary on Sand, see Leland S. Person, Jr., "Henry James, George Sand, and the Suspense of Masculinity," *PMLA* 106, no. 3 (May 1991).

13 James, *Letters*, ed. Lubbock, II, p. 181.

14 I am indebted to Goetz's *Henry James and the Darkest Abyss of Romance* for this and other subtleties concerning first-person narrative in James's writing. Goetz convincingly argues that James takes first-person narrative as auto-biographical in that it betrays the author's and not just the narrator's

presence, thereby disrupting the seamless illusion upon which the impact of romance depends (p. 20). Goetz, however, does not discuss the threat of autobiography as a sub-literary genre that I theorize here, nor does he connect the epistemological undermining associated with the form to the threats of sexual and gendered otherness.

15 Goetz, *Henry James and the Darkest Abyss of Romance*, pp. 20–3.

16 James, *Letters*, ed. Lubbock, II, p. 181.

17 In a letter to her father of 1881, Mrs. Henry Adams wrote of Henry James that "it's not that he 'bites off more than he can chaw,' as T. G. Appleton said of Nathan, but he chaws more than he bites off" (p. 306), *The Letters of Mrs. Henry Adams, 1865–1883*, ed. Ward Thoron (Boston: Little, Brown, and Co., 1937).

18 James, *Letters*, ed. Lubbock, II, pp. 181–2.

19 Ford Madox Ford records James's poke at Marlow in *Joseph Conrad: A Personal Remembrance* (London: Duckworth, 1924), pp. 160–1.

20 Henry James, "The New Novel" in *Literary Criticism: Essays on Literature, American Writers, and English Writers* (New York: Library of America, 1984), p. 148. Further quotations from this edition will be cited in the body of the chapter with the abbreviation "*LC1.*"

21 For an account of the effects of the Great War on James's writing, see Roslyn Jolly, *Henry James: History, Narrative, Fiction* (Oxford: Clarendon Press, 1993), pp. 206–23.

22 In the same year that James criticized Conrad's use of first-person narration as *risqué* modernism, the Vorticist Wyndham Lewis blasted it as *passé* realism. Ford Madox Ford records a 1914 conversation in which Lewis explosively condemned Ford's and Conrad's Impressionist principles and techniques, particularly their use of first-person narrators:

> "You try to make people believe that they are passing through an experience when they read you. You write these immense long stories, recounted by a doctor at table or a ship-captain in an inn. You take ages to get these fellows in. In order to make your stuff seem convincing. Who wants to be convinced? Get a move on. Get out or get under. This is the day of Cubism, Futurism, Vorticism. What people want is me, not you. They want to see me. A Vortex. To liven them up. You and Conrad had the idea of concealing yourself when you wrote. I display myself all over the page."

Your Mirror to My Times: The Selected Autobiographies and Impressions of Ford Madox Ford, ed. Michael Killigrew (New York: Holt, Rineheart, and Winston, 1971), pp. 188–9.
Whereas James uncomfortably perceives the author brazenly exposing himself in the "autobiographic form" of first-person narration, Lewis impatiently beholds a narrator-dummy who calls attention away from the moving lips of a bad author-ventriloquist.

23 Henry James, "The Lesson of the Master" (1888), *The Complete Tales of Henry James*, ed. Leon Edel, 12 vols. (Philadelphia: Lippincott, 1963), VII, pp. 265–6. Further citations from this edition will be cited in the body of the text with the abbreviation "*CT*" and the relevant volume number.

24 My thinking about masculinity, artistry, and discipline is indebted to Adams's *Dandies and Desert Saints* and Sussman's *Victorian Masculinities*. My reading of discipleship in "The Lesson of the Master" is also influenced by Michael A. Cooper, "Discipl(in)ing the Master, Mastering the Discipl(in)e: Erotonomies of Discipleship in James's Tales of Literary Life," *Engendering Men: The Question of Male Feminist Criticism*, ed. Joseph A. Boone and Michael Cadden (New York: Routledge, 1990).

25 *Henry James: Letters*, ed. Leon Edel, 4 vols. (Cambridge, MA: Belknap-Harvard University Press, 1984), IV, p. 5.

26 Philip Horne, *Henry James and Revision: The New York Edition* (Oxford: Clarendon Press, 1990), p. 293. Horne notes that the allusion to a "free, unhoused condition" reverses Othello's justification for marrying Desdemona to provide a rationale for James's own decision *not* to marry.

27 Like self-display, masochism can be understood as a disavowed component of normative Victorian bourgeois masculinity; see Adams, *Dandies and Desert Saints*, pp. 139–47. In *Male Masochism: Modern Revisions of the Story of Love* (Bloomington: Indiana University Press, 1995), Carol Siegel considers modernist and postmodernist literary representations of male masochism in order to elucidate how erotic submission has come to be seen as unnatural for heterosexual men. For a discussion of masochism as at the heart of all subjectivity, albeit disavowed at the site of masculinity, see Silverman, *Male Subjectivity at the Margins*, pp. 185–213; for an alternative perspective, which differentiates between masochistic submission and non-masochistic "surrender," see Emmanuel Ghent, "Masochism, Submission, Surrender: Masochism as a Perversion of Surrender," *Contemporary Psychoanalysis* 26, no. 1 (1990).

28 Leon Edel notes that James attributes this motto, the germ of *The Ambassadors*, to W. D. Howells in a notebook entry of October 21, 1895; see *Henry James: A Life* (New York: Harper and Row, 1985), p. 447.

29 In an 1888 *Century Magazine* essay, James returns to the absence of women and marriage from Stevenson's fiction. Here, however, James associates adventure with bachelorhood: "Why should a person marry when he might be swinging a cutlass or looking for a buried treasure?" (*LCI*, p. 1238). Although James is somewhat condescending here about the address of Stevenson's "boy books" to "immature minds," he generally sees Stevenson's use of male characters and appeal to a male readership as sources of his literary strength.

30 Brodhead, *The School of Hawthorne*, p. 116.

31 William Dean Howells was more comfortable than James with the notion that an author could be both "entrepreneur" and "working-man"; see Howells, "The Man of Letters as a Man of Business," *Literature and Life* (New York: Harper and Bros., 1902).

32 As noted in chapter 2, Ralph Touchett compares himself to Caliban when describing his influence over Isabel (I, p. 169). When Ralph says that he is not Prospero, Ralph implies that he is a mere functionary, not an initiator of

action or a creator of plots.

33 It is significant that this story opens with an act of proxying: one man standing in for another in relation to yet a third man. This configuration indicates a triangulation of desire within homosexual relations as well as within homosocial relations where the woman provides the point of transmission between men. It also highlights the importance of the proxy as an embodiment of representation, linking representation to sexual desire as well as to male-male relations more generally.

34 William Cohen also considers the triangulated desires at issue in these two stories in *Sex Scandal: The Private Parts of Victorian Fiction* (Durham, NC: Duke University Press, 1996), pp. 226–34. Whereas Cohen argues that the narrators' appetite for information about their literary heroes eclipses their capacity for sexual desire, I maintain that the narrators' epistemological, literary, and erotic desires are all mutually constitutive.

35 This is rather different from saying that the bachelor narrator *should* have desired Miss Tina. Such a reading would fall into the heteronormative trap that Sedgwick elucidates in her influential reading of James's "The Beast in the Jungle"; see *Epistemology*, pp. 201–2.

36 Holland, *The Expense of Vision*, pp. 142 and 146.

37 Arguably, the violent passion of the Maenads is hysteria and thus a sign of uncontrollable female passion, but I would emphasize here the control that they exert over Orpheus's fate rather than their own lack of self-control. On the multiple and changing meanings of Maenads, see Linda M. Shires, "Of Maenads, Mothers, and Feminized Males: Victorian Readings of the French Revolution," in *Rewriting the Victorians: Theory, History, and the Politics of Gender*, ed. Linda M. Shires (New York: Routledge, 1992).

38 James, *Notebooks*, p. 33.

39 Adeline R. Tintner surveys the appearance of Byronic material in three phases of James's writing in "Henry James and Byron: A Victorian Romantic Relationship," *The Byron Journal* 9 (1981).

40 James may have become aware of the controversy when W. D. Howells printed Stowe's article, "The True Story of Lady Byron's Life," in *The Atlantic Monthly* 23, no. 136 (February 1869). It also seems likely that the scandal provoked by Stowe's book may have become associated in James's mind with the 1872 scandal occasioned by the allegations of adultery between Mrs. Isabella Tilton and the Reverend Henry Ward Beecher (Stowe's brother), whom Henry James, Sr., defended in print. The sensational public debate in which Henry Sr. participated deeply embarrassed the James family and, as Alfred Habegger has discovered, many family letters from the period were destroyed, setting a prototype for the problematic letters and their destruction in "Aspern." For details on the Beecher–Tilton scandal as it pertains to the James family, see Alfred Habegger, *Henry James and the Woman Business* (Cambridge University Press, 1989), pp. 27–62. In "Henry James and Byron," p. 59, Tintner notes that in 1895 James visited the Lovelaces to look at some Byron papers that turned out to

contain proof of Byron's incest with his half-sister, but James's notebook record of this visit indicates that he already knew of the incest even though he did not know that he would see evidence of it in the letters.

41 I am indebted here to Peter Brooks's readings of *Great Expectations* and *Heart of Darkness* with respect to detective fiction in his *Reading for the Plot*; see especially pp. 135–7 and pp. 244–5.

42 The detective is both the disciple of the criminal and also the criminal's would-be master, one who represents the authority of the Law. The ambivalence of the relations between these male figures is sometimes refigured as an internal conflict within the detective, and vice versa. This divided/doubled articulation of masculine subjectivity is evident, for example, in Arthur Conan Doyle's Sherlock Holmes stories, which couple the master detective with his male disciple and sidekick, Dr. Watson, and with the criminal mastermind, Professor Moriarity.

43 Some of the most influential commentaries on the radical ambiguity or unreadability of "Figure" include Shlomith Rimmon, *The Concept of Ambiguity – The Example of James* (University of Chicago Press, 1977), pp. 95–115; J. Hillis Miller, "The Figure in the Carpet," *Poetics Today* 1, no. 3 (Spring 1980); and Shoshana Felman, "Turning the Screw of Interpretation," *Literature and Psychoanalysis: The Question of Reading Otherwise*, ed. Shoshana Felman (Baltimore: Johns Hopkins University Press, 1982). Gerard M. Sweeney emphasizes the deadliness of identifying the figure in "The Deadly Figure in James's Carpet," *Modern Language Studies* 13, no. 4 (Fall 1983).

44 The narrator's representation of Gwendolen Erme as a female decadent suggests the comparably gendered and sexual threats posed by the *fin-de-siècle* figures of the New Woman and the aesthete. Linda Dowling connects these two figures in "The Decadent and the New Woman in the 1890s," *Nineteenth-Century Fiction* 33 (1979).

45 See Lawrence Levine, *Highbrow/Lowbrow: The Emergence of Cultural Hierarchy in America* (Cambridge, MA: harvard University Press, 1988), pp. 192–200.

46 James, *Notebooks*, p. 218.

47 Edel describes this moment of reckoning as the natural outcome of the trauma of being booed off stage in 1891, a public humiliation James suffered on the opening night of his play, *Guy Domville*; see *Henry James*, pp. 414–29. For sustained reconsiderations of James's engagement with his multiple audiences, see Michael Anesko, *Friction With the Market: Henry James and the Profession of Authorship* (Oxford University Press, 1986); Freedman, *Professions of Taste*; and Strychacz, *Modernism, Mass Culture, and Professionalism*, pp. 45–83.

48 James, *Notebooks*, p. 109.

4 A WAY OF LOOKING ON

1 Zdzislaw Najder's biography *Joseph Conrad: A Chronicle* (New Brunswick, NJ: Rutgers University Press, 1983), p. 356, dates the title change sometime during January 1910, the month in which Conrad completed the novel. However, the shift of narrative focus to the narrator's point of view prob-

ably occurred during the preceding two years of the novel's composition. On the composition of the novel, see Keith Carabine, "The Figure Behind the Veil: Conrad and Razumov in *Under Western Eyes*," and David R. Smith, "The Hidden Narrative: The *K* in Conrad," both in *Joseph Conrad's* Under Western Eyes: *Beginnings, Revisions, Final Forms: Five Essays*, ed. David R. Smith (Hamden, CT: Archon Books, 1991).

2 The "decline theory" of Conrad's later work – initiated by Virginia Woolf in "Joseph Conrad," *The Common Reader* (1924; London: Hogarth Press, 1925), and reinforced by Thomas Moser in *Joseph Conrad: Achievement and Decline* (Cambridge, MA: Harvard University Press, 1957) – links the supposed lesser quality of his later work to his treatment of the apparently uncongenial subjects of women and heterosexual love. Najder, *Joseph Conrad*, only slightly modifies this theory by arguing that Conrad's later writings on these subjects "may be taken rather as a *symptom* of his weariness than as the *cause* of his decline" (p. 363). Recently, critics have begun to reassess the importance of issues of gender and sexual relations to Conrad's writing over the course of his career; see, for example, the recent collection, *Conrad and Gender*, ed. Andrew Michael Roberts (Amsterdam: Rodolpi, 1993).

3 Their almost exclusively male casts of characters, in combination with their episodic form and their exotic settings, marked *Youth* (1898), *Heart of Darkness* (1899), and *Lord Jim* (1900) as novels of incident rather than as novels of character. For an account of the contemporary reception of Conrad's early writing as adventure fiction manqué, see Andrea White, *Joseph Conrad and the Adventure Tradition: Constructing and Deconstructing the Imperial Subject* (Cambridge University Press, 1993)

4 December 5, 1903, *The Collected Letters of Joseph Conrad*, ed. Frederick Karl and Laurence Davies, 5 vols. (Cambridge University Press, 1988), III, p. 89.

5 Joseph Conrad, *Under Western Eyes* (1911; Harmondsworth: Penguin, 1987), p. 157. Further page references will be included in the body of the chapter.

6 Peter Ivanovitch is described as an "inspired man" (p. 348) in the final line of *Under Western Eyes*, but the language of inspiration appears throughout the novel.

7 On the targeting of women readers in the publicity campaign waged in *The New York Herald*, where *Chance* was serialized in the United States, see Cedric Watts, "Marketing Modernism: How Conrad Prospered," *Modernist Writers and the Marketplace*, ed. Ian Willison, Warwick Gould, and Warren Chernaik (London: Macmillan, 1996). See also Laurence Davies, "Conrad, *Chance*, and Women Readers," *Conrad and Gender*, ed. Roberts.

8 Cited in Frederick R. Karl, *Joseph Conrad: The Three Lives* (New York: Farrar, Straus and Giroux, 1979), p. 633.

9 Karl, *Joseph Conrad*, p. 722.

10 Joseph Conrad, Author's Note to *Youth*, *The Norton Edition of Heart of Darkness*, ed. Robert Kimbrough (1921; New York: Norton, 1988), pp. 3–4.

11 On Conrad's and Ford Madox Ford's collaboration, see Wayne Koestenbaum, *Double Talk: The Erotics of Male Literary Collaboration* (New York:

Routledge, 1989), pp. 166–73, and Raymond Brebach, *Joseph Conrad, Ford Madox Ford, and the Making of* Romance (Ann Arbor: University of Michigan Research Press, 1985). For first-hand accounts of their collaboration, see Joseph Conrad and Ford Madox Ford, Prefaces and Appendix to *The Nature of a Crime* (London: Duckworth, 1924), and Ford's *Joseph Conrad.*

12 The very expression (i.e., his refusal to "justify his existence") that Conrad uses in his 1920 Author's Note with respect to the narrator of *Under Western Eyes*, he also uses in his 1912 *A Personal Record* to express his distaste for Rousseau and particularly for the mode that his *Confessions* represented to him.

13 Conrad's emphasis on his impartial and fair treatment of Russia in the Author's Note resembles his stance in *Autocracy and War* (1905), his political piece on Russia written several years earlier. Najder, *Joseph Conrad*, notes that "when first printed in the *Fortnightly Review* the article carried the motto *sine ira et studio* [without anger and ardor]. The passage about the partition of Poland was even accompanied by the reservation 'without indulging in excessive feelings of indignation at that country's partition'" (p. 309).

14 In his introduction to *Under Western Eyes* (Harmondsworth: Penguin, 1985), p. 20, Boris Ford treats Conrad's intensified feelings of Polish patriotism during these years; see also Jocelyn Baines, *Joseph Conrad: A Critical Biography* (Westport, CT: Greenwood Press, 1976), pp. 373–4.

15 Much of my evidence for this reading of the conflict between, and within, Conrad's national and authorial identities comes from Karl's biography. In the same letter to John Galsworthy in which he describes being "caught between one's impulse, one's art and that question [of saleability]," Conrad attributes the failure of *The Secret Agent* to "Foreignness I suppose," thus indicating the tension between artistic success and national identity; cited in Karl, *Joseph Conrad*, pp. 633–6. He then goes on to outline his early plan for "Razumov," the manuscript title for *Under Western Eyes*. Najder, *Joseph Conrad*, discusses the conception of *Under Western Eyes* in the context of Conrad's financial problems and hopes for popular success, pp. 333–40; see also Cedric Watts, *Joseph Conrad: A Literary Life* (London: Macmillan, 1989), pp. 109–14. .

16 In his analysis of "authorial double talk," Penn R. Szittya observes that the narrator profoundly distrusts the imagination and fiction despite his ostensible praise of art, using this observation to support his suggestion that "Razumov may be an oblique figure of the novelist"; see "Metafiction: The Double Narration in *Under Western Eyes*," *English Literary History* 48, no. 4 (Winter 1981), 826–8. I emphasize, by contrast, the tension between the narrator's encomium to the realism of great art and the use of allusions in this novel to actual, historical figures, such as "de P-" who is the historical Viacheslav Konstantinovitch Plehve, assassinated by a thrown bomb in July 1904, and of fictional figures conspicuously modelled on historical figures, such as "Madame de S-" who is explicitly, though unfavorably, compared to "that other dangerous and exiled woman, Madame de Staël (p. 164).

Morton Dauwen Zabel gives a helpful account of the historical sources relevant to this period of Conrad's writing career in his Introduction and supplementary notes to *Under Western Eyes* (Garden City, NY: Anchor-Doubleday, 1963).

17 In *Joseph Conrad*, Najder argues that writing *Under Western Eyes* set Conrad "face to face with a black wall of hopelessness raised by the [political future of Poland] ... That feeling of helplessness associated with guilt might be expected to lead to a severe depression in a person of Conrad's constitution" (p. 359). Najder discounts the various attributions of Conrad's nervous breakdown offered by Bernard Meyer in *Joseph Conrad: A Psychoanalytic Biography* (Princeton University Press, 1967), particularly Meyer's attribution of the breakdown to Conrad's "sense of 'Slavonism'" (p. 358). Yet it is likely that Conrad's very resistance to pan-Slavism, including his insistence on the Westernness of Poland, may itself have added to the stresses of writing for English readers who did not always acknowledge the distinction between Russia and Poland.

18 Interestingly, Razumov is deflected from this vision of communion with Haldin by the "sidelong, brilliant glance of a pretty woman – with a delicate head, and covered in the hairy skins of wild beasts down to her feet, like a frail and beautiful savage" (p. 84). Instantaneously, another passer-by brings up the image of "Prince K -, the man who once had pressed his hand as no other man had pressed it ... like a half-unwilling caress," whereupon Razumov decides to turn in Haldin. Razumov's submission to the Law of the Father – here, in the person of his biological father – is influenced by the power of possession and of position that he associates with the pretty woman and her fur coat. For an analysis of Razumov's character along Lacanian lines, see Josiane Paccaud, "The Name-of-the-Father in Conrad's *Under Western Eyes*," *Conradiana* 18, no. 3 (Autumn 1986).

19 Conrad wrote "The Secret Sharer" between 1 and 19 December, 1909, and submitted the uncorrected typescript of *Under Western Eyes* to his literary agent on January 27, 1910. See Keith Carabine, "'The Secret Sharer': A Note on the Dates of Its Composition," *Conradiana* 19, no. 3 (Autumn 1987).

20 Bonnie Kime Scott makes an argument comparable to mine in "Intimacies Engendered in Conrad's 'The Secret Sharer'," *Case Studies in Contemporary Criticism: Joseph Conrad's "The Secret Sharer"*, ed. Daniel R. Schwarz (New York: Bedford Books, 1997).

21 Joseph Conrad, "The Secret Sharer" (1912), *The Portable Conrad*, ed. Morton Dauwen Zabel, (Harmondsworth: Penguin, 1947), pp. 58–9.

22 Karl, *Joseph Conrad*, p. 675.

23 Conrad, "The Secret Sharer," p. 60.

24 Conrad outlined the novel in a letter to John Galsworthy on January 6, 1908, marking the Russian section of the novel as "done" and the Geneva section as yet "to do": "The Student Razumov meeting abroad the mother and sister of Haldin falls in love with that last, marries her and after a time confesses to her the part he played in the arrest of Haldin and death of her

brother. The psychological developments leading to Razumov's betrayal of Haldin, to his confession of the fact to his wife and to the death of these people (brought about mainly by the resemblance of their child to the late Haldin) form the real subject of the story"; quoted in Karl, *Joseph Conrad*, p. 636.

25 Conrad cut several long passages from the typescript, including an episode in which the narrator criticizes Peter Ivanovitch's feminism to his face, then goes on to criticize his niece's marriage plans. See David Leon Higdon and Robert F. Sheard, "Conrad's 'Unkindest Cut': The Canceled Scenes in *Under Western Eyes*," *Conradiana* 19, no. 3 (Autumn 1987). Conrad made these revisions in the spring of 1910, much later than his change in plans for Razumov's and Natalia's marriage.

26 Regarding the functions of the nineteenth-century conventional epilogue, see Marianna Torgovnick, *Closure in the Novel* (Princeton University Press, 1981), p. 11.

27 In "Ford Madox Hueffer and *Under Western Eyes*," *Conradiana* 15, no. 3 (Autumn 1983), Thomas Moser links the scene in which Peter Ivanovitch abuses Tekla over some badly prepared eggs to Conrad's modelling of the "great man" on Ford Madox Ford (pp. 171–2). But Moser misses the more direct antecedent of this scene in Ford's anecdote about William Morris: "William Morris came out onto the landing in the house of the 'Firm' in Red Lion Square and roared downstairs: 'Mary, those six eggs were bad. I've eaten them, but don't let it occur again'"; *Your Mirror to My Times*, ed. Michael Killigrew (New York: Holt, Rineheart, and Winston, 1971), p. 8. Ford's emphasis on the aggressiveness of the Pre-Raphaelites in this piece – "[a]bout the inner circle of those who fathered and sponsored the Aesthetic movement there was absolutely nothing of the languishing. They were to a man rather burly, passionate creatures, extraordinarily enthusiastic, extraordinarily romantic and most impressively quarrelsome" (p. 9) – also strikingly recalls Conrad's characterization of Peter Ivanovitch.

28 Cited in Higdon and Sheard, "Conrad's 'Unkindest Cut'," p. 176.

29 Daniel R. Schwarz, for example, argues that the narrator "affirm[s] personal values" in the way that he "involves himself in Nathalie's affairs, and befriends her with a sensitivity and responsiveness that her Russian acquaintances lack" (pp. 195–6), concluding that "[h]is civilised conscience emerges as the viable ethical alternative to anarchy and fanaticism" (p. 211); *Conrad, "Almayer's Folly" to* Under Western Eyes (Ithaca: Cornell University Press, 1980). For Schwarz, the narrator exemplifies a different kind of man and a different kind of relation between men and women, a figure who translates the novel's plots of political and gendered victimization into something else, something better. Suresh Raval, *The Art of Failure, Conrad's Fiction* (Boston, Allen & Unwin, 1986), assesses the narrator as an inadequate observer of Russian life who is motivated partly by sexual interest in Natalia, thereby qualifying Schwarz's approbation. Raval minimizes, however, the impact of those "certain moments [which] suggest that [the

narrator's] interest in Nathalie Haldin derives from his impotent and jealous romantic love for her" by arguing that "these moments are not serious" (p. 128). See also Victor Luftig, *Seeing Together: Friendship Between the Sexes in English Writing from Mill to Woolf* (Stanford University Press, 1993), p. 172, for a positive appraisal of this bachelor narrator's capacity for cross-gender friendship.

30 On reevaluating narcissism, see Michael Warner, "Homo-Narcissism: or, Heterosexuality," *Engendering Men*, ed. Boone and Cadden, and Hewitt, *Political Inversions*, pp. 60–78.

31 On *tableaux vivants*, see Halttunen, *Confidence Men and Painted Women*, pp. 175–90.

32 Such a scene marks the dénouement of Thomas Southerne's *The Wives Excuse; or Cuckolds Make Themselves* (1691), whose stage directions call for an "Anti-Chamber." The second example of a discovery scene is from Shakespeare's *The Winter's Tale* (1611); this play's climactic spectacle featuring Hermione as a statue who comes to life informs my analysis of Natalia's metaphorical transformation into a statue.

33 My reading of spectatorship is indebted to the debate about gender and power that galvanized feminist film theory in the 1980s and 90s. This debate was spurred by Laura Mulvey, "Visual Pleasure and Narrative Cinema" (1975) and, later, "Afterthoughts on 'Visual Pleasure and Narrative Cinema' inspired by *Duel in the Sun*" (1981), both reprinted in *Feminism and Film Theory*, ed. Constance Penley (New York: Routledge, 1988). The contributions to this debate are too numerous to list here, but two essays particularly relevant to the issues of sexual difference and the mechanisms of pleasure in narrative cinema for men as subjects and objects of the gaze are David Rodowick, "The Difficulty of Difference," *Wide Angle: A Film Quarterly of Theory, Criticism, and Practice* 5 (1982); and Steve Neale, "Masculinity as Spectacle," *Screening the Male: Exploring Masculinities in Hollywood Cinema*, ed. Steven Cohan and Ina Rae Hark (New York: Routledge, 1993).

34 Critics in the "unreliable narrator" tradition have seized upon this moment as exemplifying this narrator's failure of imagination or perception; see, for example, Robert Secor, "The Function of the Narrator in *Under Western Eyes*," *Conradiana* 3, no. 1 (1970–1); and Tony Tanner, "Nightmare and Complacency: Razumov and the Western Eye," *Critical Quarterly* 4, no. 3 (Autumn 1962).

35 Marjorie Garber, *Vested Interests: Cross-Dressing and Cultural Anxiety* (1992; New York: Harper, 1993), p. 218.

36 Garber, *Vested Interests*, p. 338.

37 Juliet Mitchell, *Psychoanalysis and Feminism; Freud, Reich, Laing and Women* (New York: Vintage-Random House, 1975) glosses Freud on fetishism: "The instance of fetishism indicates (as does incidentally, that of the Medusa's head) the other dimension of the castration complex: fear of the mother, or rather of the mother's genitals – that first proof that castration can occur . . . There is always this oscillation between disavowal and acknowledgment;

the ego has split itself as a means of defence" (p. 85). Marjorie Garber, *Vested Interests*, elaborates on this classical formulation: "We might notice where according to Robert Stoller 'reassurance' comes for transvestites in the possession of a penis and its capacity for erection, for Rivière's fetishist the possession of the penis is itself grounds for anxiety"; Garber nevertheless offers a comparable account of the narrative "dynamics of fetishism": "the deferral of detection, the deferral of the dénouement, is part of the story" (p. 209).

38 Hal Foster, "The Art of Fetishism: Notes on Dutch Still Life," *Fetishism as Cultural Discourse*, ed. Emily Apter and William Pietz (Ithaca: Cornell University Press, 1993), p. 263.

39 Garber, *Vested Interests*, glosses Lacan's precept: "In other words, because human sexuality is constructed through repression, the signifier of desire cannot be represented directly, only under a veil" (p. 288).

40 According to both the gospels of Matthew and Mark, the death of John is seen as the desire of the mother, Herodias, not the daughter, Salome; see Garber, *Vested Interests*, p. 340. See also Charles Bernheimer, "Fetishism and Decadence: Salome's Severed Heads," *Fetishism as Cultural Discourse*, ed. Apter and Pietz. Natalia as Salome would neatly explain the narrator's emphasis on his "thinking about Natalia Haldin's life in terms of her mother's character" (pp. 300–1) and his account of Natalia "justif[ying] her action by the mental state of her mother" (p. 323).

41 I am indebted to Foster, "The Art of Fetishism," for the insight that "It is this preexistent loss in the subject that demands fetishistic perfection in the object (a recognition that puts a very different spin on 'art appreciation')" (p. 263).

42 My account of the variations on the Medusa myth is based on Edith Hamilton, *Mythology* (1940; Boston: Little, Brown, 1969) and Eleanor Wilner, "The Medusa Connection," *Triquarterly* 88 (Fall 1993).

43 The Medusa's head refutes the notion of androgyny, or of androgyny as a harmonious balance of masculine and feminine elements, since a gendered battle for preeminence is built into the narratives that it represents.

44 Sigmund Freud, "Medusa's Head," *The Standard Edition of the Complete Psychological Works of Sigmund Freud*, ed. James Strachey, 24 vols. (London: Hogarth Press, 1953–1974), XVIII, pp. 273–4.

45 Marina Warner, *Monuments and Maidens: The Allegory of the Female Form* (New York: Atheneum, 1985), pp. 108–14, traces the use of this figure. See also Neil Hertz, "Medusa's Head: Male Hysteria under Political Pressure," and Catherine Gallagher, Joel Fineman, Neil Hertz, "More About 'Medusa's Head'," both in *Representations* 4 (Fall 1983).

46 Hélène Cixous, "The Laugh of the Medusa," trans. Keith and Paula Cohen, *Signs* 1, no. 4 (Summer, 1976).

47 Freud makes no mention of Perseus in his "Medusa's Head" essay, focusing instead on the virgin goddess Athena and the male spectator that she petrifies with horror with the head of Medusa pinned to her breastplate. In

Freud's account, the petrified spectator is normatively male and human, and the petrifying object of spectatorship, she who controls the gaze, is normatively female and godly, and also doubled in her identity as Medusa/ Athena.

48 In "Brides of Opportunity: Figurations of Women and Colonial Territory in *Lord Jim*," *Qui Parle* 3, no. 2 (Fall 1989), Natalie Melas notes the portrayal of Jewel as an "unforgiving Medusa," whose stony-faced aspect Marlow mimics when he "looks hard" at Stein, the pun on whose name Melas also notes. Conrad also uses Medusa imagery in *Chance* (1913) to describe the horrified response of Flora de Barral to her rejection by the governess who is her surrogate mother.

5 THE NECESSARY MELANCHOLY OF BACHELORS

1 "Why My Uncle Was a Bachelor," *Harper's New Monthly Magazine* 8, no. 47 (April 1854).

2 On uncles as threshold figures who mark by transgressing the bounds of bourgeois familial domesticity, see Eve Kosofsky Sedgwick, "Tales of the Avunculate: Queer Tutelage in *The Importance of Being Earnest*," *Tendencies* (Durham: Duke University Press, 1993), and Eileen Cleere, "'The Shape of Uncles': Capitalism, Affection, and the Cultural Construction of the Victorian Family," PhD thesis, Rice University (1996). On the comparable discursive function of bachelor cousins, see Michael Lucey, "Balzac's Queer Cousins and Their Friends," *Novel Gazing*, ed. Sedgwick.

3 Edward K. Graham, "The Necessary Melancholy of Bachelors," *Putnam's Monthly Magazine* 4, no. 6 (September 1908), 695. Further page references will be cited in the body of the chapter.

4 David H. Lynn, *The Hero's Tale: Narrators in the Early Modern Novel* (New York: St. Martin's Press, 1989) considers these three first-person-narrated modernist novels, together with *Heart of Darkness* and *The Sun Also Rises*, in the more conventional context of the collapse of traditional values in the early twentieth century.

5 Joseph Conrad, *Chance* (1913; New York: Penguin Books, 1974), p. 125. Further page references will be given in the body of the text with "*C.*"

6 See *LC1*, p. 151.

7 The uncontrolled "sharp comical yapping" of the dog resonates with Marlow's own narrative voice, a connection suggested earlier in the text: "while waiting for [Mrs. Fyne's] answer I became mentally aware of three trained dogs dancing on their hind legs. I don't know why. Perhaps because of the pervading solemnity... In these words Mrs. Fyne answered me. The aggressive tone was too much for my endurance. In an instant I found myself out of the dance and down on all-fours so to speak, with liberty to bark and bite" (*C* 58).

8 The following is a mere sampling of popular fictions featuring the "bachelor and the baby" plot: Judith Canute, *Eros and Anteros; or The Bachelor's*

Ward (New York: Rudd and Carleton, 1857); Coyne Fletcher, *The Bachelor's Baby* (New York: Clark and Zugalla, 1891); Sarah Beaumont Kennedy, "A Bachelor's Ward" *Everybody's Magazine* 6, no. 3 (March 1902); Masson, "The Bachelor's Christmas Baby" (see chapter one, n. 77); Margaret Cameron, "The Bachelor and the Baby" *Harper's Monthly Magazine* 114, no. 681 (February 1907); Lillian Leveridge, "The Bachelor and the Baby," *The Canadian Magazine* 34, no. 4 (February 1910); Louise Bascom, *The Bachelor Club's Baby* (Franklin: Eldridge Entertainment House, 1912); and Henry James's first novel, *Watch and Ward* (Boston: Houghton, Osgood, and Co., 1878).

9 Joseph Conrad, *Heart of Darkness* (1899), *The Norton Critical Edition of* Heart of Darkness (New York: Norton, 1988), p. 12.

10 *Chance* actually has three Charlies, if we include the "Charley" who is the supposed nephew and actual lover of Flora's governess, and who courts Flora until she loses her fortune. In *"Chance* and the Secret Life: Conrad, Thackeray, Stevenson," *Conrad and Gender*, ed. Roberts, Robert Hampson also comments on *Chance*'s "patterns of reflection and repetition: the two men called Powell; the three men called Charles; three women described as governesses, the two elopements; and so on" (p. 122).

11 On intersecting perceptions of pedagogy, pederasty, and pedophilia, see Hewitt, *Political Inversions*, pp. 94–8 and pp. 141–70.

12 Anne McClintock, *Imperial Leather: Race, Gender, and Sexuality in the Colonial Contest* (New York: Routledge, 1995), pp. 44–5.

13 Admittedly, Jewel brings a female presence into the Patusan plot, although her boyishness and her portrayal as an aspect of Jim himself complicate her status as a female character. In "'Ghosts of the Gothic': Spectral Women and Colonized Spaces in *Lord Jim*," *Conrad and Gender*, ed. Roberts, Padmini Mongia argues that Jim is himself figured as a Gothic heroine, symbolically reborn in the maternal space of Patusan. Jim's emergence from the muddy bank in Patusan could equally well be interpreted as a male anal rebirth, a re-genesis of man from mud comparable to the emergence of the adventurers from the subterranean tunnel in Haggard's *King Solomon's Mines*. On the topic of women in *Lord Jim*, see also Melas, "Brides of Opportunity."

14 McClintock, *Imperial Leather*, p. 241.

15 Marianna Torgovnick, *Gone Primitive: Savage Intellects, Modern Lives* (University of Chicago Press, 1990), p. 185.

16 McClintock, *Imperial Leather*, p. 243.

17 In *Modernism and the Fate of Individuality*, Levenson analyzes the concept of the "beyond within" in *Heart of Darkness*; see pp. 5–13. He clarifies the importance of this concept for modernist and colonialist narrative, but does not connect it, as I do, to domestic and familial discourse.

18 Romantic discourse and sentimental discourse are not identical, either aesthetically or historically, but they have similarities enough – especially the priority of emotion, feeling, and imagination – to warrant their equation in this context. On the gendered intersections between these discourses, see

Anne K. Mellor, *Romanticism and Gender* (New York: Routledge, 1993), pp. 17–29. See also Suzanne Clark, *Sentimental Modernism: Women Writers and the Revolution of the Word* (Bloomington: Indiana University Press, 1991), pp. 27–8.

19 Ford paid tribute to Conrad upon many occasions, and their relationship has been extensively documented (see chapter 4, n. 11). Fitzgerald told John Galsworthy that Joseph Conrad, Anatole France, and Galsworthy himself were the three living writers he admired most, and in answer to a query from the *Chicago Tribune*, Fitzgerald pointed to *Nostromo* as "the greatest novel since *Vanity Fair* (possibly excluding *Madame Bovary*)"; see Frederick Karl, *A Reader's Guide to Joseph Conrad* (New York: Doubleday, 1960), p. 3. Jeffrey Meyers records how Fitzgerald attempted to pay homage to Conrad by dancing drunkenly with Ring Lardner on the lawn of the Doubleday estate when Conrad was a guest there in May of 1923; see *Joseph Conrad, A Biography* (New York: Scribner's, 1991), pp. 349–50.

20 Ford Madox Ford, *The Good Soldier* (1915; New York: Vintage-Random House, 1983), pp. 253–4. Further page references to be given in the body of the chapter with the abbreviation "*GS*."

21 *The Confessions of St. Augustine*, trans. Rex Warner (New York: New American Library, 1963), pp. 45–9.

22 F. Scott Fitzgerald, *The Great Gatsby* (1925; New York: Collier, 1992), pp. 63–4. Further page references will be given in the body of the chapter with "*GG*."

23 The Provencal courtly love story to which Dowell alludes in his narrative – the story of "Peire Vidal the Troubador" who "fell all over the lady's bed while the husband, who was a most ferocious warrior, remonstrated some more about the courtesy that is due to great poets" (*GS*, pp. 16–17) – reveals the centrality of adulterous desire, if not necessarily consummated adultery, to the courtly love tradition. For an overview of the threat to established order posed by this literary tradition which foregrounds devotion to a forbidden object of erotic and spiritual desire, see Boone, *Tradition Counter Tradition*, pp. 34–43.

24 See chapter 3, n. 27, for critical sources treating the paradoxical status of masochism with respect to normative masculinity.

25 Dowell also resembles Ralph Touchett, as well as *Portrait*'s other conspicuously leisurely, upper-class, transatlantic male figures, in his lack of a career: "the first question they asked me was not how I did but what did I do. And I did nothing. I suppose I ought to have done something, but I didn't see any call to do it" (*GS*, p. 15).

26 The discourse of blackmail gives an overtone of homosexual scandal to the "Kilsyte case" (*GS*, p. 149), the name by which Dowell refers to Edward's "natural but ill-timed" (*GS*, p. 50) sexual advance towards a working-class woman and its repercussions. Rictor Norton affirms that many, perhaps most, blackmail attempts in the eighteenth and nineteenth centuries involved a threat to expose a man as homosexual, whether or not he was in

fact gay; see *Mother Clap's Molly House: The Gay Subculture in England, 1700– 1830* (London: GMP, 1992), p. 135; see also pp. 134–45. The "Kilsyte case" occurs sometime between 1892 and 1895, the latter date being the year Oscar Wilde was sentenced to imprisonment under the "Labouchère Amendment" to the Criminal Law Amendment Act of 1885, commonly known as the "blackmailer's charter," further reinforcing the association of Edward's transgressions with homosexual scandal. This reckoning of dates is based on Vincent J. Cheng, "A Chronology of *The Good Soldier*," *English Language Notes* 24, no. 1 (September 1986).

27 Samuel Hynes, for example, asserts that "Passion is the necessary antagonist of Convention, the protest of the individual against the rules" (p. 233) in "The Epistemology of *The Good Soldier*," *Sewanee Review* 69, no. 2 (Spring 1961).

28 Mark Girouard describes the literary, artistic, and popular manifestations of late Victorian and Edwardian neochivalry in *The Return to Camelot: Chivalry and the English Gentleman* (New Haven: Yale University Press, 1981), pp. 250–74.

29 Michael Levenson, "Character in *The Good Soldier*," *Twentieth-Century Literature* 30, no. 4 (Winter 1984), 376. While my discussion of character is indebted to Levenson's, his conclusions – that "in an utterly improbable way Dowell becomes a compelling image of the free man" (p. 384) and that Dowell "reanimates the ethical sense that had languished in Edward, petrified in Leonora, and died in Florence" (p. 386) – seem to me overly optimistic. To champion the vision and moral rectitude of Ford's narrator is to miss the lack of resolution, both epistemological and ethical, generated in this narrative through the device of one man telling another man's story.

30 Levenson, "Character in *The Good Soldier*," p. 375.

31 Lawrence Buell has described the catalogue as a feature of American modernism in "The Pleasures of Repetition (Revisiting Whitman)," *The Breadloaf Anthology of Contemporary American Essays*, ed. Robert Pack and Jay Parini (Hanover, NH: University Press of New England, 1989).

32 David Castronovo discusses American emulation of Englishness as a class signifier in *The American Gentleman: Social Prestige and the Modern Literary Mind* (New York: Ungar-Continuum, 1991), pp. 25–34; see also his discussion of New York gentility in *The Great Gatsby*, pp. 69–75.

33 Ford's biographers have treated extensively Ford's fascination with Englishness and particularly his ambivalence toward the figure of the proper English gentleman. Ford repudiated this figure as the nemesis of true art in his literary criticism, yet often assumed the pose of the English gentleman despite the fact that he was singularly unqualified for the role by his marital infidelities and unconventional domestic arrangements; by his feminist and vaguely socialist sympathies; and by his non-English origins on his father's side and his non-landed gentry status. See Arthur Mizener, *The Saddest Story: A Biography of Ford Madox Ford* (New York: World, 1971), pp. 22 and 258–77; Thomas Moser, *The Life in the Fiction of Ford Madox Ford* (Princeton University

Press, 1980), pp. 161–95; Brita Lindberg-Seyersted, Introduction to *Pound/Ford, The Story of a Literary Friendship: The Correspondence Between Ezra Pound and Ford Madox Ford and Their Writings about Each Other* (New York: New Directions, 1982), p. viii; Alan Judd, *Ford Madox Ford* (London: Collins, 1990), p. 107; and Max Saunders, *Ford Madox Ford: A Dual Life* (Oxford University Press, 1996), I, pp. 23, 360, and 408–9.

34 Joseph Conrad, Preface to *The Nigger of the "Narcissus"; A Tale of the Sea* (1897; New York: Oxford University Press, 1984), p. xlii.

35 Adam Smith, *The Theory of Moral Sentiments*, ed. D. D. Raphael and A. L. Macfie (Oxford: Clarendon Press, 1976), p. 9.

36 Clark, *Sentimental Modernism*, pp. 5 and 35.

37 On the historical shift in the valuation of sentimentality from a term of approval to a epithet connotating degradation, see Clark, *Sentimental Modernism*, pp. 20–31.

38 One of the most influential accounts of the relations of modernism, Conrad's authorial identity, and *Lord Jim*, to mass culture is Fredric Jameson, "Romance and Reification: Plot Construction and Ideological Closure in Joseph Conrad," *The Political Unconscious: Narrative as a Socially Symbolic Act* (Ithaca: Cornell University Press, 1981), pp. 206–80. See also White, *Joseph Conrad and the Adventure Tradition*.

39 Ford Madox Ford, *The English Novel: From the Earliest Days to the Death of Joseph Conrad* (London: Constable, 1930), p. 76. The novel/nuvvle dichotomy was Ford's way of contending with the affront to the manly dedication of the true artist posed by those English gentleman nuvvelists who found it "not really gentlemanly to think of being anything but being a gentleman." Both novelist and nuvvelist have their manly honor at stake, but the nuvvelist's honor resides in simply being a gentleman whereas the novelist's lies in the integrity of his art.

40 Ford Madox Ford, "The Commercial Value of Literature: A Radio Talk Given by Ford Madox Ford," transcribed and ed. Max Saunders, *Contemporary Literature* 30, no. 2 (1989), 326.

41 Stephen Matterson, *The Great Gatsby* (London: Macmillan, 1990), observes that "it is no accident that critical interest in *The Great Gatsby* was stimulated most during the 1940s and 1950s, when the New Criticism was a dominant teaching and research practice" (p. 10).

42 My overview of Fitzgerald's early career is based primarily on Matthew Bruccoli's *Some Sort of Epic Grandeur: The Life of F. Scott Fitzgerald* (New York: Harcourt, Brace, Jovanovitch, 1981), see especially pp. 195–224.

43 Once again, I am troping upon Nina Baym's "Melodramas of Beset Manhood."

44 Nick's ambivalence towards Gatsby's sentimentalism has contributed to the long-debated question of his reliability as narrator. For a fine overview of the "Carraway Controversy" and an analysis of its ideological implications, see Elizabeth Preston, "Implying Authors in *The Great Gatsby*," *Narrative* 5, no. 2 (May 1997).

45 Only several pages before Nick avows his "intense personal interest" in Gatsby, Gatsby dismisses Daisy's love for her husband as "just personal" (*GG*, p. 152); this combination of disavowal and endorsement of the personal parallels the novel's ambivalent treatment of the sentimental. For a reading of the gendered implications of emotional investment in *Gatsby* which is compatible with my account here, see Frances Kerr, "Feeling 'Half Feminine': Modernism and the Politics of Emotion in *The Great Gatsby*," *American Literature* 68, no. 2 (June 1996).

46 My reading here owes much to Mitchell Breitwieser's intelligence concerning waste, voice, and melancholy in Fitzgerald's novel; see "*The Great Gatsby*: Grief, Jazz, and the Eye-Witness," *Arizona Quarterly* 47, no. 3 (Autumn 1991), and his "Fitzgerald, Kerouac, and the Puzzle of Inherited Mourning" (unpublished essay). Thanks also to Anne Cheng for her elucidation of the complexities of melancholic logic.

47 Keath Fraser draws on manuscript passages excluded from the published text of *The Great Gatsby* to argue that the narrative's pervasive anxiety is rooted, at least in part, in homosexual panic; see "Another Reading of *The Great Gatsby*," *F. Scott Fitzgerald's* The Great Gatsby, ed. Harold Bloom (New York: Chelsea House, 1986).

48 It was Ford, not Fitzgerald, who self-consciously aligned his own and Conrad's literary practice with painterly Impressionism, a connection suggested by Dowell who observes that "[t]he whole world for me is like spots of colour in an immense canvas" (*GS*, p. 14). Ford theorized this connection in his essay, "On Impressionism" (1914), *Critical Writings of Ford Madox Ford*, ed. Frank MacShane (Lincoln: University of Nebraska Press, 1964). Critical discussions of Ford's impressionism can be found in Levenson, "Character in *The Good Soldier*," 379–82; Charles Daughady, "Cubist Viewing with the Comic Spirit in Ford's *The Good Soldier*," *Kentucky Philological Association Bulletin* (1984); and Richard Hood, "'Constant Reduction': Modernism and the Narrative Structure of *The Good Soldier*," *Journal of Modern Literature* 14, no. 4 (Spring 1988).

49 Ford, "On Impressionism," p. 54.

50 I am indebted to Claire Kahane's reading of this passage in "Male Modernists and the Ear of the Other in *Heart of Darkness* and *The Good Soldier*," *Passions of the Voice: Hysteria, Narrative, and the Figure of the Speaking Woman, 1850–1915* (Baltimore: Johns Hopkins University Press, 1995), pp. 140–1. Whereas Kahane reads Dowell's pacific vision of communion as an illusory attempt to compensate for the betrayals he experiences, and as a cover-up for the sadistic and masochistic pleasures of narrative that he subsequently comes to enjoy, I see his fantasy as signifying that the narrative retains the ideal, if not the actuality, of redemptive communion with the other.

AFTERWORD

1 F. Scott Fitzgerald, interview with Charles C. Baldwin, originally published as "F. Scott Fitzgerald," in *The Men Who Make Our Novels* (New York: Dodd,

Mead, 1924); reprinted in *F. Scott Fitzgerald in His Own Time: A Miscellany*, ed. Matthew J. Bruccoli and Jackson R. Bryer (Kent State University Press, 1971), p. 268.

2 December 31, 1925 letter from Eliot to Fitzgerald, in *The Crack-Up: With Other Uncollected Pieces, Note-books, and Unpublished Letters, Together With Letters to Fitzgerald*, ed. Edmund Wilson (New York: New Directions, 1956), p. 310. February 20, 1926 letter from Fitzgerald to Maxwell Perkins, in *F. Scott Fitzgerald: A Life in Letters*, ed. Matthew J. Bruccoli (New York: Scribner's, 1994), p. 137.

Bibliography

Adams, James Eli. *Dandies and Desert Saints: Styles of Victorian Masculinity*. Ithaca: Cornell University Press, 1995.

Adams, Marian. *The Letters of Mrs. Henry Adams, 1865–1883*. Ed. Ward Thoron. Boston: Little, Brown, and Co., 1937.

Agnew, Jean-Christophe. "The Consuming Vision of Henry James." *The Culture of Consumption*. Fox and Lears (eds.), pp. 67–100.

"Alarming Increase of Old Maids and Bachelors in New England." *Literary Digest* 65, no. 2 (April 10, 1920), 66–70.

Alpern, Andrew. *Apartments for the Affluent: A Historical Survey of Buildings in New York*. New York: McGraw-Hill, 1975.

Andreas, Eulalie. "Apartments for Bachelor Girls." *House Beautiful* 32, no. 6 (November 1912), 168–70.

Anesko, Michael. *Friction with the Market: Henry James and the Profession of Authorship*. Oxford University Press, 1986.

Apter, Emily and William Pietz (eds.). *Fetishism as Cultural Discourse*. Ithaca: Cornell University Press, 1993.

Ardis, Ann. *New Women, New Novels: Feminism and Early Modernism*. New Brunswick, NJ: Rutgers University Press, 1990.

Armstrong, Nancy. *Desire and Domestic Fiction: A Political History of the Novel*. New York: Oxford University Press, 1987.

Arnold, Matthew. *Culture and Anarchy: An Essay in Political and Social Criticism*. London: Smith, Elder and Co., 1869.

Auerbach, Jonathan. *The Romance of Failure: First-Person Fictions in Poe, Hawthorne, and James*. New York: Oxford University Press, 1989.

Augustine, Saint, Bishop of Hippo. *The Confessions of St. Augustine*. Trans. Rex Warner. New York: New American Library, 1966.

"The Bachelor: A Modern Idyll." *Temple Bar* 25 (February 1869), 361–3.

"Bachelor Invalids and Male Nurses." *Once a Week* 8, no. 3 (October 7, 1871), 317–21.

The Bachelor Married; or the Biter Bit. Leeds: Webb and Millington, 1830.

"The Bachelor's Christmas." *Blackwood's Edinburgh Magazine* 23, no. 134 (January 1828), 14–25.

"A Bachelor's Christmas." *Harper's New Monthly Magazine* 2, no. 9 (February 1851), 399–401.

"Bachelor's Hall." *All The Year Round* 133, no. 799 (March 22, 1884), 424–8; no. 800 (March 29, 1884), 448–52.

"Bachelor's Hall." *Harper's New Monthly Magazine* 31, no. 124 (September 1860), 511–18.

"A Bachelor's Story." *Chamber's Journal of Popular Literature, Science, and Arts* 56, no. 808 (June 21, 1879), 391–5.

"Bachelors – Why?: Views of Five Hundred of Them on the Income Needed for Matrimony and the Fitness of the Girls for Household Management." *Good Housekeeping* 50, no. 3 (March 1910), 335–40; no. 4 (April 1910), 461–5.

"The Bachelors' Wing." *Living Age* 249, no. 3222 (April 7, 1906), 62–3.

Baines, Jocelyn. *Joseph Conrad: A Critical Biography*. Westport, CT: Greenwood Press, 1976.

Baldwin, Charles C. *The Men Who Make Our Novels*. New York: Dodd, Mead, 1924.

Banks, J. A., and Olive Banks. *Feminism and Family Planning in Victorian England*. University of Liverpool Press, 1965.

Barker-Benfield, G. J. *The Horrors of the Half-Known Life: Male Attitudes Toward Women and Sexuality in Nineteenth-Century America*. New York: Harper and Row, 1976.

Barrie, J. M. *My Lady Nicotine: A Study in Smoke*. London: Hodder and Stoughton, 1890.

When a Man's Single: A Tale of Literary Life. London: Hodder and Stoughton, 1888.

Barthes, Roland. *The Pleasure of the Text*. Trans. Richard Miller. New York: Hill and Wang, 1975.

Bascom, Louise. *The Bachelor Club's Baby*. Franklin: Eldridge Entertainment House, 1912.

Baym, Nina. *"The Blithedale Romance*: A Radical Reading." *The Norton Critical Edition of* The Blithedale Romance. Eds. Seymour Gross and Rosalie Murphy. New York: Norton, 1978, pp. 351–68.

"Melodramas of Beset Manhood: How Theories of American Fiction Exclude Women Authors." *American Quarterly* 33, no. 2 (Summer 1981), 123–39.

The Shape of Hawthorne's Career. Ithaca: Cornell University Press, 1976.

Bederman, Gail. *Manliness and Civilization: A Cultural History of Gender and Race in the United States, 1880–1917*. University of Chicago Press, 1995.

Bernheimer, Charles. "Fetishism and Decadence: Salome's Severed Heads." *Fetishism as Cultural Discourse*. Apter and Pietz (eds.), pp. 62–83.

Berlant, Lauren. "Fantasies of Utopia in *The Blithedale Romance*." *American Literary History* 1, no. 1 (Spring 1989), 30–61.

Bersani, Leo. "Is The Rectum a Grave?" *AIDS: Cultural Analysis, Cultural Activism*. Ed. Douglas Crimp. Cambridge, MA: MIT Press, 1988, pp. 197–222.

Bertolini, Vincent J. "Fireside Chastity: The Erotics of Sentimental Bachelorhood." *American Literature* 68, no. 4 (December 1996), 706–37.

Bird, Clement. "A Bachelor's Bedroom." *Belgravia* 62, no. 245 (March 1887), 39–47.

Boone, Joseph Allen. *Libidinal Currents: Sexuality and the Shaping of Modernism.* University of Chicago Press, 1998.

　　Tradition Counter Tradition: Love and the Form of Fiction. University of Chicago Press, 1987.

Boone, Joseph Allen and Michael Cadden (eds.). *Engendering Men: The Question of Male Feminist Criticism.* New York: Routledge, 1990.

Boscagli, Maurizia. *Eye on the Flesh: Fashions of Masculinity in the Early Twentieth Century.* Boulder, CO: Westview Press, 1996.

Braude, Ann. *Radical Spirits: Spiritualism and Women's Rights in Nineteenth-Century America.* Boston: Beacon Press, 1989.

Brebach, Raymond. *Joseph Conrad, Ford Madox Ford, and the Making of* Romance. Ann Arbor: University of Michigan Research Press, 1985.

Breitwieser, Mitchell. "*The Great Gatsby*: Grief, Jazz, and the Eye-Witness." *Arizona Quarterly* 47, no. 3 (Autumn 1991), 17–70.

　　"Fitzgerald, Kerouac, and the Puzzle of Inherited Mourning." Unpublished essay.

Brodhead, Richard H. *Cultures of Letters: Scenes of Reading and Writing in Nineteenth-Century America.* University of Chicago Press, 1993.

　　The School of Hawthorne. New York: Oxford University Press, 1986.

Brontë, Emily. *Wuthering Heights.* 1847. London: Penguin, 1986.

Brooks, Peter. *Body Work: Objects of Desire in Modern Narrative.* Cambridge, MA: Harvard University Press, 1993.

　　The Melodramatic Imagination: Balzac, Henry James, Melodrama, and the Mode of Excess. 1976. New Haven: Yale University Press, 1995.

　　Reading for the Plot: Design and Intention in Narrative. New York: Vintage-Random House, 1985.

Brown, Gillian. *Domestic Individualism: Imagining Self in Nineteenth-Century America.* Berkeley: University of California Press, 1990.

Browne, Junius Henri. "Are Women Companionable to Men?" *The Cosmopolitan* 4, no. 6 (February 1888), 452–5.

Bruccoli, Matthew J. *Some Sort of Epic Grandeur: The Life of F. Scott Fitzgerald.* New York: Harcourt, Brace, Jovanovitch, 1981.

Bruccoli, Matthew J. and Jackson R. Bryer (eds.). *F. Scott Fitzgerald in His Own Time: A Miscellany.* Kent State University Press, 1971.

Buell, Lawrence. "The Pleasures of Repetition (Revisiting Whitman)." *The Breadloaf Anthology of Contemporary American Essays.* Ed. Robert Pack and Jay Parini. Hanover, NH: University Press of New England, 1989, pp. 72–82.

Bunce, Oliver Bell. *Bachelor Bluff: His Opinions, Sentiments, and Disputations.* New York: Appleton, 1881.

　　A Bachelor's Story. New York: Rudd and Carleton, 1859.

Burnett, John. *A Social History of Housing, 1815–1985.* 2nd ed. London: Methuen, 1986.

Butler, Judith. *Bodies That Matter: On the Discursive Limits of "Sex".* New York:

Routledge, 1993.

Gender Trouble: Feminism and the Subversion of Identity. New York: Routledge, 1990.

Cameron, Margaret. "The Bachelor and the Baby." *Harper's Monthly Magazine* 114, no. 681 (February 1907), 381–91.

Canute, Judith. *Eros and Anteros; or the Bachelor's Ward.* New York: Rudd and Carleton, 1857.

Carabine, Keith. "'Bitter Honey': Miles Coverdale as Narrator of *the Blithedale Romance.*" *Nathaniel Hawthorne: New Critical Essays.* Ed. A. Robert Lee. London: Vision Press, 1982, pp. 110–30.

"The Figure Behind the Veil: Conrad and Razumov in *Under Western Eyes.*" *Joseph Conrad's* Under Western Eyes: *Five Essays.* Smith (ed.), pp. 1–37.

"'The Secret Sharer': A Note on the Dates of Its Composition." *Conradiana* 19, no. 3 (Autumn 1987), 209–13.

Carnes, Mark C. *Secret Ritual and Manhood in Victorian America.* New Haven: Yale University Press, 1989.

Carnes, Mark C. and Clyde Griffen (eds.). *Meanings for Manhood: Constructions of Masculinity in Victorian America.* University of Chicago Press, 1990.

Castronovo, David. *The American Gentleman: Social Prestige and the Modern Literary Mind.* New York: Ungar-Continuum, 1991.

Chaffee, Frank. *Bachelor Buttons.* New York: George M. Allen Co., 1892.

Chapman, Mary and Glenn Hendler (eds.). *Sentimental Men: Masculinity and the Politics of Affect in American Culture.* Berkeley: University of California Press, forthcoming.

Charvat, William. *The Profession of Authorship in America.* Columbus: Ohio State University Press, 1968.

Chauncey, George. *Gay New York: Gender, Urban Culture, and the Makings of the Gay Male World, 1890–1940.* New York: Basic Books, 1994.

Cheng, Vincent J. "A Chronology of *The Good Soldier.*" *English Language Notes* 24, no. 1 (September 1986), 91–7.

Christ, Carol. "Victorian Masculinity and the Angel in the House." *A Widening Sphere: Changing Roles of Victorian Women.* Ed. Martha Vicinus. Bloomington: Indiana University Press, 1977, pp. 146–62.

Chudacoff, Howard. *The Age of the Bachelor: Creating an American Subculture.* Princeton University Press, forthcoming.

Cixous, Hélène. "The Laugh of the Medusa." Trans. Keith and Paula Cohen. *Signs* 1, no. 4 (Summer 1976), 875–93.

Clark, Suzanne. *Sentimental Modernism: Women Writers and the Revolution of the Word.* Bloomington: Indiana University Press, 1991.

Clawson, Mary Ann. *Constructing Brotherhood: Class, Gender, and Fraternalism.* Princeton University Press, 1989.

Cleere, Eileen. "'The Shape of Uncles': Capitalism, Affection, and the Cultural Construction of the Victorian Family." PhD thesis, Rice University, 1996.

"Clubs." *Temple Bar* 51 (October 1877), 189–96.

Cohen, Ed. "The Double Lives of Man: Narration and Identification in Late

Nineteenth-Century Representation of Ec-centric Masculinities." *Victorian Studies* 36, no. 3 (1993), 353–76.

Cohen, William A. *Sex Scandal: The Private Parts of Victorian Fiction*. Durham: Duke University Press, 1996.

[Collins, Wilkie.] "The Bachelor Bedroom." *All the Year Round* 1, no. 15 (August 6, 1859), 355–60.

Conrad, Joseph. "Autocracy and War." 1905.

Notes on Life and Letters (Garden City, NY: Doubleday, Page and Co., 1924.

Chance. 1913. London: Penguin Books, 1974.

The Collected Letters of Joseph Conrad. Ed. Frederick Karl and Laurence Davies. 5 vols. Cambridge University Press, 1983–1996.

Heart of Darkness. 1899. *The Norton Critical Edition of* Heart of Darkness. Ed. Robert Kimbrough. New York: Norton, 1988.

Letters from Joseph Conrad: 1895–1924. Ed. Edward Garnett. Indianapolis: Bobbs-Merrill, 1928.

Lord Jim. 1900. New York: Penguin Books, 1989.

Preface to *The Nigger of the "Narcissus": A Tale of the Sea*. 1897. New York: Oxford University Press, 1984.

"The Secret Sharer." 1912. *The Portable Conrad*. Ed. Morton Dauwen Zabel. Harmondsworth: Penguin, 1947.

Under Western Eyes. 1911. Harmondsworth: Penguin, 1987.

Author's Note to *Youth*. 1921. *The Norton Critical Edition of* Heart of Darkness. Ed. Robert Kimbrough. New York: Norton, 1988.

Conrad, Joseph and Ford Madox Ford. *The Nature of a Crime*. London: Duckworth, 1924.

Coontz, Stephanie. *The Social Origins of Private Life*. London: Verso, 1988.

Cooper, Michael A. "Discipl(in)ing the Master, Mastering the Discipl(in)e: Erotonomies of Discipleship in James's Tales of Literary Life." *Engendering Men*. Boone and Cadden (eds.), pp. 66–83.

Corse, Sandra. "Henry James on George Eliot and George Sand." *South Atlantic Review* 51, no. 1 (January 1986), 57–68.

Craft, Christopher. *Another Kind of Love: Male Homosexual Desire in English Discourse, 1850–1920*. Berkeley: University of California Press, 1994.

Crews, Frederick. *The Sins of the Fathers: Hawthorne's Psychological Themes*. New York: Oxford University Press, 1966.

Cromley, Elizabeth C. *Alone Together: A History of New York's Early Apartments*. Ithaca: Cornell University Press, 1990.

Damon-Moore, Helen. *Magazines for the Millions: Gender and Commerce in the Ladies' Home Journal and the Saturday Evening Post, 1880–1910*. Albany: State University of New York Press, 1994.

Daughady, Charles. "Cubist Viewing with the Comic Spirit in Ford's *The Good Soldier*." *Kentucky Philological Association Bulletin* (1984), 14–24.

Davidoff, Leonore, and Catherine Hall. *Family Fortunes: Men and Women of the English Middle Class, 1780–1850*. University of Chicago Press, 1987.

Davies, Laurence. "Conrad, *Chance*, and Women Readers." *Conrad and Gender*.

Roberts (ed.), pp. 75–88.

Davis, Richard Harding. *Van Bibber, and Others*. New York: Harper, 1893.

Davis, Roderick. "Crossing the Dark Roadway: Razumov on the *Boulevard des Philosophes*." *Joseph Conrad's* Under Western Eyes: *Five Essays*. Smith (ed.), pp. 155–71.

Degler, Carl N. *At Odds: Women and the Family in America from the Revolution to the Present*. New York: Oxford University Press, 1980.

DeKoven, Marianne. *Rich and Strange: Gender, History, and Modernism*. Princeton University Press, 1991.

De Lauretis, Teresa. *The Practice of Love: Lesbian Sexuality and Perverse Desire*. Bloomington: Indiana University Press, 1994.

Deleuze, Gilles and Félix Guattari. *Anti-Oedipus: Capitalism and Schizophrenia*. 1972. Trans. Robert Hurley, Mark Seem, and Helen R. Lane. Minneapolis: University of Minnesota Press, 1983.

D'Emilio, John, and Estelle B. Freedman. *Intimate Matters: A History of Sexuality in America*. New York: Harper and Row, 1988.

DiBattista, Maria. "Introduction." *High and Low Moderns: Literature and Culture, 1889–1939*. Ed. Maria DiBattista and Lucy McDiarmid. Oxford University Press, 1996, pp. 3–19.

Dickens, Charles. *The Old Curiosity Shop*. 1840–1. London: Penguin, 1985.

Bleak House. 1852–3. London: Penguin, 1971.

Dix, Dorothy. "Bachelors." *Good Housekeeping* 57, no. 5 (November 1913), 644–8.

Douglas, Ann. *The Feminization of American Culture*. 1977. New York: Anchor-Doubleday, 1988.

Dollimore, Jonathan. *Sexual Dissidence: Augustine to Wilde, Freud to Foucault* (Oxford: Clarendon Press, 1991).

Donahue, Peter. "Collecting as Ethos and Technique in *The Portrait of a Lady*." *Studies in American Fiction* 25, no. 1 (1997), 41–56.

Dowling, Linda. "The Decadent and the New Woman in the 1890s." *Nineteenth-Century Fiction* 33 (1979), 434–53.

Doyle, Arthur Conan. "The Greek Interpreter." 1894. *The Complete Sherlock Holmes*. Garden City, NY: Doubleday, 1930.

Dunn, Waldo H. *The Life of Donald G. Mitchell (Ik Marvel)*. New York: Scribner's, 1922.

Edel, Leon. *Henry James: A Life*. New York: Harper and Row, 1985.

Fabian, Ann. *Card Sharps, Dream Books, and Bucket Shops: Gambling in Nineteenth-Century America*. Ithaca: Cornell University Press, 1990.

Faderman, Lillian. *Odd Girls and Twilight Lovers: A History of Lesbian Life in Twentieth-Century America*. New York: Penguin, 1992.

Felman, Shoshana. "Turning the Screw of Interpretation." *Literature and Psychoanalysis: The Question of Reading Otherwise*. Ed. Shoshana Felman. Baltimore: Johns Hopkins University Press, 1982, pp. 94–207.

Field, Eugene. *The Love Affairs of a Bibliomaniac*. New York: Scribner's, 1896.

Fitzgerald, F. Scott. *The Beautiful and the Damned*. New York: Scribner's, 1922.

The Crack-Up: With Other Uncollected Pieces, Note-books, and Unpublished Letters,

Together With Letters to Fitzgerald. Ed. Edmund Wilson. New York: New Directions, 1956.

F. Scott Fitzgerald: A Life in Letters. Ed. Matthew J. Bruccoli. New York: Scribner's, 1994.

The Great Gatsby. 1925. New York: Collier, 1992.

This Side of Paradise. New York: Scribner's, 1920.

Fletcher, Coyne. *The Bachelor's Baby.* New York: Clark and Zugalla, 1891.

Ford, Boris. Introduction to *Under Western Eyes.* Harmondsworth: Penguin, 1985.

Ford, Ford Madox. "The Commercial Value of Literature: A Radio Talk Given by Ford Madox Ford." Transcriber and ed. Max Saunders. *Contemporary Literature* 30, no. 2 (1989), 321–7.

The English Novel: From the Earliest Days to the Death of Joseph Conrad. London: Constable, 1930.

The Good Soldier. 1915. New York: Vintage-Random House, 1983.

Joseph Conrad: A Personal Remembrance. London: Duckworth, 1924.

"On Impressionism." 1914. *Critical Writings of Ford Madox Ford.* Ed. Frank MacShane. Lincoln: University of Nebraska Press, 1964, pp. 33–55.

Thus to Revisit: Some Reminiscences. New York: E. P. Dutton, 1921.

Your Mirror to My Times: The Selected Autobiographies and Impressions of Ford Madox Ford. Ed. Michael Killigrew. New York: Holt, Rinehart, and Winston, 1971.

Foster, Hal. "The Art of Fetishism: Notes on Dutch Still Life." *Fetishism as Cultural Discourse.* Apter and Pietz (eds.), pp. 251–65.

Fox, Richard W. and T. J. Jackson Lears (eds.). *The Culture of Consumption: Critical Essays in American History, 1880–1980.* New York: Pantheon, 1983.

Fraser, Keath. "Another Reading of *The Great Gatsby.*" *F. Scott Fitzgerald's* The Great Gatsby. Ed. Harold Bloom. New York: Chelsea House, 1986, pp. 57–70.

Freedman, Jonathan. *Professions of Taste: Henry James, British Aestheticism, and Commodity Culture.* Stanford University Press, 1990.

Freeman, Sarah. *Muttons and Oysters: The Victorians and their Food.* London: V. Gollancz, 1989.

Freud, Sigmund. "Group Psychology and the Analysis of the Ego." 1921. *The Standard Edition.* Vol. XVIII, pp. 69–143.

"Medusa's Head." 1922; published 1940. *The Standard Edition.* Vol. XVIII, pp. 273–4.

The Standard Edition of the Complete Psychological Works of Sigmund Freud. Ed. James Strachey. 24 vols. London: Hogarth Press, 1953–1974.

Fryer, Judith. *Felicitous Space: The Imaginative Structures of Edith Wharton and Willa Cather.* Chapel Hill: University of North Carolina Press, 1986.

Gallagher, Catherine and Thomas Laqueur (eds.). *The Making of the Modern Body: Sexuality and Society in the Nineteenth Century.* Berkeley: University of California Press, 1987.

Gallagher, Catherine, Joel Fineman, and Neil Hertz. "More About 'Medusa's

Head'." *Representations* 4 (Fall 1983), 55–72.

Gallop, Jane. *The Daughter's Seduction: Feminism and Psychoanalysis*. Ithaca: Cornell University Press, 1982.

Garber, Marjorie. *Vested Interests: Cross-Dressing and Cultural Anxiety*. 1992. New York: Harper, 1993.

Geary, Susan. "The Domestic Novel as a Commercial Commodity: Making a Best Seller in the 1850s." *Papers of the Bibliographical Society of America* 70, no. 3 (July–September 1976), 365–93.

Genette, Gérard. *Narrative Discourse: An Essay in Method*. Trans. Jane E. Lewin. Ithaca: Cornell University Press, 1980.

Narrative Discourse Revisited. Trans. Jane E. Lewin. Ithaca: Cornell University Press, 1988.

Gerard, Jessica. *Country House Life: Family and Servants, 1815–1914*. London: Blackwell, 1994.

Ghent, Emmanuel. "Masochism, Submission, Surrender: Masochism as a Perversion of Surrender." *Contemporary Psychoanalysis* 26, no. 1 (1990), 108–36.

Gilbert, Sandra and Susan Gubar. *The Madwoman in the Attic: The Woman Writer and the Nineteenth-Century Literary Imagination*. New Haven: Yale University Press, 1979.

Gilfoyle, Timothy. *City of Eros: New York City, Prostitution, and the Commercialization of Sex, 1790–1920*. New York: Norton, 1992.

Gillis, John R. *For Better, for Worse: British Marriages, 1600 to the Present*. New York: Oxford University Press, 1985.

Gilman, Sander L. *Disease and Representation: Images of Illness from Madness to AIDS*. Ithaca: Cornell University Press, 1988.

Gilmore, Michael. "The Commodity World of *The Portrait of a Lady*." *New England Quarterly* 3, no. 1 (1986), 51–74.

Ginsburg, Michal Peled. *Economies of Change: Form and Transformation in the Nineteenth-Century Novel*. Stanford University Press, 1996.

Girard, René. *Deceit, Desire, and the Novel: Self and Other in Literary Structure*. Trans. Yvonne Freccero. Baltimore: Johns Hopkins University Press, 1972.

Girouard, Mark. *The Return to Camelot: Chivalry and the English Gentleman*. New Haven: Yale University Press, 1981.

The Victorian Country House. New Haven: Yale University Press, 1979.

Goetz, William R. *Henry James and the Darkest Abyss of Romance*. Baton Rouge: Louisiana State University Press, 1986.

Gorn, Elliott. *The Manly Art: Bare-Knuckle Prize Fighting in America*. Ithaca: Cornell University Press, 1986.

Graham, Edward K. "The Necessary Melancholy of Bachelors." *Putnam's Monthly Magazine* 4, no. 6 (September 1908), 695–7.

Grant, Robert. "The Bachelor's Christmas." *Scribner's Magazine* 14, no. 6 (December 1893), 663–80.

The Bachelor's Christmas, and Other Stories. New York: Scribner's, 1896.

Greg, W. R. "Why Are Women Redundant?" *National Review* 14, no. 28 (April

1862), 434–60.

Habegger, Alfred. *Henry James and the Woman Business.* Cambridge University Press, 1989.

Haley, Bruce. *The Healthy Body and Victorian Culture.* Cambridge, MA: Harvard University Press, 1978.

Hall, Catherine. *White, Male, and Middle Class: Explorations in Feminism and History.* 1988. New York: Routledge, 1992.

Hall, Donald E. (ed.). *Muscular Christianity: Embodying the Victorian Age.* Cambridge University Press, 1994.

Hall, Lesley A. "Forbidden by God, Despised by Men: Masturbation, Medical Warnings, Moral Panic, and Manhood in Great Britain, 1850–1950." *Forbidden History: The State, Society, and the Regulation of Sexuality in Modern Europe.* Ed. John C. Fout. University of Chicago Press, 1992, pp. 293–315. *Hidden Anxieties: Male Sexuality, 1900–1950.* Cambridge: Polity Press, 1991.

Haller, Jr., John S. and Robin M. Haller. *The Physician and Sexuality in Victorian America.* Urbana: University of Illinois Press, 1976.

Halttunen, Karen. *Confidence Men and Painted Women: A Study of Middle-Class Culture in America, 1830–1870.* New Haven: Yale University Press, 1982.

Hamilton, Edith. *Mythology.* 1940. Boston: Little, Brown, and Co., 1969.

Hampson, Robert. "*Chance* and the Secret Life: Conrad, Thackeray, Stevenson." *Conrad and Gender.* Roberts (ed.), pp. 104–22.

Harrison, Brian. *Separate Spheres: The Opposition to Women's Suffrage in Britain.* London: Croom Helm, 1978.

Hawes, Elizabeth. *New York, New York: How the Apartment House Transformed the Life of the City, (1869–1930).* New York: Knopf, 1993.

Hawthorne, Nathaniel. *The Blithedale Romance.* 1852. *The Centenary Edition of the Works of Nathaniel Hawthorne.* Ed. William Charvat. 23 vols. Columbus: Ohio State University Press, 1964, vol. III.

Hayden, Dolores. *The Grand Domestic Revolution: A History of Feminist Designs for American Homes, Neighborhoods, and Cities.* Cambridge, MA: MIT Press, 1981.

Helsinger, Elizabeth K., Robin Lauterbach Sheets, and William Veeder. *The Woman Question: Society and Literature in Britain and America, 1837–1883.* 2 vols. New York: Garland, 1983.

Henry, Anne. *The Building of a Club: Social Institution and Architectural Type, 1870–1905.* Princeton University Press, 1976.

Herndl, Diane Price. *Invalid Women: Figuring Feminine Illness in American Fiction and Culture, 1840–1940.* Chapel Hill: University of North Carolina Press, 1993.

Hertz, Neil. "Medusa's Head: Male Hysteria under Political Pressure." *Representations* 4 (Fall 1983), 27–54.

Hewitt, Andrew. *Political Inversions: Homosexuality, Fascism, and the Modernist Imaginary.* Stanford University Press, 1996.

Hibbard, George. *The Governor, and Other Stories.* New York: Scribner's, 1892.

Higdon, David Leon, and Robert F. Sheard. "Conrad's 'Unkindest Cut': The Canceled Scenes in *Under Western Eyes.*" *Conradiana* 19, no. 3 (Autumn 1987), 167–81.

Hoeckley, Cheri Larsen. "Literary Ladies in Anomalous Positions: Victorian Women Writers and the Married Women's Property Movement." PhD thesis, University of California at Berkeley, 1997.

Holcombe, Lee. *Wives and Property: Reform of the Married Women's Property Law in Nineteenth-Century England.* University of Toronto Press, 1983.

Holland, Laurence. *The Expense of Vision: Essays on the Craft of Henry James.* 1964. Baltimore: Johns Hopkins University Press, 1982.

Homans, Margaret. *Bearing the Word: Language and Female Experience in Nineteenth-Century Women's Writing.* University of Chicago Press, 1986.

Hood, Richard. "'Constant Reduction': Modernism and the Narrative Structure of *The Good Soldier.*" *Journal of Modern Literature* 14, no. 4 (Spring 1988), 445–64.

Hopkins, Pauline. "Talma Gordon." *Colored American Magazine* 1 (October 1900), 271–90.

Horne, Philip. *Henry James and Revision: The New York Edition.* Oxford: Clarendon Press, 1990.

Horowitz, Daniel. *The Morality of Spending: Attitudes Toward the Consumer Society in America, 1875–1940.* Baltimore: Johns Hopkins University Press, 1985.

Howells, William Dean. "The Man of Letters as a Man of Business." *Literature and Life.* New York: Harper and Bros., 1902, pp. 1–35.

Hull, Raymona E. "'Scribbling Females' and Serious Males." *Nathaniel Hawthorne Journal* 5 (1975), 35–58.

Hume, Beverly. "Restructuring the Case Against Hawthorne's Coverdale." *Nineteenth-Century Fiction* 40 (1986), 387–99.

Humphreys, Mary Gay. "Women Bachelors in New York." *Scribner's Magazine* 20, no. 5 (November 1896), 626–36.

Huyssen, Andreas. *After the Great Divide: Modernism, Mass Culture, Postmodernism.* Bloomington: Indiana University Press, 1986.

Hynes, Samuel. "The Epistemology of *The Good Soldier.*" *Sewanee Review* 69, no. 2 (Spring 1961), 225–35.

Irving, Washington. *The Sketchbook of Geoffrey Crayon, Gentleman.* New York: C. S. Van Winkle, 1820–1822.

"Is Marriage a Failure?" *The Cosmopolitan* 6, no. 1 (November 1888), 93.

Jacobs, Naomi. "Gender and Layered Narrative in *Wuthering Heights* and *The Tenant of Wildfell Hall.*" *Journal of Narrative Technique* 16, no. 3 (Fall 1986), 204–19.

Jacobson, Paul H. *American Marriage and Divorce.* New York: Rinehart, 1959.

Jahn, Manfred. "Windows of Focalization: Deconstructing and Reconstructing a Narratological Concept." *Style* 30, no. 2 (1996), 241–68.

James, Henry. *The Ambassadors.* 1903. New York: Penguin, 1986.

The Complete Notebooks of Henry James. Ed. Leon Edel and Lyall H. Powers. New York: Oxford University Press, 1987.

The Complete Tales of Henry James. Ed. Leon Edel. 12 vols. Philadelphia: Lippincott, 1962–1964.

Henry James: Literary Criticism. Vol. I: *Essays on Literature, American Writers, and*

English Writers. New York: Library of America, 1984.

Henry James: Literary Criticism. Vol. II: *French Writers, Other European Writers, and the Prefaces to the New York Edition.* New York: Library of America, 1984.

Henry James: Letters. Ed. Leon Edel. 4 vols. Cambridge, MA: Belknap-Harvard University Press, 1984.

Letters of Henry James. Ed. Percy Lubbock. 2 vols. New York: Scribner's, 1920.

The Portrait of a Lady. 1880. The New York Edition, 1908. 2 vols. Fairfield, NJ: Kelley, 1976.

The Sacred Fount. New York: Scribner's, 1901.

The Sense of the Past. New York: Scribner's, 1917.

Watch and Ward. Boston: Houghton, Osgood, and Co., 1878.

Jameson, Fredric. *The Political Unconscious: Narrative as a Socially Symbolic Act.* Ithaca: Cornell University Press, 1981.

Jolly, Roslyn. *Henry James: History, Narrative, Fiction.* Oxford: Clarendon Press, 1993.

Judd, Alan. *Ford Madox Ford.* London: Collins, 1990.

Kahane, Claire. *Passions of the Voice: Hysteria, Narrative, and the Figure of the Speaking Woman, 1850–1915.* Baltimore: Johns Hopkins University Press, 1995.

Karl, Frederick R. *Joseph Conrad: The Three Lives.* New York: Farrar, Straus and Giroux, 1979.

A Reader's Guide to Joseph Conrad. New York: Doubleday, 1960.

Kelley, Mary. *Private Woman, Public Stage: Literary Domesticity in Nineteenth-Century America.* New York: Oxford University Press, 1984.

Kennedy, Sarah Beaumont. "A Bachelor's Ward." *Everybody's Magazine* 6, no. 3 (March 1902), 235–43.

Kerber, Linda. "Separate Spheres, Female Worlds, Woman's Place: The Rhetoric of Women's History." *Journal of American History* 75, no. 1 (June 1988), 9–39.

Kerr, Frances. "Feeling 'Half Feminine': Modernism and the Politics of Emotion in *The Great Gatsby.*" *American Literature* 68, no. 2 (June 1996), 405–32.

Kime, Wayne R. *Donald G. Mitchell.* Boston: Twayne Publishers, 1985.

Koestenbaum, Wayne. *Double Talk: The Erotics of Male Literary Collaboration.* New York: Routledge, 1989.

Kopelson, Kevin. *Love's Litany: The Writing of Modern Homoerotics.* Stanford University Press, 1994.

Laipson, Peter. "I Have No Genius for Marriage: Bachelorhood in Urban America, 1870–1930." PhD thesis, University of Michigan, in progress.

Langland, Elizabeth. "Nobody's Angels: Domestic Ideology and Middle-Class Women in the Victorian Novel." *PMLA* 107, no. 2 (March 1992), 290–305.

Lanser, Susan S. "Sexing the Narrative: Propriety, Desire, and the Engendering of Narratology." *Narrative* 3, no. 1 (January 1995), 85–94.

Laqueur, Thomas. *Making Sex: Body and Gender from the Greeks to Freud.* Cambridge, MA: Harvard University Press, 1990.

Larson, Magali S. *The Rise of Professionalism: A Sociological Analysis.* Berkeley: University of California Press, 1977.

Lejeune, Anthony. *The Gentlemen's Clubs of London*. London: Bracken, 1984.

Levenson, Michael. "Character in *The Good Soldier.*" *Twentieth Century Literature* 30, no. 4 (Winter 1984), 373–87.

Modernism and the Fate of Individuality: Character and Novelistic Form from Conrad to Woolf. Cambridge University Press, 1991.

Leverenz, David. *Manhood and The American Renaissance: The Subversive Imagination in the Age of Emerson and Melville*. Ithaca: Cornell University Press, 1989.

Leveridge, Lillian. "The Bachelor and the Baby." *The Canadian Magazine* 34, no. 4 (February 1910), 347–52.

Levine, Lawrence. *Highbrow/Lowbrow: The Emergence of Cultural Hierarchy in America*. Cambridge, MA: Harvard University Press, 1988.

Lewis, Wyndham (ed.). *Blast: The Review of the Great English Vortex*. London: J. Lane, 1914.

Lindberg-Seyersted, Brita (ed.). *Pound/Ford, The Story of a Literary Friendship: The Correspondence between Ezra Pound and Ford Madox Ford and Their Writings about Each Other*. New York: New Directions, 1982.

Logan, Peter M. *Nerves and Narratives: A Cultural History of Hysteria in Nineteenth-Century British Prose*. Berkeley: University of California Press, 1997.

Lombroso, Cesare. *The Man of Genius*. 1888 London: W. Scott, 1891.

Lucey, Michael. "Balzac's Queer Cousins and Their Friends." *Novel Gazing*. Sedgwick (ed.), pp. 167–98.

Luftig, Victor. *Seeing Together: Friendship Between the Sexes in English Writing from Mill to Woolf*. Stanford University Press, 1993.

Luria, Sarah. "The Architecture of Manners: Henry James, Edith Wharton, and The Mount." *American Quarterly* 49, no. 2 (June 1997), 298–327.

Lynn, David H. *The Hero's Tale: Narrators in the Early Modern Novel*. New York: St. Martin's Press, 1989.

Mackenzie, Henry. *The Man of Feeling*. London: T. Cadell, 1771.

Mangan, J. A. and James Walvin (eds.). *Manliness and Morality: Middle-Class Masculinity in Britain and America, 1800–1940*. New York: St. Martin's Press, 1987.

Marcus, Sharon. *Apartment Stories: City and Home in Nineteenth-Century Paris and London*. Berkeley: University of California Press, 1999.

"Marriage of a Medical Man Not Advisable." *British Medical Journal* (November 23, 1861), 570.

"Marriage Not à-la-Mode." *Temple Bar* 9 (November 1863), 506–21.

Marsh, Margaret. *Suburban Lives*. New Brunswick, NJ: Rutgers University Press, 1990.

"Suburban Men and Masculine Domesticity, 1870–1915." *American Quarterly* 40, no. 2 (June 1988), 165–86.

Martin, Edward Sandford. *Windfalls of Observation, Gathered for the Edification of the Young and the Solace of Others*. New York: Scribner's, 1893.

Martin, Robert K. *The Homosexual Tradition in American Poetry*. Austin: University of Texas Press, 1979.

Masson, Tom. "The Bachelor's Christmas Baby." *Ladies' Home Journal* 22, no. 1

(December 1904), 8, 54.

Matterson, Stephen. *The Great Gatsby*. London: Macmillan, 1990.

Matthews, John T. "Framing in *Wuthering Heights*." *Texas Studies in Literature and Language* 27, no. 1 (Spring 1985), 25–61.

May, Elaine Tyler. *Great Expectations: Marriage and Divorce in Post-Victorian America.* University of Chicago Press, 1980.

McCarthy, Terence. "The Incompetent Narrator of *Wuthering Heights*." *Modern Language Quarterly* 42, no. 1 (March 1981), 48–64.

McClintock, Anne. *Imperial Leather: Race, Gender, and Sexuality in the Colonial Contest*. New York: Routledge, 1995.

McElroy, John Harmon and Edward L. McDonald. "The Coverdale Romance." *Studies in the Novel* 14, no. 1 (Spring 1982), 1–16.

Melas, Natalie. "Brides of Opportunity: Figurations of Women and Colonial Territory in *Lord Jim*." *Qui Parle* 3, no. 2 (Fall 1989), 54–75.

Mellor, Anne K. *Romanticism and Gender*. New York: Routledge, 1993.

Melville, Herman. "The Paradise of Bachelors" and "The Tartarus of Maids." *The Complete Stories of Herman Melville*. Ed. Jay Leyda. New York: Random House, 1949.

Menand, Louis. *Discovering Modernism: T.S. Eliot and His Context*. Oxford University Press, 1987.

Meredith, Katherine Mary Cheever. *Green Gates: An Analysis of Foolishness*. New York: Appleton, 1896.

Merish, Lori. "Sentimental Consumption: Harriet Beecher Stowe and the Aesthetics of Middle-Class Ownership." *American Literary History* 8, no. 1 (Spring 1996), 1–34.

Meyer, Bernard. *Joseph Conrad: A Psychoanalytic Biography*. Princeton University Press, 1967.

Meyers, Jeffrey. *Joseph Conrad, A Biography*. New York: Scribner's, 1991.

Michaels, Walter Benn. *The Gold Standard and the Logic of Naturalism: American Literature at the Turn of the Century*. Berkeley: University of California Press, 1987.

Miller, D. A. *The Novel and the Police*. Berkeley: University of California Press, 1987.

Miller, J. Hillis. *The Disappearance of God; Five Nineteenth-Century Writers*. Cambridge, MA: Belknap-Harvard University Press, 1963.

"The Figure in the Carpet." *Poetics Today* 1, no. 3 (Spring 1980), 107–19.

Mitchell, Donald Grant. "A Bachelor's Reverie." *Southern Literary Messenger* 15, nos. 9 and 10 (September 1849), 601–9; *Harper's New Monthly Magazine* 1, no. 5 (October 1850), 620–7.

Dream Life: A Fable of the Seasons. New York: Scribner's, 1851.

The Lorgnette; or, Studies of the Town. New York: H. Kernot, 1850.

Reveries of a Bachelor, or A Book of the Heart (by Ik Marvel). 1850. New York: Scribner's, 1851.

Mitchell, Juliet. *Psychoanalysis and Feminism; Freud, Reich, Laing and Women*. New York: Vintage-Random House, 1975.

Mizener, Arthur. *The Saddest Story: A Biography of Ford Madox Ford*. New York: World, 1971.

Monahan, Thomas. *The Pattern of Age at Marriage in the United States*. Philadelphia: Stephenson Bros., 1951.

Mongia, Padmini. "'Ghosts of the Gothic': Spectral Women and Colonized Spaces in *Lord Jim*." *Conrad and Gender*. Roberts (ed.), pp. 1–15.

Moser, Thomas. "Ford Madox Hueffer and *Under Western Eyes*." *Conradiana* 15, no. 3 (Autumn 1983), 163–80.

Joseph Conrad: Achievement and Decline. Cambridge, MA: Harvard University Press, 1957.

The Life in the Fiction of Ford Madox Ford. Princeton University Press, 1980.

Mulvey, Laura. "Afterthoughts on 'Visual Pleasure and Narrative Cinema' inspired by *Duel in the Sun*." 1981. *Feminism and Film Theory*. Penley (ed.), pp. 69–79.

"Visual Pleasure and Narrative Cinema." 1975. *Feminism and Film Theory*. Penley (ed.), pp. 57–68.

Mumford, Kevin J. "'Lost Manhood' Found: Male Sexual Impotence and Victorian Culture in the United States." *Journal of the History of Sexuality* 3, no.1 (July 1992), 33–57.

"My Wife and My Theory about Wives." *Harper's New Monthly Magazine* 11, no. 66 (November 1855), 779–82.

Nadal, E. S. "London and American Clubs." *Scribner's Magazine* 9, no. 3 (March 1891), 289–305.

Najder, Zdzislaw. *Joseph Conrad: A Chronicle*. New Brunswick, NJ: Rutgers University Press, 1983.

Napier, Elizabeth. "The Problem of Boundaries in *Wuthering Heights*." *Philological Quarterly* 63, no. 1 (Winter 1984), 95–107.

Naremore, James, and Patrick Brantlinger (eds.). *Modernity and Mass Culture*. Bloomington: Indiana University Press, 1991.

Neale, Steve. "Masculinity as Spectacle." 1983. *Screening the Male: Exploring Masculinities in Hollywood Cinema*. Ed. Steven Cohan and Ina Rae Hark. New York: Routledge, 1993, pp. 9–20.

Nelson, Claudia. *Invisible Men: Fatherhood in Victorian Periodicals, 1850–1910*. Athens: University of Georgia Press, 1995.

"Sex and the Single Boy: Ideals of Manliness and Sexuality in Victorian Literature for Boys." *Victorian Studies* 32, no. 4 (1989), 525–50.

Nelson, Henry L. "Some New York Clubs." *Harper's Weekly* 34, no. 1 (March 8, 1890), 193–96, 211.

Nevill, Ralph. *London Clubs, Their History and Treasures*. London: Chatto and Windus, 1911.

Newfield, Christopher. "Democracy and Male Homoeroticism." *The Yale Journal of Criticism* 6, no. 2 (Fall 1993), 29–62.

The Emerson Effect: Individualism and Submission in America. University of Chicago Press, 1996.

Newman, Beth. "Narratives of Seduction and the Seductions of Narrative: The

Frame Structure of *Frankenstein.*" *ELH* 53, no. 1 (Spring 1986), 141–63.

"'The Situation of the Looker-On': Gender, Narration, and Gaze in *Wuthering Heights.*" *PMLA* 105, no. 5 (October 1990), 1029–41.

Nordau, Max. *Degeneration.* 1892. New York: Appleton, 1895.

Norton, Rictor. *Mother Clap's Molly House: The Gay Subculture in England, 1700–1830.* London: GMP, 1992.

Nunokawa, Jeff. "'All the Sad Young Men': AIDS and the Work of Mourning," *The Yale Journal of Criticism* 4, no. 2 (Spring 1991), 1–12.

"The Importance of Being Bored: The Dividends of Ennui in *The Picture of Dorian Gray.*" *Novel Gazing.* Sedgwick (ed.), pp. 151–66.

Ohmann, Richard. *Selling Culture: Magazines, Markets, and Class at the Turn of the Century.* London: Verso, 1996.

The Old Bachelor, After Southey's "Cataract of Lodore," Described and Dedicated to Bachelors and Bazaars. Tamworth: J. Thompson, 1839.

"On the Excessive Influence of Women." *Temple Bar* 49 (February 1877), 213–21.

Oppenheim, Janet. *The Other World: Spiritualism and Psychical Research in England, 1850–1914.* Cambridge University Press, 1985.

Oppenlander, Ella Ann. *Dickens' All the Year Round: Descriptive Index and Contributor List.* Troy, NY: Whitson Publishing Co., 1984.

Otter, Samuel. *Melville's Anatomies: Bodies, Discourse, and Ideology in Antebellum America.* Berkeley: University of California Press, 1999.

"Our Young Authors." *Putnam's Monthly Magazine* 1, no. 1 (January 1853), 74–8.

Owen, Alex. *The Darkened Room: Women, Power, and Spiritualism in Late Nineteenth-Century England, 1850–1914.* London: Virago, 1989.

Ownby, Ted. *Subduing Satan: Religion, Recreation, and Manhood in the Rural South, 1865–1920.* Chapel Hill: University of North Carolina Press, 1990.

Paccaud, Josiane. "The Name-of-the-Father in Conrad's *Under Western Eyes.*" *Conradiana* 18, no. 3 (Autumn 1986), 204–18.

Parker, Patricia. *Literary Fat Ladies: Rhetoric, Gender, Property.* London: Methuen, 1987.

Partridge, Eric. *A Dictionary of Slang and Unconventional English.* Ed. Paul Beale. 8th edition. New York: Macmillan, 1984.

Pater, Walter. *The Renaissance.* Ed. Donald L. Hill. Berkeley: University of California Press, 1980.

Penley, Constance (ed.). *Feminism and Film Theory.* New York: Routledge, 1988.

Person, Jr., Leland S. *Aesthetic Headaches: Women and a Masculinist Poetics in Poe, Melville and Hawthorne.* Athens: University of Georgia Press, 1988.

"Henry James, George Sand, and the Suspense of Masculinity." *PMLA* 106, no. 3 (May 1991), 515–28.

Peskin, Allan, and Arnold G. Tew. "The Disappearance of Ik Marvel." *American Studies* 33, no. 2 (Fall 1992), 5–20.

Pfister, Joel. *The Production of Personal Life: Class, Gender, and the Psychological in Hawthorne's Fiction.* Stanford University Press, 1991.

Pivar, David J. *Purity Crusade: Sexual Morality and Social Control, 1868–1900.*

Westport, CT: Greenwood Press, 1973.
"A Plea for the Men." *The Spectator.* 67, no. 3, 309 (November 28, 1891), 756–7.Pollard, Mrs. Alfred [Alice]. "Why Men Don't Marry: An Eighteenth-Century Answer." *Longman's Magazine* 23, no. 134 (November 1893), 156–62.
Pollard, Percival. "The Bachelor in Fiction." *The Bookman* 12, no. 2 (October 1900), 146–8.
Poovey, Mary. *Uneven Developments: The Ideological Work of Gender in Mid-Victorian England.* University of Chicago Press, 1988.
Porter, Carolyn. *Seeing and Being: The Plight of the Participant Observer in Emerson, James, Adams, and Faulkner.* Middletown, CT: Wesleyan University Press, 1981.
Preston, Elizabeth. "Implying Authors in *The Great Gatsby.*" *Narrative* 5, no. 2 (May 1997), 143–64.
Prince, Gerald. "On Narratology: Criteria, Corpus, Context." *Narrative* 3, no. 1 (January 1995), 73–84.
Rahv, Philip. "The Dark Lady of Salem." *Partisan Review* 8, no. 5 (September–October 1941), 362–81.
Raval, Suresh. *The Art of Failure: Conrad's Fiction.* Boston: Allen and Unwin, 1986.
Read, Donald. *The Age of Urban Democracy: England 1868–1914.* Revised edition. London: Longman, 1994.
Reade, Brian (ed.). *Sexual Heretics: Male Homosexuality in English Literature from 1850 to 1900.* London: Routledge, 1970.
Richardson, W. C. *A History of the Inns of Court: With Special Reference to the Period of the Renaissance.* Baton Rouge: Claitor's Publishing Division, 1975.
Rimmon, Shlomith. *The Concept of Ambiguity – the Example of James.* University of Chicago Press, 1977.
Robbins, Bruce. *Secular Vocations: Intellectuals, Professionalism, Culture.* London: Verso, 1993.
Roberts, Andrew Michael. "Secret Agents and Secret Objects: Action, Passivity, and Gender in *Chance.*" *Conrad and Gender.* Roberts (ed.), pp. 89–104.
Roberts, Andrew Michael (ed.). *Conrad and Gender.* Amsterdam: Rodolpi, 1993.
Robertson, James. "Some Pleas for a Special Tax on the Bachelor." *The Westminster Review* 170, no. 5 (November 1908), 531–5.
Robson, John M. *Marriage or Celibacy?: The Daily Telegraph on a Victorian Dilemma.* University of Toronto Press, 1995.
Rodowick, David N. "The Difficulty of Difference." *Wide Angle: A Film Quarterly of Theory, Criticism, and Practice* 5, no. 1 (1982), 4–15.
Rosenberg, Charles. "Sexuality, Class, and Role in Nineteenth-Century America." *American Quarterly* 35, no. 2 (May 1973), 131–53.
Ross, Mrs. *The Bachelor and the Married Man; or The Equilibrium and the "Balance of Comfort."* London: Longman, 1817.
Rotundo, Anthony. *American Manhood: Transformations in Masculinity from the Revolution to the Modern Age.* New York: Basic Books, 1993.
Rubin, Gayle. "The Traffic in Women: Notes Toward a Political Economy of

Sex." *Toward an Anthropology of Women.* Ed. Rayna Reiter. New York: Monthly Review Press, 1975, pp. 157–210.

Ryan, Mary. *Cradle of the Middle Class: The Family in Oneida County, New York, 1790–1865.* New York: Cambridge University Press, 1981.

The Empire of the Mother: American Writing about Domesticity, 1830–1860. New York: Haworth Press in association with the Institute for Research in History, 1982.

Samuels, Shirley (ed.). *The Culture of Sentiment: Race, Gender, and Sentimentality in Nineteenth-Century America.* New York: Oxford University Press, 1992.

Savage, Marmion W. *The Bachelor of the Albany.* New York: Harper, 1848.

Saunders, Max. *Ford Madox Ford: A Dual Life.* 2 vols. Oxford University Press, 1996.

"Scenes in Bachelor Life." *Harper's New Monthly Magazine* 8, no. 43 (December 1853), 141–2.

Schneirov, Matthew. *The Dream of a New Social Order: Popular Magazines in America, 1893–1914.* New York: Columbia University Press, 1994.

Schwarz, Daniel. *Conrad, "Almayer's Folly" to Under Western Eyes.* Ithaca: Cornell University Press, 1980.

Scott, Bonnie Kime. "Intimacies Engendered in Conrad's 'The Secret Sharer'." *Case Studies in Contemporary Criticism: Joseph Conrad's "The Secret Sharer".* Ed. Daniel R. Schwarz. New York: Bedford Books, 1997, pp. 197–210.

Secor, Robert. "The Function of the Narrator in *Under Western Eyes.*" *Conradiana* 3, no. 1 (1970–1), 27–37.

Sedgwick, Eve Kosofsky. *Between Men: English Literature and Male Homosocial Desire.* New York: Columbia University Press, 1985.

Epistemology of the Closet. Berkeley: University of California Press, 1990.

Tendencies. Durham: Duke University Press, 1993.

Sedgwick, Eve Kosofsky (ed.). *Novel Gazing: Queer Readings in Fiction.* Durham: Duke University Press, 1997.

Segal, Lynne. *Slow Motion: Changing Masculinities, Changing Men.* New Brunswick, NJ: Rutgers University Press, 1990.

Segal, Ora. *The Lucid Reflector: The Observer in Henry James's Fiction.* New Haven: Yale University Press, 1969.

Sennett, Richard. *Families Against the City: Middle Class Homes of Industrial Chicago, 1872–1890.* Cambridge, MA: Harvard University Press, 1970.

Shanley, Mary Lyndon. *Feminism, Marriage, and the Law in Victorian England.* Princeton University Press, 1989.

Shelton, Frederick W. "On Old Bachelors." *Southern Literary Messenger* 19, no. 4 (April 1853), 223–8.

Shires, Linda M. "Of Maenads, Mothers, and Feminized Males: Victorian Readings of the French Revolution." *Rewriting the Victorians: Theory, History, and the Politics of Gender.* Ed. Linda M. Shires. New York: Routledge, 1992, pp. 147–65.

Showalter, Elaine. *The Female Malady: Women, Madness, and English Culture,*

1830–1980. New York: Pantheon, 1985.

Sexual Anarchy: Gender and Culture at the Fin de Siècle. London: Bloomsbury, 1991.

Siegel, Carol. *Male Masochism: Modern Revisions of the Story of Love*. Bloomington: Indiana University Press, 1995.

Silverman, Kaja. *Male Subjectivity at the Margins*. New York: Routledge, 1992.

Simms, William Gilmore. *Castle Dismal: Or the Bachelor's Christmas; a Domestic Legend*. New York: Burgess, Stringer, 1844.

"Single Life Among Us." *Harper's New Monthly Magazine* 18, no. 106 (March 1859), 499–504.

Smith, Adam. *The Theory of Moral Sentiments*. Ed. D. D. Raphael and A. L. Macfie. Oxford: Clarendon Press, 1976.

Smith, David R. "The Hidden Narrative: The *K* in Conrad." *Joseph Conrad's Under Western Eyes: Five Essays*. Smith (ed.), pp. 39–81.

Smith, David R. (ed.). *Joseph Conrad's* Under Western Eyes: *Beginnings, Revisions, Final Forms: Five Essays*. Hamden, CT: Archon Books, 1991.

Smith, Francis Hopkinson. *Colonel Carter of Cartersville*. Boston: Houghton, Mifflin, 1891.

A Day at Laguerre's and Other Days: Being Nine Sketches. Boston: Houghton, Mifflin, 1892.

Smith-Rosenberg, Carroll. *Disorderly Conduct: Visions of Gender in Victorian America*. New York: Oxford University Press, 1986.

Snyder, Katherine V. "A Paradise of Bachelors: Remodeling Domesticity and Masculinity in the Turn-of-the-Century New York Bachelor Apartment." *Prospects: A Journal of American Cultural Studies* 23 (1998), 247–84.

Stevenson, John Allen. "'Heathcliff is *Me!*': *Wuthering Heights* and the Question of Likeness." *Nineteenth-Century Literature* 43 (1988), 60–81.

Stevenson, Robert Louis. *The Strange Case of Dr. Jekyll and Mr. Hyde*. 1886. London: Penguin, 1979.

Stowe, Harriet Beecher. "The True Story of Lady Byron's Life." ("Tribute of a Loving Friend to the Memory of a Noble Woman"). *The Atlantic Monthly* 23, no. 136 (February 1869), 242–50.

Uncle Tom's Cabin. 1851–2. New York: Bantam, 1981.

Strychacz, Thomas F. "Coverdale and Women: Feverish Fantasies in *The Blithedale Romance*." *American Transcendental Quarterly* 62 (December 1986), 29–46.

Modernism, Mass Culture, and Professionalism. Cambridge University Press, 1993.

Sussman, Herbert L. *Victorian Masculinities: Manhood and Masculine Poetics in Early Victorian Literature and Art*. Cambridge University Press, 1995.

Sutcliffe, Anthony. *Towards the Planned City: Germany, Britain, the United States, and France, 1780–1914*. New York: St. Martin's Press, 1981.

Sweeney, Gerard M. "The Deadly Figure in James's Carpet." *Modern Language Studies* 13, no. 4 (Fall 1983), 79–85.

Sweeting, Adam W. "'A Very Pleasant Patriarchal Life': Professional Authors and Amateur Architects in the Hudson Valley, 1835–1870." *Journal of American Studies*, 29, no. 1 (Spring 1995), 33–53.

Szittya, Penn R. "Metafiction: The Double Narration in *Under Western Eyes.*" *ELH* 48, no. 4 (Winter 1981), 817–40.

Tanner, Tony. "Nightmare and Complacency: Razumov and the Western Eye." *Critical Quarterly* 4, no. 3 (Autumn 1962), 197–214.

Thompson, F. M. L. *The Rise of Respectable Society: A Social History of Victorian Britain, 1830–1900.* Cambridge, MA: Harvard University Press, 1988.

Timbs, John. *Clubs and Club Life in London.* 1866. London: Chatto and Windus, 1908.

Tintner, Adeline R. "Henry James and Byron: A Victorian Romantic Relationship." *The Byron Journal* 9 (1981), 52–63.

Tomc, Sandra. "An Idle Industry: Nathaniel Parker Willis and the Workings of Literary Leisure." *American Quarterly* 49, no. 4 (December 1997), 780–805.

Tooley, Sarah. "Famous Bachelors." *The Woman at Home* 6 (February 1898), 470–81.

Torgovnick, Marianna. *Closure in the Novel.* Princeton University Press, 1981.
    Gone Primitive: Savage Intellects, Modern Lives. University of Chicago Press, 1990.

Trachtenberg, Alan. *The Incorporation of America: Culture and Society in the Gilded Age.* New York: Hill and Wang, 1982.

Tristan, Flora. *Promenades Dans Londres.* 1840. Excerpted in *Flora Tristan: Utopian Feminist.* Ed. Doris Beik and Paul Beik. Bloomington: Indiana University Press, 1993.

T. S. M. "Bachelors and Spinsters." *Leisure Hour* 24 (1875), 661–3.

Van Ghent, Dorothy. *The English Novel: Form and Function.* New York: Rinehart, 1953.

Vance, Norman. *Sinews of The Spirit: The Ideal of Christian Manliness in Victorian Literature and Religious Thought.* New York: Cambridge University Press, 1985.

Vernon, James (ed.). *Re-reading the Constitution: New Narratives in the Political History of England's Long Nineteenth Century.* New York: Cambridge University Press, 1996.

Vicinus, Martha. *Independent Women; Work and Community for Single Women, 1850–1920.* University of Chicago Press, 1985.

Vrettos, Athena. *Somatic Fictions: Imagining Illness in Victorian Culture.* Stanford University Press, 1995.

Walkowitz, Judith. *City of Dreadful Delight: Narratives of Sexual Danger in Late-Victorian London.* University of Chicago Press, 1992.

Wallace, James D. "Hawthorne and The Scribbling Women Reconsidered." *American Literature* 62, no. 2 (June 1990), 201–22.

Warhol, Robyn. *Gendered Interventions: Narrative Discourse in the Victorian Novel.* New Brunswick, NJ: Rutgers University Press, 1989.

Warner, Marina. *Monuments and Maidens: The Allegory of the Female Form.* New York: Atheneum, 1985.

Warner, Michael. "Homo-Narcissism: Or, Heterosexuality." *Engendering Men.* Boone and Cadden (eds.), pp. 190–206.

Watt, Ian. "Marlow, Henry James, and *Heart of Darkness.*" *Nineteenth-Century*

Fiction 33, no. 2 (September 1978), 159–74.

The Rise of the Novel. Berkeley: University of California Press, 1957.

Watts, Cedric. *Joseph Conrad: A Literary Life.* London: MacMillan, 1989.

"Marketing Modernism: How Conrad Prospered." *Modernist Writers and the Marketplace.* Ed. Ian Willison, Warwick Gould, and Warren Chernaik. London: Macmillan, 1996, pp. 81–8.

Weeks, Jeffrey. "Inverts, Perverts, and Mary-Annes: Male Prostitution and the Regulation of Homosexuality in England in the Nineteenth and Early Twentieth Centuries." *Hidden from History: Reclaiming the Gay and Lesbian Past.* Ed. Martin Bauml Duberman, Martha Vicinus, and George Chauncey, Jr. New York: New American Library, 1989, pp. 195–211.

Sex, Politics, and Society: The Regulation of Sexuality Since 1800. London: Longman, 1981.

Welch, Deshler. *The Bachelor and the Chafing Dish.* New York: F. Tennyson Neely, 1896.

Wharton, Edith. *Ethan Frome.* 1911. Harmondsworth: Penguin, 1987.

The House of Mirth. New York: Scribner's, 1905.

Wharton, Edith and Ogden Codman, Jr. *The Decoration of Houses.* New York: Scribner's, 1897.

White, Andrea. *Joseph Conrad and the Adventure Tradition: Constructing and Deconstructing the Imperial Subject.* Cambridge University Press, 1993.

White, Craig Howard. "The House of Interest: A Keyword in *The Portrait of a Lady.*" *Modern Language Quarterly* 52, no. 2 (1991), 191–207.

Whitford, Kathryn. "*The Blithedale Romance*: Hawthorne's *Reveries of a Bachelor.*" *Thoth* 15, no. 1 (Winter 1974), 19–28.

Whitman, Walt. *Democratic Vistas.* New York: J. S. Redfield, 1871.

Leaves of Grass. Brooklyn, NY: Rome Brothers, 1855.

"Why Bachelors Should Not be Taxed." *The North American Review* 184, no. 607 (February 1, 1907), 332–4.

"Why My Uncle Was a Bachelor." *Harper's New Monthly Magazine* 8, no. 47 (April 1854), 664–70.

"Why We Men Do Not Marry, By One of Us." *Temple Bar* 84 (October 1888), 218–23.

Wiegman, Robyn. "Melville's Geography of Gender." *American Literary History* 1, no. 4 (1989), 735–53.

"The Wife for Me." *Once A Week* (May 26, 1860), 507–9.

Wilde, Oscar. *The Importance of Being Earnest.* 1895. *The Picture of Dorian Gray and Other Writings by Oscar Wilde.* Ed. Richard Ellman. New York: Bantam, 1982, pp. 397–466.

The Picture of Dorian Gray. 1891. *The Picture of Dorian Gray and Other Writings by Oscar Wilde.* Ed. Richard Ellman. New York: Bantam, 1982, pp. 3–193.

Williams, Raymond. *The English Novel from Dickens to Lawrence.* New York: Oxford University Press, 1970.

What I Came To Say. London: Hutchinson, 1989.

Writing in Society. London: Verso, 1985.

Wilner, Eleanor. "The Medusa Connection." *Triquarterly* 88 (Fall 1993), 104–33.

Wilson, Christopher. "The Rhetoric of Consumption: Mass-Market Magazines and the Demise of the Gentle Reader, 1880–1920." *The Culture of Consumption.* Fox and Lears (eds.), pp. 39–64.

Winnet, Susan. "Women, Men, Narrative, and Principles of Pleasure." *PMLA* 105, no. 3 (May 1990), 505–18.

Wolff, Cynthia Griffin. "Masculinity in *Uncle Tom's Cabin.*" *American Quarterly* 47, no. 4 (December 1995), 595–618.

Wood, John Seymour. "The Story of an Old Beau." *Scribner's Magazine* 9, no. 2 (February 1891), 197–212.

Woolf, Virginia. "Joseph Conrad." 1924. London: Hogarth Press, 1925.

Zabel, Morton Dauwen. Introduction to *Under Western Eyes.* Garden City, NY: Anchor-Doubleday, 1963.

Zangwill, Israel. *The Bachelors' Club.* London: Henry, 1891.

Index

Adams, James Eli, 232–3n.6, 241–2n.24, 242n.27
Adams, Mrs. Henry, 114, 241n.17
aestheticism, 16, 42, 58, 88, 90, 102, 105, 118, 134
  fetishism and, 166–8
Anesko, Michael, 244n.47
Ardis, Ann, 215n.6, 240n.9
"Aspern Papers, The" (James), 15, 106, 108, 130–5, 137, 243n.35
  competing masculine and feminine plots in, 131
  fetishistic quest of narrator in, 131
  Orpheus myth in, 131–3
Auerbach, Jonathan, 239–40n.4
authorship
  bachelor as expressive of ambivalences inherent in, 6
  fiction of autonomy and, 102
  "masters" and, 106, 119–129 passim
  maternity and, 137, 237n.27
  modernist male, and same gender representation, 13
  novelistic, engendering gap between "high" and "low" cultural spheres, 3
  privileges and pleasures of, 6–7
  see also manhood/masculinity; narrative/narration; self-discipline
autobiography, 16, 107, 111–13, 117–18
autoeroticism, 32–3, 54–6, 206
  see also self-display; sexuality

"Bachelor Bedroom, The," 18–19
bachelor economics, 31–2
  "spermatic economy" and, 32–3
bachelor, historical figure of,
  American versus British, 25–6
  illegitimacy and, 156–7
  popular discourse of, 3, 28–31, 38–41, 232n.5
  as stock character in seventeenth- and

eighteenth-century literature, 20
  taxes on, 22
  the term "bachelor" and, 20–1, 34, 218n.3
bachelor invalids
  boundary-crossing of, 84
  bourgeois manhood of, 77
  doubled voices of, 83–4
  nursing of, 64–5, 75
  masculinity and femininity of, 15, 78
  self-difference of, 95–6
  as witnesses and onlookers, 65–6
bachelor narrators
  alternative masculinity of, 212
  as Barthesian "figure," 2–3
  ideology and form related through, 12
  liminal spaces and states of, 7, 17, 66–7, 211
  non-autodiegetic homodiegesis of, 7, 8, 9
  nostalgia and, 188, 204–5, 208
  quadrangulated desire and, 10–11, 69
  queer excesses of, 211
  self-divisions of, 7, 95–6
  as site of construction of gendered subjectivity, 212
  unreliability of, 67–8
  see also manhood/masculinity; narrative/narration
"bachelor subcultures," 21–2, 26
bachelor uncles, 172–4, 178, 188, 231n.113
"Bachelor's Christmas, A," 39–41, 227n.77
"Bachelors and Spinsters," 218n.3
Baines, Jocelyn, 246n.14
Banks, J.A., 23, 221n.19
Banks, Olive, 23, 221n.19
Barker-Benfield, G.J., 225n.56
Barrie, J.M., 1, 231n.112
Barthes, Roland, 2–3, 214n.4
Baym, Nina, 6, 216n.17, 233n.7, 255n.43
Bederman, Gail, 27–8, 93–4, 221n.22
Berlant, Lauren, 233n.8
Bersani, Leo, 232n.3
Bertolini, Vincent, 55, 231n.110

279